Legal Accountability in EU Markets for Financial Instruments

Legal Accountability in EU Markets for Financial Instruments

The Dual Role of Investment Firms

Edited by

CARL FREDRIK BERGSTRÖM AND
MAGNUS STRAND

OXFORD
UNIVERSITY PRESS

OXFORD
UNIVERSITY PRESS

Great Clarendon Street, Oxford, OX2 6DP,
United Kingdom

Oxford University Press is a department of the University of Oxford.
It furthers the University's objective of excellence in research, scholarship,
and education by publishing worldwide. Oxford is a registered trade mark of
Oxford University Press in the UK and in certain other countries

First Edition published in 2021

Impression: 1

Published in the United States of America by Oxford University Press
198 Madison Avenue, New York, NY 10016, United States of America

British Library Cataloguing in Publication Data

Data available

Library of Congress Control Number: 2021942132

ISBN 978–0–19–284928–1

DOI: 10.1093/oso/9780192849281.001.0001

Printed and bound by
CPI Group (UK) Ltd, Croydon, CR0 4YY

Foreword

It's closing in on thirty years since the EU's internal market was allegedly 'completed' and yet its intrigue, complexity, and intellectual challenge endures. In part that is because a market, any market, is never truly complete. Markets are dynamic, markets change, markets adapt. But there is a more specifically legal reason for scepticism about the notion that the EU internal market can ever reach a fixed point of equilibrium. This is because although the internal market is defined by Article 26 TFEU as an area without internal frontiers in which the free movement of goods, persons, services, and capital is ensured, this definition tells us nothing about how, in achieving that project, the balance shall be struck between the deregulatory force of free movement law and the re-regulatory energy of legislative harmonisation—between judicially driven market integration and politically shaped centralised rulemaking. Internal markets come in different shapes and sizes. Many landmark cases of the Court of Justice of the European Union are exactly concerned with interpretative choices about how far free movement law shall reach and (in consequence) what role is played by harmonisation of laws, with, in the background, associated questions about the proper scope of national regulatory autonomy. Think of Dassonville, Reyners, Cassis de Dijon, Keck & Mithouard, Alpine Investments, Centros, Viking Line and Laval, and so many more in similar vein.

I find my interest in the twists and turns of internal market law is undimmed by the passage of time, and I am delighted to welcome this collection, whose editors and authors share my fascination with inquiry into the nature of the internal market which the EU has built and continues to build.

Their particular concern is with financial markets, and I am sure their insights will be of value to specialists in that field, but I want to emphasise too that exploration of the EU's 'internal market' should always interrogate the foundations, not only the particular sector of financial markets (which in any event does not have precisely defined margins or limits). I am happy that this book does just that and I strongly encourage anyone with interests in the EU internal market to look hard at this book even if they don't (yet!) specialise in the particular area under examination. MiFID II and MiFIR, CESR, and ESMA—don't be put off by the acronyms!

What occurs in the regulation of financial markets reveals much about patterns and incentives in the rise of centralised regulation at EU level with, its inevitable corollary, suppressed room for expression of national autonomy. Regulations rather than Directives; maximum or full rather than minimum rules at EU level; regulatory frameworks supported and elucidated by subsequent rulemaking in several different forms, including non-legislative instruments; intensified administrative co-operation; agency creation. Here is rich material, providing insights into matters of weight from a constitutional, substantive, and policy perspective. It is largely a story of how markets need rules, and the gradual ratchet of centralisation is driven remorselessly by the logic that where economic integration at EU level is out of step with legal integration at EU level obstacles to trade caused by diverse national rules subvert the motivations of the system. Across the whole sweep of EU internal market law, it is orthodox that common rules encourage market freedoms, by setting the groundrules for trade applicable across the entire territory of the EU-27, but those common rules themselves establish regulatory groundrules for conduct that is permitted and conduct that is not permitted within that area. The internal market is not an unregulated free-for-all. It is based on regulated market freedom, under the unique pattern of EU rulemaking which is heavily dependent on national-level implementation, including an obligation to impose sanctions on parties who fail to observe the rules.

A major preoccupation of the book is to explore how far the rise of centralised rulemaking in the EU is accompanied by accountability. This is a rich area of inquiry and, again, I would urge those interested in accountability who might otherwise have thought their interests did not reach financial markets to think again. There is an especially intriguing strand here as a result of the impact of rulemaking and decision-making by public authorities and agencies, including courts, on private actors, and the consequent need for accountability (broadly understood) also to engage with the discharge of rights and obligations by private parties. Markets need rules, but they also need accountability in the setting of those rules and effective enforcement of those rules. This entails accountability of public authorities in the EU and the member states but also engages the role of private parties. They are granted market freedoms, but with that come obligations and responsibilities, and a key issue is how to hold private parties to the re-regulatory bargain which lies at the heart of the EU's market-making project. One of the main trends visible in the EU's functional vocation to build an internal market stretching across the territory of the twenty-seven member states is its indifference to often deeply rooted separations between public law and private law at national level, and that trend is amply demonstrated in this book.

I am really happy to welcome the publication of this book.

Stephen Weatherill
Faculty of Law and Somerville College,
University of Oxford.

Contents

Table of Cases

COURT OF JUSTICE OF THE EUROPEAN UNION

The Court of Justice

The General Court

Advocate General opinions

EUROPEAN COURT OF HUMAN RIGHTS

OTHER JUDGMENTS AND DECISIONS

Court judgments

Boards of appeal and agency decisions

Table of Legislation

EU TREATIES AND CHARTER

Treaty on European Union

Treaty on the Functioning of the European Union

Charter of fundamental rights of the European Union

Other primary law instruments

EU SECONDARY LEGISLATION

Regulations

Directives

Decisions

List of Contributors

Helene Andersson is Associate Professor in European Law at Uppsala University. She has a background in researching due process issues and fundamental rights issues in the context of competition policy. Recently her interests have begun to include similar issues with regard to the EU financial market, including the EU rules governing market abuse.

Carl Fredrik Bergström is Professor of European Law at Uppsala University. He has a background as researcher at the European University Institute in Florence, lecturer at Stockholm University and Head of Legal Research/Deputy Director at SIEPS, the Swedish Institute for European Policy Studies. His primary areas of expertise are EU constitutional law and inter-relationship to national constitutional law, EU fundamental principles and system of norms, EU rulemaking behaviour and legal method.

Merijn Chamon is Assistant Professor of EU Law at Maastricht University and Visiting Professor at the College of Europe (Bruges). He holds a doctorate in Law from Ghent University where he also was postdoctoral researcher in the past. His expertise, research interests, and publications mainly focus on EU constitutional law, EU institutional law, and the law of EU external relations.

Pieter van Cleynenbreugel is professor of European Union law at the University of Liège, Belgium, where he is also the director of the Liège Competition and Innovation Institute and a visiting professor of competition law at Paris-Dauphine University, France. His research focuses on EU administrative, internal market, and competition law. He currently leads an ERC project on national administrative autonomy in the EU legal order. Pieter holds an LLM from Harvard and a PhD from KU Leuven.

Adrienne Héritier is professor emerita of political science at the European University Institute in Florence. Her research extends to theories and empirics of institutional change in the European Union with a specific focus on the European Parliament and delegated rulemaking by the Commission, the Council, and the European Parliament. She also studied European regulatory policies in different sectors, most recently in financial markets regulation.

Britta Behrendt Jonsson is a senior lecturer in commercial law at Linköping University. She holds law degrees from Germany and a doctorate in law from Linköping University. Her research interests include the regulation of financial markets, company law, and insurance contract law. Before joining academia, she worked as an inhouse lawyer in the German insurance industry from 2002 to 2012.

Malou Larsson Klevhill is Associate Professor at Luleå University of Technology and Senior Lecturer at the Department of Business Studies, Uppsala University. Larsson

Klevhill is primarily specializing in legal issues concerning sustainability, climate, and financial markets.

Federico Della Negra is a Senior Legal Counsel at the Directorate General SSM Governance and Operations of the European Central Bank and a qualified lawyer in Italy. He holds a PhD in Law from the European University Institute and master degrees in Law from the University of Pisa, from the University Sant'Anna School of Advanced Studies of Pisa and from the European University Institute. He authored a book on MiFID II and private law and several publications on financial regulation, consumer and contract law.

Annina H. Persson is a Professor of private and commercial law, specialised in banking, property and insolvency law at the Department of Law, Psychology and Social studies at Örebro University and at the Department of Business Studies, Uppsala University. She is also Visiting Professor in real estate law at the Royal Institute of Technology in Stockholm.

Jane Reichel is Professor in Administrative Law at the Faculty of Law, Stockholm University. She is the vice head of the Department of Law, the head of the public law group and the editor of the Swedish Administrative Law Review (Förvaltningsrättslig tidskrift). She was previously Professor of Administrative Law at the Faculty of Law, Uppsala University, as well as vice dean at the same Faculty. Her primary area of expertise is in EU administrative law and its interaction with national law, especially focusing on law relating to good administration, data protection, and transparency.

Dominique Ritleng is a Professor of European Law at the University of Strasbourg and Director of the Centre d'études internationales et européennes (CEIE). He has been a Legal Clerk at the European Court of Justice (cabinets of Advocate General Poiares Maduro and Judge Safjan).

Rebecca Söderström is a Senior Lecturer in Capital Markets Law at Uppsala University. She holds a Doctorate in Law from the same university since 2017. Her area of interest is Capital Markets Law, financial regulation and supervision, law and economics, and Securities Markets Law. Especially EU regulation within these areas, as well as the economic theories behind financial regulation and supervision, is in focus in her research.

Magnus Strand is Associate Professor of European Law and Senior Lecturer in Commercial Law at Uppsala University. Strand has worked on this book as Part-time Professor at the Robert Schuman Centre for Advanced Studies at the European University Institute in Florence. Strand is also Director of Research in Law and Business at the Department of Business Studies, Uppsala University. In particular, Strand leads multiple research projects on the use of Artificial Intelligence in the financial markets.

Stephen Weatherill is the Jacques Delors Professor of European Law in the University of Oxford, a post he has held since 1998. He is also the Deputy Director of the Institute for European and Comparative Law in the Faculty of Law and a Fellow of Somerville College. His published work covers both constitutional and substantive EU law, with a special focus on matters associated with legal competence and the EU internal market.

List of Abbreviations

ACPR	Autorité de contrôle prudentiel et de résolution
ADR	alternative dispute resolution
AIM	Alternative Investment Market
BaFin	Federal Financial Supervisory Authority (Germany)
BMR	EU Benchmark Regulation
CCP	central counterparty clearing
CEBS	Committee of European Banking Supervisors
CEIOPS	Committee of Insurance and Occupational Pension Supervisors
CEO	chief executive officer
CESR	Committee of European Securities Regulators
CFD	contract for difference
CFR	Charter of Fundamental Rights of the European Union
CJEU	Court of Justice of the European Union
CMU	capital markets union
CONSOB	Commissione Nazionale per le Società e la Borsa
CPA	Consumer Protection Agency (Sweden)
CPVO	Community Plant Variety Office
CRAR	Credit Rating Agencies Regulation
CRD	Capital Requirements Directive
CRR	Capital Requirements Regulation
CRS	consumer redress scheme
CySEC	Cyprus Securities and Exchange Commission
EASA	European Aviation Safety Agency
EBA	European Banking Authority
ECB	European Central Bank
ECHA	European Chemicals Agency
ECHR	European Convention on Human Rights
ECN	European Competition Network
ECtHR	European Court of Human Rights
EIOPA	European Insurance and Occupational Pensions Authority
ELTIF	European Long-Term Investment Fund
EMA	European Medicines Agency
EMIR	European Market Infrastructure Regulation
EP	European Parliament
ESAs	European Supervisory Authorities
ESFS	European System of Financial Supervision
ESG	Environmental, Social, and Governance

ESMA	European Securities and Markets Authority
ESRB	European Systemic Risk Board
EU	European Union
EURIBOR	Euro Interbank Offered Rate
FITD	Fondo Interbancario di Tutela dei Depositi
FOS	Financial Ombudsman Service (UK)
FROB	Fondo de reestructuración ordenada bancaria
GFC	global financial crisis
HFT	high-frequency trading
ICSD	Investor Compensation Schemes Directive
IPO	initial public offering
ISD	Investment Services Directive
ISDA	International Swaps and Derivatives Association
ITS	Implementing Technical Standard
JO	justitieombudsmännen (Sweden)
LIBOR	London Interbank Offered Rate
LSE	London Stock Exchange
MAR	Market Abuse Regulation
MEP	Member of the European Parliament
MiFID	Markets in Financial Instruments Directive
MiFID II	Markets in Financial Instruments Directive II
MiFIR	Markets in Financial Instruments Regulation
MP	Member of Parliament
NCA	National Competent Authority
NOMAD	nominated adviser
OECD	Organisation for Economic Co-operation and Development
OLAF	Office européen de lutte antifraude (European Anti-fraud Office)
OTC	over-the-counter
PEPPs	Pan-European Personal Pension Products
PRIPPs	Packaged Retail and Insurance-based Investment Products
QMV	qualified majority voting
ReNEUAL	Research Network on EU Administrative Law
RTS	Regulatory Technical Standard
SG	stakeholder group
SSM	Single Supervisory Mechanism
TEU	Treaty on European Union
TFEU	Treaty on the Functioning of the European Union
VPM	The Securities Market Act

PART I
INTRODUCTION

1

EU Rulemaking in the Internal Market after the Financial Crisis

Carl Fredrik Bergström

1.1 The overall project and the book

This book is one of several publications resulting from an interdisciplinary research project that started in 2017: 'A Centralisation of Rulemaking in Europe? The Legal and Political Governance of the Financial Market'. The project was designed by myself together with Adrienne Héritier, generously funded by the Swedish Research Council and hosted by Uppsala University in collaboration with the Robert Schuman Centre for Advanced Studies at the European University Institute in Florence (within their European Governance and Politics Programme) Following the initiation of the project Magnus Strand joined us as another core member. Throughout the lifetime of the project a number of senior and junior scholars from universities in several countries have been involved.

In the project, we have studied modern patterns of centralised rulemaking in the internal market after the economic and financial crisis. Our focus has been on the EU financial market. During the first stage of the project, most efforts were directed towards the nature of centralised rulemaking. This led to a jointly authored book that was interdisciplinary in nature (and a number of individually authored publications).[1] During the second stage, we concentrated on the consequences of centralised rulemaking for the EU system of governance, considering, in particular, the issue of accountability. At this stage, we applied a clearer separation in our work, between the current book, which has a legal science profile, and another book with a political science profile.[2] But we agreed that each book should have, at the centre of their respective studies, the

[1] See Adrienne Héritier and Magnus Schoeller (eds), *Governing Finance in Europe: A Centralization of Rulemaking?* (Edward Elgar Publishing 2020).

[2] See Adrienne Héritier and Johannes Karremans (eds), *Regulating Finance in Europe: Policy Effects and Political Accountability* (Edward Elgar Publishing 2021).

Carl Fredrik Bergström, *EU Rulemaking in the Internal Market after the Financial Crisis* In: *Legal Accountability in EU Markets for Financial Instruments*. Edited by: Carl Fredrik Bergström and Magnus Strand, Oxford University Press. © Carl Fredrik Bergström 2021. DOI: 10.1093/oso/9780192849281.003.0001

same regulatory framework on markets in financial instruments (MiFID II and MiFIR).[3] For the current book, we brought together a group of scholars with expertise from different legal disciplines, but a shared interest in the EU internal market and the way that it develops. The underlying idea was to give this book added value: to integrate a high-level focus on the form and function of EU rulemaking in the internal market after the financial crisis with evaluation of core aspects of rulemaking in the financial market and, in that way, provide a cross-cutting treatment of EU law.

This chapter was originally written with the intention of providing all contributing authors with a common basis for their work on the book: to delimit the field of study, clarify the internal market context, and establish the central concepts. It has now been reworked to serve as an introduction for the reader. The structure of the chapter is intended to reflect methodological considerations, and sometimes repeats itself, while moving ahead in smaller and smaller steps, reaching, finally, the focus of study. This serves to demonstrate that the regulatory framework on markets in financial instruments is only one of many components of the internal market but also a regulatory framework that is useful to study for anyone who wants to understand the modern patterns of EU rulemaking in the internal market.

1.2 The concept of an internal market

The concept of the internal market was introduced though a reform of the EU Treaties in 1987, and is said to 'comprise an area without internal frontiers in which the free movement of goods, persons, services and capital is ensured in accordance with the provisions of the Treaties'.[4] From these provisions, it follows that the establishment and functioning of the internal market is subject to two different types of constitutional mechanism.

The first type of constitutional mechanism is (centralised) rulemaking by EU institutions and bodies. Such mechanisms are based on competences conferred on the EU by its member states, in certain provisions of the Treaties.[5]

[3] See Directive (EU) 2014/65 of the European Parliament and of the Council of 15 May 2014 on markets in financial instruments [2014] OJ L 173/349 and Regulation (EU) 2014/600 of the European Parliament and of the Council of 15 May 2014 on markets in financial instruments [2014] OJ L 173/84.

[4] See art 26 TFEU, first numbered art 8a of the Treaty establishing the European Economic Community (TEEC), inserted by the Single European Act (SEA), and, later, art 14 of the Treaty establishing the European Community (TEC). For a comprehensive study, see Stephen Weatherill, *The Internal Market as a Legal Concept* (OUP 2017).

[5] See art 26 TFEU.

Some of these provisions are derived from the original wording, in place before the introduction of the internal market, and were previously tied to the broader concept of a 'common market', but most have been inserted though later amendments.[6] None of the provisions connected to the internal market has had more significance than Article 114 TFEU, which entails a general competence to adopt 'measures for the approximation of the provisions laid down by law, regulation or administrative action in member states which have as their object the establishment and functioning of the internal market'. This Article was the centrepiece of the 1987 reforms, and it created new, more generous preconditions for EU rulemaking relating to the free movement of goods, persons, services, and capital. For the first time, legislative acts could, effectively, be pushed through by qualified majority voting in the Council (thus unblocking some governments' previous insistence on veto), and, importantly, in forms other than directives.[7]

The second type of constitutional mechanism is mutual recognition of (decentralised) rulemaking by national parliaments and authorities. It is based on provisions of the Treaties that prohibit barriers to free movement between member states, but leave these states some room for their own rulemaking, where this is justified by an interest of general public importance.[8] Typically, this type of mechanism comes into operation in situations where there have been no 'measures for the approximation' of national law relating to the free movement, ie no EU rulemaking, and seeks to ensure that goods, persons, services, and capital that comply with legal conditions in one member state are also accepted in another. The reliance on national rulemaking without approximation of national law means that many conflicts between legal conditions will come before national courts. Therefore, the second constitutional mechanism implies a (centralised) judicial system whereby the EU Court of Justice can provide authoritative interpretations to national courts. Today, that system rests on provisions of the Treaties (most notably Article 19 TEU, Article 267 TFEU and Article 47 CFR), together

[6] The original provisions tied to the concept of a common market that are most relevant in this comparison with the concept of an internal market are art 115 TFEU, first numbered art 100 TEEC, and the different sets of provisions on free movement of goods, persons (workers and establishments), services, and capital. The concept of a common market was abolished by the Lisbon Treaty (2009) and, at the same time, the concept of the internal market was broadened. For examples of modern provisions under subject-specific titles, see art 153 TFEU on social policy, art 169 TFEU on consumer protection, art 192 TFEU on environment, and art 194 TFEU on energy.

[7] The original provisions required legislative acts to have the form of directives (with original exemptions relating to workers and more recent exemptions relating to capital).

[8] See, eg arts 34, 45, 49, 56, and 63 TFEU.

with judge-made principles that seek to secure national courts' loyal enforcement of EU law.

In legal and political theory, the first type of mechanism has often been discussed in terms of positive integration, and the second in terms of negative integration. Perhaps the terms 'politically active cooperation' and 'politically passive cooperation', respectively, are more appropriate. Irrespective of this, the most important difference between the first type of mechanism and the second is the degree to which there is an effective process for rulemaking by EU institutions and bodies. Put in a historical context, the internal market reform of the EU Treaties marks a watershed. Before 1987, progress with respect to the free movement of goods, persons, services, and capital was difficult to achieve by means of centralised rulemaking and, to the extent it was made, was often a result of mutual recognition of decentralised rulemaking. Since then, centralised rulemaking has become increasingly characteristic of the development of the internal market.

The initial stage of development was launched by the Programme for Establishment of the Internal Market (1985), which presented 297 proposals for legislative acts for the Council and the European Parliament to agree upon, over an intense period between then and the end of 1992.[9] The basic strategy or 'new approach' was to combine the first and second types of constitutional mechanism mentioned above, stressing the need to make a distinction 'between what it is essential to harmonise and what may be left to mutual recognition of national regulations and standards' (minimum harmonisation). This strategy was reflected in the proposals for legislative acts and their design: these should have the form of directives that 'leave the choice of form and methods' to national authorities and they should 'off-load technical matters' through extensive use of clauses on delegation of powers to the European Commission, thus enabling it to adopt non-legislative acts.[10]

[9] See Article 8a TEEC, and Commission, 'Completing the Internal Market: White Paper from the Commission to the European Council (Milan, 28–29 June 1985)' COM (1985) 310 final, with Annex: 'Timetable for Completing the Internal Market by 1992'.

[10] See, in general, arts 288 and 296 TFEU, and n 4 above. See also the Declaration on art 100a TEEC, attached to the Single European Act [1987] OJ L 169/1. This states that proposals pursuant to art 100a TEEC (now art 114 TFEU) 'shall give precedence to the use of the instrument of a directive if harmonisation involves the amendment of legislative provisions in one or more member states.' cf the amendment to art 145 TEEC (later art 202 TEC), inserted by the Single European Act, stating that the Council should 'confer on the Commission, in the acts which the Council adopts, powers for the implementation of the rules which the Council lays down', and that the Council was entitled to impose 'certain requirements' in respect of the exercise of these powers.

1.3 The modern patterns of rulemaking

More recently, there have been striking changes in the patterns of EU rulemaking in the internal market. The most obvious expression can be seen in a shift in the type of legal instrument used for the approximation of national law: from directives to regulations that are 'directly applicable', and uniformly implemented across all member states.[11] During the first five-year-period after the entry into force of the internal market reform (1988 to 1992), the EU legislator adopted 108 directives and 25 regulations with a legal basis in Article 114 TFEU. During the period from 2001 to 2005, the corresponding numbers were 83 directives and 22 regulations. But since then the relationship has been radically reversed. During the most recent five-year period (2016 to 2020), the EU legislator adopted 24 directives and 75 regulations with a legal basis in Article 114 TFEU. The tipping point, when regulations became the principal instrument, coincides with the entry into force of the Lisbon Treaty (2009). Most of the regulations adopted since then introduce new regimes, or amend regimes in pre-existing regulations. But some of them also amend regimes that were introduced in pre-existing directives, thus supplementing or even repealing those directives.[12]

But the changes in the patterns of EU rulemaking extend far beyond the choice of legal instrument. Another important expression of these changes can be seen in the modern model of 'regulatory frameworks' (French *cadre réglementaire* or German *regelungsrahmen*). Since 1970, a legal distinction has been made between 'measures directly based on the Treaty itself and derived law intended to ensure their implementation'.[13] The Lisbon Treaty introduced a more complete system of legal acts, and a nomenclature built on the notions of legislative acts and non-legislative acts (Articles 288–97 TFEU). These reforms were intended to clarify a hierarchy of legal acts, based on the principle that 'acts which have the same nature and the same legal effect must be produced by the same democratic procedure'.[14] In compliance with this principle,

[11] See art 288 TFEU.

[12] See, eg Regulation (EU) 2017/1129 of the European Parliament and of the Council of 14 June 2017 on the prospectus to be published when securities are offered to the public or admitted to trading on a regulated market, and repealing Directive (EC) 2003/71 [2017] OJ L 168/12, and Regulation (EU) 2014/596 of the European Parliament and of the Council of 16 April 2014 on market abuse, and repealing Directive (EC) 2003/6 of the European Parliament and of the Council [2014] OJ L 173/1.

[13] See Case 25/70 *EVGF v Köster and Berodt & Co* EU:C:1970:115.

[14] See Final Report of Working Group IX on Simplification of 29 November 2002 CONV 424/02, at 2 and 8–9. For an extensive assessment of the reform and its result see Carl Fredrik Bergström and Dominique Ritleng (eds), *Rulemaking by the European Commission: The New System for Delegation of Powers* (OUP 2016).

the Court of Justice of the European Union (CJEU) has explained that '[a] systemic approach of that kind provides the requisite legal certainty in procedures for adopting EU acts, in that it makes it possible to identify with certainty the legal bases empowering the institutions of the EU to adopt legislative acts and to distinguish those bases from bases which can serve only as a foundation for the adoption of non-legislative acts'.[15]

Today, legislative acts often form part of a series of acts, both regulations and directives, that establish the basic rules or 'essential elements' for specific sectors, and leave much room for subsequent rulemaking in the form of non-legislative acts (also regulations and directives, and decisions or non-binding acts), after delegation of powers. Following the Lisbon Treaty, a considerable case law has emerged in which the CJEU has confirmed the significance of such regulatory frameworks and explained their components.[16]

Like before, non-legislative acts are, typically, adopted by the European Commission, together with comitology committees.[17] But now, a functional division is made between general implementing acts (Article 291 TFEU) and delegated acts (Article 290 TFEU), the latter of which have the purpose of supplementing or amending non-essential elements of the legislative acts and, in that way, '[to] encourage the legislator to look solely to the essential elements' of the legislative acts.[18] Besides the non-legislative acts adopted by the European Commission, there are a growing number of non-legislative acts being adopted by EU agencies.[19] These agencies are specialised bodies with their own legal personalities, set up by the EU legislator via legislative acts (always in the form of regulations). Unfortunately, there is no provision in the Treaties that describes the roles of these agencies, or the preconditions for their exercise of powers.[20] Therefore, the CJEU has stressed the importance for agencies of observing 'the bounds of the regulatory frameworks', and the design of criteria and conditions, in legislative acts.[21]

[15] See Joined Cases C-643/15 and C-647/15 *Slovak Republic and Hungary v Council* EU:C:2017:631, para 63.

[16] See eg Case C-270/12 *United Kingdom v European Parliament and Council* EU:C:2014:18, paras 84–86.

[17] cf previously Article 202 TEC (n 10).

[18] See Final Report of Working Group IX, supra note 14, at 8–12. cf Case C-427/12 *Commission v European Parliament and Council* EU:C:2014:170, paras 38–39 and 52.

[19] cf *UK v Parliament and Council* (n 16), with annotation; Carl Fredrik Bergström, 'Shaping the New System for Delegation of Powers to EU Agencies: United Kingdom v European Parliament and Council (Short Selling)' (2015) 52 Common Market Law Review 219.

[20] But arts 263, 267, and 277 TFEUF, which establish preconditions for judicial control, were all amended by the Lisbon Treaty to encompass 'acts of the institutions, bodies, offices or agencies' of the EU.

[21] cf *UK v Parliament and Council* (n 16), para 44.

Typically, EU agencies interact with national authorities and the European Commission within a permanent regulatory network. A general example can be taken from the European Medicines Agency (EMA), located in Amsterdam.[22] The EMA has tasks relating to the development, evaluation, and supervision of medicines. It operates 'at the heart' of the European Medicines Regulatory Network. The network seeks to secure coordination of the activities of national authorities in the EU that are responsible for human and veterinary medicines. It gives EMA access to experts from across the EU, but also serves as a basis for interaction with a wider group of stakeholders, including research groups and pharmaceutical companies.[23]

The extent to which EU agencies adopt legal acts[24] varies, and so does the nature of their acts. For EMA, this typically means acts having the character of soft law: scientific opinions for the European Commission or national authorities, or guidelines for research groups and pharmaceutical companies. For some other agencies, it means acts having the character of hard law: mostly acts of individual application, but sometimes also acts of general application (thus qualifying as 'regulatory acts').[25] A prominent example is the European Securities and Markets Authority (ESMA), located in Paris.[26] ESMA has tasks relating to risk assessment, standard-setting, and supervision, and forms part of the European System of Financial Supervision: a network or 'multi-layered system' that is intended to ensure consistent implementation and application of EU law in the financial market. Like EMA, ESMA also produces opinions, guidelines, and other non-binding acts. But, in addition to this, it adopts binding acts of both individual and general application, such as decisions on fines and prohibitions of financial instruments or activities.

Before 1987, there were only three EU bodies with the basic characteristics of modern agencies, and two of them had been in place since 1975.[27] Following the internal market reform, a series of new agencies were established.[28] In

[22] See Regulation (EC) 2004/726 of the European Parliament and of the Council of 31 March 2004 laying down Community procedures for the authorisation and supervision of medicinal products for human and veterinary use and establishing a European Medicines Agency [2004] OJ L 136/1.

[23] See European Medicines Agency, 'The European Regulatory System for Medicines—A Consistent Approach to Medicines Regulation across the European Union' EMA/716925/2016 (2016); 'EMA Regulatory Science to 2025—Strategic Reflection' EMA/110706/2020 (2020).

[24] In relation to the notion of 'legal acts', see n 69 and corresponding text.

[25] See art 263(4) TFEU and *UK v Parliament and Council* (n 16).

[26] See Regulation (EU) 2010/1095 of the European Parliament and of the Council of 24 November 2010 establishing a European Securities and Markets Authority [2010] OJ L 331/84. For a full study of ESMA see Niamh Moloney, *The Age of ESMA—Governing EU Financial Markets* (Hart Publishing 2018).

[27] See Carl Fredrik Bergström and Matilda Rotkirch, 'Decentralized Agencies and the IGC: a Question of Accountability', Sieps Report 2003:4.

[28] For a discussion, see, in particular, Giandomenico Majone, 'Rise of the Regulatory State in Europe' (1994) 17 West European Politics 77.

2003, there were a total of sixteen agencies. Today there are thirty-three. Of these, twenty agencies have been established or re-established since 2009, and many of these have seen their powers increased. Most EU agencies, but not all, are assigned with tasks relating to the internal market, and several, for example EMA and ESMA, have been set up via a regulation with its legal basis in Article 114 TFEU.

1.4 The process for integration in the financial market

Before 1987, little progress had been made towards integration in the financial market. Firstly, the existing competence for centralised rulemaking had been difficult to make use of: not because there were a lack of proposals for measures for the approximation of national law, but because there was not sufficient agreement among the governments to overcome the requirement for unanimous decision-making (cf the first type of constitutional mechanism described above).[29] Secondly, the conditions in which financial institutions could provide their services under the national laws of different member states varied so much that it was difficult to enforce mutual recognition of decentralised rulemaking (cf the second type of constitutional mechanism).

But in the internal market programme, the need for swift action to open up the internal market for financial services was emphasised. Therefore, proposals were made for a series of directives intended to coordinate the conditions for authorisation and supervision of financial institutions and products (such as consumer credits, and collective investment in financial instruments). In compliance with the basic strategy of the internal market programme, these directives were only to seek minimum harmonisation of national law, but were to improve the preconditions for future cooperation between national authorities.[30]

In 2001, less than ten years after formal establishment of the internal market, the conclusion was drawn by the ad hoc Lamfalussy Group that progress had been made in some sectors of the financial market, but that other sectors were still suffering from 'unnecessary bureaucracy, lack of trust, and

[29] See, in particular, the original competence for approximation of national law in art 100 TEEC (now art 115 TFEU); and Carl Fredrik Bergström, *Comitology—Delegation of Powers in the European Union and the Committee System* (OUP 2005).

[30] See Timetable for Completing the Internal Market by 1992 (n 9), points 102–07.

sometimes downright protectionism'.[31] The major problems, they said, were that the system for EU rulemaking was too slow, and produced too much ambiguity. Essentially, this was a critique of the extensive reliance on directives.[32] According to the report of the Lamfalussy Group, the transposition of directives into national law was time-consuming and uneven, which, in turn, put pressure on the European Commission to monitor and enforce them. But the Commission had been given insufficient staff to tackle 'the complex task of building an integrated financial market' and 'barely a handful' of these staff were focusing on infringement procedures.[33]

The assessment presented in the report of the Lamfalussy Group resulted in a new approach to EU rulemaking in the financial market. Perhaps most obviously, this meant that use should be made of legislative acts in the form of regulations instead of directives.[34] Furthermore, a four-level regulatory model was launched, which was to be applied in future legislative acts. To a large extent the model was not new, but, rather, it was a simplification of regulatory ideas—or ideals—that had been advanced in the past.

First it was said that the Council and the European Parliament should adopt legislative acts for different sectors of the financial market, but focus solely on 'the overarching principles', and confer powers on the European Commission to establish 'the modalities of how to implement the principles' in non-legislative acts.[35] These were levels one and two of the regulatory model. Thereafter, the need to improve the consistency of national authorities' transposition of the legislative and non-legislative acts was stressed. Therefore, existing comitology committees should be supported by committees composed of national authorities' high-level representatives. This was level three of the model. The basic idea was that the new committees should bring financial 'regulators' together within a permanent network that would give them a collective responsibility to advise the Commission, and to ensure consistent transposition of legislative and non-legislative acts.[36] Finally, the need to enforce legislative and non-legislative acts with more vigorous action than before was emphasised. This was level four of the model. Essentially, it meant that the Commission should be given resources that would enable it to make full use of existing infringement

[31] See Final Report of the Committee of Wise Men on the Regulation of European Securities Markets, chaired by Alexandre Lamfalussy, Brussels 15 February 2001, 9 ('Report of the Lamfalussy Group')

[32] ibid 14–15 and cf Annex 5, 85.

[33] ibid 18.

[34] ibid 26.

[35] ibid 22 and 94.

[36] ibid 37 and 94.

procedures, and bring actions against member states to the CJEU (Articles 258 and 260 TFEU).[37]

Overall, the report of the Lamfalussy Group was well-received, and the member state governments were quick to commit themselves to the proposed model for regulatory frameworks, which they said should make the process for rulemaking in the EU financial market more effective and transparent.[38] The first of three regulators' committees, the Committee of European Securities Regulators (CESR), was set up within a few months, in a non-legislative act adopted by the Commission.[39] Its formal task was to advise the Commission, either on the Commission's request, or on its own initiative, in the field of securities. Before transmitting its opinion to the Commission, it should 'consult extensively and at the early stage with market participants, consumers and end-users in an open and transparent manner'.

The regulatory model launched by the Lamfalussy Group was first applied to a package of legislative acts on financial instruments, and later extended to banking and insurance.[40] But like before, and against the advice of the Lamfalussy Group, most legislative acts took the form of directives. The most likely reason for this was that some governments in the Council continued to oppose a use of Article 114 TFEU that would thwart the influence that directives gave them.[41] In its review of the process, in 2007, the European Commission observed that the new model for regulatory frameworks 'has

[37] ibid 40. In this context, it was noted that investment firms and other private actors were too often 'reluctant to come forward for fear of damaging [their] market opportunities'.

[38] See European Council Resolution of 23 March 2001 on more effective securities market regulation in the European Union [2001] OJ C 138/1.

[39] See Commission Decision (EC) 2001/527 of 6 June 2001 establishing the Committee of European Securities Regulators (CESR) [2001] OJ L 191/43; and, later, Commission Decision (EC) 2004/5 of 5 November 2003 establishing the Committee of European Banking Supervisors (CEBS) [2004] OJ L 3/28; and Commission Decision (EC) 2004/6 of 5 November 2003 establishing the Committee of European Insurance and Occupational Pensions Supervisors (CEIOPS) [2004] OJ L 3/30.

[40] The package of legislative acts originally envisaged in the Lamfalussy Report led to the adoption of Directive (EC) 2003/6 of the European Parliament and of the Council of 28 January 2003 on insider dealing and market manipulation (market abuse) [2003] OJ L 96/16, with its legal basis in art 114 TFEU; Directive (EC) 2003/71 of the European Parliament and of the Council of 4 November 2003 on the prospectus to be published when securities are offered to the public or admitted to trading [2003] OJ L 345/64, with its legal basis in arts 50 and 114 TFEU; Directive (EC) 2004/39 of the European Parliament and of the Council of 21 April 2004 on markets in financial instruments (MiFID) [2004] OJ L 145/1, with its legal basis in art 53(2) TFEU; Directive (EC) 2004/109 of the European Parliament and of the Council of 15 December 2004 on the harmonisation of transparency requirements in relation to information about issuers whose securities are admitted to trading on a regulated market [2004] OJ L 390/38, with its legal basis in arts 50 and 114 TFEU.

[41] cf the Report of the Lamfalussy Group (n 32) 14, where it is asserted that proposals for directives rather than regulations were due to 'subsidiarity pressure' from the member states, and the Declaration on Article 100a TEEC (n 10). cf also European Council Resolution of 23 March 2001 on more effective securities market regulation in the European Union [2001] OJ C 138/1. Here, the Commission (in formulating its proposals) 'is invited to consider more frequent use of regulations where this would both be legally possible and would help to speed up the legislative process'.

been a pioneer in introducing and strictly applying sound regulatory principles', but had not significantly improved member states' performance with regard to the implementation of legislative and non-legislative acts. Therefore, it expressed its intention to 'propose regulations whenever appropriate and to the greatest extent possible for implementing measures'.[42]

Clearly, the introduction of CESR and the other regulators' committees were the most innovative contributions made by the Lamfalussy Group.[43] These developments, in particular, were subsequently to be built on further (discussed further below). But, parallel to their success, the significance of 'level four' and the mechanism that enables the European Commission to bring actions against member states became less important. The annual reports on the monitoring of the application of EU law show that there has been a steady decrease in such actions. Just before the Lamfalussy Group started its work, in 2000, the Commission had sent 1,317 letters of formal notice to member states and referred 172 cases to the CJEU. Ten years later, in 2010, the corresponding numbers were 1,166 and 120, and this in spite of the fact that there had been a major enlargement (from fifteen to twenty-seven member states). Most recently, in 2019, the Commission sent 797 letters of formal notice and referred 33 cases to the Court.

There are several reasons why this pattern has emerged. Perhaps most obviously, the Lisbon Treaty (2009) introduced amendments that made it easier to fine member states for failures to 'notify measures transposing a directive adopted under a legislative procedure' (Article 260 TFEU). Presumably this has been detrimental to the member states, and has had an immediate effect on the number of cases that go all the way to court. But there are also other, more indirect reasons. This can be seen, clearly, in the context of the reforms triggered by the global financial crisis.

Following the outbreak of the financial crisis in 2008, the ad hoc de Please provide full title/reference number of the report cited here. Group was requested to analyse the causes of the crisis, and to make proposals for responses covering all sectors of the financial market.[44] The report of the de Larosière Group built on a structural distinction between regulation—the set of rules

[42] See Commission, 'Communication of 20 November 2007 on review of the Lamfalussy process—strengthening supervisory convergence' COM (2007) 727 final, 3.3 and 3.4. In addition, the Commission indicated that it would 'immediately launch infringement proceedings under Article 226 of the EC Treaty for any Member State that is late in implementation'.

[43] This assessment was made by Alexandre Lamfalussy in an interview by Carl Fredrik Bergström, Frédéric Varone, and Christian de Visscher in 2004.

[44] See Report of the High-Level Group on Financial Supervision in the EU, chaired by Jacques de Larosière, Brussels, 25 February 2009 ('Report of the de Larosière Group').

that govern financial institutions—and supervision: the process designed to oversee financial institutions in order to ensure that rules are properly applied.[45]

Looking first at *regulation*, the conclusion was drawn that there was an international need for repair, relevant for 'all major jurisdictions in the world', but also that there was a specific problem in Europe: the lack of a consistent set of rules. The main cause of the latter, it was said, stemmed from 'the options provided to EU members in the enforcement of common directives', since this had '[led] to a wide diversity of national transpositions related to local traditions, legislations and practices'. According to the de Larosière Group, the use of the regulatory model launched by the Lamfalussy Group had led to good result on levels one and two described above, and the solution, now, was to proceed to introduce (and amend) regulatory frameworks in more sectors of the financial market.[46] Like the Lamfalussy Group, the de Larosière Group stressed the need to make use of legislative acts in the form of regulations, and only if this was not possible, directives (ie to seek maximum rather than minimum harmonisation).[47] Parallel to this, a new mechanism for *resolution* should be established that could limit the distress of the financial system as a whole, in the event of a future crisis.[48]

Then, looking at *supervision*, the conclusion was drawn that there was a lack of trust between national authorities that the regulators' committees had been unable to manage. In this respect, the de Larosière Group made it clear that the regulatory model launched by the Lamfalussy Group had failed on level three, and that the regulators' committees had 'clearly reached their limits in terms of informal cooperation methods'.[49] Therefore, the recommendation was made to strengthen the integrity of national authorities and transform the committees into EU agencies (or 'authorities') with their own powers.[50] This should be done within a new network: the European System of Financial Supervision (ESFS). According to the de Larosière Group:[51]

> The ESFS must be independent from possible political and industry influences, at both EU and national level. This means that supervisors should have

[45] ibid 13.
[46] ibid Annex IV.
[47] Simultaneously, a process should be launched to improve old regulatory frameworks established in directives. See ibid 27–29 and 50.
[48] ibid 4.
[49] ibid Annex IV.
[50] ibid 41–50, 55 and Annex IV.
[51] ibid 47.

> clear mandates and tasks as well as sufficient resources and powers. In order to strengthen legitimacy and as a counterpart for independence, proper accountability to the political authorities at the EU and national levels should be ensured. In short, supervisory work must be independent from the political authorities, but fully accountable to them.

Only a few months after the de Larosière Group had presented their response to the financial crisis, the national governments agreed to set the reform process in motion, recommending inter alia that the ESFS should be established as an operational network 'with shared and mutually reinforcing responsibilities', and that CESR and the other regulators' committees should be transformed into independent agencies with their own legal personalities, and their own powers.[52]

The de Larosière Group made many specific recommendations. Noteworthy, in particular, are those that followed from the observations that corporate governance had failed, allowing firms too much room to act with a short-term perspective, and to make as much profit as possible, and that member states' regimes for sanctioning breaches of existing rules had been weak and divergent. For this reason, it was concluded that national authorities should be guaranteed sufficient powers, both in respect of what they could do in terms of day-to-day supervision of individual firms, and in relation to the enforcement actions open to them when they found that firms had breached the rules.[53] But, according to the report of the de Larosière Group, there had been serious failures in the member states.[54] Therefore, the new agencies should also be given 'a significant new responsibility of ensuring that all national supervisors meet necessary standards, by being able to challenge the performance by any national supervisor of its supervisory responsibilities ... and to issue rulings aimed at ensuring that national supervisors correct the weaknesses that have been identified'.[55]

The new agencies were formally established on 24 November 2010, in legislative acts that had their legal basis in Article 114 TFEU: the European Securities and Markets Authority (ESMA), the European Banking Authority (EBA), and the European Insurance and Occupational Pensions Authority

52 See Council Conclusions of 9 June 2009 on strengthening EU Financial Supervision Doc 10862/09 ECOFIN 5. See also Presidency Conclusions from European Council in Brussels on 10 July 2009 11225/2/09 REV 2 and Commission Communication of 27 May 2009 on European Financial Supervision COM(2009) 252 final.

53 See the Report of the de Larosière Group (n 44) 23, 29–32, and 41.

54 ibid 40–41.

55 ibid 40–41 and 52–54.

(EIOPA).[56] Shortly thereafter, the European Commission issued a communication stressing the need to reinforce the sanctioning regimes relating to financial services.[57] The communication explained that there was a problem of divergence between member states' sanctioning regimes that could not be solved sufficiently by the agencies. Even if the agencies had powers 'to play an active role in building a common supervisory culture', it was still likely that the sanctioning regimes in several member states would not be dissuasive or effectively enforced. Therefore, 'member states with strong sanctioning regimes could be reluctant to fully trust those with weaker sanctioning regimes, making it difficult to ensure effective cross border supervision'.[58]

The proposition advanced by the European Commission was to extend the ongoing reforms to encompass harmonisation of member states' sanctioning regimes.[59] In essence, provisions containing standards for member states' sanctioning regimes should be introduced into each regulatory framework.[60] The standards should set out criteria for the choice of sanctions and their application, but also establish supporting mechanisms that would enable national authorities to uncover violations that would have remained undetected, or to gather additional evidence. The mechanisms that the Commission had in mind were whistle-blowing and leniency programmes. Both of these were intended to encourage persons who were aware of violations within firms to report them.[61] Over the next few years, the Commission inserted provisions that established standards for member states' sanctioning regimes in its proposals for legislative acts within the

[56] See Regulation (EU) 2010/1095; Regulation (EU) 2010/1093 of the European Parliament and of the Council of 24 November 2010 establishing a European Banking Authority [2010] OJ L 331/12; and Regulation (EU) 2010/1094 of the European Parliament and of the Council of 24 November 2010 establishing a European Insurance and Occupational Pensions Authority [2010] OJ L 331/48. In parallel, an independent unit with responsibility for the financial system as a whole was set up within the European Central Bank: the European Systemic Risk Board (ESRB). See Regulation (EU) 2010/1092 of the European Parliament and of the Council of 24 November 2010 on European Union macro-prudential oversight of the financial system and establishing a European Systemic Risk Board [2010] OJ L 331/1.

[57] See Commission, 'Communication to the Council and the European Parliament of 8 December 2010 Reinforcing sanctioning regimes in the financial services sector' COM (2010) 716 final.

[58] See Commission, 'Staff Working Paper—Impact Assessment, accompanying document to Commission Communication of 8 December 2010 Reinforcing sanctioning regimes in the financial services sector' SEC (2010) 1496 final 17–19.

[59] Support for this proposition was to be found in an action plan agreed by G20 leaders, and a then-recent reform of the US financial system. See the Communication of 8 December 2010 (n 57) 3–4, and the underlying Impact Assessment (n 58) 37.

[60] See the Communication of 8 December 2010 (n 57) 11, and the Impact Assessment (n 58) 41.

[61] See the Communication of 8 December 2010 (n 57) 15, and the Impact Assessment (n 58) 35–37.

financial market. The process was spearheaded by the new regulatory framework on market abuse (MAR).[62]

1.5 A notion of the EU financial market

There is no formal definition of the EU 'financial market', and the expression can be used more or less strictly, to include activities in a number of sectors of the internal market, and sometimes even beyond. For several years after the launch of the reforms discussed above, the European Commission made use of a complex and yet precise notion of the financial market at its web page on 'banking and finance'. But the activities reported by the Commission have become increasingly intertwined with new political initiatives, and it is therefore impossible to use this information for any systematic study of EU rulemaking. This book takes, as its starting points, the EU Official Journal, and a search in the database EUR-Lex for the period 2010 to 2020 that retrieved a total of sixty-two legislative acts relating to the free movement of financial institutions and their services. A number of interesting observations can be made. Most obviously, thirty-nine of these legislative acts took the form of regulations and twenty-three took the form of directives. Some of the acts (twelve, in total) concerned matters that cut across all sectors of the financial market, such as the regulation establishing ESMA (Regulation 2010/1095) and the regulation requiring sustainability-related disclosures (Regulation 2019/2088).[63] But most of the acts (forty, in total) concerned specific sectors; introducing twenty-one new regulatory frameworks and, later, amending them, or amending old regulatory frameworks, that existed before 2010 (ten, in total). It may be noted that many frameworks are constituted by a combination of directives and regulations. Examples are the regulatory framework on markets in financial instruments (Directive 2014/65 and Regulation 2014/600) and the regulatory framework on market abuse (Directive 2014/57 and Regulation 2014/596).

In view of the underlying competences conferred on the EU by its member states, it is noteworthy that twenty of the twenty-three directives had their legal basis in provisions setting out a subject-specific competence: Article 50 or 53 TFEU (establishment), Article 60 TFEU (services), or Article 83 TFEU

[62] See Regulation (EU) 2014/596. For more details see Niamh Moloney, *EU Securities and Financial Markets Regulation* (OUP 2014) 967–68.

[63] See, respectively, Regulation (EU) 2010/1095, and Regulation (EU) 2019/2088 of the European Parliament and of the Council of 27 November 2019 on sustainability-related disclosures in the financial services sector [2019] OJ L 317/1.

(criminalisation). These provisions explicitly restrict rulemaking thereunder to the use of directives, and exclude the use of regulations.[64] Perhaps it is unsurprising, therefore, that all regulations identified in the search had their legal basis in Article 114 TFEU (as had seven directives, of which all but two had an additional legal basis in a provision setting out a subject-specific competence). Article 114 TFEU entails a general competence to adopt unspecified 'measures' for the approximation of national law ('save where otherwise provided in the Treaties').[65]

Turning to the non-legislative acts, it can be observed, first, that the European Commission has adopted 317 binding non-legislative acts within the 21 new regulatory frameworks, consisting of 174 delegated regulations, 99 implementing regulations, 1 implementing directive, and 43 implementing decisions. The Commission has also adopted an additional number of non-legislative acts within the regulatory frameworks that existed before the reforms.[66]

It is more difficult to ascertain the number of acts adopted by EU agencies operating in the financial market. This is primarily because the system of legal acts in the Treaties is centred around the legal acts of EU 'institutions', and does not spell out how the nomenclature applies to acts of EU agencies and other bodies (Articles 288–97 TFEU).[67] For this reason, it is unclear, for example, to what extent agencies' acts are accessible, and how they might be accessed. In Article 297 TFEU a requirement is established for publication in the EU Official Journal of all legislative acts, and for binding non-legislative acts of general application. Presumably, this requirement also applies to acts of agencies. For the relevant period (2010 to 2020) there are, altogether, eight such acts from ESMA, three from EBA, and five from ESRB, in the EU Official Journal.[68] But there is no requirement for publication of binding non-legislative acts that

[64] See n 7.

[65] This should be read in conjunction with art 296 TFEU, which provides that '[w]here the Treaties do not specify the type of act to be adopted, the institutions shall select it on a case-by-case basis, in compliance with the applicable procedures and with the principle of proportionality'. It may be noted that this provision was inserted by the Lisbon Treaty. cf Final Report of Working Group IX (n 14) 7.

[66] See, eg the UCITS regulatory framework established in Directive (EC) 2009/65 of the European Parliament and of the Council of 13 July 2009 on the coordination of laws, regulations and administrative provisions relating to undertakings for collective investment in transferable securities (UCITS) [2009] OJ L 302/32. During the period from 2010 to 2020, this directive was amended eight times (in legislative acts), and provided the basis for seven binding non-legislative acts adopted by the European Commission.

[67] See, in particular, art 288 TFEU, which states that the 'institutions' shall exercise the competences and, therefore, adopt legal acts. cf art 13 TFEU, where all institutions are listed (and agencies not included). No mention is made of agencies in arts 288–97 TFEU. But at the same time their capacity to adopt acts that are judiciable is confirmed in arts 263, 267, and 277 TFEU. cf *UK v Parliament and Council* (n 16) with annotation; Bergström (n 19).

[68] See infra note 106.

only have individual application[69] (ie those that 'specify to whom they are addressed') or, indeed, for non-binding legal acts. For EU agencies, these are the most typical acts.[70]

1.6 The regulatory framework on markets in financial instruments

1.6.1 The origins of the regulatory framework

To enable us to deepen our analysis, this book has the regulatory framework on markets in financial instruments at the centre of its field of study . The regulatory framework on markets in financial instruments is constituted by two legislative acts: Directive 2014/65 on markets in financial instruments (MiFID II) and Regulation 2014/600 on markets in financial instruments (MiFIR).[71] Together, these acts establish conditions for the authorisation of 'investment firms' (and some other actors) and provision of 'investment services' in the EU. According to the underlying proposals, the overarching objective is to further the integration, competitiveness, and efficiency of the financial market.[72]

The regulatory framework on markets in financial instruments can be traced back to Directive 1993/22 on investment services in the securities field (ISD), which was one of the legislative acts envisaged in the internal market programme.[73] Before that, there had been no approximation of centralised rulemaking, and the conditions under the national law of the member states had been so different that it had been difficult to enforce mutual recognition under the provisions of the Treaties that prohibit barriers to the free movement (cf the first and second constitutional mechanism).

[69] See, eg Decision of the ESMA Board of Supervisors of 11 July 2018 to adopt a supervisory measure and impose a fine in respect of an infringement by Danske Bank A/S ESMA41-137-1145, adopted on the basis of Regulation (EC) 2009/1060.

[70] There is sometimes a requirement for publication on agencies' websites (besides notification) in the legislative acts setting up the regulatory frameworks.

[71] See Directive (EU) 2014/65 (amended by Directive (EU) 2016/1034, Directive (EU) 2019/2034, and Directive (EU) 2019/2177); Regulation (EU) 2014/600 of the European Parliament and of the Council of 15 May 2014 on markets in financial instruments [2014] OJ L 173/84 (amended by Regulation (EU) 2016/1033, Regulation (EU) 2019/2033, and Regulation (EU) 2019/2175).

[72] See Commission, 'Proposal for a directive of the European Parliament and of the Council on markets in financial instruments' COM (2011) 656 final 1, and Commission, 'Proposal for a regulation of the European Parliament and of the Council on markets in financial instruments' COM (2011) 652 final 2.

[73] See Council Directive (EEC) 1993/22 of 10 May 1993 on investment services in the securities field [1993] OJ L 141/27; Commission, 'Proposal of 3 January 1989 for a Council Directive on investment services in the securities field' COM(88) 778.

Like other directives resulting from the internal market programme, Directive 1993/22 was designed for minimum harmonisation; it was addressed to the member states and intended to coordinate their conditions for authorisation and operation of investment firms (and, to some extent, credit institutions), but it allowed each of them to set different, more stringent, standards. Interestingly, a possibility was foreseen to enable the European Commission to make 'technical amendments' to the directive in non-legislative acts (adopted together with 'the committee to be set up in the securities markets field'), but this possibility was never pursued.[74]

Following the report of the Lamfalussy Group, Directive 1993/22 was replaced by Directive 2004/39 on markets in financial instruments (MiFID).[75] It has been noted above that the new directive was part of the package of legislative acts on securities to which the model for regulatory frameworks conceptualised by the Lamfalussy Group was first applied.[76]

Similarly to Directive 1993/22, MiFID was also intended to coordinate conditions for the authorisation and operation of investment firms (as well as regulated markets and, to some extent, credit institutions) but MiFID had a broader scope, covering a more complex set of financial services and instruments, and a greater precision in many of its requirements.[77] Furthermore, it clarified that national authorities must be granted supervisory powers, including rights to demand information and carry out inspections, and must have access to sanctions that are 'effective, proportionate and dissuasive' (and that their decisions must be reasoned and subject to judicial control).[78] In compliance with the recommendations of the Lamfalussy Group, a new effort was also made to make better use of delegation of powers, enabling the European Commission to 'adapt or update' the non-essential provisions of MiFID 'by way of implementing procedures' (together with the European Securities Committee (ESC)).[79] The result was two interconnected non-legislative acts: Commission Directive 2006/73 and Commission Regulation 2006/1287.[80] Even if this might seem modest

[74] See the preamble (last recital) and art 29.

[75] See Directive (EC) 2004/39 of the European Parliament and of the Council of 21 April 2004 on markets in financial instruments [2004] OJ L 145/1.

[76] See n 40.

[77] See, eg Jean Pierre Casey and Karel Lannoo, *The MiFID Revolution* (CUP 2009).

[78] See arts 48–53.

[79] See art 64 and Commission Decision (EC) 2001/528 of 6 June 2001 establishing the European Securities Committee [2001] OJ L 191/45, with reference to Council Decision (EC) 1999/468 of 28 June 1999 laying down the procedures for the exercise of implementing powers conferred on the Commission [1999] OJ L 184/23 (see, in particular, arts 2 and 5). Note that the delegation of powers in Article 64 was very cautiously designed: not only was it based on a (regulatory) comitology procedure that reserved maximum influence for the member states, but it was also tied to a so-called 'sunset clause'.

[80] See Commission Directive (EC) 2006/73 of 10 August 2006 implementing Directive (EC) 2004/39 of the European Parliament and of the Council as regards organisational requirements and operating

in practice, the implications, in principle, were considerable, as this was the first step towards rulemaking in the form of directly applicable regulations, and towards the modern model of regulatory frameworks.

Two further aspects deserve special attention. Firstly, one of the new regulators' committees envisaged by the Lamfalussy Group, the Committee of European Securities Regulators (CESR), had an invisible role to play in the implementation of MiFID. There was no explicit reference to CESR in the directive, and the basis of its foundation was, instead, a non-legislative act applying to several sectors of the financial market.[81] This act explains that CESR 'should serve as an independent body for reflection' for the European Commission, and contribute to the implementation of legislative acts 'by securing more effective cooperation' between national authorities (and also by consulting with market participants and consumers).[82] Secondly, the suggestion from the Lamfalussy Group that the Commission should enforce centralised rulemaking against member states 'with more vigorous action' than before had an extremely limited impact in the context of MiFID. Only two such cases (ie actions for failure to fulfil obligations) are recorded in the database of the CJEU.[83] This may be compared with fourteen cases concerning the interpretation of MiFID that resulted from actions by private litigants before national courts.[84]

MiFID entered into force on 30 April 2004, and a twenty-four month period for transposition was envisaged, but this was extended to forty-two months, and it was not until 1 November 2007 that the member states were obliged to apply 'the laws, regulations and administrative provisions' necessary to comply with the directive (cf decentralised rulemaking).[85] Only two years after, a

conditions for investment firms and defined terms for the purposes of that Directive [2006] OJ L 241/26; and Commission Regulation (EC) 2006/1287 of 10 August 2006 implementing Directive (EC) 2004/39 of the European Parliament and of the Council as regards record-keeping obligations for investment firms, transaction reporting, market transparency, admission of financial instruments to trading, and defined terms for the purposes of that Directive [2006] OJ L 241/1. For an analysis, see, eg Jean Pierre Casey and Karel Lannoo, 'The MiFID Implementing Measures: Excessive Detail or Level Playing Field?' European Capital Markets Institute (ECMI) Policy Brief 1/2006.

81 See Commission Decision (EU) 2001/527 (n 39).

82 The fact that CESR was involved in the context of Directive 2004/39 was explicitly acknowledged in the preambles of Commission Directive (EC) 2006/73 and Commission Regulation (EC) 2006/1287 (recitals 84 and 27, respectively).

83 See art 258 TFEU. These cases are Case C-87/08 *Commission v Czech Republic* EU:C:2008:526, and Case C-143/08 *Commission v Poland* EU:C:2009:174.

84 See art 267 TFEU.

85 See arts 70 and 72 of Directive (EC) 2004/39; and Directive (EC) 2006/31 of the European Parliament and of the Council of 5 April 2006 amending directive 2004/39/EC on markets in financial instruments, as regards certain deadlines [2006] OJ l 114/60.

revision was initiated that led to the adoption of Directive 2014/65 (MiFID II) and Regulation 2014/600 (MiFIR).[86] This revision constituted 'an integral part of the reforms aimed at establishing a safer, sounder, more transparent and more responsible financial system working for the economy and society as a whole in the aftermath of the financial crisis'.[87]

MiFID II and MiFIR were carefully designed to form a package, and were published together on 12 June 2014. The member states were supposed to have had their measures for transposition of MiFID II in operation since 3 January 2018, which is also the date from which the provisions of Regulation MiFIR have been directly applicable.[88]

It has been explained, previously, that our notion of the financial market builds on sixty-two legislative acts adopted between 2010 and 2020, of which thirty-nine have the form of regulations, and twenty-three have the form of directives. Looking at these legislative acts, it has been observed, first, that many regulatory frameworks within the financial market are constituted by a combination of directives and regulations and, second, that directives typically have their legal bases in provisions setting out a subject-specific competence, such as Article 53 TFEU (establishment), whereas regulations have their legal basis in Article 114 TFEU. The pattern is borne out by Directive MiFID II and MiFIR. According to the legislative proposals, MiFID II has the main objective to harmonise national provisions' concerning inter alia the access to the activity of investment firms, while Regulation MiFIR is intended to establish 'uniform and directly applicable requirements which are necessary for the even functioning of the market in financial instruments'. For these reasons the proposals were based on, respectively, Article 53 and Article 114 TFEU.[89]

[86] See Directive (EU) 2014/65; and Regulation (EU) 2014/600.

[87] See Commission, 'Proposal for a directive of the European Parliament and of the Council on markets in financial instruments' COM (2011) 656 final 1.

[88] See, for MiFID II, arts 96 and 93 (which makes exceptions for art 65(2)), and Directive (EU) 2016/1034 of the European Parliament and of the Council of 23 June 2016 amending Directive 2014/65 [2006] OJ L 175/8 (which extended the original date of application for twelve months). See also, for MiFIR, art 55 (which makes numerous exceptions), and Regulation (EU) 2016/1033 of the European Parliament and of the Council of 23 June 2016 amending Regulation (EU) 2014/600 on markets in financial instruments, Regulation (EU) 2014/596 on market abuse and Regulation (EU) 2014/909 on improving securities settlement in the European Union and on central securities depositories [2016] OJ L 175/1 (which extended the original date of application for twelve months).

[89] See Commission, 'Proposal for a directive of the European Parliament and of the Council on markets in financial instruments' COM (2011) 656 final (n 72) 4, and Commission, 'Proposal for a regulation of the European Parliament and of the Council on markets in financial instruments' COM (2011) 652 final (n 72) 5. See also the preambles of Directive (EU) 2014/65 and Regulation (EU) 2014/600.

1.6.2 The legislative acts: MiFID II

Like its predecessors, MiFID II sets out the conditions for authorisation of investment firms (as well as regulated markets and data reporting services and, to some extent, credit institutions), and the conditions for their operation: how they shall behave when providing their services (such as execution of orders, portfolio management and investment advice).[90]

To a large extent, MiFID II is a recast of the original MIFID: it seeks to eliminate remaining differences in national law though full harmonisation.[91] This can be seen, clearly, in the provisions on rights of investment firms (Articles 34 and 35), under which investment firms that comply with the directive's requirements enjoy the freedom to provide investment services, or establish a branch, in any member state. Member states 'may not impose any additional requirements' (in respect of matters covered by the directive). It is still a central idea that authorisation of investment firms is granted by national authorities in their home countries, which also maintain responsibility for day-to-day supervision.

In comparison with MiFID, the conditions for authorisation of investment firms and provision of investment services are essentially the same, but, once again, the scope has been extended to comprise more services and instruments, and the requirements for transparency and consumer protection have been strengthened.[92] An example can be found in Article 9(3):

> Member States shall ensure that the management body of an investment firm defines, oversees and is accountable for the implementation of the governance arrangements that ensure effective and prudent management of the investment firm including the segregation of duties in the investment firm and the prevention of conflicts of interest, and in a manner that promotes the integrity of the market and the interest of clients.

[90] See definitions of 'investment firm' and 'investment services and activities' in Directive (EU) 2014/65, art 4(1). See also the so-called Omnibus Directive that requires ESMA to keep a list of investment firms registered in all member states, based on information received from national authorities, Directive (EU) 2010/78 of the European Parliament and of the Council of 24 November 2010 amending Directives (EC) 1998/26, 2002/87, 2003/6, 2003/41, 2003/71, 2004/39, 2004/109, 2005/60, 2006/48, 2006/49, and 2009/65 in respect of the powers of the European Banking Authority, the European Insurance and Occupational Pensions Authority and the European Securities and Markets Authority [2010] OJ L 331/120, and also the list of investment firms at <https://www.esma.europa.eu/investment-firms> (accessed 04-08-2021).

[91] See the Report of the de Larosière Group (n 44), 27–29 and 50.

[92] For a full assessment, see Danny Busch and Guido Ferrarini (eds), *Regulation of the EU Financial Markets: MiFID II and MiFIR* (OUP 2017).

This is followed by a list of specific requirements relating to an investment firm's governance arrangements, such as a risk-tolerant business policy with stress testing, and a remuneration policy aiming to encourage responsible conduct.[93]

Like MiFID, MiFID II also clarifies the member states' responsibility for securing that their national authorities have the necessary powers, and access to appropriate sanctions, but also for guaranteeing that their decisions are properly reasoned, and subject to 'the right to apply to the courts'.[94] But, importantly, the previous provisions have been replaced with new ones setting out more specific requirements for such powers and sanctions.[95] This is one of the most striking changes to the regulatory framework. There is a minimum list of infringements for which sanctions should be available, for example investment firms offering services without authorisation, or failing to cooperate in investigations. There is also a minimum list of sanctions, for example withdrawal of investment firms' authorisations, fines of 5,000,000 euros or more, temporary or permanent bans against members of management bodies, and publication (on official websites) of every decision to impose sanctions ('naming and shaming').[96] In addition to this, there are requirements to provide supporting mechanisms for the reporting of infringements ('whistle-blowing').[97]

Furthermore, as a consequence of the de Larosière Group's recommendations, MiFID II sets out the responsibilities of the new agencies and, in particular, the European Securities and Markets Authority (ESMA). This is, undoubtedly, the most far-reaching change that has been made to the regulatory framework on markets in financial instruments. It can be seen in numerous provisions stating that ESMA shall receive and coordinate information from national authorities and keep central registers, but also develop guidelines for national authorities, and draft technical standards.[98]

[93] See also reference to arts 88 and 91 of Directive (EU) 2013/36 of the European Parliament and of the Council of 26 June 2013 on access to the activity of credit institutions and the prudential supervision of credit institutions and investment firms [2013] OJ L 176/338.

[94] See Directive (EU) 2014/65 (n 3), arts 48–53.

[95] See ibid arts 69–73 and Commission, 'Proposal for a directive of the European Parliament and of the Council on markets in financial instruments' COM (2011) 656 final (n 72) subheading 3.4.14.

[96] See ibid art 70 (cf Article 51, Directive (EC) 2004/39 (MiFID)).

[97] See ibid art 73.

[98] See, eg ibid arts 9 or 21 on guidelines, and arts 7 and 17 on draft (regulatory) technical standards. The draft technical standards have been formally confirmed in binding non-legislative acts adopted by the European Commission. See also art 57, which entrusts ESMA with the tasks of settling disputes between national authorities and providing them with opinions.

1.6.3 The legislative acts: MiFIR

MiFIR establishes uniform requirements for transparency that investment firms must comply with when trading with financial instruments—for public disclosure of information, and transaction reporting to financial authorities—and also requirements for access to investment firms' trading venues.

To a large extent, the content of MiFIR is a combination of provisions that existed before, in MiFID and its implementing regulation.[99] But the scope has been extended to include new services and instruments, and more venues (adding the category 'organised trading facilities' to the existing categories of 'multilateral trading facilities' and 'regulated markets').

In addition to this, MiFIR introduces provisions relating to ESMA; some of these are similar to those found in MiFID, but there are also new provisions that entrust ESMA with supervisory powers to adopt binding legal acts in situations where national authorities are not taking sufficient action. These may be acts of either individual and general application: decisions requesting financial institutions to provide information or take action, or decisions restricting financial instruments or activities.[100]

1.6.4 The non-legislative acts

Together, MiFID II and MiFIR constitute a regulatory framework, in accordance with the modern model envisaged in the report of the de Larosière Group, and observed in other sectors of the financial market, but also the internal market in general. This means that they should be read together.[101] But it also means that the full extent of the centralised rulemaking can only be understood after additional study of the non-legislative acts adopted within the bounds of the regulatory framework. MiFID II and MiFIR both contain numerous provisions in which delegation of powers is made to the European Commission and to EU agencies: to ESMA and, exceptionally, to EBA.

[99] See Commission Regulation (EC) 2006/1287 of 10 August 2006 implementing Directive 2004/39/EC of the European Parliament and of the Council as regards record-keeping obligations for investment firms, transaction reporting, market transparency, admission of financial instruments to trading, and defined terms for the purposes of that Directive [2006] OJ L 241/1.

[100] See Regulation (EU) 2014/600, art 45 on 'position management powers' (enabling acts of individual application) and art 40 on 'temporary intervention powers' (enabling acts of general application). See also art 9(5) of Regulation (EU) 1095/2010 of the European Parliament and of the Council of 24 November 2010 establishing a European Securities and Markets Authority [2010] OJ L 331/84.

[101] See the preamble of Directive (EU) 2014/65, recital 7. cf *UK v Parliament and Council* (n 16).

Looking at the binding non-legislative acts adopted by the European Commission, it can be observed that MiFID II has given rise to twenty-five delegated and twelve implementing regulations, one delegated directive, and five implementing decisions.[102] That is more than MiFIR, which has given rise to twenty-two delegated regulations and three implementing decisions.[103] In all instances, the Commission has been required to cooperate with the ESC (comitology committee).[104]

Turning to the binding non-legislative acts adopted by EU agencies, it has already been noted that there appears to be a structural difference between the powers that ESMA exercises under MiFID II and the powers that ESMA (and exceptionally EBA) exercise under MiFIR. Only the latter powers enable the adoption of acts that have the character of hard law. There have, altogether, been eight acts of general application (published, therefore, in the EU Official Journal),[105] and they all have their legal basis in the same provision of MiFIR, establishing temporary intervention powers.[106] In addition to this, there is an unknown number of individual decisions and non-binding acts.

[102] The central provisions of Directive (EU) 2014/65 are art 89 (delegated acts) and art 89a (implementing acts).

[103] The central provisions of Regulation (EU) 2014/600 are art 50 (delegated acts) and art 51 (implementing acts).

[104] See Commission Decision (EC) 2001/528 (n 79). For the implementing acts (art 291 TFEU), a so-called examination procedure applies, in accordance with Regulation (EU) 2011/182 of the European Parliament and of the Council of 16 February 2011 laying down the rules and general principles concerning mechanisms for control by Member States of the Commission's exercise of implementing powers [2011] OJ L 55/13 (art 5). For the delegated acts (art 290 TFEU), see Interinstitutional Agreement between the European Parliament, the Council of the European Union and the European Commission of 13 April 2016 on Better Law-making ('Interinstitutional Agreement') [2016] OJ L 123/1, point 28. The agreement comprises a Common Understanding on Delegated Acts (annex), which inter alia clarifies that the Commission 'shall consult experts designated by each Member State' within existing comitology committees. See also Declaration (39) on art 290 TFEU: here, the Intergovernmental Conference that concluded the Lisbon Treaty 'takes note of the Commission's intention to continue to consult experts appointed by the member states in the preparation of draft delegated acts in the financial services area, in accordance with its established practice'. For an example, see Commission Delegated Regulation (EU) 2017/2294 of 28 August 2017 amending Delegated Regulation (EU) 2017/565 as regards the specification of the definition of systematic internalisers for the purposes of Directive (EU) 2014/65 [2017] OJ L 329/4, and the preamble (recital 6), which explains that '[t]he measures provided for in this Regulation are in accordance with the opinion of the Expert Group of the European Securities Committee'.

[105] See n 68.

[106] See Regulation (EU) 2014/600, art 40. For an example, see Decision of the European Securities and Markets Authority (EU) 2019/679 of 17 April 2019 renewing the temporary restriction on the marketing, distribution or sale of contracts for differences to retail clients [2019] OJ L 114/22. See also Decisions (EU) 2019/679, 2019/509, 2019/155, 2018/2064, 2018/1636, 2018/1466, 2018/796, and 2018/795.

1.7 The central object of the book and its structure

In the project underlying this book, we have studied modern patterns of centralised rulemaking in the EU, and focused on the financial market. This book concentrates on the consequences for the EU system of governance, considering, in particular, legal accountability. To enable the contributors to deepen their analysis, the regulatory framework on markets in financial instruments has been placed at the centre of this study.[107] This has been mapped above, and an initial description has been made of its components in terms of centralised rulemaking: the basic legislative acts, but also the non-legislative acts.

There are numerous other acts that, one way or another, come into play in the context of the regulatory framework on markets in financial instruments. The reasons for this may be historical, political, functional, or, indeed, formal. The most obvious examples can be found in legislative and non-legislative acts that relate to the operation of more than one regulatory framework. In the text above, several references have been made to such acts, for example the regulation establishing ESMA, and the directive requiring it to keep a list of investment firms, and the regulation laying down rules for control of implementing powers.[108] For the purposes of this book, such acts, which are not themselves a direct part of the regulatory framework on markets in financial instruments, are relevant, but only to the extent that each author explains how any such particular acts increase our understanding of the substance, organisation, or operation of that regulatory framework.

Importantly, there are also other forms of acts or documents that come into play in the context of the regulatory framework on markets in financial instruments, and which can increase our understanding and, indeed, the depth of our analysis. Two examples that deserve special attention are the European Ombudsman's Code of Good Administrative Behaviour (adopted by ESMA and other EU agencies, in their internal rulemaking), and the Interinstitutional Agreement on Better Law-making.[109]

The book does not assert any fixed notion of accountability (or, indeed, governance) upon its authors. To us, this is its main strength. There are many ideas

[107] See Directive (EU) 2014/65 and Regulation (EU) 600/2014.

[108] See Regulation (EU) 2010/1095 (n 63), Directive (EU) 2010/78 (n 90), and Regulation (EU) 2011/182 (n 104).

[109] See European Ombudsman, 'The European Code of Good Administrative Behaviour' (European Union 2015) and Decision of the ESMA Management Board of 11 January 2011 on Code of Good Administrative Behaviour ESMA/2011/MB; and the Interinstitutional Agreement (n 104).

about the meaning of accountability and the context in which it belongs. But, clearly, at its root lies the question of whether someone is responsible for what they have done, and is able to give a satisfactory reason for having done so.[110] In the work within our overall interdisciplinary project, a general description of accountability has been formulated by Adrienne Héritier and Johannes Karremans (discussed further in their parallel book):[111]

> Accountability is commonly understood as an obligation by one actor/institution to explain and justify its actions or decisions against a set of criteria to another actor/institution or a forum, and to accept the responsibility for its own shortcomings. The public administration literature has added a learning perspective to the definition of accountability, wherein the provision of information during accountability processes make public authorities more effective in fulfilling their mandate and more responsive to the needs and preferences of their key stakeholders. Finally, accountability also has a more legal dimension, wherein one actor may be sanctioned by another in case it does not fulfil to its mandate.

The latter, more legal, dimension was briefly elaborated upon in the original description of our overall project:

> Specifically with regard to legal accountability and, in particular, judicial control, the questions which will be discussed relate inter alia to the level and the nature of adjudication, the criteria for locus standi (for what actor), the type of remedies available (annulment or repeal type of action, infringement type of action, non-contractual liability or annulment type of action) and the intensity of the review of legality.

Traditionally, the notion of legal accountability has been reserved for use in the public law sphere, and some would even argue that it is inadequate in the private law sphere. But in our area of study—the EU financial market—we observe endless overlaps between the public law and private law spheres. Therefore, we have encouraged our authors to explore what accountability means, and why it matters.

[110] See, eg *Cambridge Dictionary* at <https://dictionary.cambridge.org/>or *Black's Law Dictionary* (Thomson Reuter 2020).
[111] See Héritier and Karremans (n 2).

In the context of the regulatory framework on markets in financial instruments, many provisions with obvious implications in terms of accountability can be found in two special chapters of MiFID II, concerning 'designation, powers and redress procedures' (Articles 67–78), and 'cooperation between the competent authorities of the member states and with ESMA' (Articles 79–87). Other provisions with obvious implications in terms of accountability can be found in Regulation 2010/1095 (ESMA), in the chapter explaining 'remedies' before the Joint Board of Appeal and the EU Court of Justice (Articles 60–61). There are numerous other provisions that have less obvious, but equally important, implications.

Even if most of these provisions explicitly address public actors—authorities, agencies, tribunals, and courts—they are centred on private actors. In this book, our assessment of accountability will seek the perspective of these private actors and focus on investment firms (thus delineating these against other financial institutions and business operators). These firms are subjects of conditions arising from centralised rulemaking and supervision, but they also have rights. Therefore, they can be held accountable for their compliance with those obligations, but they can also hold other actors accountable for infringements of their rights.

The proper functioning of the EU financial market is protected by public actors, both national and supranational, that are responsible for rulemaking and supervision of investment firms. But the EU legal system is dependent on the vigilance of private actors such as investment firms and their clients; it requires them to invoke EU law before national authorities and courts. Indeed, this has been seen in the context of MiFID.[112] It means that investment firms have a dual role within the system, turning them into subjects of control and enforcement, but also agents in the maintenance of the rule of law.

Against the above background, the thematic questions we set out to answer in this book are:

Question 1: what are the legal mechanisms for accountability within the regulatory framework on markets in financial instruments, and what is the role of investment firms in the operation of those mechanisms?

Question 2: what are the implications of the answers to Question 1 for EU law and the EU legal system?

[112] See supra n 85.

Question 3: how do our findings contribute to the understanding of the concept of accountability?

This introductory chapter will be followed and supported by a chapter giving an account of the work contained in the parallel book on political accountability.[113] Thereafter, the book will be separated into three major parts, and a concluding chapter will return to the thematic questions set out above, and seek to identify general patterns of findings. The three major parts reflect an analytical structure based on the submission that investment firms can have three different positions in accountability processes. The first two of these major parts have a predominantly public law character, and distinguish between processes where investment firms hold EU agencies and national authorities accountable for their actions (Part II), or in which investment firms are held accountable themselves (Part III). Thereafter, processes that have a private law character are explored: processes whereby different investment firms, or investment firms and other private actors, hold each other accountable (Part IV).

[113] See Héritier and Karremans (n 2).

2

Governing Finance in Europe

Policy Effects and Political Accountability

Adrienne Héritier[*]

2.1 Introduction

This chapter builds on recent work in a project on the evolution of regulatory structures in EU financial governance, in which we provided a comprehensive framework to investigate the dynamics leading to centralisation, decentralisation, and fragmentation in EU financial regulation. This generalisable theoretical account of regulatory centralisation and its counterforces was subject to an empirical assessment on the basis of major EU legislative packages in financial regulation, including the Markets in Financial Instruments Directive II (MiFID II) and capital markets union (CMU).

This chapter further builds on subsequent work asking the following questions: who benefits from the regulatory measures analysed, and how are decision makers and stakeholders held politically and administratively accountable? It focuses on all actors involved in the regulatory process, such as politicians and regulators, as well as market players such as investors, fund managers, and investment firms, and outlines the modes in which they are linked in various political and administrative accountability mechanisms. The analysis of the accountability channels is related to policy contents by asking: (a) whether specific regulatory objectives and results give rise to the mobilizing of available accountability channels; and (b) whether the use of accountability channels helps to improve regulatory decisions.

[*] This chapter builds on recent work in a project funded by the Swedish Research Council (Grant No 2016-01596).

Adrienne Héritier, *Governing Finance in Europe* In: *Legal Accountability in EU Markets for Financial Instruments*.
Edited by: Carl Fredrik Bergström and Magnus Strand, Oxford University Press.
DOI: 10.1093/oso/9780192849281.003.0002

2.2 *Governing Finance in Europe: A Centralisation of Rulemaking?*—arguments and findings

In *Governing Finance in Europe: A Centralisation of Rulemaking?*,[1] we developed hypothetical answers to this question from four research perspectives: the perspective of European legislation in the context of international agreements; the perspective of international competition between regulatory powers; the perspective of the interaction between private self-regulation and public regulation; and the perspective of technological (digital) innovation of financial instruments. To what extent were our hypothetical answers, as described below, confirmed or disconfirmed by the empirical findings made by the various contributors to 'Governing Finance in Europe' in their individual chapters? And what can we learn from the empirical findings in order to refine our arguments?

The *vertical international research perspective* starts from the fact that European financial market legislation is embedded in the context of international financial agreements and is, therefore, under a certain pressure to accommodate the regulatory expectations of international regulatory bodies to harmonise financial regulation. Hence, we would expect an increasing structural centralisation at the EU and member state level to realise a convergence of regulatory provisions. However, what we observed empirically is more complicated: in the EU, this pressure from the international level translates into a complex political process, first at the supranational European level, and then at member state level. Given that member states' economic, political, institutional, legal, and social conditions vary, the outcomes of this process of implementation of international regulations, therefore, do not result in uniform regulatory structures and policy substances at the national level. How are these general considerations playing out empirically in the legislative area of the Markets in Financial Instruments Directive?

Analysing high-frequency trading (HFT) under the Market in Financial Instruments Directive (MiFID II), Karremans and Schoeller[2] found that the Commission took important steps to comply with the expectations of the G20 agenda, and to engage in a regulatory centralisation of HFT. This confirmed our expectation that the Commission uses international agreement requirements

[1] Adrienne Héritier and Magnus G Schoeller (eds), *Governing Finance in Europe: A Centralisation of Rulemaking?* (Edward Elgar Publishing 2020).

[2] Johannes Karremans and Magnus G Schoeller, 'MIFID II between European Rule-making and National Market Surveillance: The case of High-frequency Trading' in Héritier and Schoeller (eds) (n 1) 32–51.

as a window of opportunity to advance centralisation and acquire more supervision power for itself. What we did not expect to find was that the European Parliament (EP) has joined in with these endeavours of the Commission to advance centralisation of HFT regulation. In other words, centralisation endeavours originated from *two* different actors, at the EU level.

Moreover, as we know from Europeanisation research, European legislative proposals may be proposed by pacesetter member states, which try to upload their national policy practices to the EU level in order to diminish policy adaptation costs and, hence, may engage in a competition of policy uploading.[3] Karremans and Schoeller showed that, in the case of HFT, the EU legislative initiatives were partly built on the corresponding pre-existing national regulation of HFT in Germany. Hence, one overall empirical insight is that the Commission, together with the EP, does indeed seek to use international agreements as an opportunity of regulatory centralisation, albeit using the foil of following a member state's policies.

The other crucial empirical insight is that, while there is a formal centralisation in policy formulation, the latter is seriously challenged in the course of policy implementation. It emerges empirically that when member states supervise the centrally defined technical standards, they use divergent practices and surveillance structures, due to diverse institutional, economic, and social legacies. This confirms our expectation that a centralizing policy formulation may be followed by differential implementation structures, and lead to differential outcomes (Héritier et al., 1996). In short, we find a centralisation of rulemaking at the European level, but decentralised modes of implementation at the national level.

From the same international vertical perspective, but focusing on CMU—that is, central counterparty (CCP) clearing, under the European Market Infrastructure Regulation (EMIR)—Bulfone and Smoleńska[4] confirmed that the Commission, as expected, seized the opportunity of international pressure resulting from the G20 to initiate centralizing legislation. However, they also showed that this centralizing attempt, in favour of the Commission and the European Securities and Markets Authority (ESMA), was challenged by claims from the European Central Bank (ECB), which sought to gain supervisory power over the market for itself. This attempt was successfully contained

[3] Adrienne Héritier, C Knill, and S Mingers, *Ringing the Changes in Europe: Regulatory Competition and the Transformation of the State. Britain, France, Germany* (Walter de Gruyter 1996).

[4] Fabio Bulfone and Agnieszka Smoleńska, 'The Internal and External Centralisation of Capital Markets Union Regulatory Structures: The Case of Central Counterparties' in Héritier and Schoeller (eds) (n 1) 52–78.

by the EP, which, given that it has less power to hold the ECB accountable than the Commission and ESMA, supported centralizing power within ESMA. Moreover, Bulfone and Smoleńska showed that, in the political policy formulation process, the centralisation attempt was only successful after the Brexit decision: given the existence of de facto consensus decision-making,[5] it was only after the UK's exit decision that preferences among the larger countries converged, and centralisation initiatives with respect to the regulation of third-country CCPs were successful in the political process. By contrast, regarding the internal regulation of CCPs, member states' competing economic interests in taking over part of the UK CCPs' functions in the internal market prevented moves to centralise intra-EU CCP regulation, with Germany acting as a veto player, motivated by the internal competition for a higher CCP market share after Brexit.

The empirical finding of centralisation in policy formulation, on the one hand, and decentralisation in policy implementation, on the other, described by Karremans and Schoeller, was confirmed by the findings of Bulfone and Smoleńska in the area of CCPs (EMIR). The supervisory structures at the implementation level in member states vary to a great extent, as a function of pre-existing institutional structures and the economic and political differences of member states. Not surprisingly, the pressure of the internal competition for CCP market shares (the legacy of Brexit) reinforced differences among member states.

Centralised or decentralised regulatory structures are not only reflected in the allocation of specific regulatory competences. The degree of centralisation also depends on the features of the regulatory instruments that are applied. Thus, a centrally issued standard which is very vague does not much influence the actions of the implementing actors in detail. Therefore, the chapter on the *choice of legal instruments* from the vertical international perspective by Strand[6] addressed the question of whether an increasing use of regulations (rather than directives) implies more centralised control. In his empirical analysis of regulations under MiFID II, Strand did not find confirmation of this claim, ie he did not, in general, find more 'high-density' provisions in regulations than directives. But by further differentiating rules specifically directed at institutional actors, ie regulatory authorities such as ESMA and European supervisory authorities (ESAs), he showed that regulations addressing regulatory

[5] Although EMIR is governed on a qualified majority voting (QMV) legal basis (Art 114, TFEU).

[6] Magnus Strand, 'The Choice of Instruments for EU Legislation: Mapping the System of Governance under MiFID II and MiFIR' in Héritier and Schoeller (eds) (n 1) 79–111.

authorities contained more 'high-density' provisions. He explained this by citing the legislators' wish to control the EU agencies. Furthermore, by including non-legislative acts (delegated acts) directed at other institutional actors such as national authorities, he discovered that an extensive set of such rules of centralizing financial governance was created when addressing administrations at both the European and national levels. The overall conclusion was that, if directives—which give more latitude to implementation through transposition into national legislation—are used, this latitude may subsequently be 'clawed back' through delegated legislation.

This empirical finding complemented and threw additional light on the empirical insights of the two preceding chapters, which found decentralisation, or even fragmentation, in regulatory practices, ie a differential application of formal rules by the member states. We may explain these contradictory findings by distinguishing between time periods. By adding the dimension of delegated legislation, Strand extended the time horizon of rule formation. In a first instance (t1), the pattern of centralised formal rules and decentralised implementation may emerge. In a second instance (t2), delegated legislation governing the implementation phase may seek to counter decentralizing tendencies, and lead back to more centralised implementation. Moreover, over a longer time frame, fragmented or decentralised regulatory structures in implementation tend to be levelled out by court rulings seeking to establish similar regulatory practices and structures in member states.[7]

Turning to the third horizontal perspective beyond the EU, and including the US as a regulatory power, we identify further possible forces of centralisation and decentralisation. We ask whether competition between regulatory powers leads to a centralisation of the regulatory structure within the relevant regulatory power, in our case the EU. Marjosola,[8] in his chapter, focused on the regulatory rivalry between the EU and the US in the field of over-the-counter (OTC) regulation, specifically the regulation of central counterparties (CCPs). Marjosola argued that, at the international level, regional regulation has led to a fragmentation of the regulatory structure and, consequently, to regulatory arbitrage by the regulated industry. Regulatory competition between the regional powers, and the resulting regulatory venue shopping by the industry, may—as theoretically expected—in turn lead to an internal centralisation of regulatory

[7] Carl Fredrik Bergström, oral communication, Workshop on Governing Finance in Europe, Hertie School of Governance, Berlin, November 2019.

[8] Heikki Marjosola, 'Sharing Global Regulatory Space: Transatlantic Coordination of the G20 OTC Derivatives Reforms' in Héritier and Schoeller (eds) (n 1) 112–36.

structures within *one* regulatory power seeking to better coordinate its policies in view of external competition.

Under certain circumstances, in order to reduce regulatory arbitrage, regulatory powers may refrain from competing to impose their own regulation on the rest of the world (extraterritorial application), and seek to coordinate their regulatory prescriptions; this occurs if one party takes the lead in this coordination by using strategies of regulatory equivalence or mutual recognition. Such efforts will lead to a gradual convergence of regulatory prescriptions. Empirically, however, Marjosola found that progress towards a deference-based recognition regime has been slow in bargaining an agreement between the US and the EU, the negotiations being complicated by the Brexit decision and the issue of how to regulate third-country CCPs. In this process, the EU's European Market Infrastructure legislation—as conjectured—strengthened the powers of the ESMA (the central EU administrative authority), leading to a centralisation within the EU regarding the regulation of third-country CCPs operating there.

However, as pointed out above, Bulfone and Smoleńska[9], in their chapter, differentiated that this only held for the regulation of third-country (extra-EU) CCPs which provided services in the EU market, but not for CCPs already established in one of the member states and, therefore, supervised by a national competent authority.

The third important perspective from which we capture centralizing forces and counterforces is the perspective of *public–private regulatory interaction.* This has a long tradition in the regulation of financial markets. Karremans and Héritier[10] asked whether the *self-regulation of financial services* by private actors and subsequent *public–private co-regulation* had led to centralisation or fragmentation of regulatory structure in the EU. Self-regulation rules have frequently emerged in new markets, with public actors subsequently intervening step by step, leading to a form of hybrid regulatory governance structure. While the initial forms of self-regulation may have given rise to a fragmented structure, one would expect an emergence of more centralizing features with increasing intervention by public actors. An important example of private self-regulation is the International Swaps and Derivatives Association (ISDA), whose master contract for many years formed *the* model for OTC derivatives contracts worldwide, until these became increasingly regulated, after the

[9] Bulfone and Smoleńska (n 4).

[10] Johannes Karremans and Adrienne Héritier, 'The Emergence of Transnational Hybrid Governance: How Private Risks Trigger Public Intervention' in Héritier and Schoeller (eds) (n 1) 137–63.

financial crisis. The other example, the Alternative Investment Market (AIM) of the London Stock Exchange (LSE), is an interesting example of an attempt to offer small firms access to capital markets under the conditions of more lenient regulation compared to stock exchanges. Both cases tell the story of new European rules entering two spheres of the financial markets that were previously almost entirely self-regulated. The reasons were the failures of private self-regulatory regimes to tackle excessive rent-seeking and systemic risk. In spite of public intervention, the private regulatory regimes—ISDA's 'master agreement' and the regime governed by NOMADS (nominated advisors) in the AIM—remain in place, but financial transactions in these markets are now directly subject to European regulatory requirements, hence we find steps towards regulatory centralisation. But, as we found in the chapters on MiFID II and CMU, surveillance structures vary across member states during the implementation phase.

On the one hand, the idea that private regimes will attract new members, and that these will adapt to the existing regulatory structure, is confirmed in both cases: ISDA has attracted a rapidly rising number of participants, in the case of OTC derivatives, and AIM has gathered companies under the LSE private regime. On the other hand, our expectation that private regulatory regimes emerge as a result of innovation in financial instruments only finds confirmation in ISDA's rise as a private authority linked to growing complexity and technological progress in derivatives trading. By contrast, the case of AIM, which was created by the LSE in order to avoid the heavy regulation of initial public offerings (IPOs), points to the typical pattern of the regulated seeking to eschew regulation by developing a slightly different financial product that does not correspond to the prescriptions of existing regulation.[11] As a consequence, our theoretical argument on the rise of self-regulation needs to be refined by including private actors pursuing the goal of avoiding existing regulation.

An additional general insight deriving from the empirical findings is that private actors—in this case ISDA—are not, per se, against a centralisation of rulemaking. On the contrary, especially if they operate transnationally, they tend to be in favour of homogeneous rules across different jurisdictions. At the same time, they seek, often very successfully, to claw back favourable outcomes for their clienteles, in the course of specifying the details of the legislation.[12] In

[11] Charles EA Goodhart, 'The Regulatory Response to the Financial Crisis' (2008) 4(4) Journal of Financial Stability 351.

[12] ISDA, for instance, successfully sheltered particular segments of the market from CCP regulation.

the course of implementation, their expert knowledge can easily thwart the influence of public legislators.[13]

From the fourth *technological innovation perspective,* given the rapid digital innovations featuring in ever more financial products, we ask how regulators seek to govern these new instruments, and whether they tend to have a centralisation effect on regulatory structures. Smoleńska, Ganderson, and Héritier[14] argued, in their chapter, that the type and level of uncertainties linked to a new financial product or business model were crucial factors influencing the reaction of regulators. They distinguished between substantive, legal, and cross-sectoral uncertainty, and certainty regarding compliance with regulatory prescriptions. They showed that substantive uncertainty regarding the nature of new financial instruments had induced regulators to cooperate with the industry when developing bespoke regulatory requirements, engaging in 'sandboxing', or creating innovation hubs. This led to fragmentation, in the first instance, which, in turn, was limited by regulatory convergence being sought. In cases of legal uncertainty and cross-sectoral risks regarding the provision of public goods, the regulators sought to fit the new uncertainties into pre-existing legal rules. If these rules were Mi FID II or CMU, as shown above, this implied a certain regulatory centralisation at the rulemaking level, but decentralisation or fragmentation at the implementation stage. In the case of the application of regtech, which presupposed that the regulator and the regulated market actors have at their disposal the necessary resources, the regulator had no uncertainty regarding real-time financial transactions. This meant that, if the relevant rules were detailed and strict, this led to a centralisation of regulation. This is mostly confirmed by the empirical findings. What emerges additionally from these findings is a factor that may drive centralisation, ie the collection and processing of large quantities of data on financial transactions in the course of transborder data conciliation by the competent central authority (in this case, ESMA). The role of the regulatory agency as a data gatekeeper reinforces a centralisation of regulation, even if formal regulatory structures remain decentralised.

In summary, the theoretically guided conjectures and gained empirical insights in *Governing Finance in Europe: A Centralisation of Rulemaking?* show that the formulation of rules has led to a partial centralisation of regulatory structures in Europe, due to pressure from international agreements and

[13] Karremans and Héritier (n 10).

[14] Agnieszka Smoleńska, Joseph Ganderson, and Adrienne Héritier, 'The Impact of Technological Innovation on Regulatory Structure: Fintech in Post-crisis Europe' in Héritier and Schoeller (eds) (n 1) 164–89.

European legislation, regulatory competition between regulatory powers, an increasing influence of public actors on private self-regulation, and digital technological innovations in the use of financial instruments and regulation. At the same time, at the level of the implementation of these rules, decentralizing, or even fragmenting, forces deriving from diverse economic interests and institutional traditions among the member states are impacting on regulatory structures. Technological innovation (fintech) and subsequent self-regulation tend to prompt public regulation, with the intention of harmonizing rules in a first stage, while decentralised implementation at the national level remains. Only in a second stage may divergences in the implementation of rules become subject to renewed attempts at harmonisation, through delegated technical legislation and court rulings. Centralizing legislation, which demands massive amounts of data from financial firms in order to allow for transparency, in turn reinforces technological innovation by fintech, in the form of regtech. Regtech, if widely applied, finally leads to a centralisation of regulatory structures, given the scope for real-time control of rule compliance.

The findings of partial centralisation of regulatory structures in rulemaking in almost all of the chapters, albeit attenuated by decentralisation or fragmentation during implementation, give rise to the question of how these regulatory structures can be made subject to political accountability mechanisms. European regulations imply a loss of the decision-making powers of national parliaments and, hence, less democratic accountability at the national level. In subsequent research, we therefore turned to the question of *policy effects* and *political accountability* in the second volume. As political scientists—unlike the other authors in this volume—we focused exclusively on political accountability channels, although we were aware of the fact that there are frequently links between policy effects and legal accountability. For example, political actors may bring a contested policy issue to a court to obtain a decision as to who is accountable for the policy effect in question.

2.3 Political accountability in view of regulatory effects

As already emphasised, despite extensive European regulatory reforms, national authorities still maintain a considerable degree of de facto regulatory power. Overall, this has resulted in different patterns of centralised, decentralised, and fragmented rulemaking and rule application in the EU. Regulatory standards are mostly set at the European level, and effective market supervision is carried out at the member state level.[15] In parallel, private interest groups and fintech firms provide substantial inputs to the content of European regulations.

This complex patchwork picture of the new governance of financial markets in Europe raises urgent questions about the locus of political accountability, and mechanisms whereby decision-makers and supervisors can be held accountable for their decisions, and the effects of these, in the event that the target groups of regulation are not content with these outcomes. Where, for instance, are the accountability channels that investors can turn to in relation to high-frequency trading, given the opacity of the financial transactions involved, which are based on algorithmic trading of trillions of transactions per day. Which accountability channels can institutional investors like pension funds invoke to protest against the much-criticised short-term investment strategies of fund and asset managers? How can self-regulated private fintech firms offering innovative financial products and services be held accountable by investors? To answer these questions, and to build trust in regulatory decisions, we need to know the political accountability channels[16] that are available in relation to the important financial regulatory measures that were imposed in post-crisis Europe. We also need to know how these accountability channels link up with regulatory effects resulting from these measures. Are accountability channels used on a regular basis and, if so, by whom? Or are they only used when the effects of regulation prove to be dissatisfactory, and controversial to the wider public? Further, do well-functioning accountability mechanisms help improve policy effects?

2.4 Regulatory effects and political accountability

Investigating the questions mentioned above entails exploring the modalities, scope, and policy effects of accountability mechanisms. The *concept of accountability* has been discussed in a prolific literature in the past decades, focusing on political and legal accountability mechanisms in their various forms (for example, in the Oxford Handbook on Public Accountability, published in

[15] Héritier and Schoeller (eds) (n 1).

[16] As political scientists, unlike the other authors in this volume, we focus on political accountability channels exclusively, although we are aware of the fact that there are, frequently, links between policy effects and legal accountability. For example, political actors may bring a contested policy issue to a court to obtain a decision as to who is accountable for the policy effect in question.

2014).[17] From a *procedural* aspect, political accountability in the vertical dimension (principal–agent approach) is often defined as a mechanism by which, after the delegation of a task by a political actor (the 'principal') to an executive actor (the 'agent'), the execution of this task can be monitored by the principal, if it has sufficient information on the quality of task performance. If the execution is considered to be unsatisfactory, the principal must be able to sanction the malperformance by various means, such as imposing fines or withdrawing the delegation of the task (ie dismissing the agent). These three elements—ie task delegation, monitoring of task performance, and sanctions in the event of non-performance—form one of the most extensive conceptualisations of the mechanism realizing political accountability. In practice, weaker forms of political accountability are widely used when seeking to hold regulatory authorities accountable. These may comprise acts of political delegation to an agent, and access to information (transparency) in order to control the agent. The sanctioning element is often missing, or weak in terms of its stringency.

When considering procedural accountability, it is important to first map the actors with formally defined roles in the accountability chain. This involves not only identifying which actor has been delegated which task, and to whom each is accountable, but also the target groups of the regulations that relate informally to the formally competent actors. The target group consists of the actors who are affected by a regulation when Actor B fulfils a regulatory mandate which has been formally delegated to it by Actor A. The accountability channels vary according to the number of actors involved, ranging from a short accountability relationship between A and B, on the one hand, to larger chains featuring entire networks of actors linked in accountability mechanisms, on the other.[18]

Along the vertical/horizontal dimension, it is possible to distinguish a 'vertical' principal–agent relationship, wherein actor B is the agent, and actor A is the principal, which has given actor B a formal mandate to perform a task.[19] Under the vertical stream of accountability, formal power relations are

[17] M Bovens, RE Goodin, and T Schillemans, *Oxford Handbook of Public Accountability* (OUP 2014). One problem is the so-called 'multiple accountabilities disorder', where actors become confused by the conflicting expectations of their different accountabilities and, therefore, are unable to perform their duties effectively (JGS Koppell, 'Pathologies of Accountability: ICANN and the Challenge of Multiple Accountability Disorders' (2005) 65(1) Public Administration Review 94).

[18] Colin Scott, 'Accountability in the Regulatory State' (2000) 27(1) Journal of Law and Society 38.

[19] Terry Moe, 'Political Institutions. The Neglected Side of the Story' (1990) 6 Journal of Law, Economics and Organizations (special issue); Mark Bovens, 'Analysing and Assessing Accountability: A Conceptual Framework' (2007) 13(4) European Law Journal 447.; David Howarth and Aneta Spendzarova, 'Accountability in Post-crisis Eurozone Governance: The Tricky Case of the European Stability Mechanism' (2019) 57(4) Journal of Common Market Studies, 894.

defined in the sense of traditional formal subordination and superordination to ministers, parliament, and courts, or to the European Court of Auditors or ombudsmen, at the administrative level. In the context of European financial regulation, member governments delegate a regulatory task to the Commission, and hold it accountable for the performance of this task; the Commission, in turn, delegates the task to ESMA for its performance, and holds the latter accountable.

While the principal–agent approach focuses on the vertical dimension of delegation, there may also be horizontal accountability mechanisms between public actors at the same competence level, as well as horizontal accountability relations between public and private actors, and between private actors. In the horizontal formal relationship, actors A and B are equally powerful, and share in the performance (and control thereof) of a collective task that they delegated to themselves. In the horizontal stream of political accountability, where equal formal power is vested in both actors, the European Parliament (EP), for instance, delegates a task of regulation to the Commission, and holds the Commission accountable for the outcome of this task performance. Also at the horizontal level, member states hold each other accountable in the sectoral councils, when mutually observing task performance in member states.[20]

In the public/private and formal/informal dimensions, we identify accountability streams that involve both public and private regulatory actors, , such as a formal delegation of a regulatory task to a private actor, from accountability links of an informal nature linking the self-regulation by private actors to public actors that informally monitor their performance. These accountability mechanisms may be located on a horizontal or a vertical dimension (private actors being subordinate to public ones), where private actors engaged in self-regulation are held accountable by public bodies, or, at the horizontal level, by private stakeholders. This may occur either as formal subordination/superordination, or on the basis of informal accountability mechanisms.[21] In the context of transnational financial regulation, there are many private regulators engaged in self-regulation or co-regulation with state actors[22] that, in their transnational regulatory activities, escape the vertical control of state actors when seeking to hold them accountable.[23]

[20] Adrienne Héritier, 'Composite Democracy in Europe: The Role of Transparency and Access to Information' (2003) 10(5) Journal of European Public Policy 814.
[21] Colin Scott, 'Independent Regulators in Bovens, Goodin, and Schillemans (eds) (n 17).
[22] See Karremans and Héritier (n 10).
[23] J Black, M Hopper, and C Band, 'Making a Success of Principles-based Regulation' (2007) 1(3) Law and Financial Markets Review 191.

The accountability channels may be more complicated still: is an agent held accountable by one or two bodies, or by several bodies? In other words, are we dealing with a single accountability channel or plural accountability channels? If it is the latter, how are the accountability channels linked? Are we faced with entire chains or streams of delegation, or networks of accountability channels linking public and private actors? When several public and private regulators are responsible for task performance in a fragmented field of regulation, they may be linked by a complex network of accountability mechanisms. Scott distinguishes between two different models of governance in these networks: models of interdependence and models of hierarchy.[24] The question then arises of how these modes of accountability are linked.

Another important dimension of accountability in a delegation relationship is the *type of regulatory instrument* used. Pistor,[25] speaking of the dilemma of the regulator, emphasises that soft law is more elusive vis-à-vis accountability requests. If, by contrast, rules are rigid and precise, the target groups can more easily apply political accountability mechanisms. However, rigid rules are difficult to handle for the regulator because, in cases of contingencies or crises, some flexibility of rules may be needed to deal with a financial market problem. However, this means less political accountability to the public.

Further analytical perspectives from which to examine the effects–accountability link may be gained from Bergström and Ruotsi,[26] who underlines that the main reference point of legal accountability control consists in checking whether, in a hierarchy of norms, inferior value rules conflict with higher-value rules. The monitoring may be conducted either by legal or political bodies. In the case of political accountability mechanisms, from a political science perspective, an *ex ante* and *ex post* distinction may also apply. However, this would not concern congruence with the hierarchy of norms but, instead, congruence with the regulatory objectives declared for a specific measure. Thus, the distinction between *ex ante* and *ex post* monitoring is also present in the principal–agent approach (see above). By contractually binding the agent to *ex ante* defined procedural controls (for example, regular reporting) and substantive standards (for example, keeping regulatory decisions within

[24] Might this lead to what has been called an accountability conundrum, or the so-called 'multiple accountabilities disorder', on which see Koppell (n 17): Mark Dawson and Aneta Maricut-Akbik, *Procedural and Substantive Uses of Accountability in Modern Governance: Between Payoffs and Trade-offs* (2019); Workshop Paper, 'Theorizing and Assessing Accountability in Post-Crisis EU Economic Governance' (European University Institute Florence, 25 November 2019)145; Katharina Pistor, *The Code of Capital: How the Law Creates Wealth and Inequality* (Princeton University Press 2019); Scott (n 21).

[25] Mentioned by K Pistor in a talk held at LSE.

[26] CF Bergström and M Ruotsi, 'Grundlag i gungning? En ESO-rapport om EU och den svenska offentlighetsprincipen, Rapport till Expertgruppen för studier i offentlig ekonomi' (2018) 1 Swedish Ministry of Finance.

predefined limits), the principal can ensure mechanisms of *ex ante* accountability. By contrast, in the case of *ex post* monitoring, principals may rely on information from third parties ('firebell ringing'), top-down intervention ('police patrol'), or reporting to national parliaments and the EP. An *ex ante* political monitoring system uploading national competences to the European level would consist, for instance, of an *ex ante* preview of decisions by a EP parliamentary committee, such as in the case of Sweden's constitutional committee at the national level.[27] From these considerations, a further line of research on regulatory effects and accountability mechanisms in financial markets would analyse institutional mechanisms of *ex ante* and *ex post* monitoring with respect to procedural and substantive political accountability, given the initially stated regulatory objectives.[28]

These different power relationships and modes of control in accountability channels may have different implications for the target groups of a regulation. A mapping of procedural accountability channels is important in case that the target groups of a regulation are discontented with the substance of a regulation and its implementation. Therefore, the procedural and substantive aspects of accountability mechanisms are closely linked, but this question has not yet been systematically researched.

This distinction reaches back to the original distinction in law between procedural law and substantive law.[29] In political science analysis, this distinction between substantive and procedural accountability is relevant, and raises the question of the link between regulatory effects and procedural accountability mechanisms. More specifically, how do different types of accountability mechanisms play out when used by target groups of regulation—such as investors, fund managers, and investment firms—who are dissatisfied with the effects of financial regulation in different issue areas? What is most relevant is the comparison between issues with clear redistributive effects and issue areas with win/win features. Redistributive effects of regulatory decisions tend to raise political controversy between those who 'lose out' from the regulation, as opposed to those who 'win' from the regulation. Substantive accountability mechanisms, in this context, would imply a possibility for actors affected by regulatory decisions to question the very substance of the regulation, and

[27] ibid.

[28] Of course, legal and political accountability mechanisms are often linked. Dissatisfied target groups of a regulation, in the event of a political accountability conflict, may step out of the political institutional channel, as it were, and challenge the measure in court.

[29] See, most recently, Dawson and Maricut-Akbik (n 24).

possibly to obtain a modification of that substance rather than just the procedural correctness of the underlying decision process.

When focusing on regulatory effects, a first challenge is to determine the *scope and the nature of the effects* of regulation that is subject to accountability mechanisms. Financial market transactions, in their functioning and regulation, are not easily accessible to the wider public and the target groups of regulation. In other words, financial market regulation is an informationally secluded policy area. This does not mean that financial regulation is intentionally secluded,[30] but that it is hard to grasp in its technological and economic complexity, and in view of the worldwide interdependence of financial transactions, market players, and regulators' decisions.[31]

Nonetheless, a considerable degree of financial regulation happens under the conditions of informational accessibility.[32] Individual measures can be clearly delineated and analysed in their political formation and, subsequently, in their implementation. Therefore, under the conditions of information accessibility, an important analytical question is which type of regulatory policies are most likely to be challenged through accountability channels. Are these the policies that have a clear redistributive impact, producing winners and losers, and therefore being politically salient? Or are accountability channels also used in relation to regulatory issues of a win/win nature, in which all concerned actors benefit from the regulatory decisions? This argument goes back to the distinction made by Lowi[33] between redistributive and distributive policies. In the case of redistributive policies, benefits are bestowed on specific social groups (the winners) at the cost of other social groups (the losers). This process of redistribution is linked to a contested political process, organised around a cleavage between winners and losers. Win/win policies, by contrast, in which benefits are equally distributed across social groups, do not lead to adversarial political processes, since all actors agree to adopt policies that are equally beneficial to all concerned.[34]

[30] Walter Mattli argues that there is also much intentional obfuscation in financial market transactions, in order to obtain a relative advantage over competitors (eg 'stuffing'). However, this cannot be said for regulators: Walter Mattli, *Darkness by Design: The Hidden Power in Global Capital Markets* (Princeton University Press 2019).

[31] It has been argued, for instance by Haldane and Madouros, that the overall impact of individual regulatory measures on financial transactions, with their worldwide interconnectedness, does not follow a linear causal logic but, instead, may be subject to a logic of chaos theory where, at some point, individual actions, in their systemic effect, may produce a system stability crisis: A Haldane and V Madouros, The Dog and the Frisbee (speech at 366th Economic Policy Symposium, Federal Reserve Bank of Kansas City, on 'the changing policy landscape', Jackson Hole, Wyoming, 31 August 2012).

[32] Héritier and Schoeller (n 1).

[33] Theodore J Lowi, 'American Business, Public Policy, Case Studies and Political Theory' [1964] World Politics 677.

[34] Adrienne Windhoff-Héritier, *Policy-Analyse. Eine Einfuehrung* (Campus Verlag 1987).

In the book *Regulating Finance in Europe: Policy Effects and Political Accountability*, we limit our analysis to clearly restricted measures (such as the provisions under MiFID II and MIFIR, and the CMU) that are open to a causal explanation, in order to analyse their effects on market actors and public actors. In such cases, one can investigate institutional accountability mechanisms that are available to the target groups of regulation, such as asset managers, public actors, and the public at large, vis-à-vis the regulators, in order for them to contest these effects. Furthermore, we analyse the differences that the use of accountability mechanisms make, regarding the regulatory effects in question. Does the use of accountability channels lead to better policy outcomes? Does the analysis of the accountability channels, in the course of the implementation of a regulation, reveal high intermediation costs, for example rent-seeking by intermediary actors, which diminish the benefits of a regulation meant for investors?

2.5 Some empirical results

After theorizing and empirically investigating, in previous work, the dynamics leading to centralisation, decentralisation, and fragmentation in EU financial regulation,[35] we asked (bearing these structures in mind) who benefits from the regulatory structures and measures?[36] How are decision-makers and stakeholders held politically and administratively accountable? We focus on all actors involved in the regulatory process: politicians and regulators, as well as market players such as investors, fund managers, and investment firms, and outline the modes in which they are linked, in various political and administrative accountability mechanisms. Furthermore, we explicitly link the accountability channels to policy contents by asking: (a) whether specific regulatory results, such as redistributive effects, as compared to win/win effects, give rise to the mobilisation of available accountability channels; and (b) whether the use of accountability channels leads to a change in regulatory decisions.

To empirically illustrate answers to these questions, what follows is a summary of the findings. In their chapter, Karremans and Schoeller found multiple mechanisms of procedural accountability in relation to the regulation of high-frequency trading (HFT).

[35] Héritier and Schoeller (n 1).
[36] ibid.

These mechanisms seemed to have the greatest policy effect in the initial phases of regulatory initiatives, and to lose effectiveness in the later stages of policy implementation processes. When HFT appeared on the political agenda of post-financial crisis regulation, it enjoyed considerable political attention, but as soon as policy formulation came to involve more technical details, political interest faded. The horizontal accountability mechanisms between the Commission and the EP ensured that public representatives had substantial impact in putting HFT on the policy agenda, and in framing its overall objectives. However, during the formulation of the specifics of implementation in an ESMA standard technical advice, for instance, the definition of what constitutes an HFT firm was subject to hybrid accountability mechanisms with market stakeholders, under the monitoring of the Commission and the EP. There was no substantive *ex post* accountability mechanism that could be used by the public. When issues became technical, they lost saliency and, therefore, they no longer featured on the centre stage of party politics. They became the focus of bureaucratic networks, where business organisations, with their insider expertise, had more opportunity to influence policies.[37] Thus, ESMA actively engaged as a mediator, in the shaping of standards, between MiFID II's general principles and the preferences of HFT firms. As a result, it adapted some of its initial proposals to the preferences of market participants; Technical standards hybrid accountability mechanisms are, by definition, likely to work as influence channels for the businesses having the highest stakes in the market.

In his chapter on the role of the International Swaps and Derivatives Association (ISDA) as a global regulator of over-the-counter (OTC) derivatives, Karremans[38] found a similar pattern. He showed that, in the post-crisis period, ISDA's regulatory authority in the private regulation of OTC derivatives was curbed, and confined to the role of an interlocutor of public regulators. During the post-crisis years, the EU extended the reach of public oversight to previously untouched areas, and created the conditions for public authorities to monitor more than 75 per cent of the OTC derivatives market. Today, ISDA is no longer the sole rulemaker in the OTC derivatives markets, as it was before 2008. But, in its role of interlocutor with public regulators, it can fully exploit its sectorial expertise and influence the decisions on the eligibility criteria for clearing obligations, because European regulators rely extensively on its expertise. The implication is that, in the technical specification of broader political

[37] Pepper Culpepper, *Quiet Politics and Business Power: Corporate Control in Europe and Japan* (Cambridge University Press 2012).

[38] Johannes Karremans, 'The "Quiet Politics" of Hybrid Accountability Mechanisms: Watering Down Regulation through Expertise?' in Adrienne Héritier and Johannes Karremans (eds), *Regulating Finance in Europe: Policy Effects and Political Accountability* (Edward Elgar Publishing 2021).

decisions, accountability channels are not much used, except by influential market players in the sector of regulation.

In their chapter on the role of central counterparties (CCPs) in the financial system, Smoleńska and Héritier[39] argued, and empirically showed, that CCPs, which have grown in economic volume and system stability relevance, constitute an important nerve centre of the international financial markets. Hand in hand with their growing importance, the regulation of CCPs at the international, European, and national levels has become more and more dense. At the same time, in order to allow multiple types of regulators to be held accountable, a multitude of accountability channels were created, which are centralised, decentralised, or even fragmented. In response, European political actors have sought to contain decentralisation and fragmentation, in order to ensure that the use of accountability channels allows for an improvement of regulation, and prevents regulatory and accountability venue shopping. They showed that the use of the accountability mechanisms was of particular importance if redistributive issues were at stake. The latter created conflicts between the winners and losers of a regulation, such as in the case of an unlevel playing field between member state CCPs and third country CCPs, or in the case of a possible failure of CCPs, and their recovery or resolution between financial firms and taxpayers.

Peridis and Héritier,[40] in their chapter analysing the recent MiFID II research unbundling provisions and the effects that these had on market players, asked whether MiFID II research unbundling rules help to reduce rent-seeking by intermediators. By enhancing the transactions' transparency, the regulation seeks to ban the 'soft dollar' practices of brokers and other intermediaries in the EU, in order to protect investors. Under the new rules, investment managers were forced to either pay the research fees themselves, or to transfer and disclose the research fees to their clients. Until now, brokers were charging higher transaction fees, which included research fees. Now investment managers are forced to purchase research separately, and brokers need to sell research separately from other services. Peridis and Héritier focus on the effects of the rules, and describe the accountability mechanisms that the participants can use towards each other or other public actors, in the event of discontent with the regulatory effects. Finally, they described regulatory consequences deriving from

[39] Agnieszka Smoleńska and Adrienne Héritier, 'Critical Infrastructure (CCPs): Political Accountability and the Policy Effects of EMIR' in Adrienne Héritier and Johannes Karremans (eds), *Regulating Finance in Europe: Policy Effects and Political Accountability* (Edward Elgar Publishing 2021).

[40] Promitheas Peridis and Adrienne Héritier, 'Policy Effects and Accountability: Unbundling Research and Execution under MiFiD II' in Héritier and Karremans (eds) (n 39).

the use of these accountability mechanisms. As to the substantive effects of the unbundling regulation, the authors found that investment firms have, indeed, reduced their research budgets, and are moving more towards direct corporate communications. The number of brokers has reduced, and the big brokers have reduced their fees, increasing competition, and forcing many smaller brokers and research companies to exit the market. This has led to a decrease in the quantity of research, mainly for the large companies, while for the smaller firms it has stayed almost unchanged. Research quality has increased, due to the increased competition between brokers and research firms.

Important accountability channels have emerged, to be, at the private actor level, complaints mechanisms that may lead to internal policy changes. Complaints against the national competent authorities can lead to changes in the procedures of the authorities (for example, in the Wirecard case and BaFin). The most influential accountability mechanism was the use of consultations, as used by ESMA, and in relation to which many respondents offered critical comments on the implementation of the regulation. As a consequence, ESMA made proposals to the Commission on how the regulation should be amended.

In their chapter on the EU Benchmark Regulation (BMR), Smoleńska and Peridis[41] discussed the *accountability mechanisms* under the BMR, and their use and effects. In the context of the rising importance of benchmark administrators as market gatekeepers, the control of their activities has become an ever more pressing question. The authors specifically focused on the rise and application of 'private accountability' channels: that is, the specific roles conferred by the BMR on benchmark administrators. They explained the rise and design of these accountability channels, as a result of the financial crisis, with private self-regulation under LIBOR and EURIBOR. They argue that EU legislators created a complicated regime of private accountability of benchmark administrators, in order to minimise the regulatory burden on all of the parties involved. Their empirical investigation of the use and effects of such accountability mechanisms showed that there is little use for private accountability mechanisms under the current regulatory framework, because these operated as a deterrent for private market actors.

In his chapter, Joseph Ganderson,[42] on the regulation of fintechs, raised the novel question of how different European countries—the UK, France, and

[41] Agnieszka Smoleńska and Promitheas Peridis, 'Benchmark Administrators as Gatekeepers: Accountability and Policy Effects' in Héritier and Karremans (eds) (n 39).

[42] Joseph Ganderson, 'Fighting for Fintech: Competition, Regulation and Accountability in a Europe of Financial Innovation' in Héritier and Karremans (eds) (n 39).

Germany—regulate the bottom-up race of fintechs seeking to enter and operate in financial markets. He focused on how, under the different regimes, fintechs can be held accountable by regulators, and regulators, in turn, by politicians. Given the UK's pre-existing endowments in finance and technology, in London, it has 'raced from the bottom' to create market entry standards that apply not just domestically, but around the world. The UK's Financial Conduct Authority, which has 'grown up' with fintech, faced the dual challenge of securing markets while also encouraging innovation, and has engaged in sandboxing with fintechs to develop appropriate regulations. This dual role has made it vulnerable, in relation to supervision in the accountability channel, with respect to possible security issues with a specific firm. France has established a clearer separation between its proactive industrial policy of building up the Parisian fintech centre, and the role of regulators, the latter being a small unit with a competition remit. To date, the innovation hub has had a comparatively limited focus, on potentially transformative technologies. There has not, so far, been any regulatory sandboxing. Germany's innovation facilitator has taken on an extremely narrow conception of regulation, offering contact to firms, but strongly rejecting any notion of an innovation brief. However, the opacity of BaFin's contact process prompts the question of what happens behind the scenes. The Wirecard scandal, in which Germany's, and arguably Europe's, most successful fintech was found to have persistently engaged in fraud, has led to serious repercussions, both for BaFin and for German politics.

2.6 Conclusion

Considering the link between regulatory effects and political accountability, the empirical chapters offered important insights: the overall structure of the accountability channels used in European financial regulation reveals centralised features, but also elements of decentralisation when varying across member states, and even features of fragmentation, if one includes the multiple hybrid accountability channels involving public and private actors. The overall picture is that of a patchwork of accountability channels. In response to this patchwork, the Commission and EP have made efforts to centralise accountability channels by empowering ESMA, but also by introducing new measures, such as a whistleblowing mechanism for member state actors to indicate the lack of implementation of central regulatory provisions.

These top-down endeavours are, to some extent, counteracted by the regulatory competition from the bottom, in the case of fintechs, their varying regulation across member states and the UK, and the ways in which they are held politically and privately accountable. Making the picture even more complex is the increasing reliance on self-regulation of private actors, in the context of a benchmark regime administered by administrators, as the new gatekeepers of financial markets. These administrators are subject to both public supervision and private supervision, which are linked in complex ways.

As to the link between regulatory substance and regulatory effects, on one hand, and accountability channels, on the other, it emerges that, if there is public political awareness of financial issues, such in the aftermath of the financial crisis, when redistributive issues were at stake, vertical accountability channels play an important role in bringing regulatory solutions on to the political agenda. But, in the course of implementation, where issues tend to become more and more technical when translated into practical application, public interest and political pressure both wane. This allows for the private interests of the financial industry, with their expertise, to exert more influence when the details of regulatory issues are being shaped.

PART II

INVESTMENT FIRMS AS AGENTS OF ACCOUNTABILITY

3

The Joint Board of Appeal as an Accountability Mechanism for the ESAs

Merijn Chamon

3.1 Introduction

This chapter will explore the degree to which the Joint Board of Appeal fulfils its potential as a mechanism allowing parties such as investment firms to hold to account the European Supervisory Authorities (ESAs) and, notably, the European Securities and Markets Authority (ESMA), when they fall under the ambit of MiFID II or MiFIR. Under both instruments, the ESMA has been empowered to draft level two acts and to adopt level three guidance. In addition, under MIFIR, the ESMA will also exceptionally exercise level four powers.[1] Thus, the acts adopted by the ESMA are often highly technical and/or require considerable expertise for their adoption and, consequently, for their review. From this perspective, the Joint Board of Appeal, which was established as the administrative review body for the ESAs, could possibly provide investment firms, the interests of which are affected by the acts adopted by ESMA, with an effective remedy, since the Board of Appeal combines both legal and professional expertise. As a result, the Board of Appeal could function as an accountability mechanism and forum, allowing investment firms to hold the ESMA to account, forcing ESMA to (further) explain and justify its decisions.

In line with the other contributions to this volume, accountability is understood here as a relationship between an actor and a forum, where there is an obligation for the actor to explain and justify its conduct in light of predefined objectives, and where the forum may raise questions, pass judgement, and rectify the actor's conduct.[2] Before focusing on the potential of the Board of Appeal as an accountability mechanism that is open to investment firms, this question

[1] See Section 1.4 of the introduction to this volume by Bergström.

[2] See Mark Bovens, 'Analysing and Assessing Accountability: A Conceptual Framework' (2007) 13 European Law Journal 447, 450.

Merijn Chamon, *The Joint Board of Appeal as an Accountability Mechanism for the ESAs* In: *Legal Accountability in EU Markets for Financial Instruments.* Edited by: Carl Fredrik Bergström and Magnus Strand, Oxford University Press. © Merijn Chamon 2021. DOI: 10.1093/oso/9780192849281.003.0003

will be contextualised by discussing the problematic accountability regime in relation to the EU decentralised agencies in general. This is relevant since the ESAs are part of this larger group of bodies, and because the specific mechanism of the Board of Appeal is not unique to the ESAs, but is, instead, shared with several other decentralised agencies. This more general analysis shows that the emphasis of the EU decentralised agencies' (and the ESAs') accountability regimes are placed on a form of professional accountability, but that, specifically for the ESAs, this only results in a partial accountability, since no accountability relationship is defined for the Board of Supervisors. This finding underlines the importance of being able to hold the Board of Supervisors accountable before the Joint Board of Appeal, even if the latter is not formally qualified as an accountability forum in the ESAs regulations. Finally, the rules governing the functioning of the Board of Appeal, and its body of decisions since 2011, will be analysed to determine its accountability potential for parties such as investment firms, and the degree to which that potential is being realised.

3.2 Accountability for EU agencies: Too little, too much, or ill-considered?

Since the three ESAs have been granted increasingly significant powers, the question of their accountability has also grown in importance. Ensuring the accountability of the ESAs, and the EU decentralised agencies in general, remains a significant challenge today. The starting point of this chapter is that, while the EU institutions have not been indifferent to this challenge, they have not yet lived up to it. This is not so much because there are insufficient accountability mechanisms in place, in fact there might even be too many,[3] but because, above all, the accountability regime applicable to the EU decentralised agencies is ill-considered.[4]

Looking at the horizontal framework instrument that governs the agencification process at EU level, the non-binding Common Approach on

[3] Madalina Busuioc and Martijn Groenleer, 'The Theory and Practice of EU Agency Autonomy and Accountability: Early Day Expectations, Today's Realities and Future Perspectives' in Michelle Everson, Cosimo Monda, and Ellen Vos (eds), *European Agencies in between Institutions and Member States* (Kluwer 2014) 196–97.

[4] Merijn Chamon, 'Transparency and Accountability of EU Decentralised Agencies and Agencification in Light of the Common Approach on EU Decentralised Agencies' in S Garben, I Govaere, and P Nemitz (eds), *Critical Reflections on Constitutional Democracy in the European Union* (Hart Publishing 2019) 245–66.

EU Decentralised Agencies of 2012,[5] reveals that, in their 'common approach', the three EU institutions do not share a *common view* of what accountability should entail for the agencies, which include the three ESAs. Indeed, an analysis of the Common Approach[6] reveals that its conceptualisation of accountability is both partial and incomplete. It is partial in terms of the type of accountability envisaged since the Common Approach focuses mainly on professional accountability, with a limited role for political accountability. It is also incomplete in terms of scope, since parts of the agencies' activities are not covered by accountability mechanisms.

This incomplete and partial accountability results from the Common Approach providing that the agencies' executive directors should be accountable to the agencies' management boards. Since both the directors and the members of the management boards are experts drawn from the same epistemic community, their relationship may be qualified as one of professional accountability. The Common Approach puts little emphasis on political accountability, as the relationship between the agency and the Parliament and Council is channelled through the budgetary procedure. Accountability conceptualised as such, then, is incomplete because it does not envisage a possibility or need to hold the management board to account, even though an agency's policy is determined by the board and not by the director.

3.3 Zooming in on the European Supervisory Authorities

As noted in the introductory chapter (see section 1.4), the three ESAs were established in 2010, following the outbreak of the financial crisis. The ESAs are a further development of the level three committees resulting from the Lamfalussy process, which were established in 2001.[7] These committees brought together national supervisors for banking, financial markets, and insurance to ensure that national supervisors would apply EU law more efficiently and coherently. Following the financial crisis, it became clear that further institutionalisation and centralisation of powers at EU level was necessary

[5] See the Joint Statement and the Common Approach on EU Decentralised Agencies in Council Document 11450/12 of 18 June 2012.

[6] See the analysis by Chamon (n 3) 159.

[7] At the time the committees were established, Vaccari suggested that they could be turned into fully fledged agencies: see Beatrice Vaccari, 'Le processus Lamfalussy: une réussite pour la comitologie et un exemple de "bonne gouvernance européenne"' (2005) 4 Revue du droit de l'Union Européene 807.

to manage the interdependencies and complexities of the financial sector in the European internal market. The three level three Committees were therefore 'upgraded' to EU agencies, ie independent authorities established indefinitely through EU secondary legislation, and governed by their own legal personalities.[8] In principle, this further formalisation and institutionalisation of the committees facilitates accountability, since it goes hand in hand with a greater formalisation of the relationship between actor and forum.

Looking into the ESAs' establishing regulations from an accountability perspective reveals that they go further than the Common Approach, even though they predate this approach. Article 3 explicitly provides that the ESAs should be accountable to the European Parliament and the Council. A clear relationship is, thus, spelt out between actor and forum. In contrast to the minimal provisions of the Common Approach, the European Parliament is also granted a greater role under the ESA regulations: it must confirm the appointment of the chairperson of an ESA,[9] and that of the executive director.[10] Furthermore, the chairperson can only be removed from office with the agreement of the Parliament.[11] This latter power could be an important sanctioning element (indispensable for accountability, as discussed above), but in order to fire the chairperson, the Council must also agree,[12] meaning that the Parliament cannot decide this on its own. In short, compared to the Common Approach, the accountability regime for the ESAs is a bit more refined, but still incomplete: The Board of Supervisors is still accountable to no one. Its chairperson is in an accountability relationship with the Parliament, but the Parliament cannot fully hold the chair to account without cooperation from the Board.

For the ESAs, the accountability gap seems to be even more problematic than is the case for the decentralised agencies in general, despite there being an abundance of accountability mechanisms (both for the ESAs, specifically, and the agencies, generally). Using the terminology employed in the preceding chapter by Héritier, there are plural accountability channels in relation to the ESAs, but there is no *ex post* political accountability (procedural or substantive)

[8] For a more elaborate account, see Chapter 7 of this book (by Van Cleynenbreugel). See also Merijn Chamon, *EU Agencies: Legal and Political Limits to the Transformation of the EU Administration* (OUP 2016) 10.

[9] See art 48(2) of Regulations 1093/2010, 1094/2010, 1095/2010 establishing the European Banking Authority, European Insurance and Occupational Pensions Authority, European Securities and Markets Authority [2010] OJ L 331/12 (hereafter the 'ESA Regulations'), as amended by Regulation 2019/2175. Under the original 2010 establishing regulations, the Parliament only had the opportunity to object to the appointment.

[10] ibid art 51(2).

[11] ibid art 48(2) and (5). Before the 2019 revision of the ESA Regulations, only the Parliament could remove the chairperson, following a decision by the Board of Supervisors.

[12] ibid.

for decisions taken by the Boards of Supervisors of the ESAs. The peculiar situation that the ESAs find themselves in is the result of their 'split' structure (which they share with the Energy Agency).[13] For the other EU decentralised agencies, their day-to-day functioning, and the implementation of their policies, as defined by the Board, are carried out under the authority of the director. For the ESAs (and the Energy Agency), however, the director is only responsible for the day-to-day functioning of the agency, while the Supervisory Board defines the policy of the ESA, and implements it by adopting the necessary decisions (see Article 43 of the ESA regulations). This is also the case for the decisions, opinions, and drafts which, notably, the ESMA adopts, under MiFID II and MiFIR. As with the other decentralised agencies, the (Supervisory) Boards cannot be properly held accountable, but this is even more problematic for the ESAs, given the Supervisory Boards' accrued role. The political accountability mechanisms and relationships described here were not significantly altered in the 2019 revision of the mandates of the ESAs.[14]

Of course, a full accountability picture is not presented when account is only taken of the mechanisms that the establishing regulations formally qualify as part of the ESAs' accountability regime. Going back to the definition of accountability, if there is a forum to which an actor must explain or justify its actions, and the forum may ask questions, pass judgement, and rectify actor behaviour, there is an accountability mechanism in place regardless of whether it is formally qualified as such. For instance, the Stakeholder Groups (SGs) set up within the three ESAs can also be seen as accountability mechanisms, opening up the accountability of the agencies to 'outside' professionals.[15] Another such mechanism, and one on which this chapter will focus, is the Board of Appeal. This internal review body allows affected parties to challenge agency decisions, requiring the agency to explain and justify its decision-making, and allowing the Board of Appeal to assess and annul agency decisions. In that sense, it has sanctioning powers that go beyond that of the SGs. Therefore, it is an interesting complement to the professional accountability which the director has

[13] See Regulation 2019/942 of the European Parliament and of the Council establishing a European Union Agency for the Cooperation of Energy Regulators [2019] OJ 2019 L 158/22.

[14] While art 3 of the ESA Regulations was recast, and summarises the main political accountability relations, it mainly does so by recasting existing provisions in one single Article. The main novelties under the 2019 regulations are that the Parliament now has to confirm the chairperson (art 51(2)), that it is now the Council and not the Board of Supervisors that is involved in the dismissal of the Chairperson (art 48(2) and (5)), and that there is now an explicit legal basis in art 3(7) for the Parliament and Council to direct questions to the ESAs.

[15] On the stakeholder group as an accountability forum, see C Di Noia and M Gargantini, 'The European Securities and Markets Authority: Accountability towards EU Institutions and Stakeholders' in P Iglesias-Rodriguez (ed), *Building Responsive and Responsible Financial Regulators in the Aftermath of the Global Financial Crisis* (CUP 2015) esp 151–54

vis-à-vis the Board of Supervisors, since it allows outside professionals (affected parties) to submit decisions of the Board of Supervisors for both legal and professional review by the Board of Appeal. Indeed, some years after the Board of Appeal started operating, Chiu positively assessed the Board as an accountability mechanism.[16]

In the following sections, Chiu's preliminary conclusion will be revisited, by specifically looking into how investment firms may use the Board of Appeal to hold the Board of Supervisors of ESMA to account for actions pursuant to MiFID II and MiFIR. The first stage of this will be done by looking into the rules governing the functioning of the Board of Appeal, and the body of decisions adopted by the Board of Appeal.

3.4 The mechanism of the Board of Appeal and its corpus of decisions

While an ad hoc approach has been followed in the process of agencification (even after the adoption of the Common Approach), the EU legislator has been remarkably consistent when it comes to equipping the decision-making agencies (ie EU agencies that have been granted the power to take decisions that are binding vis-à-vis third parties)[17] with dedicated internal administrative review bodies. The precise terminology (in the establishing acts of those EU agencies) varies, but these review bodies are generally referred to as Boards of Appeal.[18] Decisions adopted by the Boards of Appeal may, in turn, be appealed before the General Court.[19] While the Boards of Appeal all essentially fulfil the same function (reviewing decisions adopted by their agencies), none of them function identically. While it is, therefore, useful to compare the Joint Board of Appeal with the other Boards of Appeal (of other agencies), and an analysis of the judgments of the General Court on decisions of other Boards of Appeal

[16] Iris H-Y Chiu, 'Power and Accountability in the EU Financial Regulatory Architecture: Examining Inter-Agency Relations, Agency Independence and Accountability' (2015) 8 European Journal of Legal Studies 88.

[17] On this type of agency, see Stefan Griller and Andreas Orator, 'Everything under Control? The "Way Forward" for European Agencies in the Footsteps of the Meroni Doctrine' (2010) 35(1) European Law Review 3, 14.

[18] Generally, on the Boards of Appeal, see Jacopo Alberti, 'A New Era for EU Agencies' Boards of Appeal? A Preliminary Assessment of the Recent Reform of CJEU's Statute and its Implication on EU Administrative Adjudication' in M Conticelli, M De Bellis, and G della Cananea, *EU Executive Governance: Agencies and Procedures* (Giappichelli 2019) 204–32.

[19] See art 263(5) TFEU.

may be useful, there is always the caveat that each Board of Appeal (including the Joint Board of Appeal) has its own peculiarities.

The ESAs' Joint Board of Appeal is a unique body among the Boards of Appeal in the various agencies, since it is the only one that is shared between different agencies. In the following sections, the specific legal framework, as defined for the Joint Board of Appeal, will be assessed, in order to identify the degree to which the Joint Board of Appeal can fulfil an accountability function. As will be shown, the legislator has construed the Board of Appeal's role in a restrictive manner, greatly diminishing its accountability potential. For the Board of Appeal, the restrictive framework defined by the legislator (limiting the types of decisions reviewable by the Board, and limiting the parties having access to the Board, as described below) is to be accepted as a given. However, within that framework, the Board of Appeal has some leeway in conceptualizing its role, which may range from a minimalist to a maximalist reading of the scope and intensity of its review. Depending on how it sees its own role, it will realise its potential as an accountability mechanism to a lesser or greater degree.

To shed light on this issue, the corpus of the Board of Appeal's decisions needs to be studied. Although it has been functioning since 2011, the Board has only dealt with a small number of appeals. In addition, it is only recently that its decisions have been systematically scrutinised. Reference is made to these recent instances of scrutiny for an overview and discussion of these decisions.[20] The main point of interest in the present chapter is not the decisions as such, but the indication they give as to the degree to which the Board of Appeal may fulfil its accountability potential.

3.4.1 Establishment and composition

The Joint Board of Appeal's establishment and functioning are laid down in Articles 58 to 61 of the ESAs' founding regulations. It has been empowered to adopt its own Rules of Procedure, thus differing from the older Boards of

[20] See, in particular, Marco Lamandini and David Ramos Muñoz, 'Law and Practice of Financial Appeal Bodies (ESAs' Board of Appeal, SRB Appeal Panel): A View from the Inside' (2020) 57(1) Common Market Law Review, 119; Merijn Chamon, 'De Gemeenschappelijke Bezwaarcommissie van de Europese Toezichthoudende Autoriteiten' (2020) 68(4) Sociaal-Economische Wetgeving 171.

Appeal of other agencies, where the internal Rules of Procedure are adopted by the Commission.[21]

The Joint Board of Appeal consists of six members (and six alternates),[22] whereas the Boards of Appeal of most other agencies have only three members. How many lawyers and experts are to be appointed is not specified exactly, but the original ESA regulations provide that the members must be 'individuals of high repute with a proven record of relevant knowledge of Union law and of having international professional experience, to a sufficiently high level in the fields of banking, insurance, occupational pensions, securities markets or other financial services ... The Board of Appeal shall have sufficient legal expertise to provide expert legal advice on the legality, including proportionality, of the Authority's exercise of its powers'.[23] The 2019 revision of the ESA regulations, in light of Brexit, added that Board of Appeal members should be nationals of EU member states, and should have thorough knowledge of at least two official languages of the EU.[24]

The Supervisory Board of each ESA appoints two members from a list drawn up by the Commission (following a public call).[25] The 2019 revision also strengthened the position of the European Parliament regarding appointments, as it may now require the shortlisted candidates to appear before the Parliament before their appointment. Also, during their terms in office, Board of Appeal members may now be invited by the Parliament to make statements and answer questions.[26]

The members, who cannot hold other positions within the ESAs,[27] are appointed for a period of five years that can be extended once (for a further period of five years).[28] A member cannot be removed early, except in cases of 'serious misconduct', in which case the Management Board of the responsible ESA may decide to do so, after consulting its Board of Supervisors.[29] Members must be independent and impartial, and may be objected to by any party before the Board of Appeal.[30] Each member must publicly make a written declaration of interest ,and this must be updated annually.[31]

[21] When the functioning of the Joint Board of Appeal is compared to that of the Boards of Appeal of other agencies, the discussion in this chapter draws from earlier work, notably Merijn Chamon, 'Les agences décentralisées et le droit procédural de l'UE' (2016) 52(2) Cahiers de droit européen 541, 555.

[22] See art 58(2) of the ESA Regulations.

[23] ibid. The references to a knowledge of Union law, and to the review of proportionality, were added in the 2019 revision.

[24] ibid.

[25] See art 58(3) of the ESA Regulations.

[26] ibid.

[27] ibid, arts 58(2) and 59(1).

[28] ibid, art 58(4).

[29] ibid, art 58(5).

[30] ibid, art 59(4).

[31] ibid, art 59(6).

Unlike the Boards of Appeal of most other agencies, the Joint Board of Appeal does not have its own registry. Article 58(8) of the ESA Regulations provides that the three authorities must 'ensure adequate operational and secretarial support for the Board of Appeal through the Joint Committee'. This committee is headed by the chairpersons of the ESAs, and has its own staff, acting as a joint secretariat. This necessitates that the procedural rules of the Board of Appeal include specific safeguards that prevent the ESA chairing the Joint Committee from being responsible for handling an appeal against one of its decisions. Article 4(5) of the Rules of Procedure, thus, provides that '[t]he ESA shall ensure that there is an adequate procedure in place so that from the outset of the appeal, no information passes from the Secretariat to the respondent ESA or any of the ESAs except as specified by the Rules of Procedure'.[32]

3.4.2 Competence of the Joint Board of Appeal

The jurisdiction of the Joint Board of Appeal, like those of most other Boards of Appeal, is substantively defined: the acts that are open to challenge before the Board of Appeal are defined in Article 60(1) of the relevant ESA Regulation, based on their legal basis. For example, regarding the ESMA Regulation, only decisions adopted under Articles 17, 18, or 19 of that regulation, and 'any other decision taken by the ESMA in accordance with the acts listed in Article 1(2) of the ESMA Regulation' can be challenged before the Board of Appeal. Article 1(2) mainly consists of an explicit list of the EU legislation preceding the establishment of the ESAs. As a result, an explicit reference to the MiFIR is lacking in Articles 1(2) of both the EBA and ESMA Regulations. In contrast, the Credit Rating Agencies Regulation (CRAR) is listed in Article 1(2) of the ESMA Regulation. However, this does not mean that EBA or ESMA Decisions adopted pursuant to the MiFIR cannot be challenged before the Board of Appeal. After all, Articles 1(2) of both the ESMA and EBA regulations also provide that the ESA will act in the scope 'of any further legally binding Union act which confers tasks on the Authority'. The cross-reference to all of these acts in Article 60(1), thus, represents a rather contorted way of defining the Board of Appeal's jurisdiction.

A further question that has already been raised in this regard is how to interpret the term 'decision', used in Article 60(1). There is, of course, settled case law of the Court that holds that only binding acts can be challenged in

[32] Joint Board of Appeal, Decision 2020/01, Rules of Procedure.

the action for annulment provided for in Article 263 TFEU,[33] but nothing prevents the secondary legislator from opting for a wider category of acts that are open to challenge before a Board of Appeal. Article 19 of the original regulation establishing the EU Energy Agency also provided for the possibility of lodging an appeal before the Board of Appeal against 'decision[s] referred to in Articles 7, 8 or 9' of the regulation.[34] Did this provision allow an *opinion* of the Energy Agency adopted under Article 7(4) of the regulation to be challenged before the Board of Appeal? The Austrian energy regulator believed so, but the Board of Appeal interpreted 'decision' analogously to the settled case law of the Court of Justice under Article 263 TFEU,[35] an interpretation which the General Court confirmed, on appeal, by reference to Article 288 TFEU.[36] This clarification could be applied *mutatis mutandis* to the references to 'decisions' in the ESA Regulations; indeed, the Joint Appeal Board, drawing an analogy from the established case law of the Court, has also ruled that affirmative and preparatory acts cannot be challenged before it.[37] The potential of the Board of Appeal to act as an effective accountability mechanism is, therefore, greatly reduced, since most of the acts which the ESMA (and EBA) will adopt under MiFID II and MiFIR are non-binding (preparatory) acts (see on this the next section).

3.4.2.1 Scope of review: Exclusion of soft law

The Board of Appeal effectively reduced its accountability potential in *Creditreform Rating AG/EBA* when it was asked to review a draft implementing technical standard by the EBA under Regulation 575/2013. While the Board of Appeal's refusal to accept jurisdiction is wholly sound in light of Article 60 of the ESA Regulations, the reasoning developed by the Board fails to convince. The Board noted that, 'the appealed act is not a decision under Article 60 of the ESA Regulation because it is merely a preparatory act without immediate legal effects vis-à-vis the appellant'.[38] Recalling the EU Courts' established jurisprudence on challenging preparatory acts, the Board of Appeal continued,

[33] See Koen Lenaerts, Ignace Maselis, and Kathleen Gutman, *EU Procedural Law* (OUP 2015) 260–74.

[34] Regulation 713/2009 establishing an Agency for the Cooperation of Energy Regulators [2009] OJ L 211/1.

[35] ACER Board of Appeal, Decision A-001-2015, para 24.

[36] Case T-63/16 *E-Control v ACER* EU:T:2017:456, para 37. However, the General Court, arguably, did not properly recognise that art 288 TFEU also states that it is the institutions, and therefore *a contrario* not the EU agencies, that adopt regulations, directives, decisions, recommendations, and opinions. For a discussion of this case, see Merijn Chamon, 'General Court Confirms that the ACER's Board of Appeal cannot Review Non-binding Opinions' [2018] Revue du droit des industries de réseau 218.

[37] Decision 2015 001 *Onix Asigurări SA v EIOPA*, para 54; Decision 2019 05 *Creditreform Rating AG v EBA*, paras 60–72.

[38] *Creditreform* (n 35) para 60.

'in accordance with settled case law of the CJEU that the Board of Appeal must follow also in its interpretation of Article 60 of the ESA Regulations, acts having a preparatory nature adopted by a European agency ... are not subject to an autonomous judicial review'.[39] The Board's finding that the General Court would find such a challenge under Article 263 TFEU inadmissible is entirely correct, but, again, it does not provide clear reasoning for why 'the Board considers that this conclusion is also valid to exclude the admissibility of an appeal to the Board of Appeal against the draft implementing technical standard, because so long as the draft is not endorsed by the European Commission and therefore adopted in its final form via a decision of the European Commission, the draft developed and proposed by the ESAs, despite the negative factual consequences that can be reasonably expected by its public disclosure (as noted by the appellant), has no legal effects vis-à-vis the appellant'.[40] Even though the conclusion itself is entirely defensible, the problem with this reasoning is clear: the Board does not set out why its interpretation of an administrative remedy in Article 60 of the ESA Regulation should follow the interpretation of the judicial remedy under Article 263 TFEU. The main 'take-home' message of this case is that level two acts which ESMA (and EBA) draft pursuant to MiFID II and MiFIR will, therefore, not be challengeable before the Board of Appeal.

Based on the precedent which the General Court set for the European Energy Agency's (ACER) Board of Appeal in *E-Control v ACER*,[41] the Joint Board of Appeal would also refuse to accept jurisdiction to review the level three acts adopted by ESMA pursuant to MiFID II and MiFIR. This is the case even when a review of these measures would be useful in itself, for instance where the implementation of MiFID II by national authorities is guided by the soft law (guidelines) of ESMA (and EBA). Likewise, it could be interesting for investment firms to have the Board of Appeal review the opinions of ESMA (or EBA) under Article 43 MiFIR on whether certain product interventions by national authorities are justified and proportionate. In the same vein, the ESMA's opinions, pursuant to Article 57 MiFID II, on position limits which national authorities intend to set, are non-binding but highly determinative. In other cases, the interest which investment firms may have in having access to the Board of Appeal is even more acute: for instance, when ESMA adopts opinions on requests for waivers or suspensions pursuant to Articles 4, 9 or 11 MiFIR. These opinions, while non-binding, will typically inform national

[39] ibid para 64.
[40] ibid para 69.
[41] See n 34.

authorities, which will adopt decisions addressed to those investment firms. However, applying the case law on acts that produce legal effects under Article 263 TFEU on a *mutatis mutandis* basis to the appeal procedure before the Board of Appeal will result in appeals against all these soft law measures being rejected as inadmissible.

3.4.2.2 Intensity of review offered by the Joint Board of Appeal

Of the thirteen appeals decided, at the time this chapter was finalised, by the Joint Board of Appeal, only two hinged on substantive issues (the others turning on issues of procedure and/or admissibility),[42] even though it is precisely on issues of substance that the expert Board of Appeal has significant added value over judicial review, in the strict sense. If, for instance, an investment firm takes issue with decisions adopted under the MiFIR for policy reasons, it will be difficult to convince the EU Courts, within the framework of the annulment procedure, to quash these decisions. Under well-established case law, the EU Courts will only look for manifest errors on the part of the EU executive: when the executive has to make complex assessments based on technical and/or scientific information, it will be left a broad discretion by the judges, since 'it is not the Court's role to substitute its assessment of complex facts for that made by the institution which adopted the decision'.[43]

In contrast, the *raison d'être* of the Boards of Appeal is that they can perform a more in-depth review than the EU Courts, and can even look at how sound the policy considerations on which an EU agency has based its actions are. The 2019 revision of the ESA regulations emphasises this, as the regulations now explicitly stress that the Board of Appeal will review the proportionality of contested measures, including how appropriate they are in achieving the regulatory outcome sought. At the same time, the Boards of Appeal also have more limited means (for example, human resources) than the actual decision-making bodies of the agencies (or the EU Courts). But what does this mean for the reviews exercised by Boards of Appeal? Should Boards limit themselves to reviewing procedural correctness?[44] Should they perform a *de novo* review?[45]

[42] The cut-off date, on which this chapter was finalised, was 13 December 2020. The two appeals concerned were Decision 2013 008 *SV Capital OÜ v EBA* and its follow-up, Decision 2014 C1 02 *SV Capital OÜ v EBA II*, and Decision 2019 01-04 *Skandinaviska Enskilda Banken AB e.a. v ESMA*.

[43] See Case T-257/07 *France v Commission* EU:T:2011:444, para 89. This case concerned the Common Agricultural Policy, but the Court follows the same approach in other policy areas too. See, generally, Lenaerts, Maselis, and Gutman (n 31) 385.

[44] As suggested by Germany in Case T-755/17 *Germany v ECHA* EU:T:2019:647, para 163.

[45] As suggested by BASF in Case T-125/17 *BASF v ECHA* EU:T:2019:638, para 55.

Or should their intensity of review take a middle ground between these two extremes? In recent cases related to the Board of Appeal of the European Chemicals Agency, the General Court settled for the middle ground,[46] but, given that the Joint Board of Appeal of the ESAs functions differently from the European Chemicals Agency (ECHA) Board of Appeal, the precedential value of this case law is unclear.[47] Recently, the General Court also reviewed a decision of the ACER Board of Appeal. In *Aquind v ACER*, it held that the Board of Appeal of ACER had erred when it held that it could only strike down manifest errors of assessment. Relying on the EU Courts' established case law on this matter,[48] the General Court held that 'the provisions on the organisation and powers of the Board of Appeal of ACER support the finding that that appellate body was not established to confine itself to a limited review of complex technical and economic assessments'.[49] Those provisions, relating to the ACER Board of Appeal, are essentially the same as the ones defining the organisation and powers of the Joint Board of Appeal of the ESAs.[50] The Joint Board of Appeal is, therefore, required to perform a thorough review of contested measures.[51]

Indeed, the Joint Board of Appeal has rightly held that it cannot perform a *de novo* assessment,[52] and, instead, can only review the legality of contested measures. In *SV Capital OÜ v EBA II*, the applicant claimed that EBA had incorrectly exercised its discretion in light of its own Internal Processing Rules on Investigation. The Board of Appeal did not examine the interesting question of whether a private individual might rely on such internal organisational measures, but it did note the following:

[46] See *Germany v ECHA* (n 42) and *BASF v ECHA* (n 43), as discussed in Merijn Chamon and Annalisa Volpato, 'Sketching Out the Role and Function of the ECHA Board of Appeal: Germany v ECHA and BASF v ECHA' (2020) 45(6) European Law Review 840.

[47] If the middle ground is linked to the functional continuity of Boards of Appeal with their agencies, it should be noted that the ESA Joint Board of Appeal, unlike the Boards of Appeal of the ECHA, European Union Intellectual Property Office (EUIPO), and the Community Plant Variety Office (CPVO), cannot amend contested decisions, and only has the choice between confirming the decision or sending the decision back to the agency for revision. Confirming this functional continuity for the EUIPO, CPVO, and the European Aviation Safety Agency (EASA) (before the revision of the latter's establishing regulation in 2018), see Case T-672/17 *Mamas and Papas Ltd v EUIPO* ECLI;EU:T:2018:707, para 39; Case T-177/16 *Mema GmbH LG v CPVO* EU:T:2019:57, para 40; Case T-102/13 *Heli-Flight GmbH v EASA* EU:T:2014:1064, para 27. Alberti, however, does not link the notion of functional continuity to a Board of Appeal's power to reform contested decisions: see Alberti (n 17) 208.

[48] Decision A-001-2018 of the ACER Board of Appeal, *Aquind v ACER*, paras 51–52.

[49] Case T-735/18 *Aquind v ACER* EU:T:2020:542, para 52.

[50] The only exception being that, under the applicable legal framework at the time, the ACER Board of Appeal could exercise any power that lay within the competence of the Agency, a principle that does not apply to the Joint Board of Appeal.

[51] See *Aquind v ACER* (2020) (n 47), para 82.

[52] Decision 2017 01 *FinancialCraft Analytics v ESMA*, para 61.

> As to the test to be applied on an appeal against the EBA's decision not to initiate an 'own initiative' investigation, the respondent says that there will be a high threshold, as where the EBA based its view on materially incorrect facts, committed a manifest error of appraisal or misused its discretionary powers. Similarly, the appellant accepts that the case must be one in which the EBA incorrectly applied its discretion, resulting in a manifestly wrong decision. The Board agrees that there is a high threshold, but it need not decide this issue definitively, because on no view is the material adduced by the appellant sufficient to show that the EBA exercised its discretion wrongly.[53]

The fact that the Board of Appeal left this question open is of crucial importance, since its review should, in principle, be more in-depth than the marginal review that the General Court can exercise. If the Board of Appeal merely exercised a review that would be substitutable with that of the General Court, the added value of the Board of Appeal would be non-existent. Without making clear to what extent this played a role in its decision, the Board of Appeal in *Svenska Handelsbanken AB et al/ESMA* also noted that, '[i]t is no part of the Board of Appeal's function to decide policy, which is a matter for the Board of Supervisors'.[54] Although this is undoubtedly correct, this type of reasoning should not be used (in the future) to justify a mere marginal review by the Board of Appeal.

The few cases that hinge on substantive issues illustrate the potential added value of the Joint Board of Appeal. The most important case was the previously mentioned *Svenska Handelsbanken AB et al/ESMA* case, which raised the question of whether a group of Scandinavian banks had violated Union law by offering 'shadow ratings', in the form of investor information, without being registered as credit rating agencies. ESMA had taken this view, and had, therefore, fined the entities in question. The Board of Appeal tried to construe the proper meaning of the exception under CRAR which allows investment firms to provide 'investor information' without being deemed to have provided credit ratings. However, it could not arrive at a conclusion following either a literal or genetic interpretation.[55] It subsequently followed the consequentialist reasoning of the ESMA, agreeing with the agency that allowing investment firms to provide 'shadow ratings' through their investment information would allow market participants to avoid the application of the CRAR.[56] The Board of

[53] *SV Capital OÜ v EBA II* (n 40), paras 52–53.
[54] *Skandinaviska Enskilda Banken* (n 40), paras 12 and 194.
[55] ibid, paras 236–49.
[56] ibid para 262.

Appeal is better placed than judges in the Court to assess whether there would, indeed, be such a risk, since the Board arguably benefits from a more profound knowledge of, and affinity with, how these products are viewed in the financial markets. This applies equally to the question of whether the investment firms in question had disclosed their 'shadow ratings' to the public by making the investment reports available to 1,147 recipients.[57]

3.4.3 Active *locus standi* before the Joint Board of Appeal

Parties with standing to bring proceedings are identified by the ESA Regulations as any 'natural or legal person, including a competent authority', in so far as they are challenging decisions 'addressed to that person, or against a decision of direct and individual interest for that person, even if it is addressed to another person'.[58] This is analogous to the founding regulations of other agencies equipped with a Board of Appeal, and should be read together with paragraph 5 of Article 263 TFEU, which, since the Lisbon Treaty, provides that '[t]he acts setting up bodies, offices and agencies of the Union may lay down specific conditions and arrangements concerning actions brought by natural or legal persons against acts of these bodies, offices or agencies intended to produce legal effects in relation to them'. In concrete terms, this means that, under Article 263 TFEU, non-privileged parties like investment firms must first exhaust the appeal procedures before the Board of Appeal before they can bring an admissible appeal before the General Court against a decision by an ESA. This may, indeed, lead to remarkable situations: in order to challenge one and the same individual decision, a competent national authority might first have to appeal to the internal Board of Appeal, unless that authority can convince its own member state (privileged party) to challenge the decision's legality, in which case the member state may bring a case directly to the General Court.[59]

Although the concepts of 'direct and individual interest', as used in the ESA Regulations, are reminiscent of the concepts of direct and individual concern in Article 263 TFEU, it would be wrong to automatically interpret both in the

[57] ibid paras 270–76.

[58] See art 60(1) of the ESA Regulations.

[59] ACER's Decision 02/2019 provides a good example of this. This decision was contested simultaneously by the German regulator and Germany itself. The German regulator had to bring an appeal before the Board of Appeal (see Case A-003-2019 for the ACER Board of Appeal), while Germany had direct access to the General Court (see pending Case T-283/19 *Germany v ACER*).

same way. Indeed, in creating an entirely new and separate administrative remedy, the EU legislator is not bound by the interpretation given by the Court to similar, or even identical, provisions relating to a judicial remedy (in this case, the annulment action under Article 263 TFEU). In principle, the Joint Board of Appeal has also recognised this in *Investor Protection Europe v ESMA*:

> [W]hereas Article 263 of the TFEU provides for proceedings for a review by the Court, Article 60 of the ESMA Regulation provides for 'an appeal' to the Board of Appeal. In the Board's experience, the distinction between a judicial review by a court, and an appeal to a specialist body or tribunal, is well understood in the field of financial regulation and supervision . . .
>
> Accordingly, the Board does not agree with the respondent's analysis in this respect. The automatic application of limitations applicable to proceedings under Articles 263 and 265 TFEU . . . is, in the Board's opinion, inappropriate in the case of a right of appeal under Article 60 of the ESMA Regulation.[60]

At the same time, the Joint Board ruled, in the earlier *SV Capital OÜ v EBA* case, that the reference in the EBA Regulation to natural or legal persons who have a direct and individual interest reflects the similar provision in Article 263 TFEU.[61] This effectively means that the Board of Appeal, like other EU agencies, does not normally fulfil a function in reviewing acts of general application, despite the fact that some EU agencies, especially the ESAs, have been empowered to adopt regulatory acts (in the sense of Article 263 TFEU),[62] such as the acts which ESMA might adopt pursuant to Article 40 MiFIR. These measures of general scope will, typically, not require implementing measures, and will be of direct concern to investment firms, but it is unlikely that they would be of individual concern in the *Plaumann* sense,[63] thus barring recourse to the Joint Board of Appeal. Instead, affected investment firms would have to go directly to the General Court. In *Creditreform AG v EBA*, the Joint Board of Appeal also confirmed this view when it noted (*obiter dictum*) that the textual difference between Article 60 of the ESA Regulations and Article 263 TFEU on this point 'offers a useful indication that in the legislative intent regulatory acts

[60] Decision 2014 05 *Investor Protection Europe v ESMA*, paras 37–38.

[61] *SV Capital OÜ v EBA II* (n 40), para 27.

[62] See Case C-583/11 P *Inuit Tapiriit Kanatami e.a. v European Parliament and Council of the European Union* EU:C:2013:625, paras 60–61.

[63] The *Plaumann* sense applies *mutatis mutandis* to appeals before the Joint Board of Appeal in light of *SV Capital OÜ v EBA II* (n 40). For the *Plaumann* case and the high threshold resulting from it, see Lenaerts, Maselis, and Gutman (n 31) 325 and following pages.

drafted by the ESAs are not contemplated as the subject-matter of an appeal to the Board of Appeal'.[64]

3.4.4 Procedure before the Joint Board of Appeal

Parties who want to appeal to the Board of Appeal must do so within three months after notification or publication of the decision in question. According to the rules of procedure of the Board of Appeal, the application must be handed over personally, sent by registered mail, sent by email, or filed in accordance with the Board's directives.[65] As with the Boards of Appeal of the Energy Agency and the Single Resolution Board, the Board of Appeal itself also has a time limit to respect. It must take its decision within three months of the appeal being lodged. The Board of Appeal respects this strict period by taking the day on which the written proceedings (and a possible oral hearing) is completed as the date on which the 'appeal is lodged'.[66] This strict timing may explain why, as with the Board of Appeal of the Single Resolution Board, there is no possibility under the Regulations or the Rules of Procedure for parties to intervene[67] (although this possibility is foreseen for the Board of Appeal of the Energy Agency, which is also bound by a strict time limit). Contrary to appeals before the Boards of Appeal of some other agencies, a flat-rate fee is not charged for lodging an appeal.

Upon simple request, parties are also entitled to oral hearings of their cases.[68] In terms of procedural efficiency, it should be noted that Article 60(4) of the ESA Regulations provides that, '[i]f the objection is admissible ... the Joint Board of Appeal [examines] whether it is well-founded'. On this basis, the Board of Appeal has determined, in its internal procedures, that if the respondent (ESA) raises an objection of inadmissibility, the Board must check admissibility *before* examining the merits of the appeal.[69] In any event, the Board of Appeal can check the admissibility of its own motion, but the default rule means that the *Boehringer* case law of the Court, allowing the Courts to skip the assessment of the admissibility of the case if the pleas are manifestly

[64] *Creditreform* (n 35), para 59.

[65] See art 7(2) of the Rules of Procedure. Under the old Rules of Procedure, filing by email was not foreseen, but was still allowed in Decision 2018 02 *B v ESMA*, para 35.

[66] See art 20(1) of the Rules of Procedure.

[67] This is the case even for a member state or the Commission.

[68] See art 60(1) of the ESA Regulations and art 18 of the Rules of Procedure.

[69] See art 9(1) of the Rules of Procedure. In *Onix Asigurări SA* (n 35), the Board applied this provision, but since the applicant did not object to it, the legality of the provision was not put to the General Court: see Case T-590/15 *Onix Asigurări SA v EIOPA* EU:T:2016:374, para 67.

unfounded, cannot be applied *mutatis mutandis*.[70] As a result, and contrary to the Courts, the Board of Appeal cannot decide a case on the merits without addressing the question of a possible exception of inadmissibility, on the grounds of procedural economy.[71]

A final procedural point worth noting is that an appeal does not have automatic suspensive effect,[72] although suspension may be granted by the Board of Appeal.[73] On this point, the Board has interpreted its powers in a way that is more congenial to applicants than the EU Courts' approach on interim measures.

3.4.5 A lower threshold for suspension of challenged decisions?

Article 60(3) of the ESA Regulation allows the Joint Board of Appeal to suspend the application of an act challenged before it, 'if it considers that circumstances so require'. This language is analogous to Article 278 TFEU, which also provides that EU Courts can suspend the application of contested acts if they consider that 'circumstances so require'. Yet, differently from the notions of a challengeable act, and 'direct and individual concern', which the Joint Board of Appeal has interpreted analogously to Article 263 TFEU (see above), this wording has opened the door to a more generous test for ordering the suspension of a challenged act. In this regard, it may be recalled that, in order for the EU Courts to adopt interim measures, three conditions have to be met: *fumus boni iuris* (ie the main action must not appear unfounded), urgency (ie without interim measures, the applicant would suffer serious and irreparable harm), and a balancing of interests in favour of the applicant.[74] While, recently, the Courts seem to have been more generous in assessing these three elements, they are still applied strictly, overall.[75] Indeed, in *Svenska Handelsbanken*, where the Joint Board of Appeal was asked, for the first time, to suspend a contested decision, the ESMA argued that the Board of Appeal should apply the

[70] See Case C-23/00 P *Council v Boehringer* EU:C:2002:118, para 52.

[71] For the settled case law on this issue, see AG Jääskinen in Case C-547/10 P *Switzerland v Commission* EU:C:2012:565, paras 41–54.

[72] This in contrast to, eg appeals before the Board of Appeal of the ECHA; see art 91(2) of Regulation 1907/2006 concerning the Registration, Evaluation, Authorisation and Restriction of Chemicals (REACH) and establishing a European Chemicals Agency [2006] OJ L 396/1.

[73] See art 60(3) of the ESA Regulations and art 10 of the Rules of Procedure.

[74] See, eg Case C-619/18 R *Commission v Poland* EU:C:2018:1021, para 29.

[75] See Eric Barbier de la Serre and Claire Lavin, 'Le droit du référé européen depuis 2007: entre prudence et coups d'audace' (2019) 55(2) Cahiers de droit Européen 613.

EU Courts' established jurisprudence on interim measures.[76] The Board, however, noted that, 'it does not ... follow that such an approach is necessarily applicable in the case of a suspension decision under Article 60(3). The Board of Appeal is not a court, but an integral part of ESMA ... It is part of the system of checks and balances contained in the ESMA founding regulation ... providing participants in the financial markets with an avenue for the review of a supervisory decision, which is itself subject to appeal to the General Court of the European Union'.[77] The Board of Appeal subsequently suggested that the decisive criterion for it to decide on suspension would be the balancing of interests,[78] although it immediately added that this was not its final view on the matter since, in any event, the weighing of interests was not in favour of the applicant *in casu*.[79] In *Creditreform AG*, however, the Board of Appeal confirmed this approach (again, without granting suspension). This would mean that, under Article 60(3) of the ESA regulations, a party only needs to demonstrate that the balancing of interests tilts in its favour, and that its case is not manifestly inadmissible or unfounded, in order for the Board of Appeal to grant the interim measure of suspension.

3.5 Realizing the potential of the Joint Board of Appeal

The sections above suggest that the potential of the Board of Appeal as an accountability mechanism has been far from realised because of its limited jurisdiction, given that: (i) only non-privileged applicants can appeal decisions before the Board; (ii) the Board can only review (individually) binding decisions;[80] and (iii) the Board can only review some such decisions, but does not have general jurisdiction. As a tool to allow investment firms to hold the ESMA to account for its application and implementation of MiFID II and MiFIR it is, therefore, of limited use. More generally, it appear problematic to have an internal review body with such a meagre workload (around one case per year). Reform of the Board of Appeal, thus, seems imperative.

[76] See Decision of 30 November 2018, *SEB v ESMA*, paras 88–91.
[77] ibid para 92.
[78] ibid para 96.
[79] ibid para 97.
[80] While acts of general application can, indeed, still be of 'individual and direct concern' to a party and, therefore, not only individual acts are challengeable before the Board of Appeal, the fact that the Board follows the *Plaumann* definition of individual concern means that, in practice, it will be exceptionally rare that an admissible appeal will lie against an act of general application.

3.5.1 Enlarging the Joint Board of Appeal's jurisdiction

Exploiting the potential of the Board of Appeal to a greater degree would, thus, require reforming the ESAs on any (or all) of the three points noted above, but especially by: (i) allowing the Board of Appeal to review all binding measures, including generally binding measures; (ii) allowing the Board to review non-binding measures; and (iii) granting more hard law powers to the ESAs. Addressing point (i) would imply that the Joint Board of Appeal should also be able to review regulatory acts in the sense of Article 263 TFEU, something that it has recognised it cannot do under its current mandate.[81] For instance, under MiFIR, it would mean that the Joint Board of Appeal could review the ESMA's exercise of temporary intervention powers under Article 40.[82] Under point (ii), the Joint Board of Appeal would be competent to review the guidelines, recommendations, opinions, Q & As, and draft regulatory and implementing technical standards.[83] Under point (iii), the legislator would maximise the potential offered by the *short-selling* doctrine,[84] and allow the ESAs to adopt more hard law. For instance, some of the technical implementing standards (under MiFID II and MiFIR) could be adopted by the ESAs themselves, rather than being drafted by them and adopted by the Commission.

Another way of realizing the Joint Board of Appeal's potential would be to transform it into a specialised court, in the sense of Article 257 TFEU, which could be done by merging it with the Single Resolution Board's Appeal Panel[85] and the ECB's Administrative Board of Review,[86] creating an EU Court specialised in financial regulation.[87] However, the abolition of the Civil Service Tribunal, the doubling of the number of judges at the General Court, and the apparent lack of appetite to broaden the Joint Board of Appeal's jurisdiction (see below) all show that this will remain a mere theoretic possibility for now.

[81] *Creditreform* (n 35), para 59.

[82] Under the 'direct and individual concern' test, it is questionable whether an investment firm would be able to show individual concern under the *Plaumann* test when challenging such acts.

[83] For an earlier suggestion to this effect, see Merijn Chamon, 'EU Risk Regulators and EU Procedural Law', (2014) 5(3) European Journal of Risk Regulation 324, 334.

[84] Case C-270/12 *UK v Parliament & Council* EU:C:2014:18.

[85] See art 85 of Regulation 806/2014 of the European Parliament and of the Council establishing uniform rules and a uniform procedure for the resolution of credit institutions and certain investment firms in the framework of a Single Resolution Mechanism and a Single Resolution Fund [2014] OJ L 225/1.

[86] See art 24 of Regulation 1024/2013 conferring specific tasks on the European Central Bank concerning policies relating to the prudential supervision of credit institutions [2013] OJ L 287/63.

[87] For an earlier suggestion to this effect, see Chamon (n 20) 567.

3.5.2 The 2019 revision of the ESA Regulations

In 2017, the Commission presented a proposal for reforming the ESAs, which resulted in Regulation 2019/2175.[88] Remarkably, a revision of the jurisdiction of the Board of Appeal was not originally foreseen by the Commission, and was only put on the table, ultimately unsuccessfully, during the informal trilogues. A revision was proposed in light of the extended (or clarified) scope of soft law that the ESAs may adopt. In addition to the guidelines and recommendations that the ESAs could already adopt, the recast regulations provide for 'opinions', under Article 16a, which the ESAs may address to the EU institutions, and 'Q & As', which the ESAs may adopt to clarify the practical application or implementation of EU legislation, delegated acts, implementing acts, and guidelines and recommendations, following questions to that effect by legal and natural persons. Instead of enlarging the jurisdiction of the Board of Appeal, a new remedy has been introduced in Article 60a, as will be discussed in the following section.

3.5.3 Exceeding of competence by an ESA

Any natural or legal person may send reasoned advice to the Commission if that person is of the opinion that the Authority has exceeded its competence, including by failing to respect the principle of proportionality referred to in Article 1(5), when acting under Articles 16 and 16b, and that is of direct and individual concern to that person.

The above provision was introduced as an alternative to the provision in the Commission's original proposal that would have allowed the Stakeholder Groups (SGs) to file complaint with the Commission, if the SGs believed that the Authority had exceeded its competences when adopting guidelines or recommendations.[89] Since the Q & As, under Article 16b, were only proposed by the Council in the trilogues,[90] their inclusion in Article 60a also differs from the Commission's original proposal. Article 60a itself is problematically drafted, mixing up competence and proportionality,[91] but is indicative of legitimate

[88] See [2019] OJ L 334/1.

[89] See art 16(5) as proposed by the Commission in COM (2017) 536 final.

[90] See the four-column document for (COD) 2017-0230 of 18 March 2019, pp 60–63 (on file with the author).

[91] This is, in a way, similar to the German Constitutional Court's Weiss judgment, in which it referred to 'the order of competences on the basis of the principle of proportionality'. See BVerfG, Judgment of 5 May 2020, ECLI:DE:BVerfG:2020:rs20200505.2bvr085915, para 163.

concerns over the soft law adopted by the ESAs,[92] and the usefulness of having such law, even if it is non-binding, reviewed. In general accountability terms, however, it remains to be seen if the Commission really is the most appropriate forum to review the ESAs' soft law, or whether it would have been more effective to broaden the jurisdiction of the Board of Appeal. In this regard, it should be noted that the Commission proposed to give the Board of Appeal jurisdiction over decisions based on Articles 17, 18, 19, and 35 (the last-mentioned relating to the collection of information), but that the Council wanted to narrow this down to decisions based on Articles 17 and 19 (thus excluding the decisions taken by the ESAs in emergency situations), while the Parliament wanted to broaden it, including giving jurisdiction to review the guidelines, recommendations, and opinions adopted pursuant to Articles 16 and 16a.[93] It was also the Parliament that introduced the explicit reference to a proportionality review by the Board of Appeal.

In the end, the jurisdiction of the Joint Board of Appeal was not broadened in the course of revising the ESAs' establishing acts.[94] This seems like a missed opportunity, since proportionality is explicitly mentioned as one of the standards against which the ESAs' soft law measures may be assessed under Article 60a, and because the parties that may challenge such measures are those that already have standing before the Board of Appeal (when challenging binding measures): natural or legal persons that are directly and individually concerned by the ESA's measures.

In the actual application of the review procedure under Article 60a, however, the Commission will face serious challenges if the conditions of direct and individual concern under Article 60a are to be interpreted in the same way as direct and individual concern under Article 60. As noted,[95] the Board of Appeal has applied, by analogy, the EU Courts' jurisprudence on the admissibility requirements under Article 263 TFEU. To recall, under that established jurisprudence, the condition of direct concern implies that the legal situation of the applicant is directly affected, and that the measure leaves no discretion to the authorities entrusted with its implementation, such implementation being purely automatic, without requiring the application of other intermediate rules.[96] Conversely, the condition of individual concern implies that, by reason

[92] On the soft law adopted by the ESMA, see Marloes van Rijsbergen, *The Legitimacy and Effectiveness of ESMA's Soft Law* (Edward Elgar Publishing, forthcoming).

[93] See document (COD) 2017-0230 (n 88), p 215 (on file with the author).

[94] Procedurally, the main reform was a time limit of three months to bring an appeal, and three months to decide on an appeal. In terms of composition and appointment, the requirements imposed on Board of Appeal members were sharpened, and the role of the Parliament was reinforced.

[95] See *SV Capital OÜ v EBA II* (n 40).

[96] See, eg Case T-385/07 *FIFA v European Commission* EU:T:2011:42, para 36.

of certain attributes peculiar to the applicant, or by reason of a factual situation which differentiates it from all other persons, the applicant is individually distinguished.[97] While the guidelines, recommendations, and Q & As that the ESA will adopt under Articles 16 and 16b might, exceptionally, concern certain parties individually, it is difficult, if not impossible, to see how non-binding measures may be said to affect a party's legal situation.[98] After all, as the Joint Board of Appeal has noted, mere negative factual consequences resulting from soft law do not automatically equate with legal effects that change the legal position of an applicant.[99] In order for the review mechanism under Article 60a to work properly, the Commission will, thus, have to interpret 'direct concern' differently from how it is interpreted by the EU Courts and Joint Board of Appeal under Article 263 TFEU and Article 60 of the ESAs regulations.

In addition, it remains to be seen how the Commission will perform its review function substantively, and whether its findings will be made public, as is the case for the Board of Appeal's decisions. Finally, it is remarkable that Article 60a does not indicate the remedies that the Commission may offer, ie what the legal consequences are of the Commission finding that the ESA has indeed exceeded its competence. Does such a finding automatically result in the withdrawal of the soft law act in question? Does Article 60a empower the Commission to require the ESA to withdraw its soft law? Unfortunately, this is not spelled out in the recast regulation. In light of all this, giving legal standing to the SGs, or simply to any interested party,[100] to have guidelines, recommendations, and Q & As reviewed by the Board of Appeal would have been a legally much more elegant solution.

3.6 Concluding remarks

This analysis of the legal framework governing the Joint Board of Appeal of the three ESAs, as well as the Board's decisional practices, has revealed that it can

[97] See, eg Case T-532/08 *Norilsk Nickel Harjavalta Oy and Umicore v European Commission* EU:T:2010:353, para 97.

[98] A comparison of the different language versions of the new art 60a suggests that it is the ESA exceeding its competences that must be of direct and individual concern to the applicant rather than the measure itself, but this only complicates how the Commission is to assess the admissibility of the 'reasoned advice' it receives. After all, how can an alleged breach of competences, irrespective of the substance of the act adopted, be of direct and individual concern?

[99] *Creditreform* (n 35), para 69.

[100] Again the threshold here cannot be the same as under art 263 TFEU, since the legal interest in bringing such proceedings consists of the annulment being 'capable of having legal consequences or [procuring] an advantage for the party who has brought it'. Since soft law does not affect the legal positions of parties, the annulment of such soft law cannot change their legal position either. A party could, instead, show its interest by demonstrating that if it were to (voluntarily) follow the soft law measure, it would have to change its established practice or conduct.

be qualified as an accountability mechanism, even if that does not seem evident at first sight. Indeed, the Joint Board of Appeal may be an atypical forum, in the sense that it is passive and depends on cases being brought before it, but apart from that, it is a forum in which the agency is required to explain and justify its decisions, with the possibility of its behaviour (ie its decisions) being subject to sanctions (in the form of a remittal of the case to the ESA).

That being said, this chapter has also found that investment firms are not enjoying the full potential of the Joint Board of Appeal to hold the ESMA to account for its implementation under MiFID II and MiFIR, for two main reasons. First, while the ESAs have, indeed, been endowed with significant hard law powers, the EU legislature has also defined their mandate in such a way that a significant part of their 'regulatory output' consists of soft law, including under MiFID II and MiFIR. Secondly, as with the Boards of Appeal of other EU agencies, the jurisdiction of the Joint Board of Appeal is defined in a narrow sense whereby, in contrast to the EU Courts under Article 263 TFEU, not every act producing binding legal effects adopted by the ESAs can be challenged before the Joint Board of Appeal.

These limitations have generally resulted in an underutilisation of the Joint Board of Appeal, which has only decided thirteen cases in a ten-year period, the majority of which did not turn on substantive issues, although those substantive issues are precisely the cases where a Board of Appeal has added value compared to the EU Courts. Instead, most cases before the Joint Board of Appeal turned on procedural issues, where no such added value is to be found. In light of this, the question should be raised of whether the Joint Board of Appeal should simply be abolished.

To be clear, that is not the position taken here. Instead, the avenue suggested in this chapter is to realise more of the Joint Board of Appeal's potential by enlarging its jurisdiction, and by giving the ESAs more hard law powers. In the most recent revision of the ESAs' establishing acts, the Commission, and especially the Parliament, pursued strengthening the Joint Board of Appeal. The Council, however, favoured a restriction of the Joint Board of Appeal's jurisdiction. The end result was a maintenance of the status quo. At the same time, the EU legislature recognised that, given the practical importance of the soft law adopted by the ESAs, it is useful to have in place a review mechanism for the ESAs' guidelines, recommendations, and Q&As. As the analysis of the new Article 60a revealed, however, that new review mechanism is problematic. Not granting the Joint Board of Appeal with the power to review soft law will turn out to have been a missed opportunity.

4

Judicial Protection against the European Securities and Markets Authority (ESMA)

Dominique Ritleng

4.1 Introduction

The European Securities and Markets Authority (ESMA) was set up in the wake of the financial crisis,[1] alongside two other supervisory authorities, the European Banking Authority (EBA), and the European Insurance and Occupational Pensions Authority (EIOPA). The three European Supervisory Authorities (ESAs), together with the national supervisors,[2] form part of the European System of Financial Supervision (ESFS), whose task is to ensure consistent and effective financial supervision throughout the European Union. Within this institutional architecture,[3] ESMA has been assigned tasks relating to supervision, standard setting, and risk assessment in the financial market, as provided for in its founding regulation, and also specific tasks set out in other legislative acts[4] such as MiFID II[5] and MIFIR.[6] To fulfil these tasks, MIFID II and MIFIR empower ESMA, within the powers conferred on it by ESMA Regulation,[7] to take various types of action, and to issue various sorts of legal instrument, of both soft law and hard law character. Although the nomenclature of EU legal acts does not mention EU agencies as authors,[8] indisputable

[1] Regulation (EU) No 1095/2010 of the European Parliament and of the Council of 24 November 2010 establishing a European Supervisory Authority (European Securities and Markets Authority), as amended by Regulation (EU) No 2019/2175, hereafter 'ESMA Regulation'.

[2] And also the European Systemic Risk Board.

[3] See Eilis Ferran, 'Understanding the New Institutional Architecture of EU Financial Market Supervision' (2011) University of Cambridge Legal Studies Research Paper Series no 29/2011.

[4] See art 8(j) of ESMA Regulation.

[5] Directive 2014/65/EU of the European Parliament and of the Council of 15 May 2014 on markets in financial instruments and amending Directive 2002/92/EC and Directive 2011/61/EU (hereafter 'MiFID II').

[6] Regulation (EU) No 600/2014 of the European Parliament and of the Council of 15 May 2014 on markets in financial instruments and amending Regulation (EU) No 648/2012, as amended by Regulation (EU) No 2019/2175 (hereafter 'MiFIR').

[7] See art 1(2) of the ESMA Regulation.

[8] See art 288 TFEU.

Dominique Ritleng, *Judicial Protection against the European Securities and Markets Authority (ESMA)* In: *Legal Accountability in EU Markets for Financial Instruments*. Edited by: Carl Fredrik Bergström and Magnus Strand, Oxford University Press. © Dominique Ritleng 2021. DOI: 10.1093/oso/9780192849281.003.0004

signs of their capacity to adopt legal acts can be found in the Treaties[9] upon which the European Court of Justice (ECJ) relied to confirm that, in the ESMA Regulation, the EU legislator could confer on ESMA the power to enact binding measures, even of general scope.[10]

This chapter shall deal with the judicial remedies available to litigants, in particular investment firms, both on national and EU levels, against ESMA action taken under MiFID II or MiFIR. As has rightly been pointed out, 'given the extensive powers of agencies, most visibly exemplified in some cases by their power to adopt decisions binding on third parties, judicial review as a check on agency power becomes central in a discussion of agency accountability'.[11] The most significant aspect of legal accountability is, indeed, that of judicial review. The challenge is to identify which judicial remedies may be used against these various types of action and legal instrument, and to assess whether, and to what extent, they ensure an effective judicial protection against such actions and instruments. Before proceeding to address this issue, it is necessary to make two preliminary remarks.

Article 61 of the ESMA Regulation sets out some of the judicial proceedings that may be instituted against ESMA. It mentions the possibilities of seeking annulment of a decision taken by ESMA, and bringing before the ECJ proceedings for failure to act against ESMA. In so doing, the ESMA Regulation does not add anything new to the Treaties, because Articles 263 and 265 TFEU already provide for such possibilities. These two provisions have indeed been amended by the Lisbon Treaty to explicitly make available the possibilities of filing an action for annulment or an action for failure to act, against EU agencies.[12] As the provisions of the Treaties permit, Article 61 of the ESMA Regulation merely lays down specific conditions and arrangements governing actions for annulment and actions for failure to act, brought against ESMA by private parties.[13]

[9] See arts 263, 267, and 277 TFEU.

[10] Case C-270/12 *United Kingdom v Parliament and Council (ESMA)* EU:C:2014:18. For commentary, see Carl Fredrik Bergström, 'Shaping the New System for Delegation of Powers to EU Agencies' (2015) 52 Common Market Law Review 219; Brunessen Bertrand, 'La compétence des agences pour prendre des actes normatifs: le dualisme des pouvoirs d'exécution' (2015) Revue Trimestielle de droit Européen 21. On the allocation of regulatory tasks to EU agencies, see, more generally, Marta Simoncini, *Administrative Regulation beyond the Non-delegation Doctrine. A study on EU Agencies* (Hart Publishing 2018).

[11] Madalina Busuioc, *European Agencies: Law and Practices of Accountability* (OUP 2013) 191.

[12] In the pre-Lisbon era, the Court of First Instance had already ruled that, although EU agencies were not among EU institutions listed in art 230 EC, the general principle that any act of a Community body intended to produce legal effects vis-à-vis third parties must be open to direct judicial review should be inferred from the rule of law on which the Community is based (see CFI Case T-411/06 *Solgema* EU:T:2008:419, para 37).

[13] See in particular, art 263(5) TFEU: 'Acts setting up bodies, offices and agencies of the Union may lay down specific conditions and arrangements concerning actions brought by natural or legal persons against acts of these bodies, offices or agencies intended to produce legal effects in relation to them.'

Furthermore, Article 61 of the ESMA Regulation does not provide an exhaustive list of available judicial remedies. The Treaties provide for other means of redress against ESMA action. Articles 267 and 277 TFEU explicitly open up the possibility of an indirect legality review of ESMA's legal acts. As regards actions for damages, Article 69 of ESMA Regulation provides for non-contractual liability on ESMA's part.[14] In so doing, secondary law does not add to primary law either. To be sure, even after the Lisbon Treaty, Article 340 TFEU has not been amended to mention the harmful conduct of EU agencies; it mentions only the harmful conduct of EU institutions as a source of the Union's non-contractual liability. The Court of Justice, however, ruled that the term 'institution' must be understood as referring not only to the EU institutions, but also to all bodies of the European Union.[15] The European Union[16] may, thus, be compelled to make good any damage caused by its agencies,[17] such as ESMA.

The principle of effective judicial protection, which is also a fundamental right, was initially imposed on member states and their national courts, when acting within the scope of EU law.[18] Sometime later, its requirements were extended to EU courts[19] as well, and today EU courts must respect Article 47 of the EU Charter.[20] This means that the provisions relating to judicial remedies must be applied and interpreted by EU courts in the light of Article 47 of the Charter.[21]

In order to ascertain whether this is also the case as regards the judicial remedies that may be used to challenge ESMA action taken under MiFID II and MiFIR, the direct legality review of ESMA's legal acts shall, firstly, be examined in this chapter. Second, the indirect legality review will be assessed. Third,

[14] Art 69 of ESMA Regulation: 'In the case of non-contractual liability, the Authority shall, in accordance with the general principles common to the laws of the Member States, make good any damage caused by it or by its staff in the performance of their duties. The Court of Justice of the European Union shall have jurisdiction in any dispute over the remedying of such damage.'

[15] See, inaugurating this line of jurisprudence, ECJ Case C-370/89 *SGEEM and Etroy v EIB* EU:C:1992:482, about an action for damages against the European Investment Bank. See also Case C-234/02 P *European Ombudsman v Lamberts* EU:C:2004:174.

[16] Whether the EU or the agency itself is held liable, the exact source of the funds from which the compensation is payable is of secondary importance, from the perspective of the claimant.

[17] See GC Case T-12/08 P *M v EMEA* EU:T:2009:143, about an action for damages against the European Agency for the Evaluation of Medicinal Products; *Solgema* (n 12), about an action for damages against the European Agency for Reconstruction; GC Case T-838/16 *BP v FRA*, EU:T:2019:494 and, on appeal, ECJ Case C-669/16 P *BP v FRA* EU:C:2020:713, about an action for damages against the Fundamental Rights Agency. See also Merijn Chamon, *EU Agencies: Legal and Political Limits to the Transformation of EU Administration* (OUP 2016) 355–61.

[18] See ECJ Case 222/84 *Johnston* EU:C:1986:206.

[19] See ECJ Case C-399/95 R *Germany v Commission* EU:C:1996:193, para 46; Case C-445/00 R *Austria v Council* EU:C:2001:123, para 111.

[20] See ECJ Case C-385/07 P *Die Grüne Punkt* EU:C:2009:456, para 179.

[21] See Case C-583/11 P *Inuit Tapiriit Kanatami* EU:C:2013:625, paras 97–98.

the intensity of the legality review of ESMA's acts will be explored, and so, finally, will be the possibility of filing an action for damages caused by ESMA.[22] It must, however, be borne in mind from the outset that, so far, no judicial proceedings, save staff cases, have been directly or indirectly brought against ESMA before the EU courts.

4.2 Direct legality review by EU courts

The legal acts that ESMA is empowered to enact under MiFID II and MIFIR are mostly[23] technical standards, guidelines, regulatory acts, and individual decisions. Whether, to what extent, and under which conditions, these legal acts are reviewable under Article 263 TFEU needs to be ascertained.

4.2.1 Draft regulatory technical standards (RTSs) and draft implementing technical standards (ITSs)

Numerous provisions of MiFID II and MiFIR confer on ESMA the power to develop draft regulatory technical standards (RTSs) or draft implementing technical standards (ITSs), which then take on the form of delegated acts (Article 290 TFEU) and implementing acts (Article 291 TFEU), respectively, when adopted by the Commission. To mention just a few examples, ESMA may develop draft RTSs and ITSs relating to the authorisation and operating conditions for investment firms,[24] or relating to the information which must be notified by investment firms wishing to provide services or activities, or to establish a branch, within the territory of another member state.[25] It may develop draft RTSs specifying the obligation to supply financial instrument reference data,[26] and draft RTSs specifying the information which must be provided by a third-country firm applying for registration in order to provide investment services or perform investment activities.[27]

Draft RTSs or ITSs adopted by ESMA are not amenable to judicial review through the direct route of Article 263 TFEU, since they are merely

22 The action for failure to act will not be dealt with in this chapter, because this remedy is rarely used.
23 ESMA can also issue opinions (see art 57(5) and (13) of MiFID II; arts 11(2) and 43 of MiFIR).
24 See art 7 of MiFID II.
25 See arts 34 and 35 of MiFID II.
26 See art 27 of MiFIR.
27 See art 46 of MiFIR.

preparatory acts. Under Articles 10 and 15 of the ESMA Regulation, the European Commission is not bound by draft RTSs or ITSs submitted by ESMA, and has a certain amount of discretion[28] as to the final determination of the content of such standards, at the stage of their endorsement. The requirement for the Commission's endorsement reveals that the Commission remains the ultimate decision maker. Draft RTSs or ITSs cannot, therefore, undergo autonomous judicial review, since they form part of a compound procedure, being just one element of the ordinary process of adoption of the final decision by the European Commission. Those wishing to challenge these acts can do so only by filing an application for annulment under Article 263 TFEU against the final decision authored by the Commission, asking the General Court to consider, additionally, the alleged errors in fact or in law of ESMA's preparatory act that may vitiate the Commission's final decision.[29]

4.2.2 Guidelines

Pursuant to several provisions of MiFID II,[30] ESMA may or shall enact guidelines. Addressed to competent authorities or financial market participants, guidelines aim at establishing consistent, efficient, and effective supervisory practices within the ESFS, and at ensuring the common, uniform, and consistent application of Union law. For instance, ESMA may develop and issue guidelines regarding the methods used by member states to monitor compliance with conditions imposed when authorizing investment firms to provide investment services or perform investment activities; guidelines for the assessment and supervision of investment firms' cross-selling practices; or guidelines specifying the criteria for assessment of the knowledge and competence required from employees of investment firms in charge of giving investment advice or information about financial instruments, investment services, or ancillary services to clients.[31]

Guidelines, like recommendations, as a rule lack binding character. They are soft law instruments. As a consequence, the guidelines issued by ESMA are not

[28] Not a very high level of discretion; however, see Madalina Busuioc, 'Rule-making by the European Financial Supervisory Authorities. Walking a Tight Rope' [2013] European Law Journal 111.

[29] See, by analogy, CFI Joined Cases T-74/00, 76-, 83-, 85-, 132-, 13-7, 141/00 *Artegodan* EU:T:2002:283, para 197; Case T-326/99 *Nancy Fern Olivieri* EU:T:2003:351, paras 51–55. Both of these cases concern opinions issued by the European Agency for the Evaluation of Medicinal Products. See also Decision of 13 September 2019 BoA/2019/05 *Creditreform AG v EBA*, about an appeal before the Board of Appeal against draft ITSs adopted by EBA.

[30] See also art 26(6) of MiFIR.

[31] See, respectively, arts 21(2), 24(11), and 25(9) of MiFID II.

amenable to an action for annulment under Article 263 TFEU. Only EU legal acts which 'are intended to have binding legal effects'[32] are challengeable acts for the purposes of Article 263 TFEU.

However, this holds true only for genuine guidelines. It is well-known that, in order to determine the binding force of an EU legal act and hence its challengeable character within the meaning of Article 263 TFEU, it is ultimately to be relied, whatever the form or designation of the act may be, on its wording and context, its content, and the intention of its author. The assessment of those criteria will reveal whether the act concerned has a mandatory nature. This is the lesson transpiring from consistent case law about the admissibility of actions for annulment. To give but one telling example, the ECJ recently had to rule on the classification of a 'recommendation' adopted by the Commission as a reviewable act under Article 263 TFEU. Although Article 263 TFEU expressly excludes recommendations from the class of acts amenable to actions for annulment, in connection with the failure of Article 288 TFEU to confer binding force on that type of act, the Court found it necessary to examine whether the contested recommendation constituted a genuine recommendation, or an act producing binding effects, and hence an actionable measure within the meaning of Article 263 TFEU. The Court came to the conclusion that the challenged recommendation was not intended to have binding legal effects, on the basis of the following considerations: it was drafted in an essentially non-binding manner; the content revealed that the Commission, which authored the act, had no intention of conferring such effects on it, and the absence of will to legislate on the subject matter emerged from the context.[33]

It could be argued that the case law of the ECJ puts the threshold for establishing the challengeable nature, under Article 263 TFEU, of soft law instruments like guidelines or recommendations too high. This seems to be the view of the French Conseil d'État (supreme administrative court). In a case where the validity of guidelines issued by the EBA pursuant to Article 16 of Regulation 1093/2010 was called into question,[34] the Conseil d'État, very recently, referred to the ECJ the more general question as to whether guidelines adopted by the ESAs may be the subject of an action for annulment under

[32] See ECJ Case C-599/15 P *Romania v Commission* EU:C:2017:801, para 47; ECJ Case 22/70 *Commission v Council (ERTA)* [1971] EU:C:1971:32, para 42.

[33] See ECJ Case C-16/16 P *Belgium v Commission* [2016] EU:C:2018:79. For commentary, see Anthony Arnull, 'EU Recommendations and Judicial Review' (2018) 14 European Constitutional Law Review 609.

[34] See Guidelines EBA/GL/2015/18 on product oversight and governance arrangements for retail banking products, 22 March 2016.

Article 263 TFEU.[35] For the 'rapporteur public' of the Conseil d'État, the guidelines issued by the ESAs could be regarded as having enough normative density and binding character to be reviewable under Article 263 TFEU.[36] The likely answer to this reference seems, however, to be predictable, should the settled case law described above be followed. Guidelines issued by ESAs, provided that they are genuine guidelines, are not reviewable by EU courts by means of an action for annulment, as they do not in themselves give rights or impose obligations for their addressees and/or third parties. Deciding that guidelines issued by ESAs fall inside the scope of the direct legality review would, thus, require a relaxation of the notion of the challengeable act, within the meaning of Article 263 TFEU. There are some arguments in favour of such a relaxation.[37] Already, in its seminal *Grimaldi* judgment, the ECJ has acknowledged that soft law instruments 'cannot be regarded as having no legal effect'.[38] In particular, albeit perhaps not being endowed with binding force in the traditional narrow sense of the term, guidelines produce legal effects, and are expected to be complied with, as revealed by the 'comply or explain' mechanism provided for in Article 16(3) of ESAs regulations. This mechanism requires that, within two months of the issuance of a guideline, each competent authority shall confirm whether it complies with that guideline or not, and, in the latter case, state its reasons for non-compliance; if required by the guideline, financial institutions must report, in a clear and detailed way, whether they comply with it.[39] Such a jurisprudential change could be inspired by the evolution concerning the admissibility of the action for annulment in French administrative law.[40] In order to enhance the judicial protection of persons concerned by the activities of

[35] See Conseil d'État, 4 December 2019, *Fédération bancaire française*, n° 415550; ECJ Case C-911/19 *Fédération bancaire française*.

[36] See Opinion of E Bokdam in the *Fédération bancaire française* case, n° 415550.

[37] See, also, for a thorough and forceful plea, Giulia Gentile, 'Ensuring Effective Judicial Review of EU Soft Law via the Action for Annulment before the EU Courts: a Plea for a Liberal-Constitutionalist Approach' [2020] European Constitutional Law Review 466.

[38] See ECJ Case C-322/88 *Grimaldi* EU:C:1989:646, para 18, about recommendations.

[39] See art 16(3) of the ESMA Regulation: 'The competent authorities and financial market participants shall make every effort to comply with those guidelines and recommendations.

Within 2 months of the issuance of a guideline or recommendation, each competent authority shall confirm whether it complies or intends to comply with that guideline or recommendation. In the event that a competent authority does not comply or does not intend to comply, it shall inform the Authority, stating its reasons.

The Authority shall publish the fact that a competent authority does not comply or does not intend to comply with that guideline or recommendation. The Authority may also decide, on a case by case basis, to publish the reasons provided by the competent authority for not complying with that guideline or recommendation. The competent authority shall receive advanced notice of such publication.

If required by that guideline or recommendation, financial market participants shall report, in a clear and detailed way, whether they comply with that guideline or recommendation.'

[40] See also examples of similar solutions from courts of other member states, cited by Advocate General Bobek (Opinion in Case C-16/16 P *Belgium v Commission* EU:C:2017:959, para 84).

regulatory agencies, the French Conseil d'État has recently ruled that not only acts having binding force, but also soft law instruments issued by regulatory authorities, are amenable to actions for annulment 'if they are liable to produce significant effects, especially of economic character or if they intend to influence significantly the behaviour of the persons to whom they are addressed'.[41]

It may, however, be doubted that the ECJ will follow the path of the Conseil d'État, for at least two reasons. First, the *Belgium v Commission* ruling did not take up the suggestion of the Advocate General. In his Opinion, Advocate General Bobek had recommended the widening of the conditions for standing and judicial review under Article 263 TFEU to render them in sync with the evolution of the EU's normative landscape, which is now marked by a proliferation of various soft law instruments 'generating significant legal effects that find themselves beyond the binary logic of binding/non-binding legal rules'. But, as we have seen, the ECJ stuck to its case law, and assessed the reviewable nature of the impugned recommendation according to the divide between binding and non-binding legal effects. Second, the unavailability of direct legality review does not necessarily run the risk of allowing a deficit in judicial protection, since it does not amount to an absence of any judicial reviewability of guidelines. Indeed, it emerges from established case law that the requirements of the rule of law, in particular the requirements of an effective judicial protection, are satisfied even though access to direct legality review is closed, provided that the indirect legality review is available.[42] With respect to ESAs' guidelines, the indirect legality review is, as a rule, available. The first reason for this is that the ECJ has held that Article 267 TFEU confers on the Court of Justice jurisdiction to deliver a preliminary ruling on the interpretation and validity of all EU legal acts, without exception.[43] The second reason is that it stems from settled case law that the duty imposed on member states by Article 19(1) TEU to provide remedies sufficient to ensure effective legal protection in the fields covered by Union law[44] implies that national courts are bound to

[41] My translation. See French Conseil d'État, Ass, 21 March 2016, *Sté Fairvesta International*, n° 368082; French Conseil d'État, Ass, 21 March 2016, *Sté NC Numericable*, n° 390023: 'Les avis, recommandations, mises en garde et prises de position adoptés par les autorités de régulation ... peuvent être déférés au juge de l'excès de pouvoir ... lorsqu'ils sont de nature à produire des effets notables, notamment de nature économique, ou ont pour objet d'influer de manière significative sur les comportements des personnes auxquelles ils s'adressent'.

[42] See ECJ Case C-50/00 P *Unión de Pequeños Agricultores* EU:C:2002:462, paras 34–40; *Inuit Tapiriit Kanatami* (n 21), paras 90–104. For a thorough criticism of this line of jurisprudence, see Jonathan Wildemeersch, *Contentieux de la légalité des actes de l'Union européenne. Le mythe du droit à un recours effectif* (Bruylant 2019).

[43] See *Grimaldi* (n 38), para 8; Case C- 11/05 *Friesland Coberco Dairy Foods* EU:C:2006:312, para 36; Case C-258/14 *Florescu and Others* EU:C:2017:448, para 30; *Belgium v Commission* (n 33), para 44.

[44] See, already, *Unión de Pequeños Agricultores* (n 42).

regard as admissible actions brought against national acts taken within the scope of EU law that are capable of adversely affecting third parties, even if the domestic rules of procedure do not so provide;[45] or, alternatively, it obliges member states to create new remedies before the national courts if their domestic legal systems do not provide any remedy making it possible, even indirectly, to ensure respect for the rights which individuals derive from EU law.[46]

The prediction has been borne out. In the *Fédération bancaire française* case, the ECJ replied to the French Conseil d'État that the guidelines issued by the EBA are not challengeable acts for the purposes of Article 263 TFEU. The ECJ has however confirmed that it has jurisdiction to give a preliminary ruling on the validity of such guidelines.[47]

4.2.3 Individual decisions

ESMA is vested with the power to take individual decisions by several provisions of MiFID II and MiFIR. To mention but a few, with respect to MiFID II, an investigation initiated by ESMA for breach of EU law committed by a competent authority may end up with individual measures being addressed to an investment firm, if the competent authority does not comply with the formal opinion issued by the Commission.[48] ESMA is empowered to take precautionary measures addressed to an investment firm.[49] The settlement of any dispute arising from a disagreement between competent authorities about the exercise of their respective supervisory responsibilities may lead to the enactment of decisions addressed to a competent authority, and decisions addressed to an investment firm.[50] MiFIR grants ESMA the power to address individual measures to investment firms, on the basis of its position management powers,[51] powers to grant or refuse the registration of a third-country firm which has applied for the provision of investment services or the

[45] See ECJ Case C-97/91 *Oleificio Borelli* EU:C:1992:491; Case C- 269/99 *Carl Kühne and Others* EU:C:2001:659, paras 57–58; Case C-219/17 *Berlusconi* EU:C:2018:1023, para 46. This duty concerned national preparatory acts adopted in the course of a composite procedure leading to the adoption of a definitive EU legal measure, but the solution can be extended beyond, especially when read in the light of the subsequent *Inuit Tapiriit Kanatami* case (n 21), para 104.

[46] See *Inuit Tapiriit Kanatami* (n 21), para 104.

[47] See ECJ Case C-911/19, *Fédération bancaire française*, EU:C:2021:599

[48] See art 57(5) of MiFID II and art 17 of the ESMA Regulation.

[49] See art 86 of MiFID II, in conjunction with art 19 of the ESMA Regulation.

[50] See arts 57(6) and 82 of MiFID II, in conjunction with art 19 of the ESMA Regulation. See also arts 4(4), 7(1), and 9(2) of MiFIR, in conjunction with art 19 of the ESMA Regulation.

[51] See art 45 of MiFIR.

performance of activities throughout the Union,[52] and the power to withdraw such a registration.[53]

With regard to individual decisions addressed to competent authorities or investment firms, the main issue is how to combine the administrative remedy provided for in Article 60 of the ESMA Regulation and an action for annulment in accordance with Article 263 TFEU, whose availability is recalled by Article 61 of the ESMA Regulation. More precisely, the question is whether access to the Article 263 TFEU avenue is subject to the prior exhaustion of the administrative remedy.

In that respect, it should first be observed that this question does not concern all individual decisions taken by ESMA. Indeed, the possibility of an appeal to the Board of Appeal of the ESA is, pursuant to Article 60(1) of ESMA Regulation, open to any natural or legal person, including competent authorities, only against: (1) a decision of ESMA referred to in Articles 17, 18, or 19, or any other decision taken by ESMA in accordance with the Union acts referred to in Article 1(2), that is addressed to such a person; or (2) a decision which, although in the form of a decision addressed to another person, is of direct and individual concern to such a person. Invited to interpret Article 60(1) of the ESA Regulations,[54] the EU courts have confirmed that, in order for an appeal to the Board of Appeal to lie against a decision of the EBA, for the purpose of Article 60 of Regulation 1093/2010, the decision must either have been taken in accordance with the EU acts referred to in Article 1(2) of that regulation, or be one of the decisions referred to in Articles 17 to 19 of the Regulation. Otherwise the Board of Appeal lacks competence.[55]

The question is, thus, whether decisions taken by ESMA under MiFID II and MiFIR may be appealed to the Board of Appeal. Noteworthy in this regard is that, while Article 1(2) of the ESMA Regulation refers to MiFID II, it does not contain a reference to MiFIR. This does not, however, mean that decisions of ESMA adopted pursuant to MiFIR cannot be challenged before the Board of Appeal, since Article 1(2) also provides that ESMA shall act in the scope 'of any further legally binding Union act which confers tasks on the Authority'.

However, even if a decision of ESMA not to open a formal investigation against a national financial supervisory authority (under Article 17 of the

[52] ibid, art 46 .

[53] ibid, art 49.

[54] art 60(1) of the Regulation (EU) No 1093/2010 of the European Parliament and of the Council of 24 November 2010 establishing a European Supervisory Authority (European Banking Authority) [2010] OJ L 331/12..

[55] See GC Case T-660/14, *SV Capital OÜ v EBA* EU:T:2015:608, confirmed on appeal by ECJ Case C-577/15 P *SV Capital OÜ v EBA* EU:C:2016:947, paras 35–42.

ESMA Regulation) is an act reviewable by the Board of Appeal,[56] only the entities expressly referred to in Article 17(2) of ESMA Regulation, which may request the ESMA to initiate an investigation into an alleged breach or failure to apply EU law,[57] have a right of appeal,[58] as they are 'addressees' of the contested decision within the meaning of Article 60(1) of the ESMA Regulation. The Board of Appeal, thus, found inadmissible an appeal against a decision of ESMA's chair *not to* open a formal investigation on its own initiative against the Cyprus Securities and Exchange Commission (CySEC), under Article 17 of the ESMA Regulation, for alleged infringements of MiFID and EU rules on capital adequacy, because the appellant was not entitled to request an investigation pursuant to Article 17(2) of the ESMA Regulation.[59] Consequently, an investment firm may directly challenge the ESMA's decision not to initiate an investigation under Article 17 of ESMA Regulation into an alleged breach or failure to apply MiFID or MiFIR rules before EU courts.

In the event that a decision of ESMA is open to challenge before the Board of Appeal, it is not clear whether the administrative remedy must be used before filing the case before the General Court. Such an obligation seems to flow from Article 61(1) of the ESMA Regulation, which provides that 'proceedings may be brought before the Court of Justice in accordance with Article 263 TFEU contesting a decision taken by the Board of Appeal or, in cases where there is no right of appeal before the Board of Appeal, by the Authority', implying that the institution of a proceeding before the General Court must follow a decision of the Board, unless 'there is no right of appeal before the Board of Appeal'. Also, the legal scholarship tends to be in favour of the prior exhaustion of the administrative remedy. Authors have pointed out advantages of procedural economy: the requirement for prior recourse to the Board of Appeal would filter the judicial proceedings, and even if the matter ultimately ended up going to the EU Courts, the expertise of the Board of Appeal would have helped to find facts and narrow the issues, thereby doing much to save time and expense in further hearings.[60] And it is true that, to date, only two cases dealt with by

[56] See Decision of 10 November 2014, *Investor Protection Europe/ESMA*, BoA D/2014/05.

[57] That is, the European Parliament, the Council, the Commission, and the Securities and Markets Stakeholder Group.

[58] See Case C-577/15 P *SV Capital OÜ v EBA*, para 40.

[59] See Decision of 10 September 2018, *B v ESMA*, BoA D/2018/02.

[60] See Marco Lamandini and David Ramos Munoz, 'Law and Practice of Financial Appeal Bodies (ESAs' Board of Appeal, SRB Appeal Panel): A View from the Inside' (2020) 57 Common Market Law Review 119, 147–48; William Blair and Grace Cheng, 'The Role of Judicial Review in the EU's Financial Architecture and the Development of Alternative Remedies: The Experience of the Board of Appeal of the European Supervisory Authorities' in Bank of Italy, 'Judicial Review in the Banking Union and in the EU Financial Architecture', Quaderni di Ricerca Giuridica della Consulenza Legale, no 84 (June 2018) 17, 24; Miroslava Scholten and Michiel Luchtman (eds), *Law Enforcement by EU*

the Board of Appeal have been then brought before EU courts.[61] Moreover, the ECJ has ruled, with respect to national proceedings, that the obligation to exhaust administrative remedies, albeit being a limitation on the right to an effective judicial remedy within the meaning of Article 47 of the EU Charter, is justified by the general interest of relieving the courts of disputes that can be decided directly before the administrative authority concerned, and of increasing the efficiency of judicial proceedings as regards disputes in which a legal action is brought despite the fact that a complaint has already been lodged.[62]

Yet, Article 61(2) of the ESMA Regulation does not expressly subject the right of recourse to the EU courts to the condition of pre-emptive exhaustion of the appeal remedy under Article 60. It provides that 'Member States and the Union institutions, as well as any natural or legal person, may institute proceedings before the Court of Justice of the European Union against decisions of the Authority, in accordance with Article 263 TFEU.' This seems to contrast with the wording of Article 61(1) of the ESMA Regulation. The only way to reconcile the two statements is to consider that, as allowed by Article 263(5) TFEU, Article 61(1) of the ESMA Regulation sets out specific conditions concerning actions brought by private parties, by subjecting access of private parties to Article 263 TFEU to the prior use of the administrative remedy, whereas Article 61(2) of ESMA Regulation sets out the litigants who are entitled to seek annulment of ESMA's legal acts before EU courts.

4.2.4 Measures of general scope

MiFIR endows ESMA with the power to enact measures of general scope on the basis of temporary intervention powers. The legality of this delegation of powers to ESMA was upheld by the ECJ in the *Short selling* case.[63] Pursuant to Article 40(1) of MiFIR , ESMA may, in accordance with Article 9(5) of the ESMA Regulation, temporarily prohibit or restrict, in the Union, the marketing, distribution, or sale of certain financial instruments or financial instruments with certain specified features, or certain types of financial activity or practice. ESMA has already made use of these powers. It has, in particular,

Authorities: Implications for Political and Judicial Accountability (Edward Elgar Publishing Limited 2017), 76; Chamon (n 17) 349.

[61] See *SV Capital OÜ v EBA*, GC and ECJ cases (n 54); *Onix Asigurări v EIOPA* EU:T:2016:374.
[62] See ECJ Case C-73/16 *Puskar* EU:C:2017:725, paras 62–67.
[63] See *United Kingdom v Parliament and Council (ESMA)* (n 10).

adopted decisions restricting the marketing, distribution, or sale of contracts for differences to retail clients,[64] and prohibiting the marketing, distribution, or sale of binary options to retail clients.[65] The condition imposed on the legality of the delegation of temporary intervention powers in the *Short selling* case was that the powers must be 'precisely delineated and amenable to judicial review'.[66]

This is the case within the context of MiFIR. The exercise of rulemaking powers is subject to the fulfilment of the conditions set out in Article 40 (2) and (3) of MiFIR, and further specified by a delegated regulation of the Commission.[67] With respect to judicial scrutiny, as appeals to the Board of Appeal are not open against ESMA's measures of general scope, litigants may, in any event, immediately seek annulment of those measures before the General Court. As is well known, the main obstacle for non-privileged applicants will be to fulfil the *locus standi* conditions set out in Article 263(4) TFEU. In particular, they will most often come up against the *Plaumann* test, according to which an EU legal act is of individual concern to natural or legal persons within the meaning of Article 263(4) TFEU when it affects them by reason of certain attributes peculiar to them, or by reason of a factual situation that differentiates them from all other persons and distinguishes them individually in the same way as the addressee.[68] Indeed, an investment firm will, most of the time, be unable to establish that it is being affected differently from all other investment firms by ESMA's measures prohibiting or restricting the marketing, distribution, or sale of certain financial instruments or types of financial activity. For instance, the decision restricting the marketing, distribution, or sale of contracts for differences to retail clients affects not only all investment firms which currently offer contracts for differences to retail clients, but also investment firms which may offer contracts for differences to retail clients in the future. The direct legality review avenue, thus, being in all likelihood closed, the litigants will have to pursue the indirect route.

[64] See European Securities and Markets Authority Decision (EU) 2018/796 of 22 May 2018 to temporarily restrict contracts for differences in the Union, in accordance with art 40 of Regulation (EU) No 600/2014 of the European Parliament and of the Council.

[65] See European Securities and Markets Authority Decision (EU) 2018/795 of 22 May 2018 to temporarily prohibit the marketing, distribution or sale of binary options to retail clients in the Union in accordance with art 40 of Regulation (EU) No 600/2014 of the European Parliament and of the Council.

[66] *United Kingdom v Parliament and Council (ESMA)* (n 10), para 53.

[67] See Commission Delegated Regulation (EU) 2017/567 of 18 May 2016 supplementing Regulation (EU) No 600/2014.

[68] See Case 25/62 *Plaumann* EU:C:1963:17, para 107.

4.3 Indirect legality review

As the Court of Justice constantly reiterates, in order to ensure that the EU is a Union based on the rule of law, the Treaty has established a complete system of judicial remedies and procedures designed to permit EU courts to review the legality of EU legal acts. Natural and legal persons are, thus, protected against the application of EU measures, even where they cannot challenge these directly before EU courts by reason of the stringent conditions of admissibility laid down in Article 263(4) TFEU. In particular, where the implementation of EU legal acts falls to the national authorities, such persons may plead the invalidity of EU legal acts in support of an action against the implementing national measures brought before the national courts, in accordance with the conditions laid down by national rules,[69] and cause the national courts to request a preliminary ruling from the ECJ.[70] Indeed, pursuant to the *Foto-Frost* case,[71] the national court in charge of the main proceedings is, in principle, bound to refer the question to the ECJ under Article 267 TFEU if in doubt about the validity of an EU legal act raised before it. The national court will also be entitled, under strict conditions, to grant interim relief.[72] It is incumbent upon member states to ensure that such indirect legality review of EU legal acts is available to claimants who cannot challenge them directly. Member states are, thus, under a duty to provide legal remedies that make it possible to review the legality of these EU legal acts by means of a reference for a preliminary ruling under Article 267 TFEU. It is to be stressed, in that regard, that Article 74 of MiFID II obliges the member states to ensure that any national decision taken under the provisions of MiFIR or MiFID II, and therefore also in implementation of an ESMA's act adopted in accordance with MiFIR or MiFID II, is subject to the right of appeal before a tribunal.[73] In particular, national courts are required, so far as possible, to interpret and apply national procedural rules in a way that enables claimants to challenge, before the courts, the legality of any national measure relative to the application to the claimant of an EU legal act, by pleading the invalidity of such an act.[74] Furthermore, even though Article 19 TEU does not,

[69] Provided that these respect the principles of equivalence and effectiveness and the right to effective judicial protection enshrined in art 47 of the EU Charter (for a reminder, see ECJ Case C-12/08 *Mono-Car Styling* [2009], EU:C:2009:466, para 49).

[70] See Case 294/83 *Les Verts* EU:C:1986:166, para 23.

[71] Case 314/85 *Foto-Frost* EU:C:1987:452, para 17.

[72] Especially to order suspension of enforcement of the national supervisory decision based on the contested instruction (see Case C-465/93 *Atlanta Fruchthandelsgesellschaft* EU:C:1995:369; Joined Cases C-143/88 and 92/89 *Zuckerfrabrik Süderdithmarschen* EU:C:1991:65).

[73] See art 74 of MiFID II.

[74] See *Unión de Pequeños Agricultores* (n 42), para 42; see also Case C-84/14 P *Forgital Italy* EU:C:2015:517, para 66.

as a rule, intend to create new remedies before the national courts to ensure the observance of EU law, in addition to those already laid down by national law, it would be otherwise if the structure of the domestic legal system concerned were such that there was no remedy making it possible, even indirectly, to ensure respect for the rights that individuals derive from EU law.[75]

As indicated above, the indirect route will be, save in exceptional circumstances, the only one available to natural or legal persons to challenge the legality of measures of general scope adopted by ESMA.

Likewise, even if the ECJ, in response to the previously mentioned question referred by the French Conseil d'État,[76] has ruled that ESAs' guidelines do not constitute actionable measures within the meaning of Article 263 TFEU because of lack of binding legal effects, indirect challenge might be brought against those guidelines through the preliminary reference procedure. As mentioned above, the range of measures that can be challenged indirectly through a question of validity is wider than those that are amenable to judicial legality review in direct actions.[77] And the French Conseil d'État, by including the soft law instruments used by the national regulatory authorities in the category of acts whose annulment may be sought before it, has made it possible for applicants to invoke the invalidity of ESAs' guidelines in support of an action of annulment against an act of soft law that has been adopted by a competent authority in order to implement those guidelines. For example, in the *Fédération bancaire française* case, it has been possible for the applicant to raise the plea of invalidity of the EBA's guidelines because his action for annulment against the notice by which the national supervisory authority (Autorité de contrôle prudentiel et de résolution (ACPR)) had declared that it complied with those guidelines was deemed admissible, on the ground that the challenged notice 'has as its object and effect to incite credit institutions to modify significantly their practices regarding the governance and oversight on retail banking products'.[78]

With regard to individual measures taken by ESMA, the admissibility of a request for a preliminary ruling about their validity will depend on the answer to the question as to whether the claimant had undoubted standing to challenge the contested decision under Article 263 TFEU and failed to do so. If this

[75] See *Inuit Tapiriit Kanatami* (n 21), paras 103–04.

[76] See *Fédération bancaire française* (n 47).

[77] See *Belgium v Commission* (n 33), para 44; *Grimaldi* (n 38), paras 7–8; *Fédération bancaire française* (n 47); Case T-193/04 *Tillack* EU:T:2006:292, para 80.

[78] My translation. See *Fédération bancaire française* (Conseil d'État) (n 35) para 5: 'l'avis attaqué ... a pour objet et pour effet d'inciter ces établissements à modifier de manière significative leurs pratiques concernant la gouvernance et la surveillance des produits bancaires de détail'.

question is answered in the affirmative, the request for a preliminary ruling will be rejected as inadmissible.[79] The ECJ has recently specified that the possibility for a person to rely, in an action brought before a national court, on the invalidity of provisions contained in a measure of the EU that constitutes the basis of a national decision concerning him, presupposes either that he has also brought, pursuant to Article 263(4) TFEU, an action for annulment of that EU measure within the prescribed time limits, or that he has not done so, as a result of not having an undoubted right to bring such an action.[80]

4.4 Intensity of legality review

How thorough and deep will judicial scrutiny of ESMA's legal acts be? The intensity of review is related to the amount of discretion granted to the author of the challenged act. More precisely, discretion is the leeway left by the judge to the holder of public authority, which, accordingly, falls outside the ambit of judicial review. The reason why the reviewing court leaves a margin of discretion to the holder of public authority lies primarily in the separation of powers doctrine, according to which the court must stay within the limits of its judicial activity, and cannot interfere in what is considered to be the province of the executive or the legislative.[81] The granting of a margin of discretion is the necessary corollary of the specific tasks entrusted to the executive and the legislative in correlation with the amount of legitimacy those two branches of government bring into the process of governance, without which the latter would not be able to fulfil them.[82]

[79] See Case C-188/92 *TWD Textilwerke Deggendorf* EU:C:1994:90; Case C-441/05 *Roquette Frères*, EU:C:2007:150, paras 35–48; Case C-343/07 *Bavaria and Bavaria Italia* EU:C:2009:415, paras 37–46; Case C-143/14 *TMK Europe*, EU:C:2015:236 para 18.

[80] See Case C-135/16 *Georgsmarienhütte* EU:C:2018:582.

[81] See Charles Baron de Montesquieu in *The Spirit of Laws*: 'there is no liberty, if the judiciary power be not separated from, the legislative and executive. Were it joined with the legislative, the life and liberty of the subject would be exposed to arbitrary control; for the judge would be then the legislator. Were it joined to the executive power, the judge might behave with violence and oppression' (English translation available at <www.constitution.org/cm/sol.htm> accessed 14 October 2021): Charles Baron de Montesquieu, *De l'esprit des lois*, ch VI, Livre XI (Bibliothèque de la Pléiade, Gallimard 1951): 'Il n'y a point encore de liberté si la puissance de juger n'est pas séparée de la puissance législative et de l'exécutrice. Si elle était jointe à la puissance législative, le pouvoir sur la vie et la liberté des citoyens serait arbitraire: car le juge serait législateur. Si elle était jointe à la puissance exécutrice, le juge pourrait avoir la force d'un oppresseur'; see also J Madison, *The Federalist Papers* no 47. Madison says of 'the political maxim, that the legislative, executive, and judiciary departments ought to be separate and distinct' that 'accumulation of all powers, legislative, executive, and judiciary, in the same hands, whether of one, a few, or many, and whether hereditary, self-appointed, or elective, may justly be pronounced the very definition of tyranny' (text available at <www.congress.gov/resources/display/content/The+Federalist+Papers> accessed 14 October 2021).

[82] See Alexander Fritzsche, 'Discretion, Scope of Judicial Review and Institutional Balance' (2010) 47 Common Market Law Review 361; Dominique Ritleng, 'Judicial Review of Administrative

That being recalled, it is well known that, pursuant to the *Meroni* doctrine,[83] EU agencies cannot be allocated discretionary powers. They can only, ruled the Court, be vested with 'clearly defined executive powers'.[84] The reason for this limitation is that the delegation of powers to EU agencies, which cannot be derived from an explicit provision in the founding Treaties and, thus, is not constitutionally legitimised, would, if the powers granted were of discretionary nature, affect the Treaty-conferred responsibilities of the delegating authorities, and hence distort the institutional balance. *Meroni*'s legacy is that 'agencies cannot be given the power to adopt general regulatory measures. They are limited to taking individual decisions in specific areas where a defined technical expertise is required, under clearly and precisely defined conditions and without genuine discretionary power'.[85]

In the *Short selling* case, the ECJ mellowed the democratic constraints on the powers of EU agencies set by the *Meroni* doctrine. For the first time, it allowed the EU legislature to endow EU agencies with rulemaking powers, and acknowledged that ESMA can be granted a 'margin of discretion', provided that the exercise of this discretion will be subject to a series of conditions and criteria and, therefore, 'amenable to judicial review'.[86]

Nevertheless, it follows from the recognition of a margin of discretion that, as a matter of principle, only limited judicial review should be performed. In the EU courts' case law, when a margin of discretion must be afforded, as a consequence of the complex technical, scientific, or economic assessments required by the making of an administrative measure, judicial review is confined to verifying either 'whether the rules on procedure and on the statement of reasons have been complied with, whether the facts have been accurately stated, and, whether there has been any manifest error of assessment or misuse of powers'[87] or 'whether there has been a manifest error of appraisal or a misuse of powers, or whether [the administrative authorities] have manifestly

Discretion: How far does the Separation of Powers Matter?' in Joana Mendes and Ingo Venzke (eds), *Allocating Authority: Who should do what in European and International Law?* (Hart Publishing 2018), 183.

[83] Case 9/56 *Meroni* EU:C:1958:7.

[84] ibid.

[85] Commission, 'Communication from the Commission to the European Parliament and the Council 'European agencies—The way forward' COM (2008) 135 final, 5.

[86] *United Kingdom v Parliament and Council* (n 10), paras 45–53.

[87] See, eg Case 42/84 *Remia* EU:C:1985:327, para 34, about a decision of the Commission; Case C-77/09 *Gowan* EU:C:2010:803, paras 55–56, about a directive of the Commission; Case T-541/13 *Albertis Telecom* EU:T:2015:898, para 122, about a decision of the Commission.

exceeded the limits of their discretion'.[88] Moreover, to counterbalance the limitations on substantive review, the EU judicature has strengthened the procedural guarantees. Pursuant to a jurisprudence inaugurated by the *Technische Universität München* judgment, when the administration has a margin of discretion and, accordingly, the substantive legality of the acts adopted in the exercise of that discretion is subject to only light scrutiny, 'respect for the rights guaranteed by the Community legal order in administrative procedures is of even more fundamental importance. Those guarantees include, in particular, the duty of the competent institution to examine carefully and impartially all the relevant aspects of the individual case, the right of the person concerned to make his views known and to have an adequately reasoned decision'.[89] The reason for such a dialectical relationship resides in the aims of formal and procedural rules, which are to enable the administration to make the best possible discretionary assessments and, thus, to ensure the substantive legality and, further, the merits of its measures.[90] More stringent procedural requirements have been imposed, initially on individual decisions,[91] and then on general measures.[92]

The control over the exercise of ESMA's margin of discretion will most likely follow the same standard of review. The 'manifest error' standard has been already applied to EU agencies' measures.[93] Whether this standard of review will be liable to ensure effective judicial protection is hard to tell. Under the disguise of the 'manifest error of appraisal' standard, different degrees of review may be performed.[94] In any event, extended scrutiny shall be exerted over fines or periodic penalty payments imposed by ESMA on investment firms.[95]

[88] See, eg Case C-425/08 *Enviro Tech* EU:C:2009:635, para 47, about a directive of the Commission; Case T-13/99 *Pfizer Animal Health* EU:T:2002:209, para 166, about an implementing regulation of the Council.

[89] Case C-269/90 *Technische Universität München* EU:C:1991:438, para 14.

[90] For a reminder of that rationale, see Opinion of AG Bot in Case C-584/10P *Kadi II*, EU:C:2013:176, para 97.

[91] See *Technische Universität München* (n 89); Case T-44/90 *La Cinq SA* EU:T:1992:5, para 86; Case T-109/02 *Bolloré SA* EU:T:2007:115, para 92; *Albertis Telecom* (n 87), para 123.

[92] See *Pfizer Animal Health* (n 88), para 171; *Gowan* (n 87), para 57; *Enviro Tech* (n 88), para 62; Case T-285/03 *Agraz and others v Commission* EU:T:2005:109, paras 49–50, about a regulation of the Commission.

[93] See Case T-187/06 *Schräder v CPVO* EU:T:2008:511, paras 60–62, concerning the intensity of review of a decision of the Community Plant Variety Office rejecting an application for a plant variety right; Case T-102/13 *Heli-Flight* EU:T:2014:1064, para 89, on a decision of the European Aviation Safety Agency.

[94] See Alexander H Türk, 'Oversight of Administrative Rulemaking: Judicial Review' (2013) 19 European Law Journal 126; Joana Mendes, 'Discretion, Care and Public Interests in the EU Administration: Probing the Limits of Law' (2016) 53 Common Market Law Review 419.

[95] For breach of data reporting obligations, for instance (see art 38(h) of MiFIR).

Under Article 38(m) of MiFIR, EU courts 'shall have unlimited jurisdiction to review decisions whereby ESMA has imposed a fine or a periodic penalty payment', and 'may annul, reduce or increase the fine or periodic penalty payment imposed'.

4.5 Damages actions

Investment firms that have suffered damage caused by ESMA action under MiFID II or MiFIR may wish to claim for compensation.

The more thorny issue relates to cases where the allegedly damaging ESMA action forms part of composite administrative procedures, where EU and national bodies contribute to the making of the decision, or to the action. This raises the issue of joint or concurrent liability:[96] situations where both an EU body and a national body may be held liable. For instance, by virtue of Article 80(2) of MiFID II, ESMA participates in on-site verifications or investigations, carried out jointly by two or more competent authorities in accordance with Article 21 of Regulation (EU) No 1095/2010.[97] Also, ESMA makes use of the temporary intervention powers granted by Article 40 of MiFIR to prohibit the marketing, distribution, or sale of certain financial instruments, or types of financial activity or practice, prohibition of which is then enforced by the competent authorities at national level. In those situations, the question is that of the allocation of liability between ESMA and the competent authority for losses incurred by a third party. To whom should the allegedly harmed investment firm turn for compensation: ESMA or the competent authority? Should it sue ESMA before the General Court, in accordance with the liability conditions laid down in EU law,[98] or should it, instead, bring an action against the competent authority in a national court, which will be governed by national law, albeit to some degree Europeanised?[99]

[96] See Trevor C Hartley, 'Concurrent Liability in EEC Law: A Critical Review of the Cases' (1977) 2 European Law Review 249; Wouter Wils, 'Concurrent Liability of the Community and a Member State' (1992) 17 European Law Review 191; Peter Oliver, 'Joint Liability of the Community and the Member States' in Ton Heukels and Alison McDonnell (eds), *The Action for Damages in Community Law* (Kluwer 1997), ch 16.

[97] See also arts 38(d) and 48(d) of MiFIR, concerning on-site inspections carried out by ESMA with the assistance of the national competent authority.

[98] For those conditions, see Case C-352/98 P *Bergaderm* EU:C:2000:361. The conditions are also applicable to the liability of EU agencies: see Case T-556/11 *European Dynamics Luxembourg* EU:T:2016:248, para 264.

[99] See Joined Cases C-46 and 48/93 *Brasserie du pêcheur* EU:C:1996:79.

It transpires from the case law that several situations are to be distinguished.

The first situation is that of an unlawful national implementation of a ESMA legal act. An example of such a scenario would be where, in order to punish a violation by an investment firm of the prohibition of a type of financial activity, the competent authority has imposed administrative penalties in breach of the enabling national legislation. In such a situation, since the competent authority retains some leeway in determining the content of the measure to be adopted, the damage does not result from a measure or unlawful conduct attributable to ESMA. As a consequence, the investment firm that claims to have been injured has to proceed against the competent authority in a national court. As the held, 'the question of compensation … for damage caused to private individuals by the agencies and servants of Member States, either by reason of an infringement of Community law or by an act or omission contrary to national law, in the application of Community law … must be determined by the national courts in accordance with the national law of the Member State concerned'.[100]

The second situation is that of the correct application of an unlawful EU act. Suppose that ESMA has prohibited a type of financial activity without regard for the conditions set out in Article 40 of MiFIR, prohibition which is then enforced by the national competent authority. To allocate liability in such a situation, it must be determined to whom the unlawful conduct alleged, in support of the application for compensation, is to be attributed. The principle is that any damage ensuing from the implementation of EU legislation by national authorities that had no discretion in that regard will be attributable to the EU.[101] Thus, in the *Krohn* case, the Court ruled that, where the decision adversely affecting the claimant was adopted by the national body on the allegedly unlawful instruction of the Commission, the damages action had to be brought against the Commission, since the EU law provisions did not merely confer on the Commission the right to give an opinion on the national decision to be adopted, but empowered it to dictate that decision by way of instructions that the national authority was bound to comply with.[102] In such a case, the damage suffered can, in principle, only give rise to non-contractual liability of ESMA in an action brought before the General Court. However, in cases where ESMA's allegedly unlawful measure leaves the competent authority a margin

[100] Case 101/78 *Granaria* EU:C:1979:38, para 14; See also Case 12/79 *Wagner* EU:C:1979:286.

[101] See Joined Cases C-104/89 and C-37/90 *Mulder* EU:C:1992:217, para 9; Case T-174/00 *Biret* EU:T:2002:2, para 33.

[102] Case 175/84 *Krohn* EU:C:1986:85, paras 18–23; for a recent reminder, in a case concerning the role of the ECB and other EU institutions in the award of conditional financial assistance, see Case T-786/14 *Bourdouvali* EU:T:2018:487, paras 80 and 99.

of discretion on how to implement it, there is no direct causality between the ESMA measure and the loss: the harmful conduct must be regarded as attributable to the national competent authority, and the national courts retain sole jurisdiction to order compensation for such losses.[103]

The third situation is that where ESMA either fails to perform its task of overseeing the proper national implementation of EU law by the competent authorities,[104] or participates in harmful on-site inspections carried out by those competent authorities. Those types of conduct on the part of ESMA are capable of causing the EU to incur liability.[105] But in such cases there are two instances of harmful conduct: one attributable to ESMA, the other to the competent authority. To obtain compensation for its losses, the investment firm harmed would, therefore, have to bring two separate damages actions, one against the competent authority in the national court, and another against ESMA before the General Court. If the investment firm simultaneously brings these two actions seeking compensation for the same damage, the EU court will wait until the national court has given judgment before ruling on the amount of the damages for which ESMA will be held liable, in order to avoid the applicant being insufficiently or excessively compensated because of different assessments of that damage by the two different courts.[106] This will nonetheless not call into question the admissibility of the action brought before the General Court, but merely, where relevant, the final decision on the amount of the compensation that it should grant.[107] Moreover, the General Court may, even before the national court has given its ruling, determine whether the conduct alleged against ESMA is capable of giving rise to its non-contractual liability.[108]

4.6 Conclusion

The question whether the remedies available to litigants, especially investment firms, to challenge action taken by ESMA under MiFID II or MiFIR are liable to ensure effective judicial protection cannot be answered definitively. These are the same remedies as those provided for in the Treaties and, as such, they

[103] See Case T-54/96 *Oleifici Italiani* EU:T:1998:204, para 67.

[104] See, eg art 57(5) of MiFID II, in conjunction with art 17 of the ESMA Regulation.

[105] See Joined Cases 5-24, 7-24, and 13-24/66 *Kampffmeyer* EU:C:1967:31; Case T-546/13 *Šumelj and Others/Commission* EU:T:2016:107; *Bourdouvali* (n 102), paras 197–203.

[106] See *Kampffmeyer* (n 104) at 344; *Bourdouvali* (n 101), para 240; Case T-138/03, *ÉR and Others v Council and Commission* EU:T:2006:390, para 42.

[107] See *ÉR and Others* (n 106), para 42.

[108] See *Bourdouvali* (n 101), para 240.

present the same possible faults as regards the effectiveness of the judicial protection they guarantee. All will depend on whether EU courts maintain the same interpretation of these remedies, within the regulatory context of MiFID II and MiFIR. Some adjustments would certainly be welcome for meeting the needs of effective judicial protection, in particular with respect to the direct reviewability of guidelines issued by ESMA, whose effects make it clear that they are the result of quasi-regulatory powers.

5

Protecting Investors at all Costs? Due Process Aspects of the Investigatory Powers Granted to Competent Authorities under MiFID II

Helene Andersson

5.1 Introduction

The financial crisis of 2008 pushed the world's financial systems towards the edge of collapse, and exposed weaknesses in both the functioning and transparency of financial markets. The crisis triggered a number of regulative responses from legislators around the world, including in the EU. One such response was to replace the Markets in Financial Instruments Directive (MiFID) with two new pieces of legislation: a directive and a regulation. The two acts aim at restoring trust in the financial system by strengthening the framework for regulation and supervision of markets in financial instruments. They impose a number of obligations on those authorised to operate in these markets, and failure to comply with the rules is not without risk. Not only can national supervisory authorities issue public warnings, withdraw authorisations, or require the removal of natural persons from their managerial functions, they may also impose substantial administrative fines on both natural and legal persons. Yet, while the two acts provide national authorities with far-reaching enforcement powers, they provide few safeguards against abuse of these powers.

This chapter provides a due process examination of the investigatory powers granted to national supervisory authorities. In particular, it will focus on the power to carry out on-site inspections, and the possibilities of holding the supervisory authorities accountable for any arbitrary or disproportionate measures taken in relation to these inspections. It is concluded that, absent clear and adequate procedural safeguards, there is an apparent risk that any measures

Helene Andersson, *Protecting Investors at all Costs? Due Process Aspects of the Investigatory Powers Granted to Competent Authorities under MiFID II* In: *Legal Accountability in EU Markets for Financial Instruments*. Edited by: Carl Fredrik Bergström and Magnus Strand, Oxford University Press. © Helene Andersson 2021. DOI: 10.1093/oso/9780192849281.003.0005 taken will infringe both the right to privacy and the defence rights of those targeted. Without adequate safeguards, any decisions taken by the authorities risk being contestable on procedural grounds. Furthermore, the threat of having to pay hefty fines may already deter some from accepting a managerial function in an investment firm. If the enforcement rules are allowed to be applied in an arbitrary or inconsistent way, allowing the supervisory authorities to escape accountability, it will no doubt become even more difficult to recruit managers and board members in the future. Thus, while lenient procedural safeguards would, in theory, further the interests of effectiveness and efficiency, the reality may be the opposite.

5.2 Background

The original Markets in Financial Instruments Directive (MiFID) became effective in November 2007,[1] and was intended as the cornerstone of the EU's Financial Services Action Plan. Its aim was to establish a single market for investment services and activities by ensuring not only a level playing field for firms to compete in the financial markets, but also a consistent level of consumer protection across the EU.[2] The pace of technological change and innovation in financial instruments and markets, combined with calls for reform following the financial crisis, soon prompted the European Commission to propose a new legislative package to replace the MiFID regime. In October 2011, the Commission presented a proposal in the form of a revised directive and a new regulation, and, after more than two years of deliberations, a new directive (MiFID II) and a new regulation, the Market in Financial Investments Regulation (MiFIR),[3] were eventually adopted. As noted in the directive's recitals, the new legislative package reflected the Union's commitment to minimise, where appropriate, the level of discretion available to member states in relation to EU financial services law. The reasons for doing so were to contribute to the establishment of a single rule book for financial markets in the

[1] This directive was adopted in April 2004 and was initially to become effective on 30 April 2006. However, the original timetable was extended in 2006 through the adoption of an amending directive, which extended the implementation deadline to 31 January 2007, and provided that MiFID should be applied from 1 November 2007. For a more detailed description of the legislative process, see, eg Niamh Moloney, *EU Securities and Financial Markets Regulation* (3rd edn, OUP 2014) 327–35.

[2] ibid.

[3] Directive 2014/65/EU of the European Parliament and the Council of 15 May 2014 on markets in financial instruments and amending Directive 2002/92/EC and Directive 2011/61/EU (hereafter 'MiFID II'); Regulation (EU) no 600/2014 of the European Parliament and of the Council of 15 May 2014 on markets in financial instruments and amending Regulation (EU) no 648/2012 (hereafter 'MiFIR').

EU, to help further develop a level playing field, and to enhance investor protection, but also to improve supervision and enforcement.

Indeed, the 2008 financial crisis resulted in a major reconsideration of many rules and assumptions underpinning financial systems across the globe. While many of the reforms, MiFID II and MiFIR included, have focused on addressing these problems through the imposition of new substantive rules, the institutional set-up in place before 2008 was considered to be partly responsible for the failure to mitigate the extreme effects of the crisis. This highlighted the need to also improve the supervisory framework.[4] In February 2009, the high-level group on financial supervision in the EU presented its report to the Commission, stating that a sound prudential and conduct of business framework must rest on strong supervisory and sanctioning regimes. Supervisory authorities should be equipped with sufficient powers to act when financial institutions have inadequate risk management and control mechanisms, or inadequate solvency of liquidity positions, the report stated. There should also be equal, strong, and deterrent sanctions regimes against all financial crimes: sanctions that should be enforced effectively.[5] At the time, these were not considered to exist in the EU. On the contrary, the high-level group considered national sanctioning regimes to be both weak and heterogeneous. Sanctions for insider trading ranged from a few thousand euros, in one member state, to millions of euros, or imprisonment, in another. This could induce regulatory arbitrage in the internal market, the report declared. It was, therefore, considered urgent that sanctions were not only strengthened, but harmonised.

The legislator appears to have acted on the suggestions presented in the report, as MiFID II acknowledges the need to enhance convergence of the powers at the disposal of competent authorities of the member states (the NCAs), so as to pave the way towards an equivalent intensity of enforcement across the EU financial market. A common minimum set of powers, coupled with adequate resources, should guarantee supervisory effectiveness, the directive declares. Accordingly, it provides for a minimum set of supervisory and investigatory powers to be granted to the NCAs.[6] While most of the investigatory powers were already in place under the old MiFID regime, the old directive did not

[4] Wolf-Georg Ringe, Luis Morais, and David Ramos, 'A Holistic Approach to the Institutional Architecture of Financial Supervision and Regulation in the EU' in Veerle Colaert, Danny Busch, and Thomas Incalza (eds), *European Financial Regulation: Levelling the Cross-Sectoral Playing Field* (Hart Publishing 2019) 405.

[5] The High-level group on financial supervision in the EU, chaired by Jacques de Larosière, Report of 25 February 2009, 83.

[6] MiFID II, recital 137.

spell out the sanctions to be imposed. Instead, it required member states to ensure, in conformity with their national law, that appropriate administrative measures could be taken, or administrative sanctions could be imposed, against those responsible for infringements. While the member states were to ensure that these measures were effective, proportionate, and dissuasive, there were no requirements as to the nature or severity of any sanctions. Nor were there any explicit requirements to provide sanctions or remedies against natural persons. As a result of MiFID II, member states are now required to provide their NCAs with a number of sanctioning powers against both investment firms and members of their management bodies, raising the stakes for both natural and legal persons. This increases the importance of ensuring a fair procedure, which duly respects the fundamental rights of those targeted by the NCAs' investigations, and where the NCAs are held accountable for any arbitrary or disproportionate measures taken.

As will be further discussed below, the investigatory powers provided for in the directive are far-reaching, and have been framed in such a way that they allow for, or even encourage, a broad interpretation and application by the member states. Yet, with a few exceptions, the operative parts of the two acts are silent on the rights of those targeted by the investigations. The absence of procedural safeguards is remarkable, given that fundamental rights are protected by EU primary legislation, and that all member states have acceded to the European Convention on Human Rights (ECHR). That said, while the operative parts of the directive make no mention of the Charter of Fundamental Rights of the European Union (Charter), the recitals declare that the supervisory powers granted to the NCAs should be exercised within a complete system of national law that guarantees the respect for fundamental rights, including the right to privacy.[7] The directive, thus, acknowledges the importance of ensuring adequate fundamental rights protection. However, there is a catch. While requiring member states to provide adequate and effective safeguards against abuse, it also states that they should allow the NCAs to exercise the supervisory powers to the extent necessary for the proper investigation of serious cases, where there are no equivalent means for effectively achieving the same result. Thus, according to the wording of the directive, in serious cases, the objective of ensuring the aims of the directive should be allowed to trump fundamental rights. The question is, of course, whether this can be done without infringing EU rules of a higher rank. Before discussing this issue in

[7] ibid, recital 138.

more detail, the following section provides a brief presentation of the EU fundamental rights regime.

5.3 EU fundamental rights protection

While the Treaty of Rome was silent on fundamental rights, the legal landscape has gradually been redesigned as fundamental rights eased their way into the EU legal system. Today, Article 2 of the Treaty on European Union (TEU) declares that the Union is founded on the values of respect for human dignity, freedom, democracy, equality, the rule of law, and respect for human rights. Article 6 TEU protects fundamental rights under three diverse and complementary perspectives: as general principles of EU law, as defined by the Charter, and as protected by the ECHR. Article 6(1) TEU gives the Charter the same legal value as the Treaties, Article 6(2) commits the EU to accede to the ECHR, and Article 6(3) confirms general principles as a source of fundamental rights.

The Charter contains all the rights encompassed in the ECHR, together with a number of additional, third-generation rights, such as the right to good administration, as discussed by Reichel in the following chapter.[8] According to Article 51 of the Charter, its provisions are directed not only at the EU institutions, but also at the member states, when they are implementing EU law.[9] This means that the NCAs are bound by the Charter when they apply MiFIR, or the national rules adopted pursuant to MiFID II.

An important feature of the Charter is its Article 52(3). This article stipulates that, to the extent that the Charter affords rights that correspond to ECHR rights, the meaning and scope of those rights shall be the same as those laid down by the ECHR. EU law may only derogate from the ECHR standard if such derogation means more extensive protection. As a result, the ECHR and the case law of the European Court of Human Rights (the 'Strasbourg court' or 'ECtHR') now provide a 'floor' to EU fundamental rights protection.[10]

[8] Charter of Fundamental Rights of the European Union art 41.

[9] Much has been said about the term 'implementing EU law'. In *Åklagaren v Hans Åkerberg Fransson*, the Court made it clear that the term should be interpreted so as to cover national authorities' application of EU law. Thus, the Charter may come into play whenever a member state acts within the scope of EU law. See Case C-617/10 *Åklagaren v Hans Åkerberg Fransson* EU:C:2013:105, and Case C-205/15 *Direcția Generală Regională a Finanțelor Publice Brașov (DGRFP) v Vasile Toma and Biroul Executorului Judecătoresc Horațiu-Vasile Cruduleci* EU:C:2016:499.

[10] See, eg the explanations to the Charter, stating that the scope of the rights is determined not only by the wording of the ECHR, but also by the case law of the Strasbourg court. See also Case C-400/10 PPU *JMcB v LE* EU:C:2010:582, where the CJEU held that, where Charter rights correspond to those in the ECHR, the Court should follow the clear and consistent jurisprudence of the ECtHR.

More or less through the back door, the EU has not only committed itself to ensuring a minimum standard of protection, but has also, indirectly, left it to the ECHR to state what that standard should be. To use the words of Groussot and Stavefeltdt, Article 52(3) creates a situation of informal accession to the ECHR.[11] According to Weiss, the article not only requires harmony between Charter rights and corresponding ECHR rights, but absorbs these rights into the EU legal order.[12] The obligation to observe the standards of fundamental rights protection that flow from the ECHR has a constitutional status in the EU.

When the NCAs enforce EU rules, they will, thus, have to respect the requirements imposed by the Charter, and this standard should not fall short of the ECHR standard. However, while the Charter may constitute an informal accession of the EU to the ECHR, all member states have also formally acceded to the Convention and are, thus, directly bound by its provisions. When enforcing the national rules adopted pursuant to MiFID II, they will, therefore, have to make sure that both the Charter and the ECHR standards are met. As will be discussed in the following section, the level of protection required varies depending on whether the procedures laid down in MiFID II are considered criminal or purely administrative.

5.4 The criminal nature of any available sanctions

Article 70 of MiFID II stipulates that the NCAs should be empowered to impose sanctions that are effective, proportionate, and dissuasive. While this was already a requirement under the original MiFID, the replacement directive goes further than its predecessor and identifies certain powers that need to be included in the NCAs' arsenal. NCAs must be empowered to issue public statements and cease and desist orders, to suspend or withdraw authorisations, and to ban natural persons from exercising managerial functions in investment firms. Furthermore, the NCAs should be able to impose substantial fines. For natural persons, the maximum fine is 5,000,000 euros, and for legal persons it is 5,000,000 euros or ten per cent of annual turnover. These thresholds may be pushed upwards as the maximum fines are to be at least twice the amount of the benefit derived from the infringement.

[11] Xavier Groussot and Eric Stavefeldt, 'Accession of the EU to the ECHR: A Legally Complex Situation' in Joakim Nergelius and Eleonor Kristoffersson (eds), *Human Rights in Contemporary European Law* (Hart Publishing 2015).

[12] Wolfgang Weiss, 'Human Rights in the EU: Rethinking the Role of the European Convention on Human Rights After Lisbon' (2011) 7(1) European Constitutional Law Review 67.

MiFID II explicitly defines these sanctions as administrative. This definition is of great significance for two reasons. First, if the fines are considered administrative, this allows national courts to impose custodial sentences in addition to any fines already imposed on natural persons without thereby infringing the principle of *ne bis in idem*, according to which no one should be liable to be tried or punished twice for the same offence. Second, if the sanctions are considered administrative, the standard of protection to be afforded is lower than would otherwise be the case. Fundamental procedural rights are broader, and apply much more strictly when 'criminal sanctions' are imposed than when civil remedies or administrative sanctions are imposed.[13] Thus, the nature of the sanctions will determine the extent of the rights afforded to those targeted by the NCAs' investigations.

While MiFID II defines the sanctions as administrative, this by no means implies that the Charter or the ECHR will define them as such. In fact, it is clear from the case of *Grande Stevens v Italy*[14] that the criminal head of Article 6 ECHR applies to the fines provided for under MiFID II. While *Grande Stevens* concerned market abuse, the sanctions imposed in that case bear a striking resemblance to those available under MiFID II. In the case at hand, the Italian Companies and Stock Exchange Commission ('CONSOB') had imposed substantial administrative fines not only on two companies (Exor and Giovanni Agnelli), but also on two of the companies' managers, as well as an external lawyer consulted by the companies. In addition to these pecuniary sanctions, the three natural persons were banned from administering, managing, or supervising listed companies for periods varying from two to four months. CONSOB also reported the case to the prosecuting authorities, and Messrs Gabetti and Grande Stevens were later convicted of having provided false information capable of triggering a significant change in the value of financial instruments.[15]

An application was later filed with the Strasbourg court. Relying on Article 6 ECHR the applicants claimed that the proceedings before CONSOB had not been fair. Referring to the ruling of the CJEU in *Åkerberg Fransson*,[16] they argued that the sanctions imposed by CONSOB, despite being classified as

[13] Treschel notes that, although the principle of equality of arms and the right to adversarial proceedings laid down in art 6 of the ECHR apply indistinctly in civil and criminal cases, there is a slight difference in the application of the article depending on the nature of the case, and that the contracting states have greater latitude when dealing with cases concerning civil rights and obligations than they have when dealing with criminal cases: Stefan Treschel, *Human Rights in Criminal Proceedings* (OUP 2006) 85.

[14] *Grande Stevens v Italy*, judgment of 4 March 2014, App no 18640/10.

[15] Contrary to art 187 *ter* of Legislative Decree no 58 of 1998.

[16] *Åkerberg Fransson* (n 9).

administrative, should be considered criminal in nature, thereby triggering the application of the *ne bis in idem* principle. To this, the Strasbourg court responded that, in determining the existence of a 'criminal charge', it is necessary to have regard to three factors: the legal classification of the measure in national law, the very nature of the measure, and the nature and severity of the penalty. These criteria are alternative and not cumulative.[17]

The Strasbourg court noted that market manipulation did not constitute a criminal offence in Italian law. However, the court continued, the national classification was not decisive for the purposes of the applicability of the criminal head of Article 6 ECHR, as the indications furnished by domestic legislation have only a relative value.[18] As to the nature of the offence, the Strasbourg court noted that the rules allegedly infringed were intended to guarantee the integrity of the financial markets and to maintain public confidence in the security of transactions. CONSOB was entrusted with the task of protecting investors and ensuring the effectiveness, transparency, and development of the stock market: all general interests of society, and usually protected under criminal law.[19] In addition, the fines imposed were essentially intended to punish—to prevent repeat offending—and were, thus, based on rules whose purpose was both deterrent and punitive. Any penalties were imposed on the basis of the gravity of the infringement and not on the harm caused to investors, the court noted further.[20]

As to the nature and severity of the penalty, the Strasbourg court noted that the fines could go up to 5,000,000 euros, and this ordinary maximum amount could, in certain circumstances, be tripled or fixed at ten times the proceeds or profit obtained through the unlawful conduct. Imposition of such fines entailed the temporary loss of honour for the representatives of the companies involved, and they could also be forbidden from administering, managing, or supervising listed companies for periods ranging from two months to three years. CONSOB could also prohibit listed companies, management companies, and auditing companies from engaging the services of the offender, for a maximum period of three years, and request professional associations to suspend, on a temporary basis, the individual's right to carry out his or her professional activities. Lastly, the imposition of financial administrative sanctions

[17] *Grande Stevens* (n 14), para 94. These criteria were first established during the mid seventies, in the case of *Engel and Others v the Netherlands*, judgment of 8 June 1976, Apps nos. 5100/71; 5101/71; 5102/71; 5354/72; 5370/72.

[18] *Grande Stevens* (n 14), para 95. It is worth noting that if the applicable national law classifies an offence as criminal, it automatically takes the same classification for the purposes of art 6 ECHR.

[19] ibid, para 96.

[20] ibid.

entailed confiscation of the proceeds or profits of the unlawful conduct, and of the assets that made it possible.[21]

The Strasbourg court also noted that, while the maximum fines had not been imposed, the criminal connotations of proceedings depended on the degree of severity of the penalty to which the person concerned was *a priori* liable, and not the severity of the penalty ultimately imposed. Furthermore, in the present case the applicants had received fines ranging from 500,000 to 3,000,000 euros, and the three natural persons had been prohibited from administering, managing, or supervising listed companies for periods ranging from two to four months. This last penalty was such as to compromise their integrity, and, given their amounts, the fines were of undeniable severity, and had significant financial implications for the applicants. The Strasbourg court, thus, considered that they were criminal in nature, with the result that Article 6(1) ECHR was applicable under its criminal head.[22]

To conclude, as both the overarching aim of the legislation in question—to guarantee the integrity of the financial markets and to maintain public confidence in the security of transactions—and the sanctions available under MiFID II bear a striking resemblance to the sanctions defined as criminal in the case of *Grande Stevens*, it can be established that the procedures, as well as the sanctions available under MiFID II, are criminal in nature.[23] This will affect the level of protection to be afforded to legal and natural persons targeted by the NCAs' investigations.

Another aspect that may also influence the intensity of any fundamental rights protection is the fact that the provision of investment services requires prior authorisation. The following section will discuss the possibility that investment firms could, depending on the terms of their authorisations, be considered to have waived certain rights, and might thereby be afforded a lower standard of protection.

[21] ibid, para 97.

[22] ibid, para 100. The consequence of this was that, while the Strasbourg court considered that the sanctions imposed by CONSOB pursued an aim that was in the general interest, and did not appear disproportionate to the conduct with which the applicants were charged, the new criminal proceedings against Mr Gabetti and Mr Grande Stevens were considered to infringe the principle of *ne bis in idem* and, therefore, had to be closed.

[23] In the recent case of *DB v CONSOB*, the CJEU followed the reasoning of the ECtHR. In a Grand Chamber ruling, it declared that, while it was for the referring court to assess whether the administrative fines imposed by CONSOB were criminal in nature, the fines pursued a punitive purpose and presented a high degree of severity, such that they were liable to be regarded as criminal in nature. See Case C-481/19 *DB v Commissione Nazionale per le Società e la Borsa (CONSOB)* EU:C:2021:84, para 43.

5.5 Supervision in the context of financial markets regulation

Any examination of the scope and level of fundamental rights protection afforded to investment firms will have to consider the possibility that such firms, by operating in a market subject to strict regulation, have waived certain rights, and may not enforce these rights against measures taken by the NCAs, at least not with as much force as otherwise might have been the case. This section examines the merits of such an argument and concludes that, while investment firms may indeed have to accept certain obligations, such as extensive reporting duties, or obligations to record telephone conversations, the strict regulation of the market, combined with the far-reaching enforcement powers and the broad margins of discretion and appreciation granted to the NCAs, actually make the need for strict procedural safeguards all the more urgent. This is especially true since MiFID II has introduced a number of sanctions targeted not only at investment firms, but also at natural persons. Furthermore, and also of relevance, it should not be ignored that the MiFID II authorisation requirement constitutes, in and of itself, a limitation of a fundamental right: the right to conduct a business.

5.5.1 The right to conduct a business

As noted by Oliver, EU law has been suffused with economic rights ever since its inception.[24] It is, therefore, not surprising that the Court of Justice of the European Union (CJEU) recognised the existence of a right to conduct a business as early as 1974,[25] and that the Charter, unlike the ECHR, contains a provision explicitly protecting this right. Article 16 of the Charter recognises the right to conduct a business in accordance with Union law and national law and practices, thereby granting the right constitutional status.[26]

However, while the right is on a par with other fundamental rights, and may serve as a counterweight against them, as well as against other public interests, the phrase 'in accordance with Union law and national laws and practices'

[24] Peter Oliver, 'What Purpose does Article 16 of the Charter Serve?' in Ulf Bernitz, Xavier Groussot, and Felix Shulyock (eds), *General Principles of EU Law and European Private Law* (Kluwer Law International 2013) 281.

[25] Case 4/73 *Nold KG v European Commission* EU:C:1974:51.

[26] According to the Charter Explanations, art 16 comprises the freedom to exercise an economic or commercial activity, freedom of contract, and the right to free competition.

weakens its intensity. Indeed, in *Sky Österreich*,[27] the CJEU declared that the freedom to conduct a business is not absolute, but must be viewed in relation to its social function. This means that it may be subject to a broad range of interventions on the part of public authorities, which may limit the exercise of economic activity in the public interest.[28] That said, while the right may be set aside in order to promote or protect other interests, it is not possible to prohibit the conduct of a business unless there is a justified reason for such prohibition, and that reason is considered to outweigh the individual's right to carry out business activities. It is clear from MiFID II that the legislators considered the public interest in ensuring efficient, transparent, and resilient financial markets to outweigh the right to conduct a business. As financial crises may be liable to cause economic 'tsunamis' in affected economies, the public interest in preventing these crises bears considerable weight. Accordingly, MiFID II requires the provision of investment services and/or the performance of investment activities to be subject to prior authorisation.[29] The authorisation should specify the investment services or activities that the firm may provide, and an NCA may not grant authorisation unless, and until such time, as it is fully satisfied that the applicant complies with the directive's requirements. An authorisation may be withdrawn if the investment firm seriously and systematically infringes the provisions adopted pursuant to the directive, or if it no longer meets the conditions under which authorisation was granted.[30]

Thus, as a general rule, providing investment services or activities is prohibited in the EU: unless the investment firm can satisfy the relevant NCA that the requirements for authorisation are satisfied, it may not operate in the EU market. Furthermore, investment firms are required to comply with the conditions for initial authorisation at all times, and also have to adjust to, and accept, any new conditions for authorisation.[31] While this may be a challenging task for the firms, it, admittedly, also puts a heavy burden on the supervisory authorities. Member states need to ensure that the NCAs monitor the activities of investment firms so as to assess compliance with the operating conditions provided for in MiFID II. This requires that the NCAs are provided with adequate means to obtain the necessary information.[32] Given the ever-expanding scope of financial market regulation and the apparent importance of ensuring

[27] Case C-283/11 *Sky Österreich GmbH v Österreichischer Rundfunk* EU:C:2013:28.
[28] ibid, para 46.
[29] MiFID II, art 5.
[30] ibid, art 8(d).
[31] ibid, art 21.
[32] ibid, art 22.

sound financial markets, it is understandable that the powers of the NCAs are far-reaching, and that investment firms may have to submit to certain obligations that would otherwise constitute an undue interference with their rights.[33] The weights placed on the scale when assessing the proportionality of any measures taken are, thus, not necessarily the same as for companies active in non-regulated markets. However, this does not mean that the public interest in monitoring the activities of investment firms should, at all times, be allowed to trump the rights of targeted undertakings or their managers: it cannot serve as a carte blanche for the NCAs.

The Strasbourg court's case law on the privilege against self-incrimination can be used as to illustrate the effects that regulatory regimes may have on the standard of protection. In the case of *O'Halloran and Francis,* the Strasbourg court paid regard to the fact that the applicants had subjected themselves to a regulatory regime and could, therefore, be taken to have accepted certain responsibilities and obligations that could otherwise be considered as infringing their fundamental rights.[34] In the case at hand, the two applicants were both registered owners of cars that had been caught on speed cameras driving in excess of the speed limit. Both were requested by the police to identify the driver, and failure to comply with such request constituted a criminal offence. While Mr O'Halloran first admitted to being the driver but later sought to exclude his confession from the trial, Mr Francis refused from the outset to reveal the driver's identity. They were later convicted—Mr O'Halloran for driving in excess of the speed limit and Mr Francis for refusing to identify the driver.

Applications were made to the Strasbourg court where the applicants argued that the obligation to reveal the driver's identity under penalty of a fine violated Article 6 ECHR and the privilege against self-incrimination enshrined therein. The Strasbourg court acknowledged that, in all previous cases in which 'direct compulsion' had been applied to require a suspect to provide possibly incriminating information, the court had established a violation of Article 6 ECHR. However, it continued, this did not mean that direct compulsion would automatically result in the finding of an infringement.[35] While the right to a fair trial is an unqualified right, what constitutes a fair trial cannot be the subject of

[33] That said, and as noted by Busch and van Dam, the scope of the duty of care seems to have expanded from protection of consumers against unclear risks of complicated products, to protection of professional parties, and against more obvious risks of relatively straightforward products. If the financial institutions' duties are expanding and also becoming more blurred, the need for protection against arbitrary or disproportionate measures from the supervisory authorities appears more urgent and legitimate. See Danny Busch and Cees van Dam (eds), *A Bank's Duty of Care* (Hart Publishing 2017) 3.

[34] *O'Halloran and Francis v the United Kingdom*, judgment of 29 June 2007, Apps no 1589/02 and 25624/02, para 57.

[35] ibid, para 53.

a single unvarying rule; it must depend on the circumstances of the particular case, the court declared.[36]

Such assessment should be dependent on: (i) the nature and degree of compulsion; (ii) the existence of any safeguards in the procedure; and (iii) the use to which any material so obtained was put.[37] The Strasbourg court acknowledged that direct compulsion had been used to obtain the evidence. However, the court also took notice of the fact that, by owning a car, the applicants had subjected themselves to a regulatory regime that had been imposed by the State because the possession and use of cars are recognised to have the potential to cause grave injury. Those who choose to keep and drive cars can, therefore, be taken to have accepted certain obligations and responsibilities, the court declared. While accepting that direct compulsion to provide possibly incriminating evidence should not automatically constitute a violation of Article 6 ECHR, this did not mean that the privilege was inapplicable to these cases.

A further aspect of the compulsion applied was the limited nature of the inquiry that the police were authorised to undertake. The relevant national legislation only applied where the driver was alleged to have committed a relevant offence, and only 'as to the identity of the driver'. Here, the court explicitly distinguished the situation at hand from earlier cases where the applicants had been subjected to statutory powers requiring the production of large amounts of information, such as 'production of papers and documents of any kind relating to the operations of interest to the department' or 'any matter which appeared to the investigator to relate to the investigation'.[38] Furthermore, the court noted, the penalty for refusing to reveal the identity of the driver was 'moderate and non-custodial'.[39] It then examined the safeguards available, noting that there was no strict liability, and that the risk of unreliable admissions was negligible.

The Strasbourg court also considered the use made of the evidence obtained. In Mr O'Halloran's case, it remained for the prosecution to prove the offence beyond reasonable doubt. Mr O'Halloran had also been free to give evidence and call witnesses. Furthermore, the court noted, the identity of the driver was only one element in the offence of speeding. As for Mr Francis, the court noted that, as he had refused to make a statement, it could not be used in the

[36] ibid.

[37] ibid, para 54.

[38] ibid, para 58, where reference is made to inter alia the cases *Funke v France*, judgment of 25 February 1993, App no 10828/84 and *Shannon v United Kingdom*, judgment of 4 October 2005, App no 6563/03.

[39] *O'Halloran and Francis* (n 34), para 58.

underlying proceedings, and indeed the underlying proceedings had not been pursued.[40] Given all of the above, the Strasbourg court found no violation of Article 6 ECHR.[41]

Thus, while the applicants were unsuccessful in this case, the Strasbourg court, nevertheless, explicitly acknowledges that those who have subjected themselves to a regulatory regime may have accepted certain obligations and responsibilities, but this does not mean that they are without rights. In fact, it could be argued that the procedural safeguards should be even stronger in regulated markets, as the consequences of any arbitrary or disproportionate measures taken by the authorities may have severe consequences. Decisions taken by NCAs may be devastating for investment firms, which may not only have to pay a hefty fine, but may even be forced to exit the market. Add to this the fact that MiFID II also requires member states to impose sanctions of a criminal nature on natural persons.

5.5.2 The margin of appreciation

The need to protect targeted firms and the members of their management bodies from arbitrary or disproportionate intervention is further motivated by the fact that the NCAs have been entrusted with a very broad scope of supervision, as well as broad margins of both discretion and appreciation. A decision to deny or withdraw an authorisation will, by necessity, have far-reaching consequences for an investment firm which may be prevented from entering, or perhaps even worse, be compelled to exit the market. While the rules and requirements imposed on investment firms are sizeable in both number and detail, not all are 'black and white', and many require assessments of 'suitability' or 'honesty' which, by necessity, involve a certain degree of value judgement.

A firm's duty of loyalty to its clients can be used to illustrate how difficult it may be for both the NCAs and the firms themselves to assess compatibility with MiFID II. The directive requires investment firms to act honestly, fairly, and professionally, in accordance with the best interests of their clients.[42] While this duty of loyalty has, to some extent, been defined in more specific conduct of business rules, its actual scope and meaning may often be hard to define. Some measures undertaken by an investment firm may clearly be categorised

[40] ibid, paras 60–61.
[41] ibid, para 63.
[42] MiFID II, art 24(1).

as dishonest, but it is not always immediately evident whether certain other measures meet this criterion.[43]

On a similar note, and as discussed by Reichel and Behrendt Jonsson in Chapters 6 and 9 of this book, an authorisation is not only dependent on the actual conduct of the investment firm, but also on the suitability of shareholders and company representatives.[44] An NCA is required to refuse authorisation unless it is satisfied that the members of the management body are of 'sufficiently good repute', and that the shareholders with qualifying holdings are suitable.[45] There is an apparent risk that these assessments may vary between jurisdictions, and over time. As noted by Behrendt Jonsson, the UK authorities decided to prohibit the managing director in the UK division of one of the world's largest investment firms, BlackRock, from 'conducting any function in relation to any regulated activity carried on by any authorised or exempt persons'.[46] The reason for this was that he had been caught travelling to London without a valid train ticket, and had admitted having evaded his train fare on a number of occasions. What if he had been caught driving in excess of the speed limit, or had received a parking ticket? Would that have led to the same result? As noted by Behrendt Jonsson, being deemed unfit or improper for an existing or future management position in the financial industry may be regarded by some as more severe than any administrative sanctions.[47] It is, therefore, crucial that the NCAs take reasoned and balanced decisions, and that they may be held accountable for any arbitrary decisions.

Thus, the duty to supervise investment firms' compliance with the provisions in MiFID II requires much of the NCAs, but it also allows them considerable room for manoeuvre, leaving them to perform a number of balancing exercises. Not only may they decide that the conditions for authorisation are not met, but they also have the power to withdraw any authorisation granted to an investment firm at any time, should they consider that the firm has seriously and systematically infringed the provisions adopted pursuant to the directive, or that it no longer meets the conditions under which authorisation

[43] Likewise, and as noted by Enriques and Gargantini, the duty to act in the best interests of the client may not always be reconciled with other requirements in MiFID II, such as those regarding services characterised by an 'at arm's length relationship between the investment firm and its clients'. See Luca Enriques and Matteo Gargantini, 'The Expanding Boundaries of MiFID's Duty to Act in the Client's Best Interest: The Italian Case' (2017) 3(2) Italian Law Journal 485.

[44] See the Financial Conduct Authority's Final Notice Against Jonathan Burrows (15 December 2014). Available at https://www.fca.org.uk/publication/final-notices/jonathan-paul-burrows.pdf.

[45] MiFID II, arts 9 and 10.

[46] Being prohibited from conducting any function, and not just managerial functions, will effectively force him to leave the firm.

[47] The fit and proper test is, admittedly, a different test to whether a member of the management is of 'sufficiently good repute', but both tests allow the NCAs a considerable margin of appreciation.

was granted. Such withdrawal will effectively shut down the business.[48] While a 'serious and systematic infringement' requires both gravity and persistence, thereby limiting the possibilities of withdrawing an authorisation on this ground, finding that 'the conditions for authorisation are no longer met' is not equally restrictive, and would, in theory, allow an NCA to withdraw an authorisation in those situations where the effects of an infringement are insignificant. In practice, however, the principle of proportionality would prevent this.

The powers granted to the NCAs may be considered necessary to achieve the aims of MiFID II, but there is no doubt that they may have extremely serious consequences for the company forced to exit the market, or the manager who is no longer allowed to carry out managerial functions, or is forced to pay a fine of up to 5,000,000 euros. NCAs must, therefore, tread carefully, and, while it is important to allow them to carry out their duties properly, investment firms need adequate protection against abusive or arbitrary measures. Before discussing the safeguards provided under the directive, the following section describes the investigatory powers granted to the NCAs in more detail.

5.6 The competent authorities' enforcement powers

Article 69 of MiFID II governs supervisory powers. While this chapter focuses on the investigatory powers, or, more precisely, the power to carry out on-site inspections, it is nevertheless worth noting that Article 69 also requires member states to grant the NCAs the powers to impose far-reaching remedies, declaring that they should be able to require the freezing or sequestration of assets, or the temporary prohibition of professional activity, and to 'adopt any type of measure to ensure that investment firms, regulated markets and other persons to whom the Directive applies, continue to comply with legal requirements'. These rather draconian remedies, which do not seem to require the formal finding of an infringement, coupled with the sanctions available for established infringements, highlight the need to ensure that any investigatory powers granted to the NCAs are applied in conformity with the Charter and the ECHR.

MiFID II declares that, in order to ensure compliance with the rules, and to accomplish a level playing field, member states should grant the NCAs a minimum set of investigatory powers. These are listed in Article 69, and range from the power to have access to any document or other data that the NCA

[48] MiFID II, art 8.

may consider could be relevant, to the power to require existing recordings of telephone conversations. Among the listed powers is the power to carry out on-site inspections or investigations.[49] Article 69 itself provides no guidance on which sites may be inspected, whether such inspections can be carried out without prior notice, whether the decisions preceding such inspections should be adopted by a court,[50] or whether the authorities should be allowed to use force when carrying out inspections, thus leaving the member states considerable room for manoeuvre when drafting national legislation pursuant to the provision. However, the recitals provide some guidance, declaring that it may be necessary to carry out inspections at the premises of legal and natural persons when there is reasonable suspicion that documents and other data relating to the subject matter of the investigation exist, and may be relevant to prove an infringement, or when a person who has received a demand for information has failed to comply with such request, or where there is reasonable suspicion that the documents or data may be removed, tampered with, or destroyed if a request was sent out to the person in question.[51] While the recitals, thus, give some guidance by providing examples of situations when the NCAs should be able to carry out inspections, the operative parts are silent on the matter. Accordingly, there is an apparent risk that the power to carry out on-site inspections may take different shapes in different member states.[52]

Furthermore, the consequences of questioning these powers and their compatibility with the Charter may be grave. NCAs are encouraged to strike down hard on anyone questioning their investigatory measures. Article 70(6) of MiFID II stipulates that failure to cooperate or comply in an investigation, or with an inspection or request covered by Article 69, shall be regarded as an infringement of the directive, and that the sanctions available under Article 70 shall also apply to this type of infringement.[53] In member states where inspections are allowed to be carried out in private homes, the consequences for

[49] ibid, art 69(2)(c).

[50] According to ibid, art 72(1), member states may choose whether these decisions should be taken by the NCAs or national courts.

[51] ibid, recital 143.

[52] In Sweden, the national legislation adopted pursuant to MiFID II more or less mirrors the wording of art 69 of the directive, leaving the NCA ample room for manoeuvre. However, interestingly enough, it does not empower the Swedish NCA, *Finansinspektionen*, to carry out inspections in private homes, thus failing to reflect the directive's recitals. In practice, the NCA carries out on-site inspections during the course of its investigations when this is considered necessary. In most cases, the authority informs the firm in writing when it opens an investigation. If an on-site inspection is considered necessary, the authority will contact the firm in advance of any visit. See the manual of procedure, *Processbeskrivning för undersökningsprocessen*, available at https://www.fi.se/contentassets/5e009a7c9fb640058882907fb9dbdb3c/undersokningsprocessen-20-12-18.pdf.

[53] MiFID II, art 70(6).

a manager questioning the measures taken by the NCAs may, thus, be devastating. While the principle of proportionality should prevent NCAs from imposing sanctions that are too harsh, the fact remains that, according to the wording of the Directive, the maximum fine available for obstruction during the investigation is 5,000,000 euros. In theory, questioning the scope of the authorities' powers of investigation may also result in the withdrawal of authorisation, or in a temporary ban on exercising managerial functions. Anyone targeted by an investigation is, therefore, likely to think twice before questioning the authorities' actions, as this may be regarded as failure to comply in the investigation.

5.7 On-site inspections from a due process perspective

While case law surrounding on-site inspections carried out in accordance with MiFID II may still be scarce, on-site inspections are frequently carried out within another area of EU law: EU competition law.[54] When the Commission suspects a company of infringing Articles 101 or 102 TFEU, and the prohibitions against anti-competitive agreements or abuse of market power contained therein, it may carry out unannounced inspections at the premises of targeted companies.[55] In some circumstances, such inspections may also be carried out at the homes of company employees or representatives, but these are surrounded by stricter procedural safeguards.[56] Over the years, the CJEU has been given ample opportunity to define the boundaries of these inspections and how they should be framed, in order to ensure adequate fundamental rights protection. Also, the Strasbourg court has been asked to rule on the boundaries surrounding inspections, on more than one occasion, with regard to inspections carried out by national competition authorities, but also with regard to inspections carried out under other areas of law and by other authorities, such as national tax authorities or public prosecutors.[57]

[54] The sanctions imposed by the Commission on competition law offenders are also considered criminal in nature. See, eg *A Menarini Diagonistics SRL v Italy*, judgment of 27 September 2011, App no 43509/08; Case C-272/09 P *KME v European Commission* EU:C:2011:810 and Case C-389/10 P *KME v Commission* EU:C:2011:816.

[55] Art 20 of Council Regulation (EC) No 1/2003 of 16 December 2002 on the Implementation of the rules on competition laid down in Articles 81 and 82 of the Treaty, [2003] OJ L1 1–25.

[56] ibid, art 21.

[57] See, eg *Société Colas Est and Others v France*, judgment of 16 April 2002, App no 37971/97, para 41; *Bernh Larsen Holding SA and Others v Norway*, App no 24117/08; *Robathin v Austria*, judgment of 3 July 2012, App no 30457/06.

Depending on how it is framed, an on-site inspection may be a very powerful investigatory method. It is its intrusive character that makes it so powerful, but the intrusiveness also entails an inherent risk that fundamental rights are not properly safeguarded.[58] First, the inspection suggests, by its very nature, that an infringement has been committed, and this may have major repercussions on targeted firms or persons.[59] Furthermore, the fact that large amounts of data are gathered and possibly also shared with sister agencies in other member states, or even with public prosecutors, may cause damage that goes far beyond the boundaries of the case at hand, and perhaps also far beyond what is possible to envisage at the time of the inspection. In the field of competition law, it has become increasingly common for authorities to make image copies of large amounts of electronic data—in many cases, entire servers—for review back at the authorities' headquarters. While this is often motivated by efficiency concerns and a wish to minimise intrusion at company premises, the fact remains that most of the data gathered will lack relevance to the investigation, and there is also an apparent risk that the data gathered will not be duly protected. It is, therefore, crucial that adequate procedural safeguards are in place for these inspections, and that the NCAs respect these safeguards.

This is acknowledged by both the CJEU and the Strasbourg court. Article 7 of the Charter and Article 8 of the ECHR both provide a right to privacy. The Strasbourg court has declared, in a string of rulings, that this right is not reserved to natural persons, but may also be invoked by legal persons.[60] Compliance with Article 7 of the Charter and Article 8 ECHR requires that there are procedural safeguards in place that provide adequate protection against abusive or arbitrary measures. However, the courts have provided no list of safeguards. Instead, both the Strasbourg court and the EU courts make an overall assessment of the safeguards available in each case. It may be that certain safeguards that are usually required in competition cases may not be considered necessary in investigations concerning compliance with MiFID II. The requirement that the Commission must suspect a company of wrongdoing before carrying out an on-site inspection may, for example, not apply within the frame of MiFID II, at least not if the company is informed of the

[58] Wouter P J Wils, 'Powers of Investigation and Procedural Rights and Guarantees in EU Antitrust Enforcement: The Interplay between European and National Legislation and Case-law' (2006) 29(1) World Competition 3.

[59] Case T-296/11 *Cementos Portland Valderrivas SA v European Commission* EU:T:2014:121, para 35.

[60] See, eg *Société Colas* (n 57), para 41 ; *Bernh Larsen* (n 57); *Vinci Construction et GTM Génie Civil et Services v France*, App nos. 63629/10 and 60567/10. Also, the EU Courts acknowledge that legal persons enjoy a right to privacy. See, eg Case C-94/00 *Roquette Frères* EU:C:2002:603; Case T-135/09 *Nexans France SAS and Nexans SA v European Commission* EU:T:2012:596, para 40; Case T-140/09 *Prysmian SpA and Prysmian Cavi et Sistemi Energia Srl v European Commission* EU:T:2012:597, para 35.

inspection beforehand. In *Bernh Larsen Holding*, the Strasbourg court accepted the legislator's view that tax audits complemented the duty of the tax subject to provide accurate information, and that a review of archives was a necessary means of ensuring efficiency in the checking of the information provided.[61]

Likewise, stricter safeguards are required when the inspection is carried out at the home of a natural person. Within the frame of competition law investigations, the Commission is only allowed to carry out inspections at private homes if it suspects a company of a serious violation of the EU competition rules, and has reason to believe that evidence is located at the home of the person in question. Furthermore, the search requires prior judicial authorisation.[62] While it may be accepted that the NCAs can carry out pre-announced inspections at the premises of investment firms without any ground for suspicion, it is not equally evident that these powers should extend to the homes of their managers, especially not since sanctions of a criminal nature may be imposed on natural persons.[63] In those cases, inspections should not be allowed unless the requirements listed in the recitals are met.[64]

However, as concerns legal persons, the Strasbourg court often takes a rather flexible and pragmatic approach, not requiring any *ex ante* review of inspection decisions, and allowing for rather broad searches, as well as the making of image copies for review and selection back at authority premises. In *Bernh Larsen Holding*, the court explicitly acknowledged that considerations of efficiency suggested that the tax authorities' possibilities to act should be relatively wide at the preparatory stage, and that interpreting Article 8 ECHR to also protect legal persons would not unduly hamper the contracting states, as they would retain their entitlement to 'interfere', to the extent permitted by the article. It also noted that such rights may well be more far-reaching where professional or business premises were involved than would otherwise be the case.[65] However, this pragmatic, flexible, and, to some extent, arguably lax approach is conditioned upon the existence of an effective and timely *ex post* control of any decisions taken by the investigating authorities, as well as of any measures taken on their basis. In the Strasbourg court's view, the proportionality *stricto sensu* test cannot be met, absent the possibility for an effective judicial review,

[61] *Bernh Larsen* (n 57), judgment of 14 March 2013, para 164. However, the Strasbourg court also noted that the powers granted to the Norwegian tax authorities were not unfettered, notably with regard to such matters as the nature of the documents that the authority was entitled to inspect.

[62] Art 21 of Council Regulation (EC) No 1/2003 (n 55), pp 1–25.

[63] It is also necessary to ensure that any evidence gathered at the premises of an investment firm is not used against natural persons unless the procedural safeguards surrounding the collection of such evidence are sufficiently strict.

[64] MiFID II, recital 143.

[65] *Bernh Larsen* (n 57), judgment of 14 March 2013, para 104.

as there would then be no effective protection against abuse or arbitrariness. The following section examines MiFID II's provisions on judicial review, and concludes that they fail to guarantee compliance with the ECHR standard. There is, thus, a risk that certain NCAs may escape accountability for violations of applicable fundamental rights.

5.8 The right to an effective remedy

Article 74 of MiFID II provides a right of appeal. It requires member states to make sure that any decision taken pursuant to MiFIR or MiFID II is properly reasoned, and subject to the right of appeal before a tribunal. While these requirements are necessary to guarantee the protection of targeted persons' defence rights, and to ensure the right to a fair trial, they are not sufficient to ensure national systems' compliance with Article 6 ECHR or Article 47 of the Charter. As will be discussed below, more is required.

Admittedly, the recitals require member states to ensure that their systems meet the requisite fundamental rights standard, and it may seem unnecessary to explicitly provide for more than a right to appeal any decisions taken, especially since the Charter trumps MiFID II. Against this background, it could be argued that Article 74 could be deleted altogether, as member states are required to ensure adequate protection anyway. It is evident that the legislator has considered it necessary to spell out the basic elements of the right to a fair trial, and it may, therefore, also be necessary to ensure that other aspects of this right are guaranteed throughout the Union.

5.8.1 *Ex ante* control

MiFID II leaves it to the member states to decide whether the powers provided under Articles 69 and 70 shall be exercised directly, or by application to the competent judicial authorities.[66] This means that, in some member states, the decision to carry out an inspection will be taken by a court and, in other member states, by the NCAs themselves. Both options are, thus, acceptable from the directive's perspective, but are they also acceptable from a fundamental rights perspective? The short answer to this question is yes; there is no strict requirement of *ex ante* control. The right to carry out inspections without

[66] MiFID II, art 72.

prior judicial authorisation has been challenged on numerous occasions, and both the EU Courts and the ECtHR have consistently accepted this practice, provided, however, that there other procedural safeguards are in place.[67]

While this chapter focuses on the rights of investment firms, it should be noted that there is nothing in MiFID II that prevents on-site inspections from also taking place at private dwellings. In these cases, where a manager risks having to pay fines of up to,000,000 euros, and may also be prohibited from exercising managerial functions, should the NCA establish an infringement, the procedural safeguards must be strict. That said, the Strasbourg court has accepted searches carried out at private homes without prior judicial authorisation, but it has also been prone to stress that special vigilance is then required, and that the margin of appreciation needs to be limited.[68] In *Harju v Finland* the Strasbourg court acknowledged that the absence of a prior judicial warrant may be counterbalanced by the availability of an *ex post* judicial review, where both the lawfulness of, and the justification for, the search may be properly reviewed[69] Thus, to conclude, there are no strict requirements of prior judicial authorisation for on-site inspections, irrespective of whether they are carried out at the premises of a legal person or the home of an employee.

5.8.2 Interim measures

While MiFID II provides an explicit right to appeal any decisions taken by the NCAs, it provides no right to apply for interim measures or suspension of any decisions taken. Yet, Article 69 grants the NCAs far-reaching investigatory powers, and also empowers them to impose a number of rather draconian remedies without requiring any formal finding of an infringement. Interim measures safeguard the effectiveness of the fundamental rights protection system by preventing particularly harmful violations that would not be reparable by decisions on the merits. Given the nature and scope of the enforcement powers

[67] See, eg *Delta Pekárny v The Czech Republic*, judgment of 2 October 2014, App no. 97/11 and the General Court's ruling in Joined Cases T-289 and 290/11 and T-521/11 *Deutsche Bahn and Others v European Commission* EU:T:2013:404.

[68] See, eg *Harju v Finland*, judgment of 15 February 2011, App no 56716/09, para 39. In this case, the applicant was under suspicion of having organised illegal immigration, a criminal offence with a maximum penalty of two years imprisonment. In July 2009, the Finnish Border Guard conducted a search at her domicile. During the search, which was carried out without prior judicial authorisation, and without informing the applicant, who was not at home, the inspectors seized a number of items, including the applicant's computer. When the applicant returned home, she found a handwritten note indicating that a search had been carried out, and that objects had been seized.

[69] ibid, para 44. In this case, the applicant had not had effective access, a posteriori, to a court. An infringement of art 8 ECHR was, therefore, established.

granted to the NCAs, it is likely that situations will occur where the rights of targeted companies and managers may be irreversibly impaired, absent the possibility of applying for interim measures.

The NCAs may, for example, decide to collect and review documents that firms consider to be protected by legal professional privilege, and therefore out of reach to the NCAs. The privilege, which is considered necessary for a proper administration of justice, prevents the investigating authorities from seizing or reviewing correspondence with lawyers. Thus, if receiving a visit from an NCA, the firm should not have to be afraid that the inspectors will make copies of documents containing legal advice. The privilege, which encourages candour between client and lawyer, is motivated by the belief that the lawyer will neither be able to secure effectively the full measure of the client's rights nor the proper administration of justice if the client withholds information for fear of disclosure.[70] This means that if an NCA's inspectors are allowed to even have a glance at such advice, the damage is done and cannot be repaired. This was acknowledged by the president of the General Court in the case of *Akzo Nobel*, where he established that companies must be provided with the means of preventing the irreversible consequences that would result from improper disclosure of documents protected under legal professional privilege.[71] Thus, absent the possibility for interim measures, there is a clear risk of investment firms not being adequately protected against fundamental rights infringements. While there is nothing in MiFID II that prevents national legislators from adopting rules on interim measures, there is nothing that ensures it either.

5.8.3 Review of measures taken during the investigation

On a similar note, there may be situations where the NCAs adopt measures during the course of an investigation which affect firms' legal positions without formally qualifying as decisions. In competition cases, the General Court refers to these measures as 'implementing measures', and has established that they may not be challenged on a stand-alone basis. MiFID II appears to take a similar approach, as it provides no right for investment firms to challenge

[70] Edna Selan Epstein, *The Attorney-Client Privilege and the Work Product Doctrine* (American Bar Association 2007) 5; Hock Lai Ho, 'Legal Professional Privilege and the Integrity of Legal Representation' (2006) 9(2) Legal Ethics 171.

[71] Joined Cases T-125/03 and T-253/03 *Akzo Nobel Chemicals Ltd and Akcros Chemicals Ltd v Commission of the European Communities* EU:T:2007:287, para 3.

implementing measures. Yet, the Strasbourg court has established that, in order for a system to be compliant with Article 6 ECHR, there should be a right to challenge both the inspection decisions and any measures taken on their basis. This was first established in the case of *Ravon*,[72] where the French tax authorities suspected two companies controlled by Mr Ravon of tax evasion. During the course of the investigation, the authorities searched the premises of the companies and the home of Mr Ravon. Suspecting that the inspections had been vitiated by irregularities, the applicants challenged the operations in their entirety before the French courts.[73] The complaints were considered inadmissible because the courts were not empowered to review the measures taken by the tax authorities once the inspections had been effected.[74] An application was filed with the Strasbourg court, which ruled in favour of the applicants, and concluded that the right of judicial access:

> [i]mplies with respect to premises searches, that the persons sought may obtain an effective judicial review, in fact and law, of the decision authorizing the search and, if any, of the measures taken on its basis; the remedy or remedies available must allow, in the event irregularities are uncovered, either to prevent the upcoming search or, in the event a search deemed unlawful has already taken place, to provide the relevant party with an appropriate remedy.[75]

The court did not consider the requirement of a judicial authorisation to compensate for the lack of an *ex post* review, as, at the time of the *ex ante* review, the targeted company or person is not yet aware of the procedure, and is, therefore, unable to invoke its rights.[76] The stance taken in *Ravon* has been confirmed by the Strasbourg court on numerous occasions. In the two cases of *Canal Plus*[77] and *Primagaz*,[78] concerning inspections carried out by the French competition authorities, the court referred to its ruling in *Ravon*, and declared that targeted companies must be granted the possibility of obtaining an effective judicial review, not only of the inspection decisions, but also of any measures taken

[72] *Ravon v France*, judgment of 21 February 2008, App no 18497/03.
[73] ibid, para 8.
[74] ibid, paras 8–10.
[75] ibid, para 28.
[76] ibid, para 30.
[77] *Société Canal Plus and Others v France*, judgment of 21 December 2010, App no 29408/08.
[78] *Compagnie des Gaz de Pétrole Primagaz v France*, judgment of 21 December 2010, App no 29613/08.

on their basis. In addition, it established that any judicial review must be both timely and guaranteed.

5.9 Joining the dots

The EU legislator has found it necessary to provide detailed rules on how to conduct business, how to supervise and investigate infringements of these rules, and on the sanctions that should be available to the NCAs. As the EU legislator is bound by the principles of proportionality and subsidiarity laid down in Article 5 TEU, it can be assumed that these detailed provisions are considered necessary to establish and maintain a single market for investment services and activities, and that, without these rules, there would be no level playing field for firms to compete in the EU's financial markets or consistent level of consumer protection across the EU. It is, therefore, surprising that the legislator has not considered it necessary to provide any guidance on how these rules should be applied in order to protect the fundamental rights of targeted companies and persons. While the member states are, apparently, not trusted to ensure effective enforcement of the rules in place, absent detailed guidance, the legislator appears confident that a general reference to the Charter in the recitals, combined with a right to appeal, is sufficient to ensure adequate fundamental rights protection. This absence of explicit safeguards is remarkable for a number of reasons. First, given the strict regulation of these markets, defining the appropriate level of protection may, at times, be difficult. While this may exclude the possibility of providing for detailed procedural safeguards in MiFID II, there should, nevertheless, be some guidance or minimum requirements. Second, member states have also been required to introduce extremely tough sanctions against natural persons, and this calls for even stricter safeguards against abusive or arbitrary measures from the NCAs. By excluding any due process aspects from the operative parts of the directive, some member states may take this as a signal that due process aspects carry little weight. That would be very unfortunate.

Absent minimum safeguards, and effective possibilities of holding supervisory authorities accountable for any transgressions of these safeguards, there is an apparent risk that the level of protection will vary between member states. This, in turn, means that the desired level playing field will not materialise, as the risks involved in carrying out financial services are not consistent throughout the Union. While deterrence cannot be achieved unless the NCAs are viewed as tough and diligent enforcers of the rules in place, it is equally important that the application of the supervisory powers is consistent, predictable, and fair. Otherwise, firms may be reluctant to enter national markets, and may also find it difficult to attract competent persons to their management bodies. Furthermore, if the national systems fail to protect the rights provided under the Charter, any decisions taken by the competent authorities may be contestable on procedural grounds, and this would further undermine the effectiveness of the system.

6

Ensuring the Principle of Good Administration in EU Financial Markets Law

*Jane Reichel**

6.1 Introduction: The principle of good administration as an accountability tool

One of the more striking features of EU financial markets law and each of the ESMA Regulation,[1] MiFID II,[2] and MIFIR,[3] is their profound effect on the factual modes of operation of the European and national administrative authorities, as well as decision-making of these authorities, in individual cases. Administrative actions are undertaken in a true multilevel administrative environment, where public power based on the constitutional frameworks of the EU and the member states, respectively, are exercised in mixed, composite administrative procedures.[4]

The principle of good administration has been identified as a fundamental right in EU law, and codified in Article 41 of the Charter of Fundamental

* I would like to express my gratitude to the editors, Carl Fredrik Bergström and Magnus Strand; to Dominque Ritleng, Strasbourg University; Gustaf Sjöberg and Helen Andersson, Stockholm University; and to Aron Szugalski Verständig, Finansinspektionen, for valuable input on this chapter.

[1] Regulation (EU) No 1095/2010 of the European Parliament and of the Council of 24 November 2010 establishing a European Supervisory Authority (European Securities and Markets Authority) [2010] OJ L 331/84 (hereafter the 'ESMA Regulation').

[2] Directive 2014/65/EU of the European Parliament and of the Council of 15 May 2014 on markets in financial instruments [2014] OJ L 173/349 (hereafter 'MiFID II').

[3] Regulation (EU) No 600/2014 of the European Parliament and of the Council of 15 May 2014 on markets in financial instruments [2014] OJ L 173/84 (hereafter 'MiFIR').

[4] The ReNEUAL project has defined a composite procedure as 'an administrative procedure where the EU authorities and the authorities of a Member State or different Member States have distinct functions which are interdependent. A composite procedure may also mean a combination of two administrative procedures that are directly linked', in Paul Craig and others (eds), *ReNEUAL Model Rules on EU Administrative Procedure* (OUP 2017) (hereafter Craig and others (eds), 'ReNEUAL Model Rules') 50. For an overview of possible categorisations, see Mariolina Eliantonio, 'Judicial Review in an Integrated

Jane Reichel, *Ensuring the Principle of Good Administration in EU Financial Markets Law* In: *Legal Accountability in EU Markets for Financial Instruments*. Edited by: Carl Fredrik Bergström and Magnus Strand, Oxford University Press. © Jane Reichel 2021. DOI: 10.1093/oso/9780192849281.003.0006

Rights of the European Union.[5] According to the first paragraph of the article, the principle contains the duty of care: to ensure that every person's affairs are handled impartially, fairly, and within a reasonable time. The second paragraph ensures a right to be heard, a right to access to files, and a right to reasoned decisions.[6] The aim of the principle is, thus, to safeguard that individuals and their affairs are treated efficiently, impartially, and fairly when affected in one way or another by the EU institutions, as well as to ensure that basic administrative procedural guarantees are upheld. In case law, the principle has also been applied to aspects of the performance of the administration other than the handling of individual matters, for example factual administration and rulemaking.[7]

The principles of good administration and the duty of care, thus, obligate administrations to take into account the rights and interests of the individuals concerned—in this case, investment firms on the internal market—as well as to the public at large, in carrying out their duties in an efficient, correct, and prudent manner.[8] In a constitutional democracy, public power is presumed to be exercised in accordance with the rule of law, ie it must be limited, applied in a law-bound and predictable manner, and exercised within a framework of constitutional rules that ensure the protection of fundamental rights.[9] There is, further, a connection between Article 41 of the Charter and the right to good administration, and Article 47 and the right to an effective remedy.[10] In this sense, the principle of good administration serves the dual purposes of, firstly, providing citizens and others within an constitutional setting with guarantees against the arbitrary or improper exercise of power, and, secondly, holding the administration accountable. If the principle of good administration has been

Administration: The Case of "Composite Procedures"' (2014) 7(2) Review of European Administrative Law 65, 69 ff.

[5] Charter of Fundamental Rights of the European Union [2012] OJ C 326/2 (hereafter 'the Charter').

[6] The third paragraph includes a right to have the Union make good any damage caused by its institutions or servants in the performance of their duties, and the fourth includes a right to communicate with the institutions of the Union in one of the languages of the Treaties. These rights will not be addressed further here.

[7] See T-231/97 *New Europe Consulting and Brown v Commission* EU:T:1999:146 and C-16/90 *Nölle v Hauptzollamt Bremen-Freihafen* EU:C:1991:402. A more recent example of the latter may be found in Case C-62/14 *Gauweiler and Others v Deutscher Bundestag (OMT)* [2015] EU:C:2015:400.

[8] Herwig CH Hofmann, 'The Duty of Care in EU Public Law—A Principle Between Discretion and Proportionality' [2020] Review of European Administrative Law 87 (hereafter Hofmann, 'Duty of Care'), 98 ff.

[9] Harlow refers to 'the twin ideals of democracy and rule of law' as the legitimating principles of any Western system of administrative law: Carol Harlow, 'Global Administrative Law: The Quest for Principles and Values' (2006) 17(1) European Journal of International Law 187, 212. See, further, Martin Loughlin, 'What is Constitutionalism?' in Petra Dobner and Martin Loughlin (eds), *The Twilight of Constitutionalism?* (OUP 2010) 47.

[10] Explanations relating to the Charter of Fundamental Rights [2012] OJ C 303/02, art 41.

transgressed, this may render enacted decisions invalid, provide grounds for an action for damages, or induce a critical decision from the EU ombudsman.[11] Via these channels, both the individuals concerned and the public at large can ensure that the administration is working efficiently, and with respect to the rule of law.

One much debated question has been whether the right to good administration is also applicable to the member states when applying EU law, since Article 41 expressly refers to the EU institutions and bodies. The Court of Justice of the European Union (CJEU) has long since held that member states must apply certain minimum procedural requirements in their administrative decision-making within the sphere of application of EU law,[12] and, in 2014, the CJEU confirmed that the principles underlying Article 41 of the Charter are applicable to the member states.[13] However, as will be discussed in this contribution, the CJEU has been careful to leave room for national administrative traditions, and the case law regarding EU requirements on national implementation of the principle of good administration is scarce. The doctrine of procedural autonomy, allowing the member states to apply national procedural law when implementing EU law at the national level is, thus, still relevant.

The overarching question raised here is how the principle of good administration is to be applied within the composite administrative structure of EU financial markets law. Composite administrative procedures are not new in EU secondary law, and are well known in the case law of the CJEU.[14] However, financial markets law differs from traditional composite administrative procedures in that it does not merely link decision-making, but also aspires to establish a common supervisory culture, as stated in Article 29 of the ESMA Regulation. Supervision, in its entirety, is shared between EU and member state bodies, both in regard to factual administration, ie information sharing, standard setting, training programmes, peer review mechanisms and the like, and decision-making procedure in individual cases, where different parts of the administrative decision-making procedure are taking place within different jurisdictions, European and national. Since the financial crisis at the end of the first decade of this millennium, a coherent and efficient supervision of

[11] Cases C-269/90 *TU München v Hauptzollamt München-Mitte* EU:C:1991:438; T-167/94 *Nölle v Council and Commission* EU:T:1995:169, 76; T-105/96 *Pharos v Commission* EU:T:1998:35, 73–78, confirmed in case C-151/98 P *Pharos v Commission* EU:C:1998:440, but without the mentioning of the principle of good administration. See, further, Marc Clement, Breach of the Right to Good Administration: So What? (2018) ELTE Law Journal 19.

[12] Case C-222/86 *Unectef v Heylens* EU:C:1987:442, and see, further, section 6.2.3 below.

[13] Case C-604/12 *HN v Minister for Justice, Equality and Law Reform* EU:C:2014:302.

[14] *TU München* (n 11); C-97/91 *Borelli v Commission* 1992 EU:C:1992:49; Eliantonio (n 4).

the integrated European financial market has, in itself, been identified as an overriding aim.[15] However, even though administrative cooperation and composite procedure are regulated in MiFID II and MiFIR, central components of the principle of good administration, for example the duty of care and the right to be heard, are not addressed.

The 'fit and proper' test in MiFID II will be used as an illustration of a composite decision-making procedure. The test is representative, in the sense that it is a commonly performed assessment, often based on information collected from several different national competent authorities (NCAs). Further, the test can be perceived as sensitive, from a personal point of view, for members of management bodies of regulated undertakings in the financial sector, since it includes an evaluation of their personal conduct, moral standards, and 'independence of mind'.[16] These qualities are not easily measured in an administrative procedure, and a negative assessment may lead to serious consequences for investment firms and individual members of staff.[17] The correct application of the right to good administration is, therefore, essential. The CJEU recently reviewed a decision on a fit and proper test undertaken by the European Central Bank (ECB), in the 2018 *Berlusconi* case, which gives rise to some further queries in relation to the application of the principle of good administration.[18]

It is a central feature in any legal order based on the rule of law that the law is known in advance, in order for public power to be exercised under transparent legislative, administrative, and judicial procedures that are identifiable for both the public authorities and the individuals concerned.[19] It is, further, a necessary component in a functioning accountability regime that the public authority knows in advance what it is it is being held accountable for.[20] The more closely defined questions to be analysed are the following: who is responsible for defining the right to good administration for investment firms within the sphere of application of EU law? Which courts—national or European—are competent to hear appeals of decisions that have been adopted? Is this diversity in the realisation of the principle of good administration a threat to the effective functioning of accountability within EU financial markets law?

[15] See section 6.3.1 below.

[16] See section 6.3.2 below.

[17] See, further, the contribution of Britta Behrendt Jonsson in Chapter 9 of this book.

[18] Case C-219/17 *Silvio Berlusconi v Banca d'Italia* EU:C:2018:1023. See, further, section 6.4.2 below.

[19] See, eg European Commission for Democracy Through Law (Venice Commission), 'Report on the Rule of Law', Study no 512/2009, CDL-AD(2011)003rev, 10 ff.

[20] Compare Napoleon Xanthoulis, 'Administrative Factual Conduct: Legal Effects and Judicial Control in EU Law' (2019) 12(1) Review of European Administrative Law 39, 40 ff.

Due to limits of space, this study will focus on the supervisory functions within the composite administration of EU financial markets law.

6.2 Identifying the relevant administrative law regime

6.2.1 Administrative law as a tool for the sovereign state?

As stated by way of introduction, public power in a democracy based on the rule of law is presumed to be limited, and applied in a law-bound and predictable manner, and must be exercised within a framework of constitutional rules that ensure the protection of fundamental rights. Administrative law has a key function in ensuring that the law is applied in an efficient manner, so that the policies of the democratically enacted legislator can be put into practice, and that, in doing so, public powers are exercised with due respect to fundamental rights and procedural guarantees for the persons concerned.[21] The principle of good administration recognises both of these functions in relation to the persons concerned, such as an investment firm. Matters are to be dealt with efficiently within a reasonable time, and impartially and fairly.

Both of these functions of administration have traditionally been carried out within the nation state, following the connection between the development of administrative law and the development of the modern nation state.[22] It is a basic notion in public international law that nation states are sovereign vis-à-vis each other, meaning that states may exercise their public power independently of other states.[23] Traditionally, it has been uncommon for national authorities to implement policies from foreign states or international organisations. Equally, sovereign states will not be bound by legal acts enacted elsewhere, whether these are administrative decisions or court judgments, unless it has so agreed through international agreements, treaties, or conventions.[24]

[21] Sabino Cassese, 'New Paths for Administrative Law: A Manifesto' (2012) 10(3) International Journal of Constitutional Law 603, 605 and Craig and others (eds), ReNEUAL Model Rules (n 4) 28.

[22] Susan Rose-Ackerman, 'Administrative Law and Democracy' in Peter Cane and others (eds), *The Oxford Handbook of Comparative Administrative Law* (OUP 2020) 1077, and Mats Kumlien, *Professorspolitik och samhällsförändring—En rättshistorisk undersökning av den svenska förvaltningsrättens uppkomst* (Institutet för rättshistorisk forskning 2019) 163.

[23] Henrik Wenander, 'Recognition of Foreign Administrative Decisions: Balancing International Cooperation, National Self-Determination, and Individual Rights' (2011) 71 ZaöRV (Heidelberg Journal of International Law) 755, 762.

[24] ibid.

The notion of sovereignty is also closely linked to the principles of self-determination and territoriality, entailing that it is the task of each state and its administration to handle administrative issues concerning the state, its citizens, and activities carried out within state borders.[25] An equivalent to private international law 'conflict of law' mechanisms for finding the competent jurisdiction is, thus, necessary; in administrative law, this matter has been discussed within the field of international administrative law, namely the application of the public law of one jurisdiction in another jurisdiction.[26]

Developments within EU financial markets law have come a long way from these basic principles. Today, the function of administrative law is no longer merely to cater to the needs of national governments, within their national constitutional frameworks. Globalisation and Europeanisation have transformed administrative law, but no novel role for administrative law has yet been defined.[27] Within the EU, there is at least an ambition that administrative law should fulfil the same functions as it does in the member states: to ensure the efficiency of public action, and to safeguard the rights and legally protected interests of private persons.[28]

6.2.2 Division of functions between EU and national administrations

Traditionally, the implementation of EU law can be divided into three categories: direct or centralised administration carried out by EU organs, implementation via member states' administrations, and implementation via shared administrations.[29] In the first category, defining the applicable law is rather straightforward: EU law applies. This category will not be discussed further here. In the second category, national administrative law applies, under the limitations and conditions set forward in the case law of the CJEU, discussed below. In the third category, functions are shared. EU law is applicable

[25] Cedric Ryngaert, *Jurisdiction in International Law* (2nd edn, OUP 2015) 49 and Herwig CH Hofmann, 'Dealing with Trans-territorial Executive Rule-making' (2013) 78 Missouri Law Review 423 (hereafter Hofmann, 'Trans-territorial Executive Rule-making'), 423–24.

[26] Hofmann, 'Trans-territorial Executive Rule-making' (n 25) 427.

[27] Carlo Maria Colombo and Mariolina Eliantonio, 'The Changing Nature of the Public Administration: Innovations and Challenges for Public Lawyers' (2018) 24(3) European Public Law 403, 404.

[28] Joana Mendes, 'The EU Administrative Institutions, Their Law and Legal Scholarship' in Peter Cane and others (eds), *The Oxford Handbook of Comparative Administrative Law* (OUP 2020) 537.

[29] Carol Harlow, 'Three Phases in the Evolution of EU Administrative Law' in Paul Craig and Grainne de Búrca (eds), *The Evolution of EU Law* (OUP 2011) 443; Hervig CH Hofmann, Gerard C Rowe, and Alexander H Türk, *Administrative Law and Policy of the European Union* (OUP 2011) 259.

to the EU organs involved, and national law is applicable to the national organs, under the same conditions as in the second category.

Thus, EU law also recognises the basic premises of national autonomy of internal administrative and judicial functions and, consequently, the diversity of the administrative functions of the member states. According to the doctrine of institutional and procedural autonomy, it is for the member states to appoint competent public authorities to handle specific policy areas under EU law, and, in the absence of EU regulation, to decide what procedures public authorities and courts are to apply, under the condition that these are effective and applied equivalently.[30] Member states will, thus, normally steer and control their public authorities, and apply their own administrative procedures in areas covered by EU law, as long as there is no specific secondary EU law providing specific requirements, that EU general principles of law are upheld, and that the principles of effectiveness and equivalence are upheld.[31] From the point of view of national administrative law, there are sound arguments for this. Even though there is a basic core of general administrative principles that more or less all member states adhere to, the details of the rules and their functions within administrative law systems differ between member states.[32] The national administrative law systems vary with regard to the forms of actions, the administrative and legal sources, and the organisation of courts competent to review administrative actions.[33] A uniform application of the same version of the principle of good administration is not easy to achieve.

Further, up until the end of the last millennium, the EU itself had not prioritised general administrative law issues, either at the EU level itself or in relation to the member states.[34] An important reason for this was that the EU

[30] The principle of the institutional autonomy of the member states was introduced in Case 51–54/71 *International Fruit Company v Produktschap voor groenten en fruit* EU:C:1971:128, 4, and the principle of procedural autonomy in case 33/76 *Rewe-Zentralfinanz v Landwirtschaftskammer für das Saarland* EU:C:1976:188, 5.

[31] See, further, C-205–215/82 *Deutsche Milchkontor GmbH and others v Federal Republic of Germany* EU:C:1983:233, 17; C-201/02 *Delena Wells v Secretary of State for Transport, Local Government and the Regions* EU:C:2004:12, 65.

[32] The Council of Europe enacted a resolution in 1977 with core administrative principles for all member states to respect: see Council of Europe, Resolution (77) 31 on the Protection of the Individual in relation to the Acts of Administrative Authorities. See, further, FIDE XVII, *Procedures and Sanctions in Economic Administrative Law* (Nomos 1996); Koen Lenaerts and Jan Vanhamme, 'Procedural Rights of Private Parties in the Community Administrative Process' (1997) 34(3) Common Market Law Review 531, 531 ff; Statskontoret 2005:4, 'Rules and Principles of Good Administration in the Member States of the European Union' 71 ff.

[33] Craig and others (eds), ReNEUAL Model Rules (n 4) 35; Paul Craig, *EU Administrative Law* (OUP 2018) 265.

[34] Craig, EU Administrative Law (n 33) 36 et seq.

lacked general competence to regulate administrative law matters at either level. However, after the fall of the Santer Commission, following allegations of fraud, mismanagement, and nepotism,[35] and the consolidation of EU administrative law in the Lisbon Treaty, where the EU was conferred further legislative competence in the area of administrative law,[36] the scenery has changed.

6.2.3 Applying the principle of good administration within the sphere of EU law

As mentioned in the introduction to this chapter, the CJEU has, since the 1980s, developed requirements for the member states to apply certain minimum procedural requirements in their administrative decision-making within the sphere of application of EU law. More recently, it has also held that the principles underlying Article 41 of the Charter are applicable to the member states. The member states are obligated to respect these principles when acting within the sphere of application of EU law.[37] Precisely what this means, with respect to the way in which administrative procedural rules are to be upheld, is not quite clear.

An early and groundbreaking case for both the right to good administration and the right to an effective judicial remedy is the *Heylens* case on free movement of workers, from 1987.[38] The case was brought before the CJEU within criminal proceedings against Georges Heylens, a football trainer, and the directors of the Lille Olympic Sporting Club, for having infringed the provisions of French criminal law on the organisation and promotion of physical and sporting activities, as well as the wrongful assumption by Mr Heylens of a title. Mr Heylens had applied to have his Belgian football trainer's diploma recognised, but a member of the French government had rejected the application without providing any reasons. It was when Mr Heylens continued to work as a

[35] See Committee of Independent Experts, 'First Report on Allegations regarding Fraud, Mismanagement and Nepotism in the European Commission' (15 March 1999); Commission, 'Reforming the Commission—White Paper' COM (2000) 200 final.

[36] See, in particular, art 6 TEU, turning the Charter (n 5) into binding law, and arts 6(g), 197, and 298 TFEU, conferring powers on the EU to take actions within the field of administrative cooperation, and enacting secondary law for administrative procedures at the EU level, respectively.

[37] Cases 5/88 *Wachauf v Bundesamt für Ernährung und Forstwirtschaft* EU:C:1989:321; C-260/89 *Elliniki Radiophonia Tiléorassi (ERT) v Dimotiki Etairia Pliroforissis* EU:C:1991:254; C-617/10 *Criminal proceedings against Åkerberg Fransson* EU:C:2013:280; art 51(1) of the Charter (n 5).

[38] *Heylens* (n 12).

football trainer that he and the directors of the club were was charged with the above-mentioned crimes.[39] The CJEU famously held that:[40]

> Effective judicial review, which must be able to cover the legality of the reasons for the contested decision, presupposes in general that the court to which the matter is referred may require the competent authority to notify its reasons. But where, as in this case, it is more particularly a question of securing the effective protection of a fundamental right conferred by the Treaty on Community workers, the latter must also be able to defend that right under the best possible conditions and have the possibility of deciding, with a full knowledge of the relevant facts, whether there is any point in their applying to the courts. Consequently, in such circumstances the competent national authority is under a duty to inform them of the reasons on which its refusal is based, either in the decision itself or in a subsequent communication made at their request.

Since Mr Heylens was subject to the right to free movement of workers, French law could not limit his right without providing for a judicial remedy, and requiring the competent authority to state reasons for its decision.

Another interesting case for this study is the *Sopropé* case, where the question arose of whether an effective right to be heard had been provided within a customs matter. The CJEU held that, in accordance with the principle of the right to be heard, 'the addressees of decisions which significantly affect their interests must be placed in a position in which they can effectively make known their views as regards the information on which the authorities intend to base their decision', and 'they must be given a sufficient period of time in which to do so', but referred to national law for more specific procedural details.[41] The Court made it clear that member states must uphold the right to be heard, also in cases where there is no express grounds in secondary EU law. In a later judgment, the Grand Chamber case *Sabou*, the CJEU clarified that the principle of the right to be heard does not include a right for the individual concerned to take part in the request for information sent from a national authority, a tax authority, to a tax authority in another member state, nor when inquiries are carried out in the requested member state.[42] Since the relevant secondary law did not address the taxpayer's right to challenge the accuracy of the information

[39] ibid, paras 2–4.
[40] ibid, para 15.
[41] C-349/07 *Sopropé v Fazenda Pública* EU:C:2008:746, 36–38.
[42] Case C-276/12 *Sabou v Finanční ředitelství pro hlavní město Prahu* EU:C:2013:678, para 44.

conveyed to the requesting authority, the CJEU held that this was a question for national law to resolve.[43]

Lastly, the case of *HN*, where the CJEU pronounced that the principle underlying Article 41 of the Charter is applicable to the member states, shall be mentioned briefly.[44] *HN* was a migration law case, and the question was whether it was contrary to the right to good administration, including the right of any person to have his or her affairs handled impartially and within a reasonable period of time, to include, in national law, a procedural rule to the effect that an application for subsidiary protection must be covered by a separate procedure, and can be made only after an asylum application has been refused. The CJEU found that this was not the case, as long as the entire procedure for considering an application for international protection did not exceed a reasonable period of time.[45]

In comparison to the right to an effective remedy, which has been elaborated in case law over the years,[46] the case law on the right to good administration, and the related requirements on the member states, remains scarce and inconsistent.[47]

6.2.4 EU law regulating factual and procedural administrative law of the member states

With the Lisbon Treaty, the EU gained some competence to take actions regarding administrative cooperation with national administrative authorities. According to Article 6 (g) TFEU, the EU's competence in the field of administrative cooperation is, however, limited. The EU may carry out actions to 'support, coordinate or supplement the actions of the Member States'. Article 197(2) TFEU, where EU competence under Article 6(g) TFEU is specified, adds in its first paragraph that 'the effective implementation of EU law by the

[43] ibid, paras 48–49.
[44] *HN* (n 13).
[45] ibid, paras 52–56.
[46] See, eg in regard to effectiveness, cases C-312/93 *Peterbroeck* EU C:1995:437; C-430/93 and C-431/93 *van Schijndel* EU:C:1995:441; C-432/05 *Unibet v Justitiekanslern* EU:C:2007:163. In regard to equivalence, see, eg C-261/95 *Palmisani mot INPS* EU:C:1997:351; C-200/14 *Câmpean* EU:C:2016:494; and C-69/14 *Dragoş Constantin Târşia v Statul român* EU:C:2015:662.
[47] Clement (n 11) 22; Ton Duijkersloot, 'Consequences of the Violation by Administrative Authorities of the Right to be Heard under EU Law: The Case MG and NR' (2014) 7(1) Review of European Administrative Law 81. This is, to a certain extent, also the case in regard to application of the principle at the EU level: Herwig HC Hofmann and others, 'The General Principles of EU Administrative Law—An In-depth Analysis' [2015] Revista Italiana Di Diritto Pubblico Comunitario 1425–26.

Member States, which is essential for the proper functioning of the Union, shall be regarded as a matter of common interest'. It is for the member states to implement EU law, but it is a matter of common interest that it is done. However, although the EU does not have any independent competence to regulate administrative law at member state level, EU legislative competence within sector-specific areas has been considered a possible legal basis to also adopt rules of administrative character. For example, Article 114 TFEU confers the power on the EU to 'adopt the measures for the approximation of the provisions laid down by law, regulation or administrative action in Member States which have as their object the establishment and functioning of the internal market', and has been used to introduce minimum rules on administrative procedures, at the national level, in different policy areas.[48] The ESMA Regulation and MiFIR were also enacted on the basis of Article 114 TFEU, whereas MiFID II was enacted on the basis of Article 53 TFEU, on the taking-up and pursuit of activities as self-employed persons.

However, it should be underlined that EU laws on administrative procedural requirements to be applied by the member states are generally formulated in an open-ended manner. For example, such laws might require that an individual concerned should be given an opportunity to be heard,[49] or access to files,[50] and that decisions should be reasoned,[51] or possible to appeal,[52] without specifying, in each case, how this is to be done. In other pieces of legislation, there is merely a statement in the preamble that procedural safeguards are to be upheld.[53] National administrative law will, thus, supplement and fill out the EU secondary law in regard to how the procedural rules are to be applied in

[48] eg Directive 2004/38/EC of the European Parliament and the Council of 29 April 2004 on the right of citizens of the Union and their family members to move and reside freely within the territory of the Member States [2004] OJ L 158/77; Directive 2006/123/EC of the European Parliament and the Council of 12 December 2006 on services in the internal market [2006] OJ L 376/36; Directive 2005/36/EC of the European Parliament and the Council of 7 September 2005 on the recognition of professional qualifications [2005] OJ L 255/22, among others.

[49] Regulation (EC) No 764/2008 of the European Parliament and the Council of 9 July 2008 laying down procedures related to the application of certain national technical rules to products lawfully marketed in another Member State [2008] OJ L 218/21, art 6(1).

[50] Directive (EU) 1/2019 of the European Parliament and the Council of 11 December 2018 to empower the competition authorities of the Member States to be more effective enforcers and to ensure the proper functioning of the internal market [2018] OJ L 11/3, art 31.

[51] MiFID II (n 2) art 74.

[52] Regulation (EU) 2016/679 of the European Parliament and the Council of 27 April 2016 on the protection of natural persons with regard to the processing of personal data and on the free movement of such data, and repealing Directive 95/46/EC (General Data Protection Regulation) [2016] OJ L 119/1, art 78.

[53] See recitals 45 and 48 of the preamble to Directive 2014/67/EU of the European Parliament and the Council of 15 May 2014 on the enforcement of Directive 96/71/EC concerning the posting of workers in the framework of the provision of services [2014] OJ L 159/11.

individual cases. Even when administrative procedure is regulated under secondary law, EU law still gives member states quite some leeway.

On the other hand, national rules may have to be applied in a different context than usual, since EU rules on factual administrative actions and the composite environment may affect the work of national public authorities. Authorities may, therefore, be required to act in situations where national procedural law does not really fit, and may need to be inventive. In the next section, administrative cooperation under MiFID II and MiFIR will be analysed more closely.

6.3 Good administration in composite procedures of financial markets supervision?

6.3.1 ESMA at the centre of the composite administration of financial markets in the EU

ESMA has been equipped with extensive powers in the regulatory and supervisory fields.[54] The two fields may also function in a mutually reinforcing manner: the organ writing the rule book will also be influential, in its supervisory role, in interpreting the rules, and the supervisory role will inform the rulemaking function, from experiences in the field. In this context, it may be noted, both from the ESMA Regulation and ESMA's own description of its mission, that efficiency in supervision is clearly of key importance.[55] Financial stability seems to be an overriding objective.[56]

ESMA's supervisory tasks have a factual, administrative, governance-oriented character, as well as a decision-making function. Within the first category fall ESMA's tasks of playing an active role in building a 'common supervisory culture': establishing consistent supervisory practices, and ensuring uniform procedures and consistent approaches throughout the Union.[57] The ESMA Regulation provides two specific tools: peer reviews of competent

[54] Elizabeth Howell, 'EU Agencification and the Rise of ESMA: Are its Governance Arrangements Fit for Purpose?' (2019) 78(2) Cambridge Law Journal 330, 333.

[55] ESMA Regulation (n 1), art 1(5) and <https://www.esma.europa.eu/about-esma/who-we-are>, accessed 8 September 2020. The soundness in regulating financial markets as such has been convincingly argued, see, eg Gustaf Sjöberg, 'Reglering av banker' [2018] Jure 264, in regard to banks. See also Päivo Leino, 'Accountability Dilemmas of Regulating Markets through the European Supervisory Agencies' in Carol Harlow, Päivo Leino, and Giacinto della Cananea (eds), *Research Handbook on EU Administrative Law* (Edward Elgar Publishing 2017) 209, 221–22.

[56] Compare Case C-270/12 *UK v Parliament and Council* EU:C2014:18, 85.

[57] ESMA Regulation (n 1), art 29.

authorities, and coordination functions, especially exchange of information between competent authorities.[58] Beyond coordinating and steering the NCAs, ESMA is further tasked with functions relating to control of the NCAs, and may enact binding measures towards an NCA, if it is considered to have breached EU law. In Article 17 of the ESMA Regulation, a procedure has been laid down allowing ESMA, after having addressed the authority with a recommendation and, in collaboration with the Commission, a formal opinion, to step into the NCA's shoes and take the relevant actions against an investment firm. ESMA may, thus, 'adopt an individual decision addressed to a financial market participant requiring the necessary action to comply with its obligations under Union law including the cessation of any practice'.[59]

According to Article 19 of the ESMA Regulation, NCAs may also refer to ESMA questions brought up within horiontal composite procedures, namely where an NCA has asked for the cooperation or intervention of the competent authority of another state. If the issue cannot be resolved between the national authorities themselves, ESMA may 'take a decision requiring them to take specific action or to refrain from action in order to settle the matter, with binding effects for the competent authorities concerned, in order to ensure compliance with Union law'.[60] Article 20 of the ESMA Regulation contains an equivalent procedure for cross-sectoral disagreements between NCAs, under the European Bank Authority, EBA, or European Insurance and Occupational Pensions Authority, EIOPA. ESMA is, further, the only EU agency with direct enforcement powers vis-à-vis private parties.[61] In the context of MiFID II and MiFIR, ESMA may conduct certain types of supervision directly, such as temporarily prohibiting or restricting 'the marketing, distribution or sale of certain financial instruments or financial instruments with certain specified features' or 'type[s] of financial activity or practice', under Article 40 MiFIR.

Accordingly, there is a thin line between ESMA's softer factual administrative tasks of coordination and information sharing, and its powers to enact binding measures in the place of an NCA. In the words of ESMA, its role as facilitator, coordinator, and coach is complemented by its policing role, where

[58] ibid, arts 30–31.

[59] ibid art 17(6).

[60] ibid art 19(3).

[61] Regulation (EU) No 648/2012 of the European Parliament and of the Council of 4 July 2012 on OTC derivatives, central counterparties and trade repositories [2012] OJ L 201/1 (hereafter 'EMIR'); Annex III of Regulation (EU) No 513/2011 of the European Parliament and of the Council of 11 May 2011 amending Regulation (EC) No 1060/2009 on credit rating agencies [2011] OJ L 145/30 (hereafter the 'CRA Regulation'); Marloes van Rijsbergen and Miroslava Scholten, 'ESMA Inspecting: The Implications for Judicial Control under Shared Enforcement' (2016) 7 European Journal of Risk Regulation 569, 571.

non-convergence is found to be harmful to market participants or other member states.[62] Administrative procedures under MiFID II and MiFIR will be discussed next.

6.3.2 Administrative procedures for cooperation in MiFID II and MiFIR procedures

The ESMA Regulation, like MiFID II and MiFIR, presupposes close co-operation between the ESMA and the NCAs, as well as between the NCAs themselves. According to Article 79 MiFID II, the NCAs are under an obligation to cooperate with each other when carrying out their duties under the directive, and under MiFIR. This includes cooperation between competent authorities in supervisory activities, on-site verifications, or investigations;[63] exchange of information with other national competent authorities and ESMA,[64] and the collection of relevant information when handling individual matters.[65] This cooperation is to be carried out when making use of the extensive investigatory powers provided for in the directive, as discussed by Andersson in the preceding chapter of this book.[66]

Further, if the NCAs cannot agree on any relevant matter, MiFID II provides a mechanism allowing ESMA to enact a binding act resolving the issue, including, if necessary, overriding decisions already adopted by the NCA.[67] Even more elaborate administrative cooperation can be found in the so-called supervisory colleges, but neither MiFID II nor MiFIR provide any decision-making procedures based on supervisory colleges.[68]

[62] ESMA Strategic Orientation 2016–2020, 15 June 2015, ESMA/2015/935, 14.
[63] MiFID II (n 2), art 80.
[64] ibid, arts 81 and 87.
[65] ibid, art 84.
[66] ibid, art 69; Helene Andersson, 'Protecting Investors at all Costs' (Chapter 5).
[67] MiFID II (n 2) arts 82 and 83, referring to arts 19 or 20 of the ESMA Regulation (n 1).
[68] See ESMA Regulation (n 1), art 21; EMIR (n 61), arts 17–18. The colleges consist of representatives from the competent authorities concerned forming a new entity, a supervisory college, where an individual administrative matter is discussed and resolved in the form of an agreement, which is then implemented via an administrative decision by the lead authority. However, according to art 80(2) of MiFID II, with the objective of converging supervisory practices, ESMA may participate in the activities of the colleges of supervisors, including on-site verifications or investigations, carried out jointly by two or more competent authorities.

This entails different versions of decision-making procedures, depending on whether the decision is adopted based on input from another administrative organ, or ESMA adopts a measure binding an NCA, as follows:

- An NCA adopts a decision after input from ESMA[69]
- An NCA adopts a decision after input from another NCA.[70]
- ESMA adopts a decision binding and overriding any decision adopted by an NCA.[71]

The fit and proper test in MiFID II can be used to illustrate the procedures.[72] As discussed by Behrendt Jonsson in Chapter 9 of this book, the test constitutes a cornerstone in EU financial markets law, and includes an assessment of the trustworthiness of key actors, such as members of management boards, in order to safeguard financial stability and investors.[73] The assessment includes the collective knowledge, skills, and experience of the management body, as well as individual traits of members of the management board, such as honesty, integrity, and independence of mind.[74]

The ESMA and EBA have adopted joint guidelines on suitability assessments, including a section on cooperation between NCAs.[75] According to the joint guidelines, the lead NCA may request information from other NCAs about the entity under assessment, either in form of the results of a suitability assessment carried out by another NCA, or any other information an NCA might be in position to provide, such as details of a refused registration, or criminal records.[76]

According to Behrendt Jonsson, minor breaches of societal rules without connection to the financial market, such as repeated failures to buy bus tickets, can also be included in assessments.[77] When information of this kind is gathered from a

[69] eg art 57.5 of MiFID II (n 2), and art 43(2) and (3) of MiFIR (n 3).
[70] eg art 84 of MiFID II (n 2); art 4 MiFIR (n 3).
[71] eg arts 19 and 20 of ESMA Regulation (n 1), and arts 82 and 83 of MiFID II (n 2). ESMA may also, by its own initiative, take measures that override decisions adopted by an NCA: art 9 (5) of ESMA regulation (n 1), and arts 45(9) and 18(3)–(5) MiFIR (n 3).
[72] MiFID II (n 2) art 9, and Directive 2013/36/EU of the European Parliament and of the Council of 26 June 2013 on access to the activity of credit institutions and the prudential supervision of credit institutions and investment firms [2013] OJ L 176/338 (hereafter 'Capital Requirements Directive IV'), art 91.
[73] See the contribution by Britta Behrendt Jonsson in Chapter 9 of this book.
[74] MiFID II (n 2) art 45(2) (a)–(b); Capital Requirements Directive IV (n 72) art 91(7)–(8).
[75] EBA and ESMA, 'Final Report: Joint ESMA and EBA Guidelines on the assessment for the suitability of members of the management body and key function holders under Directive 2013/36/EU and Directive 2014/65/EU' (hereafter, the 'Joint Guidelines').
[76] ibid, paras 194 and 196.
[77] See the contribution by Britta Behrendt Jonsson in Chapter 9 of this book.

potentially large number of NCAs, the participation of the individual in the handling of the matter is crucial. This issue will be discussed in the following section.

6.3.3 Rules implementing the principle of good administration

The ESMA regulation sets out some basic rules for ESMA's internal decision-making procedures in Article 39, providing for a right to be heard, and a right to reasoned decisions.[78] However, neither the duty of care nor the right to access files are mentioned. Further, ESMA has enacted a code where the rules are set out in more detail, including, amongst others, requirements for staff members of ESMA to act lawfully, impartially, fairly, and reasonably (Articles 4, 8, 9, and 11), and a duty to adopt decisions within a reasonable time limit (Article 17).[79] The right of access to files is not mentioned here either. These rules are, however, not applicable in decision-making procedures in the member states, even though it is clear that ESMA's decision-making powers could be extended to also involve national decision-making in composite procedures.[80]

Neither MiFID II nor MiFIR contain any coherent rules on matters falling under Article 41 of the Charter. The preambles to MiFIR and MiFID II both emphasise the respect for fundamental rights in the Charter, but without mentioning Article 41 and the right to good administration.[81] One exception is Article 74 MiFID II, where a general right to reasoned decisions, as well as a right of appeal before a tribunal, is included, for all decisions adopted under the directive.

Other than Article 74, MiFID II contains only a very few, scattered rules on administrative procedures implementing the right to good administration. According to Article 12(4) of MiFID II, if an NCA wants to oppose a proposed acquisition notified under Article 11, the NCA must 'inform the proposed acquirer in writing and provide the reasons for that decision'. Thus, no full right to be heard, , which would have entailed a right for the acquirer to make known their views as regards the information on which the authorities intended to base their decision, is guaranteed.[82] In regard to the fit and proper

[78] See also recital 51 of the preamble to the ESMA Regulation (n 1).
[79] ESMA, 'Decision of the Management Board—Code of Good Administrative Behaviour', 11 January 2011, ESMA/2011/MB/6.
[80] See, eg recital 32 of the ESMA regulation (n 1), and section 6.3.2 above.
[81] Recital 54 in the preamble to MiFIR (n 3), and recital 166 in the preamble to MiFID II (n 2).
[82] Compare *Sopropé* (n 41) paras 36–38.

tests discussed above, neither MiFID II nor the ESMA and EBA joint guidelines give any guidance on how the information collected from other NCAs is to be processed. The guidelines do, however, include rules on data protection, stating that the requesting NCA must seek consent, from the members of the management board involved, in order to request information about individuals from other NCAs, and to process and use the information for their own suitability assessment, unless national law permits this without consent.[83]

Even if it is not openly stated, both MiFID II and MiFIR, thus, presuppose that the NCA applies national administrative procedural law, even where decision-making procedures are composite in nature.[84] As seen above, according to the case law of the CJEU, the member states are still obliged to ensure that their internal administrative law fulfils the rights guaranteed in the EU principle of good administration. The exact content of the principle will, however, vary from one state to another. This is of relevance when moving on to consider the next step: judicial review of the administrative organs implementing EU law.

6.4 Jurisdiction of the European and national courts in composite administration

6.4.1 Division of competence between the European courts and the national courts

The division of competence between the European and national courts in EU law is, on paper, rather straightforward: neither the CJEU nor the national courts have any competence to review acts emanating from legal orders other than their own.[85] This division of competence is, thus, based on the traditional international administrative law/conflict of law approach.[86] In composite administrative procedures, where different parts of the decision-making have taken place within different national and/or European administrative authorities, the question of from where a decision has emanated is, however, not

[83] Joint Guidelines (n 75) para 193.

[84] van Rijsbergen and Scholten (n 61) 573. See also Malou Larsson Klevhill and Annina H Persson, in Chapter 8 of this book.

[85] See art 19 TEU and art 267 TFEU, in regard to the competence of the CJEU, and Case 314/85 *Foto-Frost v Hauptzollamt Lübeck-Ost* EU:C:1987:452, in regard to the CJEU view on the competence of national courts.

[86] See Hofmann, Trans-territorial Executive Rule-making (n 25) 427; Wenander (n 23) 760; section 6.3.1 above.

always straightforward. Different solutions may be utilised for different situations. In this section, the main strands in the CJEU case law will be drawn from the *TU München* and *Borelli* cases.[87]

When a national authority enacts a decision based (wholly or partially) on an act taken by an EU authority, the preliminary ruling mechanism may be used. This was the situation in the *TU München* case, also a seminal case for elaborating the principle of good administration at EU level.[88] A German customs authority had taken a decision to deny an exemption from customs, based on a decision from the Commission, and the question arose of whether the Commission had respected the rights of the applicant when handling the matter. On an appeal of the decision of the German customs authority, the Commission decision was reviewed, and declared invalid, within a preliminary ruling.[89] The CJEU found that the Commission had breached its duty of care, the applicant's right to be heard, and the right to reasoned decision.[90]

The opposite situation may also occur, namely that a national authority adopts a decision binding an administrative organ at the EU level. In the *Borelli* case, an Italian administrative organ issued an opinion in an agricultural aid matter, which the Commission, according to applicable law, could not deviate from. The CJEU, thus, held that there is an obligation on member states to ensure that their measures can be reviewed by a national court, even if their domestic rules of procedure would not normally provide for this in an equivalent national case.[91] Even non-final decisions may, therefore, need to be appealable, if the final decision is to be taken at the EU level.

6.4.2 Decision-making with non-binding contribution from another authority

The division of power between courts in the *TU München/Borelli* line of cases presupposes that the acts being reviewed can be separated clearly: specifically, it presupposes that the decision-making authority (either European or national) is bound by the act adopted by the contributing authority. If the contributing authority has merely recommended that the decision-making authority take particular action, or consider certain aspects, in their decision-making,

[87] *TU München* (n 11) and *Borelli* (n 14).
[88] *TU München* (n 11) paras 14–15.
[89] ibid paras 28–29.
[90] ibid paras 22, 25–26.
[91] *Borelli* (n 14) para 13.

the division of competence in judicial reviews, as outlined above, has not been upheld by the CJEU. In this regard, the *Tillack* and *Berlusconi* cases will be discussed in some detail.[92]

In the *Tillack* case, a German journalist, Hans-Martin Tillack, had published articles in the *Stern* magazine on alleged irregularities regarding the activities of OLAF, the EU anti-fraud organ. OLAF initiated an investigation against Tillack, based on the suspicion that he had bribed officials at OLAF, as a result of which OLAF contacted judicial authorities in Belgium and Germany under the regulation concerning investigations conducted by OLAF.[93] These suspicions were also included in a press release from OLAF.[94] The Belgian police initiated a search at the applicant's home and office, and seized professional documents and personal belongings. Tillack lodged a complaint with the EU Ombudsman, who found that OLAF, by making allegations of bribery without a factual basis that was both sufficient and available for public scrutiny, had gone beyond that which was proportionate to the purpose pursued by its action, and that this constituted an instance of maladministration.[95] Tillack then turned to the General Court, seeking annulment of the act by which OLAF forwarded information to the German and Belgian judicial authorities, and compensation for the alleged damages.[96] However, the General Court found that the measures undertaken by OLAF—asking for assistance from national judicial authorities—had not produced any legal effects and, therefore, could not be appealed.[97]

The same reasoning was applied in the *Berlusconi* case, where the question was whether Silvio Berlusconi was 'fit and proper', according to the Single Supervisory Mechanism (SSM) Regulation, to acquire, via his company Fininvest, a qualified holding in an Italian bank, Banca Mediolanum.[98] The decision was enacted by the ECB after a request for a decision by the competent national bank, the Bank of Italy. The Bank of Italy gave an adverse opinion, and invited the ECB to oppose the acquisition. The ECB concurred with the Bank of Italy's arguments and approved the draft decision.[99] Berlusconi and

[92] Case T-193/04 *Tillack v Commission* EU:T:2006:292; *Berlusconi* (n 18).

[93] Regulation (EC) No 1073/1999 of the European Parliament and of the Council of 25 May 1999 concerning investigations conducted by the European Anti-Fraud Office (OLAF) [1999] OJ L 136/1.

[94] As recorded in *Tillack* (n 92) para 19.

[95] Decision of the European Ombudsman on complaint 1840/2002/GG against the European Anti-Fraud Office, 20 November 2003.

[96] *Tillack* (n 92) para 43.

[97] ibid para 72.

[98] *Berlusconi* (n 18), and Council Regulation (EU) No 1024/2013 of 15 October 2013 conferring specific tasks on the European Central Bank concerning policies relating to the prudential supervision of credit institutions [2013] OJ L 287/63.

[99] *Berlusconi* (n 18) paras 32–33.

Fininvest used three different avenues to challenge the decision: first, an action for annulment was brought against the ECB's decision at the General Court;[100] second, Fininvest brought proceedings before the Tribunale amministrativo regionale per il Lazio (Regional Administrative Court of Lazio, Italy) for annulment of the Bank of Italy's acts preparatory to the ECB's decision; lastly, Mr Berlusconi and Fininvest both brought an action before the Consiglio di Stato (Council of State).[101] It was the last court, the Italian Council of State, that asked for a preliminary ruling from the CJEU.

In regard to the question of division of powers between the EU courts and the national courts, the CJEU took, as its point of departure, Article 263 TFEU, stating that this article conferred upon the court exclusive jurisdiction to review the legality of acts adopted by the EU institutions, such as the ECB. The CJEU referred to the *Sweden v Commission (IWAF)* case, on the appeal of a decision to deny public access to German official documents held by EU Commission, according to the EU Transparency Regulation.[102] According to the applicable procedure in the EU Transparency Regulation, the CJEU interpreted the decision-making procedure as having, as its sole object, the determination of whether access to a document should be refused under the list of exceptions in the regulation, 'a decision-making procedure in which both the Community institution and the Member State concerned play a part'.[103] Since the objects of the European and national authorities were, in this case, the same, the CJEU found that the member state's intervention in the decision-making procedure did not affect the EU dimension of the outcome of the procedure, and that the EU courts were competent to review the enacted decision in its entirety.[104] The decision of the national authority did not have any binding legal effect on the EU decision-making procedure, and so the EU institution holding the member state's official document could take its decision independently. The CJEU did not explicitly comment on whether it would be possible to initiate a review before national courts regarding any actions taken by the national authorities in the matter (what may be called the 'Borelli side' of the review). However, AG Campos Sánchez-Bordona concluded in his opinion in the *Berlusconi* case that this would not be possible, adding that 'measures of national authorities in

[100] Case T-913/16 *Fininvest and Berlusconi v ECB*, pending.

[101] *Berlusconi* (n 18) para 36.

[102] Case C-64/05 P *Sweden v Commission* EU:C:2007/802, and Regulation (EC) No 1049/2001 of the European Parliament and of the Council of 30 May 2001 regarding public access to European Parliament, Council and Commission documents [2001] OJ L 145/43.

[103] ibid para 93.

[104] ibid para 94.

such procedures are of a purely preparatory nature, and therefore as a general rule they will not need to be reviewed either by national courts or by the Court of Justice.'[105]

This step was explicitly taken in the *Berlusconi* case, where the CJEU defined a specific type of composite procedure, which was to be under the exclusive competence of the EU Courts:[106]

> In such a situation, where EU law does not aim to establish a division between two powers—one national and the other of the European Union—with separate purposes, but, on the contrary, lays down that an EU institution is to have an exclusive decision-making power, it falls to the EU Courts, by virtue of their exclusive jurisdiction to review the legality of EU acts on the basis of Article 263 TFEU (see, by analogy, judgment of 22 October 1987, *Foto-Frost*, 314/85, EU:C:1987:452, paragraph 17), to rule on the legality of the final decision adopted by the EU institution at issue and to examine, in order to ensure effective judicial protection of the persons concerned, any defects vitiating the preparatory acts or the proposals of the national authorities that would be such as to affect the validity of that final decision.

The CJEU further clarified that it is at the discretion of the EU institution to either follow or disregard the decisive national act. Under these circumstances it is necessary to apply this specific form of 'single judicial review', conducted by the EU courts alone.[107] Otherwise, the risk of divergent assessments in one and the same procedure could not be ruled out, thereby compromising the EU courts' exclusive jurisdiction to rule on the legality of the final decision. The EU courts should, therefore, also be competent to examine the parts of the procedure that had taken place at the national level.[108] Interestingly, in 2021, the CJEU has found that a non-binding contribution by EBA, a recommendation, which a national authority, the Bulgarian National Bank, had relied upon in its decision-making, could be reviewed and declared invalid within an preliminary ruling proceeding.[109]

[105] AG Campos Sánchez-Bordona opinion in C-219/17 *Silvio Berlusconi v Banca d'Italia* EU:C:2018:502, 74. See, further, Simona Demková, 'The Grand Chamber's Take on Composite Procedures under the Single Supervisory Mechanism. Comments on Judgment of 27 June 2018, C-219/17 *Silvio Berlusconi v Finanziaria d'investimento Fininvest SpA (Fininvest) v Banca d'Italia and others* EU:C:2018:502' (2019) 12(1) Review of European Administrative Law 209, 215.

[106] *Berlusconi* (n 18) para 44.

[107] ibid para 49 and Xanthoulis (n 20) 69–70.

[108] *Berlusconi* (n 18) para 52.

[109] C-501/18 *Balgarska Narodna Banka*, EU:C:2021:249, p. 101. See also C-911/19 *Fédération bancaire française*, EU:C:2021:599.

The solution found by the CJEU raises a further question: if the EU courts are to review national parts of the composite procedure, does this not necessitate a common standard of what the administrative organs are to uphold, for example when it comes to the principle of good administration? This question will be addressed in the next section.

6.5 Which principle of good administration for EU financial markets supervision?

6.5.1 Who defines good administration within the sphere of application of EU law?

In the introduction to this chapter, three question were identified for analysis. The first two will be analysed in this section: first, who is responsible for ensuring the right of financial actors to good administration when several jurisdictions are involved in the handling of a single matter? Second, which courts—national or European—are competent to hear appeals of decisions that have been adopted? The third question—whether this diversity in realisation of the principle of good administration is a threat to the effective functioning of accountability within EU financial markets law—will be addressed in the conclusive sixth section.

As discussed above, national authorities are obliged to uphold the EU principle of good administration within the sphere of the application of EU law.[110] When and how general principles of EU law are to be applied at the national level has been debated in legal doctrine for a long time.[111] In this section, two steps will be addressed. First, which courts, the EU or the national, ought to decide on the more precise content of the principle to be applied in an individual matter: more specifically, which courts should decide when a part of the principle (duty of care, right to be heard, right to reasoned decisions) has been breached? Second, what effect is a breach of the principle to have in the concrete case: in other words, what function is the principle to have in the review of an administrative matter?

[110] See section 6.2.3 above.

[111] Koen Lenaerts, 'Respect for Fundamental Rights as a Constitutional Principle of the European Union' (2000) 6(1) Columbia Journal of European Law 1; Piet Eeckhout, 'The EU Charter of Fundamental Rights and the Federal Question' (2002) 39(5) Common Market Law Review 945; Michael Dougan, 'Judicial Review of Member State Action under the General Principles and the Charter: Defining the "Scope of Union Law"' (2015) 52(5) Common Market Law Review 1201.

In the *Åkerberg Fransson* case, the CJEU made it clear that the leeway enjoyed by the member states to adjust the application of EU law to national traditions depends on the extent to which national law has been harmonised, ie on how intensively a policy area is governed by Union law.[112] This must be understood as encompassing both steps: identifying when the principle of good administration has been breached, and deciding what effect the breach is to have, in the concrete case.

On the other hand, if the effective and uniform application of EU law is challenged, the leeway for member states to decide on the content of the principle to apply may shrink.[113] An administrative law example of this situation can be found regarding the principle of legitimate expectations, and its application in matters concerning reimbursement of EU funds paid out to individuals in the member states. The revocation of positive administrative decisions is a well-known concept in the administrative law of all member states[114] and, generally, a national authority will apply its own internal administrative and procedural arrangements, provided that the usual limitations on procedural autonomy are observed.[115] However, in cases of reimbursement of EU funds, where the requirements for wrongly paid-out monies being recovered are laid down in EU law, the CJEU has, on the contrary, held that the reimbursement of the aid should be assessed solely on the basis of the Union's principles of legal certainty and legitimate expectation.[116]

So far, no similar tendencies can be seen in the CJEU case law on the principle of good administration. The CJEU has, in its case law, been careful to allow member states some room for manoeuvre when implementing the right to good administration on a national level, and requirements have often been left open-ended.[117] Since administrative law traditions at national level vary, this means that the application of the principle of good administration will vary, also, in different parts of a single composite procedure.[118] However, the

[112] *Åkerberg Fransson* (n 37) 29.

[113] Case C-399/11 *Melloni v Ministerio Fiscal* EU:C:2013:107 para 63.

[114] See, for an early example, Joined Cases 7/56 and 3- to 7/57 *Algera v Common Assembly of the European Coal and Steel Community* EU:C:1957:7.

[115] Case C-453/00 *Kühne & Heitz NV v Produktschap voor Pluimvee en Eieren* EU:C:2004:17.

[116] Case C-383/06–385/06 *Vereniging Nationaal Overlegorgaan Sociale Werkvoorziening* EU:C:2008:165, para 53; Case C-568/11 *Agroferm A/S v Ministeriet for Fødevarer, Landbrug og Fiskeri* EU:C:2013:407, para 49. See also Jane Reichel, 'Sanctions against Individuals and the Rule of Law: Can the Member States let the EU Decide?' in Antonina Bakardjieva Engelbrekt, Karin Leijon, Anna Michalski, and Lars Oxelheim (eds), *The European Union and the Return of the Nation State, Interdisciplinary European Studies* (Palgrave Macmillan 2020) <doi.org/10.1007/978-3-030-35005-5_8, 204-205>.

[117] Clement (n 11) 21 ff.

[118] See section 6.2.2 above

EU version of the principle seems to be used as some sort of minimum requirement. In many cases, for example the above-mentioned cases of *Sopropé* and *HN*, the CJEU has referred to leading case law relating to administrative procedures at the EU level, where Commission decisions had been appealed.[119] The EU version of the principle of good administration does, thus, seem to be relevant when defining the requirements of the member states, at least to a minimum level. The role of the EU principle of good administration as the fallback version is also underlined in another line of cases, where the CJEU has found that, in composite procedures where the final decision has been enacted by an EU institution, the responsibility to ensure that good administration is upheld ultimately falls on that institution. If the national authority, in a preparatory stage, has not given the individual concerned a right to be heard, for example, this must be granted by the EU institution before the final decision is enacted.[120] As will be discussed in the following section, the CJEU has not applied the same reasoning in horizontal composite procedures involving national authorities.

In regard to the function of the principle of good administration in the review procedure, what effect ought a breach of the principle have in the individual case? This is a question that is also rather uncertain at the EU level. At the national level, the CJEU has provided the member states with considerable leeway. In the *Valsts* case, the CJEU held:[121]

> it is for the Member States, exercising their procedural autonomy, to regulate the consequences of a failure by the customs authorities to fulfil their obligation to state reasons and to determine whether and to what extent such a failure may be remedied in the course of legal proceedings, subject to observance of the principles of equivalence and effectiveness.

The answer to the first question posed in this chapter—whether it is, ultimately, for the EU or the national legal order to define the content and function of

[119] Case *Sopropé* (n 41) 37 and *HN* (n 13) para 52.

[120] Case T-346/94 *France Aviation v Commission* EU:T:1995:187, paras 30 ff; Case T-42/96 *Eyckeler & Malt AG v Commission* EU:T:1998:40, paras 84–86. See, further, Christina Eckes and Joana Mendes, 'The Right to be Heard in Composite Administrative Procedures: Lost in between Protection?' (2011) (36) European Law Review 651 ff; Marco Lamandini, David Ramos Muñoz, and Javier Solana Álvarez, 'Depicting the Limits to the SSM's Supervisory Powers: The Role of Constitutional Mandates and of Fundamental Rights' Protection' (2015) 79 Quaderni di Ricerca Giuridica della Consulenza Legale 82. In the cases C-135/92 *Fiskano* EU:C:1994:267, para 39 and *TU München* (n 11) paras 14–15, the EU institution—the Commission in both cases—was, on the other hand, criticised for not having afforded the individual concerned a right to be heard within the procedure at the EU level before providing an opinion to the national authority.

[121] Case C-46/16 *Valsts ieņēmumu dienests v 'LS Customs Services' SIA* EU:C:2017:839, para 46.

the principle of good administration when applied within the sphere of EU law—remains fuzzy. The version of the principle applicable at the EU level may be relevant when defining minimum requirements for the member states, but, currently, there is no concrete common standard on either the content or function of the principle of good administration in the sphere of application of EU law.

6.5.2 Who reviews the principle of good administration in composite EU financial law matters?

If there is no common standard for the principle of good administration, this means that it may vary from one member state to another, and between the national and European level. In a composite procedure, where more than one administrative law standard may be involved, it is, therefore, essential to know which court is responsible for reviewing an administrative decision, in order to know what standard is applicable to the procedure at hand. Even when administrative procedures are composite, the judicial accountability regimes provided for in the EU Treaties remain binary—either EU or national—with the exception of the preliminary ruling mechanism. The EU and national administrative authorities, thus, remain subject to the jurisdiction of their respective court systems, under their respective constitutional settings. As the case law stands today, there are different routes depending on whether the composite procedure is made up of separable parts that are, in themselves, binding on the other administrative authorities involved in the procedure, or if the contributing parties are merely recommending or providing information for the decision-making authority to assess independently. The first of these routes is referred to as the *TU München/Borelli* line of cases, and the second as the *Tillack/Berlusconi* line of cases.

It is clear that the *TU München/Borelli* line of cases, based on a separation of power and an international administrative law/conflict of law approach, is not always convincing.[122] There will always be aspects falling between the jurisdictions involved. The lack of a preliminary ruling mechanism in cases of horizontal cooperation may be problematic.

Also, the *Tillack/Berlusconi* line, with its single judicial review, has its weak points. First, the *Tillack* and *Berlusconi* cases both illustrate the fact that is not

[122] Hervig CH Hofmann and Morgane Tidghi, 'Rights and Remedies in Implementation of EU Policies by Multi-jurisdictional Networks' (2014) 20(1) European Public Law 147, 164.

always easy to trace who has done what in a procedure, and where decisions ought to be appealed.[123] Even for resourceful appellants such as Berlusconi, it was hardly evident to which court the negative decision on his fit and proper test was to be appealed. If the relevant test for when the single judicial review is applicable is whenever 'EU law does not aim to establish a division between two powers—one national and the other of the European Union—with separate purposes, but, on the contrary, lays down that an EU institution is to have an exclusive decision-making power', this could potentially include a wide range of policy areas.

Secondly, it is inherently difficult for a court from one jurisdiction to fully review informal but highly influential investigatory contributions from an administrative authority from another jurisdiction.[124] In both the *Tillack* and *Berlusconi* cases, it seems clear that the real controversies were between Tillack and the Commission, and Berlusconi and the Bank of Italy, respectively, but that the formal decisions were adopted by administrative organs in another jurisdiction. It remains to be seen whether the 2021 cases *Balgarska Narodna Banka* and *Fédération bancaire française* , where the CJEU reviewed non-binding contributions from EBA to national authorities, will open a new path in case law.[125]

Turning to composite procedures under MiFID II and MiFIR, the three different types of procedures identified in section 6.3.2 above may be recalled:

- An NCA adopts a decision after input of ESMA.
- An NCA adopts a decision after input from another NCA.
- ESMA intervenes in an administrative procedure at national level and adopts a decision binding and overriding any decision adopted by an NCA.

In many ways, the single judicial review is uncontroversial in these procedures. When an NCA adopts a decision after contribution from either ESMA or another NCA, it seems difficult to see how the decision could be reviewed by any court other than the competent national court. The same logic applies to decisions adopted by ESMA, even if one or more NCA has been heavily involved

[123] There are several examples in the case law of the CJEU where individuals have sought redress from the incorrect court system, eg Case C-462/98 *P Mediocurso v Commission* EU:C:2000:480 and Case C-119/05 *Ministero dell'Industria, del Commercio e dell'Artigianato v Lucchini* EU:C:2007:434. See, further, Xanthoulis (n 20) 70.

[124] Compare van Rijsbergen and Scholten (n 61) 576.

[125] See C-501/18 *Balgarska Narodna Banka* and C-911/19 *Fédération bancaire française* (n 109).

in the procedure. The questions, however, are what standard of the principle of good administration should be applied to the case, and how can a court in one jurisdiction review parts of the procedure that have taken place elsewhere. This is especially relevant in matters such as the fit and proper tests, where potentially sensitive information is collected from several different NCAs, perhaps without the involvement of the investment firm in question.

In the *Berlusconi* case, the CJEU held that it fell on the EU Courts to rule on the legality of decisions enacted within the composite administration of EU banking law, including 'any defects vitiating the preparatory acts or the proposals of the national authorities that would be such as to affect the validity of that final decision'. The Court did not explicitly state whether the national procedures are to be examined against a national or a European version of administrative procedural law, but Demková has suggested that the review should be carried out through the lens of EU institutions' compliance with essential procedural requirements in preparing a final measure with the duty of care, enshrined in Article 41(1) of the EU Charter.[126] The main reason put forward for this is to avoid competence creep: namely, to avoid the EU courts taking upon themselves the power to review national law.[127]

There are several sound arguments for this conclusion, in addition to competence creep. First, Article 41 EU Charter already binds the member states and is, therefore, a common denominator for the EU composite administration. Even the CJEU has not required the member states to uphold a common version of the principle: its core values should be respected.[128] The influence of EU general principle on national law is, by now, a well-known and largely accepted phenomenon; as held by Tridimas, the general principles of law are one of the strongest forces of the Europeanisation of national laws.[129] With a 'common supervisory culture' being advanced by ESMA, it may be natural to also advance a common understanding of the content of the principle of good administration. Secondly, it would be compliant with the earlier CJEU case law, where the EU version of the principle of good administration constitutes a fallback version of the principle.[130]

[126] See Demková (n 105) 217.
[127] ibid.
[128] Compare *Åkerberg Fransson* (n 37) para 29, where the court held that the member states have a wider discretion to apply general principles in accordance with national traditions within areas that are not 'entirely determined by European Union'.
[129] Takis Tridimas, 'The General Principles of EU Law and the Europeanisation of National Laws' (2020) 13(2) Review of European Administrative Law 5, 30.
[130] See section 6.2.3 above.

On the other hand, such development would entail a competence creep of another nature. If EU courts are to review procedures applied by authorities in the member states on the basis of the EU version of the principle of good administration, this seems to presuppose that the national competent authorities are bound to apply this version of the principle. If it was legally correct to handle the preparatory parts of a composite procedure according to a national version of good administration, this would entail the review of the actions of the national competent authorities against a standard other than the one applicable at the time.[131] Further, the functions of the general principles in the review of administrative decisions differs between EU and national law. Hofmann has held that the principle of the duty of care in the case law of the CJEU has been developed as an essentially information-based concept by which the court attempts to uphold a rule of law-based judicial review whilst, at the same time, respecting the discretion of decision makers.[132] This function is not necessarily upheld in national administrative procedure law.

Lastly, if the corresponding reasoning is to be applied in horizontal situations, where national courts review administrative procedures applied in other member states, the situation is even more unclear. In the *Sabou* case, the CJEU held that the principle of right to be heard (or right to defence, as it was referred to in the case) did not include a right for the individual concerned to be involved in enquiries carried out by a contributing authority in another member state.[133] Unfortunately, the CJEU did not take the opportunity to declare that the decision-making authority was responsible for ensuring that the individual concerned was able to make his or her views known on the accuracy of the information conveyed by the contributing authority, but merely referred to national law.[134]

Even though it would have been beneficial for the protection of individuals in composite administrative procedures if the CJEU had come to such a conclusion, it must be submitted that a requirement on national authorities

[131] Compare Enrico Gagliardi and Laura Wissink, 'Ensuring Effective Judicial Protection in case of ECB Decisions based on National Law' (2020) 13(1) Review of European Administrative Law 41, 46.

[132] Hofmann, 'Duty of Care' (n 8) 88. Hofmann gives a topical example of how courts may understand the function of the duty of care differently: the CJEU case C-493/17 *Weiss and others* EU:C:2018:1000, 36–42 and the German Constitutional Court response in the *PSPP* case, German Constitutional Court (Bundesverfassungsgericht) of 5 May 2020 (Joined Cases 2 BvR 859/15, 2 BvR 1651/15, 2 BvR 2006/15, 2 BvR 980/16, 156). English version at <https://www.bundesverfassungsgericht.de/SharedDocs/Entscheidungen/EN/2020/05/rs20200505_2bvr085915en.html> 105, accessed 15 October 2020.

[133] *Sabou* (n 42) 44.

[134] ibid 48–49. It should, however, be noted that the CJEU also stated that nothing prevented a member state from extending the right to be heard to other parts of the investigation stage, by involving the taxpayer in various stages of the gathering of information, in particular the examination of witnesses (ibid 45).

to control the application of the principle of good administration in other member states would be a difficult and rather inconvenient task, in practice. National authorities are to cooperate under the principle of loyal cooperation specified in Article 4(2) TEU, often supplemented by loyalty clauses in secondary law, which will rarely include obligations to question each other's administrative standards.[135] Also vis-à-vis opinions and information conveyed by EU administrative organs, it is not entirely clear that a national authority would be in a position to question the application of administrative procedures at the EU level. The situation can be contrasted with the one in *TU München*, where the Commission adopted a final decision to be applied in a matter being handled by the German customs authority.[136] Here, the Commission was fully responsible, and accountable, for upholding the principle of good administration independently from the German authorities involved. If the contribution of the Commission had been merely informal (yet influential), it is questionable whether the German customs authority, or German courts in a subsequent review, would have been able to identify and correct the breaches of the principle at EU level.

Applying a European version of the principle of good administration to horizontal national administrative cooperation without a clear legal basis risks causing confusion in regard to both the content and the function of basic rules for exercising public power within the member states.

6.6 Conclusions

The question, raised in the previous section, of who is responsible for ensuring the principle of good administration in composite EU financial law matters has to be answered in a somewhat unsatisfying manner: it is difficult to say. The state of general administrative law in composite procedures within the sphere of application of EU law must be described as complex and unclear.[137] The final question to be analysed is, thus, whether this diversity in the realisation of the principle of good administration constitutes a threat to the effective functioning of accountability within EU financial markets law.

[135] ESMA Regulation (n 1), art 2(4) holds that: '[i]n accordance with the principle of sincere cooperation under art 4(3) of the Treaty on European Union, the parties to the European System of Financial Supervision (ESFS) shall cooperate with trust and full mutual respect, in particular in ensuring the flow of appropriate and reliable information between them.'

[136] Case *TU München* (n 11).

[137] Compare Xanthoulis (n 20) 40 ff and Edoardo Chiti, 'Is EU Administrative Law Failing in some of its Crucial Tasks' (2016) 22 European Law Journal 576, 581.

As held in the introduction, accountability presupposes that the organ being held accountable is able to identify the legal requirements that it is to uphold, in order for the accountability regime to be effective. A public authority cannot be expected to follow rules that it has, on good grounds, found to be inapplicable. Accordingly, the relevant question seems to be, why has the EU legislator not laid down at least minimum rules to ensure that the principle of good administration can be upheld within composite decision-making procedures? Even if hardly a quick fix, the most apparent way forward seems to be to use EU administrative procedural rules as the common denominator, and as a basis for development of a common standard for the principle of good administration within the sphere of application of EU law. Another evident problem is that EU administrative procedural law today is fragmented and mostly policy-specific.[138] Rather than reinventing the wheel, and constructing another policy-specific version of the principle of good administration for EU financial markets law, an Administrative Procedural Act for the EU would constitute an important step forward. The European Parliament has already drafted a proposal.[139] Further, the ReNEUAL project has explained how an EU Administrative Procedural Act could be extended to also include composite, or even national administrative, procedures.[140]

Administrative cooperation is central for ESMA to achieve its mission and objective, but focus seems to have been placed on efficiency in carrying out the supervision, whereas the need for legal certainty, transparency, and good administration has been underestimated. However, as held by Sjöberg, there is merely a perceived contradiction between the interests of maintaining an efficiently regulated financial market, and providing legal certainty and foreseeability for financial actors.[141] In the end, the prioritisation of efficiency may not only undermine the conditions for an adequate judicial accountability regime, but, further down the line, the legitimacy of EU financial markets law.

[138] Craig and others (eds), ReNEUAL Model Rules (n 4) 29.

[139] European Parliament resolution of 9 June 2016 for an open, efficient and independent European Union administration (2016/2610(RSP)).

[140] Craig and others (eds), ReNEUAL Model Rules (n 4) 71. See, eg art III-24.4–5 on the right to be heard in composite procedures.

[141] Sjöberg (n 55) 299. See also Leino (n 55) 221–22.

PART III

INVESTMENT FIRMS AS SUBJECTS OF ACCOUNTABILITY

7

Compliance Requirements in EU Investment Services Regulation

Towards a more Coherent Accountability Framework?

Pieter van Cleynenbreugel

7.1 Introduction

The increasing regulation of financial markets and services within the EU internal market[1] has given rise to the emergence of a 'Single Rulebook' that applies to all investment services providers established in one of the EU member states.[2] Putting into practice a four-layered regulatory approach inspired by the 2001 Lamfalussy Report, and refined by the 2009 De Larosière Report, the EU has pioneered an interesting combination of principles- and rules-centred regulation in the fields of banking, insurance, and investment services regulation.[3] At level one, regulations and directives contain general principles. Those general instruments are further developed or implemented through delegated and implementing acts at level two. At level three, a coherent interpretation and implementation of both level one and level two instruments has been the main objective.[4] At the outset, three networks of national supervisory authorities

[1] See, for an extensive overview up to 2014, Niamh Moloney, *EU Securities and Financial Markets Regulation* (3rd edn, OUP 2014).

[2] See Pieter van Cleynenbreugel, 'Conduct of Business Rules in EU Financial Services Regulation: Behavioural Rules Devoid of Behavioural Analysis?' in Alberto Alemanno and Anne-Lise Sibony (eds), *Nudge and the Law: A European Perspective* (Hart 2015) 255, 263–64.

[3] For background, see Christian de Visscher and Olivier Maiscocq, 'The Lamfalussy Procedure and the EC Institutional Balance: From Comitology Procedures to Policy Levels' <http://www.eu-newgov.org/database/DELIV/D07D07b_Lamfalussy_Process_and_the_EC_Institutional_Balance.pdf> accessed 11 August 2021.

[4] For the Lamfalussy Report, see Final Report of the Committee of Wise Men on the Regulation of European Securities Markets, available at < https://www.esma.europa.eu/sites/default/files/library/2015/11/lamfalussy_report.pdf > accessed 11 August 2021. The High Level Group on Financial Supervision in the EU chaired by Jacques de Larosière Report is available at <https://ec.europa.eu/economy_finance/publications/pages/publication14527_en.pdf> accessed 11 August 2021.

Pieter van Cleynenbreugel, *Compliance Requirements in EU Investment Services Regulation* In: *Legal Accountability in EU Markets for Financial Instruments.* Edited by: Carl Fredrik Bergström and Magnus Strand, Oxford University Press. © Pieter van Cleynenbreugel 2021. DOI: 10.1093/oso/9780192849281.003.0007

were created to make this happen: the Committee of European Securities Regulators (CESR), the Committee of European Banking Supervisors (CEBS), and the Committee of European Insurance and Occupational Pensions Supervisors (CEIOPS).[5] Originally having no formal coordinating powers, these networks of national supervisory authorities were upgraded into three European Supervisory Authorities (ESAs) in 2010: the European Securities and Markets Authority (ESMA), the European Banking Authority (EBA), and the European Insurance and Occupational Pensions Authority (EIOPA).[6] In accordance with their mandates, outlined in their founding regulations, these agencies ensure supervisory convergence, and can intervene in cases of persistent disrespect for EU legal rules by, or conflict between, national authorities.[7] They also provide the necessary expertise and input for the development of level two rules, and can adopt supplementary level three guidelines, which are formally non-binding.[8] Originally conceived of as having only soft law coordinating powers, level four envisaged the actual enforcement and supervision of EU financial regulation as lying with the supervisory authority of a financial institution's home state.[9] That national supervisory authority would maintain the principal responsibility for the enforcement of EU rules vis-à-vis the financial institution concerned. Over time, EU law has conferred supplementary sanctioning powers on the EU agencies in the realm of credit rating agencies[10]

[5] For CESR, see Commission Decision 2001/527/EC [2001] OJ L191/44, replaced by Commission Decision 2009/77/EC [2009] OJ L25/18. For CEBS, see Commission Decision 2004/5/EC [2004] OJ L 3/28, replaced by Commission Decision 2009/78/EC [2009] OJ L25/23. For CEIOPS, see Commission Decision 2004/6/EC [2004] OJ L3/30, replaced by Commission Decision 2009/79/EC [2009] OJ L25/28.

[6] Regulation 1093/2010 of the European Parliament and of the Council of 24 November 2010 establishing a European Supervisory Authority (European Banking Authority) amending Decision 716/2009/EC and repealing Commission Decision 2009/78/EC [2010] OJ L331/12; Regulation 1094/2010 of the European Parliament and of the Council of 24 November 2010 establishing a European Supervisory Authority (European Insurance and Occupational Pensions Authority) amending Decision 716/2009/EC and repealing Commission Decision 2009/79/EC [2010] OJ L331/48; Regulation 1095/2010 of the European Parliament and of the Council of 24 November 2010 establishing a European Supervisory Authority (European Securities and Markets Authority) amending Decision 716/2009/EC and repealing Commission Decision 2009/77/EC [2010] OJ L331/84 (hereafter the 'ESMA Founding Regulation'). The three Regulations essentially follow the same structure, and will collectively be referred to hereafter as the 'ESA Regulations'.

[7] See art 17–19 of the ESA Regulations.

[8] ibid, arts 10–11 and 16.

[9] On this principle, see Eva Lomnicka, 'The Home Country Control Principle in Financial Services Directives and the Case Law' in Mads Andenas and Wulf Henning Roth (eds), *Services and Free Movement in EU law* (OUP 2001), 295–320.

[10] See, in that regard, Regulation 1060/2009 of the European Parliament and of the Council of 16 September 2009 on credit rating agencies [2009] OJ L302/1, as amended by Regulation 513/2011 of the European Parliament and of the Council of 11 May 2011 amending Regulation 1060/2009 on credit rating agencies [2011] OJ L145/30.

and short selling.[11]. As a result of those developments, EU authorities now also engage in direct enforcement activities at level four,[12] giving rise to potential overlaps and conflicts with national supervisors and requiring regular coordination between the ESAs.

Within the set-up of that regulatory framework, attention has, above all, focused on creating a series of uniformly applicable principles and rules at levels one and two, on the one hand, and ensuring smooth coordination and regular consultation on the application and enforcement of those principles and rules at levels three and four, on the other hand. Questions that have been less at the forefront of attention concern the way in which financial institutions themselves have to comply with the increasingly detailed Single Rulebook requirements, and to what extent such internalisation can play a role in holding them to account via national and EU supervisory authorities.[13] Although increasing attention has been paid, and detail has been devoted, to investment firm compliance, it cannot be denied that this compliance framework has remained in the background of the overall EU financial regulatory project, and detached from overall reflections on sanctioning and other legal accountability mechanisms. As a result, the legal set-up of compliance obligations within EU financial services regulation may not have been thought through as much as it could have been, at this stage.

In its barest essence, compliance refers to the set of internal management programmes within a firm aimed at improving their 'ability to monitor the conduct of their own divisions and employees [in order to] reduce the risks of illegal behaviour being undertaken (*ex ante*), and identify and promptly put to an end [to] (*ex post*) violations incurred despite the company's commitment to abide by the . . . rules'.[14] Within the context of financial regulation, making firms responsible for internalizing such features can be an important tool to promote a culture of self-accountability, whereby firms proactively seek to comply with

[11] See Regulation 236/2012 of the European Parliament and of the Council of 14 March 2012 on short selling and certain aspects of credit default swaps [2012] OJ L86/1. The CJEU validated this approach in Case C-270/12 *UK v Council and Parliament* EU:C:2014:18. See also Pieter van Cleynenbreugel, '*Meroni* Circumvented? Article 114 TFEU and EU Regulatory Agencies' (2014) 21 Maastricht Journal of European and Comparative Law 64.

[12] On the increasingly varied roles of these authorities, see, among others, Pierre Schammo, 'The European Securities and Markets Authority: Lifting the Veil on the Allocation of Powers' (2011) 48 Common Market Law Review 1879; Niamh Moloney, *The Age of ESMA: Governing EU Financial Markets* (Hart 2018).

[13] Iris Chiu, *Regulating (From) the Inside—The Legal Framework for Internal Control in Banks and other Financial Institutions* (Hart 2015) 41–60.

[14] Federico Ghezzi, 'The Italian Guidelines on Antitrust Compliance Programs and the Difficult Goal of Matching Deterrence, Education, and Business Ethics' in Catalin Rusu and others (eds), *New Directions in Competition Law Enforcement* (Wolf 2020) 20.

rules.[15] From that point of view, promoting compliance can be a tool to empower financial institutions to show that they can respect rules, and to hold them accountable without having to resort exclusively to sanctions or supervisory decisions.[16] In a regulatory framework such as EU financial regulation, where legal accountability structures are constantly evolving, paying closer attention to the legal features of compliance as a complementary accountability mechanism could, therefore, prove useful.

Against that background, this chapter will uncover and conceptualise the ways in which compliance mechanisms have been embedded, as a matter of EU financial services law. Rather than focusing on the entire field of EU financial markets regulation, it will zoom in on the field of EU investment firm regulation. Within this field, analysis will centre more specifically on the compliance management features that investment firms have to respect, in terms of the framework of the Markets for Financial Instruments Directive (MiFID). From its adoption in 2004, MiFID contained particular organisational requirements to ensure and enhance compliance with its provisions.[17] Those specific requirements imposed particular obligations on the organisation of the compliance functions that were generally already present in most investment firms. The 2004 Directive was replaced by an upgraded version, in 2014. That successor Directive 2014/65 (MiFID II) has maintained and refined those requirements,[18] which have been detailed further in a 2017 delegated regulation,[19] and in 2020 ESMA guidelines.[20]

The first section of this chapter will revisit the particular compliance requirements specified in MiFID II, and the ways in which those requirements have been given shape by means of a delegated regulation and ESMA guidelines. The purpose of its analysis is not to offer an exhaustive analysis of those

[15] See John H Walsh, 'Institution-based Financial Regulation: A Third Paradigm' (2008) 49 Harvard International Law Journal 381.

[16] For this approach, see already Christine Parker, *The Open Corporation* (CUP 2002).

[17] Directive 2004/39/EC on markets in financial instruments, as regards the implementing powers conferred on the Commission [2008] OJ L76/33, art 13(2).

[18] Directive 2014/65/EU of the European Parliament and of the Council of 15 May 2014 on markets in financial instruments and amending Directive 2002/92/EC and Directive 2011/61/EU [2014] OJ L173/349 (hereafter 'MiFID II'), art 16(2).

[19] Commission Delegated Regulation (EU) 2017/565 of 25 April 2016 supplementing Directive 2014/65/EU of the European Parliament and of the Council as regards organisational requirements and operating conditions for investment firms and defined terms for the purposes of that Directive [2017] OJ L87/1 (hereafter 'Delegated MiFID II Regulation').

[20] ESMA Guidelines of 5 June 2020 on certain aspects of the MiFID II compliance function (hereafter 'ESMA 2020 Compliance Guidelines'). The Guidelines have been published first as annex V to the Final Report – Guidelines on certain aspects of the MiFID II compliance function requirements, 5 June 2020, ESMA35-36-1946 available at < https://www.esma.europa.eu/sites/default/files/library/esma35-36-1946_final_report_guidelines_on_certain_aspects_of_the_mifid_ii_compliance_function.pdf> accessed 11 August 2021.

obligations,[21] but only to highlight their key features. To do so, the chapter will summarise, in a succinct way, how EU law has envisaged the setting up of compliance strategies by investment firms, and the obligations those firms have to comply with as a result. It will be submitted, subsequently, that the framework put in place has been made to fit a principle- and rules-centred regulation framework. Notwithstanding its inherent values in integrating financial markets, this type of framework misses the mark on what are supposed to be the key objectives of compliance: to encourage certain outcomes in investment firms' processes, and to reward firms for having reached these outcomes. Having established a compliance culture, this could become an element that is embedded in the overall assessment of whether a sanction needs to be imposed on a firm in a particular context. So far, however, the MiFID II framework has not established such a link between compliance and sanctions.

The second section of the chapter, therefore, analyses whether respect for compliance obligations could be taken into account, as a matter of EU law, in potential sanctioning procedures. The example of EU competition law compliance shows that this is, indeed, a possibility, albeit one that is to be treated with caution. With this possibility in mind, the chapter questions whether the MiFID II framework imposes any clear legal limits on such linkage, before arguing that ESMA could play a more enhanced role, at this stage.

7.2 Compliance management in EU investment firm regulation

The first MiFID already contained provisions relating to compliance with its various obligations. Article 13(2) of that directive clearly stated that an investment firm was to establish adequate policies and procedures sufficient to ensure compliance of the firm, including its managers, employees, and tied agents, with its obligations under the provisions of the directive, as well as appropriate rules governing personal transactions by such persons. That principle was complemented by a series of general obligations that were rendered more specific in an implementing directive,[22] and in ESMA guidelines published in

[21] A useful overview is provided in Malte Wundenberg, 'Organisational Requirements for Investment Firms' in Rüdiger Veil (ed), *European Capital Markets Law* (2nd edn, Hart 2017) 621.

[22] Commission Directive 2006/73/EC of 10 August 2006 implementing Directive 2004/39/EC of the European Parliament and of the Council as regards organisational requirements and operating conditions for investment firms and defined terms for the purposes of that Directive [2006] OJ L241/26.

2012.[23] The same compliance obligations have been included and updated in MiFID II (see section 7.2.1 below) and have also given rise to more concrete obligations outlined in a delegated regulation. The provisions of this regulation have, in addition, been interpreted coherently by ESMA guidelines published on 5 June 2020 (see section 7.2.2). Three layers of hard and soft law norms, thus, shape a series of requirements that investment firms have to respect when setting up compliance mechanisms. Overall, those legal norms structuring and outlining the scope of MiFID II compliance obligations are faithful to the multi-layered principles-based, yet increasingly rules-centred, EU financial services regulatory framework of which they form part (see section 7.2.3).

7.2.1 Compliance as a distinctive feature in MiFID II

Just like its predecessor, MiFID II contains a provision imposing specific organisational compliance requirements on investment services providers, subject to its conduct of business rules, and other behavioural rules.[24] Faithful to the four-level regulatory structure, member states' home authorities are predominantly responsible for guaranteeing the correct implementation of those organisational requirements. Amongst those organisational requirements covered by Article 16 of MiFID II, setting up a compliance strategy also figures.

Generally speaking, that provision requires an investment firm to establish adequate policies and procedures sufficient to ensure compliance of the firm, including its managers, employees, and tied agents with its obligations under MiFID II, as well as appropriate rules governing personal transactions by such persons. In that regard, the investment firm shall maintain and operate effective organisational and administrative arrangements, with a view to taking all reasonable steps designed to prevent conflicts of interest from adversely affecting the interests of its clients. In the same way, the firm is to take reasonable steps to ensure continuity and regularity in the performance of its investment services and activities.[25] It is to have sound administrative and accounting procedures, internal control mechanisms, effective procedures for risk assessment, and effective control and safeguarding arrangements for information

[23] Guidelines on certain aspects of the MiFID compliance function requirements, 28 September 2012, ESMA/2012/388, available at <https://www.esma.europa.eu/sites/default/files/library/2015/11/2012-388_en.pdf> accessed 11 August 2021.

[24] These principles are also valid for credit institutions offering investment products, see art 1(3) and (4) of MiFID II; ESMA 2020 Compliance Guidelines, para 1.

[25] MiFID II, art 16(3).

processing systems.[26] To that end, the investment firm is also required to employ appropriate and proportionate systems, resources, and procedures.[27]

In addition, an investment firm may outsource some of its operational functions. However, such outsourcing may not be undertaken in such a way as to impair materially the quality of its internal control, or the ability of the supervisor to monitor the firm's compliance with all of its obligations.[28]

It is interesting to note that the obligation to set up a compliance strategy is somewhat hidden, among a wide variety of other organisational requirements. These requirements vary between keeping records of all conversations and transactions,[29] and algorithmic trading security measures.[30] Each of these other measures is characterised by the fact that it mandates certain procedures or tools to be in place within an investment firm. These procedures or tools directly serve as instruments that would enable national supervisory authorities to more easily hold those firms to account. This, in itself, is an interesting observation, as it gives some indications as to how legal accountability is conceived of in this particular context.[31] Such accountability is to be ensured externally by competent supervisory authorities, rather than internally by investment firms themselves. The increasingly detailed and varied organisational requirements imposed on these firms are means to allow supervisory authorities to better control and, if necessary, sanction the firms. The fact that compliance obligations feature among those more general organisational requirements indicates that compliance is becoming a central nexus of investment firms' accountability. Given its place among other organisational requirements, it could be inferred that the obligation to institutionalise compliance mechanisms would be considered indeed as a tool to make firms more accountable to external supervisory authorities. It could, thus, be argued that the organisational compliance requirements constitute, above all, a tool to facilitate external supervision, rather than a way to empower investment firms to set up internal accountability mechanisms that could either replace, or at least gain priority over, external accountability mechanisms spearheaded by the national supervisory authorities.

[26] ibid, art 16(5), second part.

[27] ibid, art 16(4).

[28] ibid, art 16(5), first part.

[29] ibid, art 16(6) and (7).

[30] ibid, art 17.

[31] For the concept of legal accountability, see section 1.7 of Chapter 1 by Carl Fredrik Bergström in this book.

7.2.2 Organizing firms' compliance: Delegated Regulation 2017/565 and ESMA guidelines

The organisational requirements regarding compliance outlined in MIFID II have been rendered more specific by means of delegated Regulation 2017/565. According to Article 22 of that regulation, Article 16(2) of MiFID II is to be understood as requiring investment firms to establish, implement, and maintain adequate policies and procedures designed to detect any risk of failure by the firm to comply with its obligations under that directive, as well as the associated risks, and put in place adequate measures and procedures designed to minimise such risks, and to enable the competent authorities to exercise their powers effectively.

To make this happen, the regulation imposes particular organisational requirements on the structuring of the compliance function. The firm has to maintain a permanent and effective compliance function that operates independently, and which is to:

(1) monitor on a permanent basis and assess, on a regular basis, the adequacy and effectiveness of the measures, policies and procedures put in place, and the actions taken to address any deficiencies in the firm's compliance with its obligations;
(2) advise and assist the relevant persons responsible for carrying out investment services and activities to comply with the firm's obligations under MiFID II;
(3) report to the management body, on at least an annual basis, on the implementation and effectiveness of the overall control environment for investment services and activities, on the risks that have been identified and on the complaints-handling reporting as well as remedies undertaken or to be undertaken;
(4) monitor the operations of the complaints-handling process and consider complaints as a source of relevant information in the context of its general monitoring responsibilities.[32]

To do so, a risk-based monitoring programme has to be set up. That programme serves to establish priorities determined by means of compliance risk assessment, ensuring that compliance risk is comprehensively monitored.[33]

[32] Delegated MiFID II Regulation, art 22(2).
[33] ibid.

To allow the compliance function to discharge its responsibilities properly and independently, investment firms shall ensure, additionally, that:

(1) the compliance function has the necessary authority, resources, expertise and access to all relevant information;
(2) a compliance officer is appointed and replaced by the management body and is responsible for the compliance function and for any reporting as to compliance required by MiFID II and its implementing instruments;
(3) the compliance function reports on an ad-hoc basis directly to the management body where it detects a significant risk of failure by the firm to comply with its obligations under MiFID II;
(4) the relevant persons involved in the compliance function are not involved in the performance of services or activities they monitor;
(5) the method of determining the remuneration of the relevant persons involved in the compliance function does not compromise their objectivity and is not likely to do so.[34]

The last two conditions do not have to be met where an investment firm is able to demonstrate that, in view of the nature, scale, and complexity of its business, and the nature and range of its investment services and activities, imposing these conditions would be disproportionate, and that its compliance function continues to be effective. If it can be established that this is the case, the investment firm shall assess and review regularly whether the effectiveness of its compliance function is compromised.[35]

On top of these requirements, investment firms shall, when allocating functions internally, ensure that senior management are responsible for ensuring that the firm complies with its obligations under MiFID II. In particular, senior management shall be required to assess and periodically review the effectiveness of the policies, arrangements, and procedures put in place to comply with the obligations under MiFID II, and to take appropriate measures to address any deficiencies.[36] A complaints-handling procedure is to be put in place as well, in order to ensure that clients or potential clients can flag compliance problems. Such problems need to be addressed as rapidly as possible.[37] Safeguards have to be put in place when operational functions or key services are outsourced to third parties.[38]

[34] ibid, art 22(3).
[35] ibid.
[36] ibid, art 25(1).
[37] ibid, art 26.
[38] ibid, art 30.

The regulatory obligations that are made explicit by the delegated regulation (setting up a risk monitoring programme, independence of the compliance function, procedures in place for outsourcing) have given rise to slightly different practices in different member states. This should not be surprising, as the legal status of a compliance function is not explicitly addressed by the delegated regulation. On the one hand, a compliance officer is an employee of the investment firm that she is charged with controlling, operating directly under the auspices of senior management. In doing so, the compliance officer plays a role that is complementary to, yet also distinct from, other controlling bodies such as (external) auditors and (senior) management itself.[39] On the other hand, the delegated regulation makes it clear that this officer is to act in the public interest, and in close relationship with the senior management that has appointed her.[40] As a result, the compliance officer is a private firm employee fulfilling some kind of public interest mandate, which is not as detached as that of an independent auditor, but which requires at least some limited independence.[41] It goes without saying that this public/private interaction results in different ways of organizing the legal status of a compliance officer. By way of example, the German supervisory authority has asked investment firms to inform them of the appointment and qualifications of compliance officers. France even asks for those officers to be registered with the competent authority.[42]

To ensure a sufficient amount of streamlining throughout the implementation of the compliance function, ESMA has adopted a series of guidelines. These guidelines do not take away all diversity, but seek to streamline the ways in which national supervisory authorities implement and enforce the compliance obligations in MiFID II. As per the 2020 guidelines, ESMA recognises the diversity of member states' engagement with the concurrent public mandate and private employee statuses of compliance officers. Although some diversity can be tolerated in this regard, the guidelines also make it clear that the functioning of compliance officers has to follow certain guidelines.[43] ESMA

[39] Compliance fits in the three lines of defence model, a conceptual framework aimed at assuring firms respect legal and regulatory obligations imposed on them. For background, see Richard Alleyne and Pete Maloney, 'Lawyers and Enterprise Risk Management: Balancing Business and Independence' (2015) 33 New York State Bar Association—Inside Newsletter 12.

[40] On the dual role of a compliance officer, see Chiu (n 13) 64–75.

[41] As compatible with the 'three lines of defence' model as presented by the Institute of Internal Auditors. See, for its 2013 position paper 'The Three Lines of Defence in Effective Risk Management and Control'<https://na.theiia.org/standards-guidance/Public%20Documents/PP%20The%20Three%20Lines%20of%20Defense%20in%20Effective%20Risk%20Management%20and%20Control.pdf> accessed 11 August 2021, 2.

[42] See Wundenberg (n 21) 599, 653.

[43] ESMA 2020 Compliance Guidelines, paras 5–6.

expounds on twelve key principles, which are also more or less explicitly present in the directive and delegated regulation:

(1) the compliance function shall establish a risk-based monitoring programme on the basis of this compliance risk assessment to determine its priorities and the focus of the monitoring, advisory and assistance activities;[44]
(2) The aim of the risk-based monitoring programme should be to evaluate whether the firm's business is conducted in compliance with its obligations under MiFID II as well as whether its internal policies and procedures, organisation and control measures remain effective and appropriate to ensure that compliance risk is comprehensively monitored;[45]
(3) The mandatory compliance reports should cover all business units involved in the provision of investment services, activities and ancillary services provided by a firm. Where the report does not cover all of these activities and services of the firm, it should clearly state the reasons;[46]
(4) Firms should ensure that the compliance function fulfils its advisory and assistance responsibilities, including providing support for staff and management training; providing day-to-day assistance for staff and management and participating in the establishment of policies and procedures within the firm (eg the firm's remuneration policy or the firm's product governance policies and procedures);[47]
(5) When ensuring that appropriate human and other resources are allocated to the compliance function, firms should take into account the scale and types of investment services, activities and ancillary services undertaken by the firm. The number of staff required for the tasks of the compliance function depends to a large extent on the nature of the investment services, activities and ancillary services and other services provided by the firm;[48]
(6) Firms' compliance staff shall have the necessary skills, knowledge and expertise to discharge their obligations. Furthermore, the compliance

[44] ibid, para 14.
[45] ibid, para 19.
[46] ibid, para 27.
[47] ibid, para 33.
[48] ibid, paras 43–44.

function shall have the necessary authority to fulfil its role. These requirements should in particular be taken into account by firms when appointing the compliance officer. Having regard to the function and tasks assigned to the compliance officer, he or she should demonstrate high professional ethical standards and personal integrity;[49]

(7) Firms should establish adequate arrangements for ensuring that the responsibilities of the compliance officer are fulfilled when the compliance officer is absent, and adequate arrangements to ensure that the responsibilities of the compliance function are performed on an ongoing basis. These arrangements should be in writing;[50]

(8) Firms should ensure that the compliance function holds a position in their organisational structure that ensures that the compliance officer and other compliance staff act independently when performing their tasks. While senior management is responsible for establishing an appropriate compliance organisation and for monitoring the effectiveness of the organisation that has been implemented, the tasks performed by the compliance function should be carried out independently from senior management and other units of the firm;[51]

(9) Firms should decide which measures, including organisational measures and the level of resources, are best suited to ensuring the effectiveness of the compliance function in the firm's particular circumstances;[52]

(10) A firm should favour an organisation where control functions are properly separated. The combination of the compliance function with other control functions may be acceptable if this does not compromise the effectiveness and independence of the compliance function. Any such combination should be documented, including the reasons for the combination so that competent authorities are able to assess whether the combination of functions is appropriate in the circumstances. However, where an internal audit function has been established and is maintained within the investment firm, such function may not be combined with other control functions such as the compliance function;[53]

[49] ibid, paras 49–50.
[50] ibid, para 55.
[51] ibid, paras 49–51: any deviation from the compliance officer's findings by the senior management needs to be mentioned explicitly in a report.
[52] ibid, para 62.
[53] ibid, para 69.

(11) Firms should ensure that all requirements applicable to the compliance function continue to be fulfilled where all or part of the compliance function is outsourced;[54]

(12) Competent authorities should review how firms plan to meet, implement and maintain the applicable compliance function requirements. This should apply in the context of the authorisation process, as well as, following a risk-based approach, in the course of on-going supervision.[55]

It is important to stress that the ESMA guidelines are not binding as such. As explained in the guidelines themselves, competent authorities to which these guidelines apply should comply by incorporating them into their national legal and/or supervisory frameworks as appropriate, including where particular guidelines are directed primarily at firms. In this case, competent authorities should ensure through their supervision that firms comply with the guidelines. The ESMA Founding Regulation does not force those authorities to comply; they can also explain and motivate their non-compliance with certain guidelines (comply or explain).[56] In case of non-compliance, competent authorities must also notify ESMA within two months of the date of publication of the guidelines on ESMA's website in all EU official languages of their reasons for non-complying with the guidelines.[57] Should they simply wish to comply with them, a notification of this fact or of their intention to comply with them shortly has to be made to ESMA.[58] The ESMA guidelines are formally only addressed to those national supervisory authorities. Firms are not required to notify any such non-compliance.[59]

7.2.3 A framework made to fit principles-based, rules-centred regulation

It follows from the cursory overview in the previous sections that the compliance function has not only been acknowledged explicitly by MiFID II, but that it has also been made subject to increasingly detailed requirements and

[54] ibid, para 75.
[55] ibid, para 86.
[56] ESMA Founding Regulation, art 16(3).
[57] ESMA 2020 Compliance Guidelines, para 10.
[58] ibid, para 9.
[59] ibid, para 12.

conditions, which impose certain outcomes on the ways in which investment firms have to be organised. It would, therefore, seem that the EU believes that the best way to achieve the set-up of a compliance function is to regulate its organisation in an increasingly detailed manner, implementing the general organisational requirements. However, and somewhat remarkably, those organisational requirements of the compliance function are laid out in accordance with the principles-based yet rules-centred, multi-layered regulation approach, just like any other investment service operation or transaction. As a result, the organisation of compliance management is, above all, conceived of as a regulatory obligation imposed externally on investment firms. Failure to comply with this obligation will result in sanctions being imposed, as if failure to put in place compliance measures is similar to the performance of transactions not executed in the best interests of clients.

It may be useful to clarify what we mean by principles-based, rule-centred regulation. Traditionally, principles- and rules-based approaches have been seen as opposites, in financial services regulation. Principles-based regulation can be defined as a regulatory mechanism in which the government defines desired outcomes for regulated entities and then provides guidance on how these entities can meet those goals.[60] Those principles incorporate particular outcomes for firms to achieve: rather than imposing rules or processes on them, they have to design their own processes so that they can abide by the principles formulated by the regulator.[61] This type of regulation presupposes a significant amount of mutual trust between regulator and regulated firm, and requires a willingness at firm level to do more than the mere minimum to comply with what the regulator wants.[62] In practice, this kind of regulation, although in vogue in the early 2000s, has been discredited, as a result of the 2008 financial crisis.[63] By contrast, rules-based regulation refers to a framework in which the government establishes binding rules that regulated firms must obey, and then uses the power of the State to enforce those rules.[64] Such a framework requires particularly detailed rules, and an important sanctioning apparatus to hold firms to account.[65] Rules-based regulation has been criticised for imposing rules that are too detailed and too easy to circumvent, and for creating

[60] Walsh (n 15) 384.

[61] Julia Black, 'Forms and Paradoxes of Principles-based Regulation' (2008) 3 Capital Markets Law Journal 428.

[62] Marianne Ojo, 'Building on the Trust of Management: Overcoming the Paradoxes of Principles-based Regulation' (2011) 30 Banking and Financial Services Policy Report 1, 1.

[63] See Cristie Ford, 'Principles-based Securities Regulation in the Wake of the Global Financial Crisis' (2010) 55 McGill Law Journal 258.

[64] Walsh (n 15) 386.

[65] Black (n 61) 440.

a culture of law and order, discouraging any mutual trust between regulator and regulatees.[66] It is submitted that neither of those two extremes has been chosen as the preferred or only regulatory approach at EU level. The four-level regulatory structure proposed in the wake of the Lamfalussy Report has mixed and matched elements of both approaches. At level one, general principles are meant to guide financial firms, but those principles are complemented by very detailed rules at level two, and increasing supervisory guidance at level three. At level four, respect for both rules and principles is ensured. Ultimately, rules derived from principles are the backbone of the EU financial services regulatory framework. From that perspective, we consider the EU framework to be principles-based, yet rules-centred.

Within MiFID, compliance requirements have also been regulated in accordance with this principles-based but, above all, rules-centred EU regulatory approach. Since the introduction of the Lamfalussy four-level regulatory strategy, EU financial regulation has relied on a mix of principles and detailed rules to establish, maintain, and reinforce its Single Rulebook project. At level one, basic financial regulation principles have been developed and imposed, as a matter of EU law. Absent any other implementing measures, it would seem that financial firms would benefit from a wide discretion to implement and comply with those principles. However, the focus on principles at level one has not been on designing principles that would have to be implemented by firms. The idea behind this first level was, rather, to facilitate the adoption of legislative instruments at the EU level. It is, indeed, unsurprising that vague general principles are likely to trigger fewer discussions between the representatives of different member states, which only have to agree on general principles that can be interpreted flexibly.[67] The idea behind the use of principles has, rather, been to delegate the power to develop more detailed rules to the European Commission, supported by the ESAs, in which the national supervisory authorities are all represented.[68] At that level, more detailed rules have been adopted. The third and fourth levels are meant to allow for swifter and more coordinated enforcement of those rules. Enforcement, as envisaged by the Lamfalussy and de Larosière reports, has mainly centred on classical 'command and control' enforcement. The detailed rules adopted at EU level have to

[66] Ojo (n 62) 6.

[67] A similar idea underlies the emergence of principle-based financial regulation, where firms would only have to comply with certain of those principles. On that type of regulation, see Black (n 61); Ojo (n 62).

[68] On that delegation issue, Yannis Avgerinos, 'Essential and Non-essential Measures: Delegation of Powers in EU Securities Regulation' (2002) 8 European Law Journal 269.

be respected. Lack of respect for those rules implies that sanctions can be imposed. To facilitate convergence among different national supervisory authorities, level three envisages the adoption of yet another layer of principles that explain how detailed rules are to be interpreted and applied.

In the end, two sets of principles, general level one principles and level three common supervision and enforcement principles, accompany the adoption and interpretation of detailed rules imposed on financial market operators. The compliance organisational requirements summarised in the previous sections fully reflect this approach. MiFID II postulates the establishment of a compliance function, the details of which can be found in the delegated Regulation 2017/565. ESMA has adopted guidelines in an attempt to increase convergence in the ways in which those detailed rules are interpreted and enforced by national supervisory authorities.

An important gap that comes to light against that background is the lack of a clear linkage between respect for compliance requirements and the imposition of fines or other sanctions by national supervisory authorities. Directive 2014/65 only confirms that failure to comply with the compliance organisational requirements constitutes an infringement of MiFID II that results in the imposition of a criminal law or administrative law sanction by a national authority.[69] However, MiFID II remains silent as to whether having a dedicated compliance framework in place could be a mitigating circumstance that could have an impact on the type of sanction or the amount of the fine imposed. The fact that not having such a framework constitutes an infringement of the MiFID II obligations does not mean that having a well-functioning compliance framework in place will automatically be looked upon in a favourable way. Although it has not been explicitly ruled out that member states retain some possibility of treating the presence of a compliance framework as a mitigating factor, EU law does not require them to take that position. The ESMA guidelines interpret and render more specific the compliance organisational requirements, but do not, as such, link respect for them to the sanctioning framework that also underlies MiFID II. The word 'sanction' is not mentioned even once in these guidelines. As a result, it would seem that having a compliance framework in place and truly internalised in an investment firm's corporate culture does not count in holding the firm concerned to account, at least not from the EU's regulatory perspective. The legal accountability framework put in place by MiFID II, above all, remains focused on a 'command and control' style of enforcement

[69] MiFID II, art 70(1) read in conjunction with 70(3)(a)(iv).

by public enforcement authorities, and appears to leave little room for other types of coordinated regulatory enforcement overseen or stimulated by ESMA.

7.3 Towards a more coherent legal accountability framework?

The previous section outlined that the principles-based, rules-centred approach to MiFID II compliance has been drafted in such a way that the objective to instil an internalised compliance culture in investment firms has not been made as explicit as it could have been. The compliance organisational requirements covered by MiFID II foresee no possibility of rewarding such internalised compliance-oriented behaviour; neither do the ESMA guidelines make any link whatsoever with the sanctioning apparatus at the disposal of member states' supervisory authorities, and to the relationship between respect for compliance and the consequences this may have for the imposition of sanctions.

It is submitted that the absence of such an explicit link may have severe repercussions on the development of a coherent legal accountability framework in the context of investment services regulation. To the extent that the main purpose of the EU Single Rulebook is to ensure that investment firms are subject to a set of rules protective of investors and financial consumers,[70] it would be useful not only for firms to be penalised for having failed to put in place a compliance framework, but also for them to be rewarded for having taken sufficient or noteworthy steps in the right direction. In that context, having made an effort to internalise those values by means of a compliance framework could be seen as such a step. When a firm needs to be held to account as a matter of law, all initiatives taken, or lack thereof, should be taken into account, at least if a relationship of mutual trust between a firm and a regulator is to be created. The fact that MiFID II demands the implementation of compliance obligations seems to reinforce that conclusion. When a firm makes genuine efforts to do so, and to show supervisory authorities that it can be trusted, it would seem inappropriate not to take that effort into account throughout the sanctioning process.

To do so, establishing a more explicit link between the presence of a compliance culture and the extent to which sanctioning mechanisms are applied would seem most welcome. In practice, however, linking compliance and

[70] This objective is reiterated in recital 3 of MiFID II.

sanctioning mechanisms is not self-evident. Existing political science and economics literature links compliance, above all, to the presence of sanctions, rather than focusing on the positive effects compliance may have on avoiding or limiting such sanctions.[71] In the same way, the (theoretical) legal literature remains largely silent on those questions. In the context of EU competition law compliance, moderate steps have recently been taken in that direction (see section 7.3.1 below). In light of this experience, this chapter argues that it is possible, as a matter of EU law, to move forward in that direction without significant legal problems (section 7.3.2). ESMA holds the key to developing a more explicit policy in that regard, and could implement a more coherent follow-up strategy to streamline and further refine a legal accountability framework in this context (section 7.3.3).

7.3.1 Linking compliance to sanctions: The example of competition law

The increasing importance of, and attention to, compliance by firms is not limited to EU financial services regulation. The same issues have also arisen recently in the field of competition law. Whereas EU competition law and financial services regulation have different objectives, one cannot deny at least some similarities in their regulatory set-up. To some extent, the regulatory set-up of competition law resembles the four-level structure of EU financial services law. The Treaty on the Functioning of the European Union contains the key provisions that outline the principles on which competition law has been based: anti-competitive agreements and abuses of a dominant economic position are prohibited, unless they can be justified by overriding (economic) reasons.[72] These general provisions, comparable to level 1 financial services legislation, have been interpreted and specified by the European Commission by means of regulations[73], directives,[74] and soft law

[71] See, eg Michelle Welsh, 'Continuous Disclosure: Testing the Correspondence between State Enforcement and Compliance' (2009) 23 Australian Journal of Corporate Law 206.

[72] Arts 101 and 102 TFEU. For an overview of these provisions, see Alison Jones, Brenda Sufrin, and Niamh Dunne, *Jones & Sufrin's EU Competition Law* (7th edn, OUP 2019).

[73] See, eg Commission Regulation 330/2010 of 20 April 2010 on the application of Article 101(3) of the Treaty on the Functioning of the European Union to categories of vertical agreements and concerted practices [2010] OJ L102/1 and Commission Regulation (EU) No 461/2010 of 27 May 2010 on the application of Article 101(3) of the Treaty on the Functioning of the European Union to categories of vertical agreements and concerted practices in the motor vehicle sector [2010] OJ L129/52.

[74] See, eg Directive 2014/104/EU of the European Parliament and of the Council of 26 November 2014 on certain rules governing actions for damages under national law for infringements of the competition law provisions of the Member States and of the European Union [2014] OJ L349/1.

instruments.[75] Those instruments outline, in more detail, the practices that are prohibited, and could be said to resemble, in some ways, the level two provisions in financial services law. The enforcement of those provisions is the responsibility of the European Commission and of national competition authorities, which united in a European Competition Network (ECN). The purpose of that network is to ensure coherent enforcement.[76] It is no surprise, therefore, that the ECN issues supervisory and enforcement convergence guidelines as well, resembling level three practices.[77] In practice, however, national competition authorities also have to apply EU competition law, and the majority of infringement decisions are taken at member state level, as is the case with level four in financial services regulation.

The accountability framework put into action by EU competition law additionally also relies on 'command and control' enforcement of the EU competition law provisions. The European Commission and the national competition authorities can impose administrative fines (and criminal sanctions at national level) for any infringement. It has only been over the past two decades that increased attention to alternative ways of holding businesses to account has emerged. Attention has been paid to private damages actions,[78] settlements and commitments,[79] and to businesses having in place compliance programmes.[80] Despite this attention to compliance, the European Commission has not established a clear link between having in place compliance structures and the impact that this may have on the scope and extent of sanctions imposed on a business in the event of a violation of EU competition law.[81]

At first sight, the absence of a link between compliance organisation and sanctioning mechanisms is, therefore, not limited to the field of investment services regulation. Having in place compliance programmes has, above all, been considered necessary in order to educate employees about the need to

[75] See, eg Commission Notice—Guidelines on the effect on trade concept contained in Articles 81 and 82 of the Treaty [2004] OJ C101/81.

[76] Kris Dekeyser and Maria Jaspers, 'A New Era of ECN Cooperation—Achievements and Challenges with a Special Focus on Work in the Leniency Field' (2007) 30 World Competition 3.

[77] For information on the network, see <https://ec.europa.eu/competition/ecn/index_en.html> accessed 11 August 2021.

[78] For background, Ioannis Lianos, Peter Davis, and Paolisa Nebbia, *Damages Claims for the Infringement of EU Competition Law* (OUP 2015).

[79] Wouter Wils, 'Settlements of EU Antitrust Investigations: Commitment Decisions under Article 9 of Regulation No 1/2003' (2006) 29 World Competition 345.

[80] As highlighted by the European Commission: see <https://ec.europa.eu/competition/antitrust/compliance/index_en.html> accessed 11 August 2021. On compliance, see also Wouter Wils, 'Antitrust Compliance Programmes and Optimal Antitrust Enforcement' (2013) 1 Journal of Antitrust Enforcement 52.

[81] See also Ghezzi (n 14) 22.

respect EU competition law.[82] As an educational tool, having compliance programmes in place has not been envisaged as impacting on the amount of the fines being imposed.[83]

The European Commission has, indeed, promoted having a compliance programme in place, yet has explicitly stated that having such a programme will not have an impact on the ways in which fines will be calculated. At EU level, detailed guidelines have been published on how fines are to be calculated.[84] Those guidelines clearly confirm that deterrence is considered the best way to hold businesses to account.[85] Although mitigating circumstances may result in a decreased fine, the European Commission does not take compliance programmes into account in that regard.[86] There has, more generally, been a clear distaste at Commission level for rewarding businesses simply for having a compliance framework in place.[87] It is believed that doing so would diminish the deterrence that the competition law sanctioning apparatus wants to instil.

However, the European Commission's tough stance on deterrence has not been followed everywhere at member state level. As with financial services regulation, member states retain some liberty to decide how to organise their competition law enforcement frameworks. As a result, they remain free to take the presence of compliance guarantees into account when determining the amount of fines to be imposed. The most notable example in this regard is Italy. The Italian competition authority adopted compliance programme guidelines in 2018.[88] In accordance with those guidelines, the presence of a compliance programme may result in a reduction of the fine of up to 15 per cent.[89] The Italian authorities, governing a market structure consisting of many small enterprises, decided, in an attempt to stimulate more awareness of EU competition law, that having a compliance programme in place ought to be rewarded.[90]

[82] See also Anne Riley and Daniël Sokol, 'Rethinking Compliance' (2015) 3 Journal of Antitrust Enforcement 31.

[83] See also, for that position, the following paper by the US Department of Justice, 'Compliance is a Culture, not just a Policy' <https://www.justice.gov/atr/file/517796/download> accessed 11 August 2021.

[84] See Commission, Guidelines on the method of setting fines imposed pursuant to Article 23(2)(a) of Regulation No 1/2003 [2006] OJ C210/2.

[85] ibid, para 4.

[86] See Commission, 'Compliance Matters' 21, available at <https://op.europa.eu/en/publication-detail/-/publication/78f46c48-e03e-4c36-bbbe-aa08c2514d7a/language-en> accessed 11 August 2021.

[87] Ghezzi (n 14) 22 refers to Commissioners' speeches going in that direction. Wouter Wils, a Commission official writing in his personal capacity, also seems to hint at that position: see Wils (n 80) 81.

[88] The Italian guidelines are available at <https://www.agcm.it/media/comunicati-stampa/2018/10/Linee-guida-compliance-Antitrust> accessed 11 August 2021.

[89] See also Ghezzi (n 14) 19.

[90] ibid 34.

Italy felt that its particular market structure and the businesses active therein could benefit from such a strategy.

Two relevant observations can be drawn from this succinct overview. First, the example of EU competition law confirms that establishing a link between the presence of compliance structures and the level of sanctions is not necessarily self-evident. When the aim of an enforcement framework is to guarantee deterrence, rewarding compliance is difficult. The Italian example nevertheless shows that the link between both programmes can be made, if it turns out to be useful in establishing a workable accountability relationship between regulator and regulatees. Second, the fact that EU competition law and its enforcement framework are more mature, having been around much longer than EU financial services regulation in its current format, highlights that it might to be too early, at this stage, to link compliance and sanctions in investment services regulation. However, an important difference is in place between the two fields of EU law. In EU competition law, compliance has never been prescribed as a matter of hard law. It has only been mentioned in non-binding documents. In the context of investment services protection, MiFID II itself prescribes the need for compliance structures to be in place. Prescribing such compliance as a legal requirement would seem to attach more importance to it. From that point of view, it would only be a little step to also reward investment firms respecting those hard law compliance obligations.

Despite the relative ease with which a legal change could be made in that respect, introducing such a reward system is not something the EU has much experience with. Moreover, the effects of introducing such a system have not been studied in depth. By contrast, political science and economics literature emphasises either the need for deterrent sanctions as a tool to enhance compliance,[91] or the ways in which compliance can best be ensured by focusing on factors other than pure sanctioning.[92] Studies on the specific potential for rewarding compliance with fewer or no sanctions have received little or no attention. It would therefore seem useful, first, to empirically test to what extent linking respect for compliance with decreased sanctions could be feasible, from a political or behavioural point of view. This dimension is unfortunately missing from the debate so far.

[91] See, eg Rob Nelissen and Laetitia Mulder, 'What Makes a Sanction "Stick"? The Effects of Financial and Social Sanctions on Norm Compliance' (2013) 8 Social Influence 70; John Armour, Colin Mayer, and Andrea Polo, 'Regulatory Sanctions and Reputational Damages in Financial Markets' (2017) 52 Journal of Financial and Quantitative Analysis 1429.

[92] See John Worrall and others, 'The Moderating Effects of Informal Social Control in the Sanctions–Compliance Nexus' (2014) 39 American Journal of Criminal Justice 341.

7.3.2 EU law limits on a more coordinated legal accountability approach

The previous section showed that the idea of linking the presence of compliance guarantees with sanctioning decisions has not been developed much in European Union law, or in political science and economics studies devoted to compliance. This apparent lack of interest does not mean, however, that such a linkage would be illegal. The Italian example shows that EU law seemingly tolerates a closer embedding of respect for compliance decisions within sanctioning procedures. Against that background, this section enquires whether, in the context of MiFID II, any such obstacles exist. The first part of this chapter has already highlighted that neither MiFID II nor its implementing measures would seem to impede the coupling of respect for compliance with lower fines or other sanctions. This section analyses whether the overall set-up of the particular enforcement mechanism centred on ESMA would impose additional legal obstacles, as a matter of EU law.

Under current EU law, no formal legal obstacles exist. Despite the setting up of the four-level regulatory framework, EU law has intervened only moderately in the ways in which national supervisory authorities have to be organised, and have to set their enforcement priorities.[93] As a result, those authorities retain a significant amount of discretion to determine how they organise their sanctioning procedures, whether they envisage the establishment of a mutual trust or a command and control relationship with their regulatees, and whether or not they take into account certain mitigating circumstances when adopting sanctioning decisions. So far, EU law has not interfered with these powers, as long as EU regulatory provisions are enforced effectively, and in compliance with the general objectives that have been set.

The liberty accorded to member states does not automatically exclude any potential coordination or convergence within the framework of ESMA. It is well known that, according to Article 16(1) of the ESMA Founding Regulation, and with a view to establishing consistent, efficient, and effective supervisory practices, and to ensuring the common, uniform, and consistent application of Union law, ESMA may 'issue guidelines addressed to all competent authorities or all financial market participants and issue recommendations to one or more competent authorities or to one or more financial market participants'.[94]

[93] See on the types of interventions made, Pieter van Cleynenbreugel, *Market Supervision in the European Union—Integrated Administration in Constitutional Context* (Nijhoff 2014).

[94] ESMA Founding Regulation, art 16(1).

Making use of this power, ESMA could recommend the linking of compliance respect to sanctioning decisions, or could, conversely, recommend that a national supervisory authority should no longer maintain such a framework. ESMA opinions and recommendations are not binding, yet they allow the majority of national supervisory authorities to take and publish common positions in relation to a particular issues. ESMA, thus, seems to hold the keys to taking a position on the question of linking compliance and sanctioning accountability mechanisms. Absent any clarification at this level, member states remain free to implement such measures. When a common position is adopted, a member state is still not obliged to follow it. However, at that point, it will have to explain why it is not following the ESMA recommendation or opinion at hand.[95] Absent EU legislative provisions imposing a certain framework in this respect, ESMA can, thus, play an important steering role in either tolerating or prohibiting the linkage of compliance and sanctioning frameworks in the design of an overall legal accountability regime for investment firms.

7.3.3 A future role for ESMA?

It follows from the foregoing that ESMA, in practice, holds the keys to formulating a clearer position on the question of designing a more coherent accountability framework, linking compliance and sanctioning approaches more explicitly. Against this background, the question arises of how ESMA could go about promoting, discouraging, or developing such links, should it no longer wish to maintain the status quo. Two alternative policy strategies can be envisaged in that respect: 'wait and see' and 'coordinated experimentalism'.

First, a 'wait and see' approach could be taken. This strategy resembles the situation as it is, but would call for an explicit communication by ESMA to allow national supervisory authorities to address the question of linking respect for compliance with setting up an effective sanctioning mechanism, and to report to ESMA how they see that relationship, in the context of the regulatees they oversee and the markets they supervise. As with the case of the Italian competition authority, some supervisory authorities might be likely to reward respect for compliance provisions, whereas others would resist this idea. On the basis of the outcomes of the different positions taken by the different national supervisory authorities, ESMA could take a more informed position, either leaving diversity to persist in this regard, or nudging national authorities into a more

[95] ESMA Founding Regulation, art 16(3).

convergent legal accountability framework. In the longer run, the search for a more convergent solution might even result in a draft technical standard modifying one of the level two instruments, to that extent.

Second, a more 'coordinated experimentalism' approach could also be envisaged. Rather than leaving it up to national supervisory authorities, ESMA could take a common position at the outset, either in favour of, or against, linking compliance to the organisation of sanctions. The common position could take the format of an opinion or recommendation, in accordance with Article 16 of the ESMA Founding Regulation. On the basis of this common position, the different national supervisory authorities would then be invited to see whether they could, in their day-to-day supervisory practice, agree with the position taken. This 'coordinated experimentalism' approach would require dissenting national authorities to explain why they did not accept the common position. The dialogues between member state and EU-level actors that emerged as a result of this coordinated experimentalism could then lead ESMA to take a better-informed, firmer position on this debate, modifying its recommendations, or suggesting a modification of level two rules, in the wake of the outcomes of the coordinated experimentalism approach.

It is clear from the foregoing that, in any of those instances, ESMA could engage in a more thorough reflection on how compliance obligations fit the overall framework of legal accountability and sanctions enacted by the EU legislator. It is submitted that, where national supervisory authorities succeed in finding common ground, level two or level one rules could be modified in order to better reflect the potential link that might exist between respect for compliance obligations and the level of sanctions imposed. ESMA clearly holds the key to opening and furthering that debate, at this stage, and it can be hoped it might be willing to take on that challenge.

7.4 Conclusion

This chapter has revisited the status of compliance organisational requirements as a tool for legal accountability in EU financial services regulation. Zooming in on such requirements, in the context of MiFID II, the chapter found that the compliance organisational requirements, in that context, have, above all, been made to fit the principles-based, rules-centred framework of EU investment services law. As a result, compliance obligations are merely seen as external obligations imposed by public authorities. Failure to meet these obligations may result in administrative or criminal sanctions being imposed. As a consequence, very little attention is being paid to how having a well-functioning compliance framework in place could be a sign of a firm having internalised a culture of respect for the Single Rulebook. A side effect of that lack of attention is the absence of any link between the compliance obligations and their impact on the way in which sanctions are to be imposed.

The chapter subsequently showed that, as a matter of law, such a link could be made without clear obstacles. In practice, and as a matter of policy, linking compliance to sanctions is not self-evident, as the example of EU competition law compliance demonstrates. It was submitted that those obstacles should not limit ESMA from at least considering linking compliance and sanctioning tools more explicitly. At the same time, however, setting up such a linked and more coherent legal accountability framework would require a more elaborate conceptualisation of, and reflection as to how, accountability can best be ensured within the framework of EU financial services regulation as a whole. Although such reflections go beyond the mandate of ESMA, nothing impedes bottom-up reflections as to the outlook of the legal accountability framework underlying EU investment services law from taking place there. The chapter identified and distinguished between two policy approaches ESMA could take to move that debate forward. It remains to be seen, with the maturing of enforcement experiences within the EU investment regulation framework, whether the coherence of the current legal accountability regime will, indeed, receive more attention.

8

Supervisory Arbitrage

The Case of Sweden

Malou Larsson Klevhill and Annina H. Persson

8.1 Introduction

The EU Commission has, during the last ten years, worked on the basis of imposing administrative sanctions on both legal and physical persons, instead of penalty-based sanctions in criminal law. The intention has been to apply efficient and transparent sanctions on delinquent behaviour, and to prevent serious violations that could have an impact on the stability of the financial system. The rules in MiFID II[1] on the supervisory powers of the competent authority are, in principle, unchanged from those in the original MiFID.[2] However, the rules have changed significantly regarding sanctions (see Articles 70 and 72 of MiFID II). Administrative sanctions may be imposed, not only on a legal person that fails to fulfil its obligations, but also on members of the governing body of the legal person, and on all other persons who were responsible for such violation, under national law. Member states must ensure that the competent authorities have at their disposal a set of certain types of sanctions and measures, and that there are certain minimum levels of fines for infringements of several specified rules.[3] An important purpose of MiFID II and MiFIR[4] is to achieve harmonised and effective rules.[5] A prerequisite for the desired harmonisation is that the member states' national regulations do

[1] Directive 2014/65/EU of the European Parliament and of the Council of 15 May 2014 on markets in financial instruments and amending Directive 2002/92/EC and Directive 2011/61/EU (hereafter 'MiFID II').

[2] Directive 2004/39/EC of the European Parliament and of the Council of 21 April 2004 on markets in financial instruments amending Council Directives 85/611/EEC and 93/6/EEC and Directive 2000/12/EC of the European Parliament and of the Council and repealing Council Directive 93/22/EEC.

[3] Governmental Proposal to the Parliament, 'Proposition 2016/17:162 Nya regler för marknader för finansiella instrument (MiFID II och MiFIR)' (hereinafter 'prop 2016/17:162') 235.

[4] Regulation (EU) No 600/2014 of the European Parliament and of the Council of 15 May 2014 on markets in financial instruments and amending Regulation (EU) No 648/2012 Text with EEA relevance (hereafter 'MiFIR').

[5] MiFID II, preamble, paras 3 and 7; MIFIR preamble, paras 2, 3, and 5.

Malou Larsson Klevhill and Annina H. Persson, *Supervisory Arbitrage* In: *Legal Accountability in EU Markets for Financial Instruments*. Edited by: Carl Fredrik Bergström and Magnus Strand, Oxford University Press. © Malou Larsson Klevhill and Annina H. Persson 2021. DOI: 10.1093/oso/9780192849281.003.0008

not set additional rules or requirements other than those that follow from the common regulatory framework.

However, the successful introduction of the new financial market governance system depends not only on the faithful incorporation of the new rules, but also on effective supervision, and compliance with these rules. Importance must also be attached to application of the rules in an equal or similar way.

A basic goal of the model of regulation contained in MiFID II—the so-called Lamfalussy model[6]—is, among other things, to improve supervisory coordination and cooperation. The model divides the regulation and follow-up activities into four levels.

The first level consists of frameworks adopted under the normal regime of EU law: directives and regulations proposed by the EU Commission and adopted by the European Parliament and the Council. On the security market, the first level corresponds to MiFID II and MiFIR. MiFID has been implemented in Swedish law, primarily by the Securities Market Act (2007:528), VPM. MiFIR, which is a regulation, is directly applicable in Swedish law.

At the second level, the Commission adopts implementation measures that specify the details of the legislation on the first level. Implementing measures can be adopted in the form of both directives and regulations. The implementation directives have been introduced into Swedish law through regulations of the Financial Supervisory Authority (FSA).[7]

The third level consists of common guidelines and recommendations. On the securities market, these are issued by the European Securities and Markets Authority (ESMA). The Authority works, among other things, on designing the supervision of investment firms and markets in operation in several countries, and promoting equal application of EU rules by supervisory authorities in different countries. These guidelines are to be equated with what in Sweden are called general advices (*allmänna råd*).

Finally, at the fourth level, the Commission is responsible for ensuring that member states implement EU law in a similar way. The EU Commission, thus, supervises the member states that the implementation is correct.

In Swedish law, both MiFID II and MiFIR have led to changes in domestic legislation. To the extent that new rules were not fully in harmony with, for

[6] See Regulatory process in financial services. Https://ec.europa.eu/info/business-economy-euro/banking-and-finance/regulatory-process-financial-services/regulatory-process-financial-services_en, visited 2021-08-09.

[7] The Financial Supervisory Authority's rules (FFFS (2017:2) regarding securities businesses (Finansinspektionens föreskrifter (FFFS 2017:2) om värdepappersrörelse).

example, MiFID II, changes were made in laws, ordinances, and government regulations, ie at the first and second levels.

At level three, there may be room for improvement in Swedish law due to the following issues. If an investment firm breaches the obligations arising from law, ie the VPM, the FSA has both the obligation and the opportunity to intervene against the firm with various measures and sanctions. The legislation gives the FSA access to a whole catalogue of measures from which the supervisory authority can choose, at its discretion, the kind of intervention that appears to be the most appropriate in a particular case.

The measures and sanctions that are available are listed in Chapter 25 VPM.[8] The rule in Chapter 25, section 1(2) VPM stipulates that FSA, if VPM or another relevant law is violated, intervene by issuing an injunction to limit or reduce the risks in the business in some way, limit or completely omit dividends or interest payments, or take any other action to remedy the situation. Intervention can also be in the form of the FSA announcing a ban on execute decisions or by making a remark. Finally, the FSA can also intervene by issuing an injunction if it is probable that, within twelve months, a securities institution will no longer fulfil its obligations according to VPM or other regulations governing the company's operations (Chapter 25, section 1(3)). However, if the firm's infringement is serious, FSA can revoke the firm's authorisation or, if it considers this sufficient, issue a warning. In addition, if an investment firm has received a complaint or warning, the FSA may decide that the firm must pay a fine (Chapter 25, section 8 VPM).

The legislator's purpose, in the regulations, is to give the FSA access to several different types of penalties from which the FSA can, in each case, choose which to apply, in the event of a violation of the rules applicable to the firm in question.[9] In choosing the measure to be applied, the FSA must consider how serious the infringement is, based on the consequences it has had, or could have, for the functioning of the securities market in general, and for individual investors.[10]

However, although FSA has these powers, and the MiFID regime presupposes their application, it is not mandatory to use them. Instead of fully using the MiFID sanctions regime, the FSA has developed a communicative

[8] Compare MiFID II. In prop 2016/17:162, 525 it is stated that it cannot be required for the proper implementation of the directive that the various infringements are listed in the same way as in the directive. Thus, a general provision instead specifies when an intervention may be made.

[9] See Governmental Proposal to the Parliament, 'Proposition 2013/14:228 Förstärkta kapitaltäckningsregler' (hereafter 'prop 2013/14:228'), 232.

[10] See ibid, 238, and Governmental Proposal to the Parliament, 'Proposition 2014/15:57 Nya administrativa sanktioner på finansmarknadsområdet' (hereafter 'prop 2014/15:57'), 33.

dialogue with market actors, ending with a 'Final Letter' containing recommendations for the future, rather than a formal decision applying penalties for wrongful actions. This behaviour can result in what may be called 'supervisory arbitrage', which (as opposed to regulatory arbitrage) does not refer to the design of the rules, but to the relative rigour or leniency of supervisory practices. Supervisory arbitrage can, however, result in inconsistency, from a supervisory perspective.

However, the whole purpose of MiFID II and MiFIR was to increase transparency, improve investor protection, and strengthen confidence in the European securities market. The intention was to apply efficient and transparent sanctions on unacceptable behaviour, and to prevent serious violations that could have an impact on the stability of the financial system.

The FSA is also obliged, according to the Swedish Public Administrative Act[11] to treat individuals fairly and democratically when exercising its authority, and to demand responsibility in a predictable manner. If different investment firms are sanctioned in different ways for the same behaviour, this may pose a problem for the coordination of the governance of the financial markets, and for maintaining a level playing field for investment firms operating on the European securities markets.

This chapter addresses the application of the administrative sanctions in the MiFID regime by the FSA, but, firstly, describes some of the mentioned penalties, and provide examples of how they are used in practice in Sweden.

8.2 Regular practice: Intervention against investment firms

8.2.1 When should an intervention take place?

Chapter 25, section 1(1) VPM stipulates that the FSA shall intervene where a Swedish investment firm has violated its obligations under the VPM, another statutory instrument governing the company's operations, the company's articles of association, statutes or regulations, or internal instructions that are based on legislation which governs the company's operations.[12] The FSA will also intervene against such a company in certain special cases (Chapter 25, Sections 3–5) (see below). The rules in Chapter 25, sections 1a and 1b, state

[11] Förvaltningslag (2017:900).

[12] FSA may intervene against a foreign investment company. See, further, section 8.2.2 below. See prop 2016/17:162 p. 524.

that the FSA shall intervene against a natural person who is a member of an investment company's board of directors, or its managing director, or a replacement for any such person, where the firm has committed a violation.

The list of violations that can lead to FSA intervening against the firm includes, for example, the acquisition of an authorisation permit due to false information, breach of notification obligations in respect of qualified holdings, or breached investor protection rules.[13] However, intervention against a natural person may be made only if the firm's violation is serious, and the person in question, intentionally or through gross negligence, caused the violation (Chapter 25, section 1c). The legislative text does not specify any criteria for when the violation is so serious that an intervention is justified.[14] However, guidance can be found in the FSA's practice.

In a case from 2018, the FSA decided to give a company, Solidar Fonder AB, a warning and a penalty fee because it had insufficient procedures in place for dealing with conflicts of interest. The company also had deficiencies in its procedures aimed at ensuring that the company acted exclusively in the mutual interest of the unitholders, and that it achieved the requirements for the best possible result when placing orders. The company also had inadequate routines and controls when it came to risk assessment and risk management of the funds.[15] The FSA argued that the rules on conflicts of interest, conduct, the best possible results, and risk management were among the most central rules that a company such as Solidar Fonder was obliged to follow. The infringements committed by the company were so serious that there was reason to consider a revocation of its authorisation. In light of the measures taken by the company to ensure that the infringements were not repeated, the FSA considered it sufficient that the company was given a warning and a fine of SEK 10 million.

The activities of FSA are aimed, inter alia, at preventing an investment firms from engaging in risk-taking that may threaten the stability of the financial system. As a result, the FSA has the opportunity to review the firm's activities. For example, the FSA has the right to request documents and information concerning the business (Chapter 23, sections 2–3 and 15). The FSA may also conduct an inspection at the investment firm under scrutiny (Chapter 23, section 4). If an investment firm does not provide prescribed information on its activities on time, a delay fine of up to SEK 100,000 can be imposed (Chapter 25, section 11). The FSA itself determines how high this fine should be.

[13] See prop 2014/15:57 p. 41.
[14] ibid.
[15] See the decision from FSA, *Solidar Fonder AB* FI Dnr 16-3001, 17 April 2018.

In determining the size of the fine, the size of the investment firm must be taken into account. However, in some cases the FSA refrain from imposing the fine or sets it at a lower amount. Of course, a longer delay is more serious than a shorter one, but smaller delays repeated on several occasions may be considered serious. In repeated cases of delayed or failed reporting, it may be necessary to issue a warning or a remark.[16]

8.2.2 Against whom should the intervention be made?

The FSA can intervene not only against investment firms that operate in Sweden (Chapter 25, sections 12–15a-c). The FSA may, for example, order a foreign investment company that is domiciled in the European Economic Area (EEA), and which conducts operations from a branch in Sweden, to effect rectification where it violates the rules of conduct, rules on reporting of transactions, or other obligations under VPM, Chapter 25, section 12 (1).[17] If rectification does not take place, the FSA may prohibit the firm from commencing new transactions in Sweden (Chapter 25, section 12(4)). Before issuing such an injunction, the FSA must notify the competent authority in the firm's home state (Chapter 25, section 12(3)).[18]

In relation to a foreign company that is domiciled outside the EEA, and which conducts securities operations from a branch in Sweden, or a foreign company that is authorised to operate a regulated market or clearing operation from a branch in Sweden, the FSA can intervene if the company breaches its obligations under VPM or any other statutory instrument that regulates the company's operations in Sweden (Chapter 25, sections 15(1) and 16(1) VPM).[19]

It is also possible for the FSA to revoke the authorisation of an investment firm if any person who serves on the board of directors of the company, as its managing director, or serves as a replacement for any such person, no longer fulfils the requirements imposed on him or her, according to VPM. For example, the authorisation may be revoked when such a person does not possess the sufficient level of insight and experience required to participate in the

[16] See Governmental Committee (Statens Offentliga Utredningar) 2006:50 'En ny lag om värdepappersmarknaden' (hereafter 'SOU 2006:50') Författningsbilaga, 323.
[17] ibid, pt 1, 458.
[18] ibid.
[19] See prop 2016/17:162, 524.

management of the institute, or is otherwise inappropriate and unsuitable for the task (Chapter 3, Section 1 § (1)(5)).[20]

However, revocation may only take place if FSA first decides to inform the investment firm that the person, who may be a board member or the chief executive officer (CEO), does not meet the requirements, and the person in question nevertheless remains in his or her post following the expiry of a period of time fixed by the FSA, which shall not exceed three months (Chapter 25, section 4 § (1) (second sentence)). The purpose of this rule is to have the firm ensure that the requirements for suitability are met by all persons in management positions. Instead of revoking the authorisation of an otherwise viable firm, however, the FSA may decide that a board member or the CEO may no longer hold that position. Usually there is an alternative person who can step in for the person who has resigned, but if there is not, FSA may appoint a replacement. The replacement's mandate is valid until the company has appointed a new board member or CEO.[21]

According to the *travaux préparatoires* of the VPM, the intention is that this alternative should be chosen instead of revocation in cases where there are shortcomings in the management of an otherwise viable investment firm, but it has been unable change the situation. However, the FSA is not required to choose this alternative instead of revoking the authorisation, and may make case-by-case assessments.[22]

8.2.3 Choice of action

As mentioned above, if the FSA detects deficiencies in an investment firm's regulatory compliance, the authority may intervene by means of an injunction or prohibition, or by issuing remarks. A prohibition or injunction may be combined with a fine. However, if the violation of the rules is serious, the FSA will revoke the firm's authorisation or, if it considers it to be sufficient, issue a warning. The FSA has the opportunity, though not entirely freely, to choose which sanction should follow from the infringement. However, it should be pointed out that there is no difference between natural and legal persons as to the circumstances to be taken into account when choosing the penalty and fine.[23]

[20] See also VPM, Chapter 12, s 2 (p 4), and Chapter 19, s 3 (p 4).

[21] See SOU 2006:50 Författningsbilaga, 317–18, and pt 1, 444.

[22] ibid, Författningsbilaga, 317–18 and Governmental Proposal to the Parliament, 'Proposition 2006/07:115 Ny lag om värdepappersmarknaden' (hereinafter 'prop 2006/07:115'), 638.

[23] See prop 2014/15:57, 53.

Chapter 25, section 2 VPM stipulates that, in conjunction with the determination of sanctions, the FSA shall take into consideration the gravity of the infringement and its duration. Furthermore, particular consideration should be given to the nature of the infringement, its tangible and potential effects on the financial system, the losses that arose, and the degree of responsibility. Chapter 25 section 2a states that a previous infringement by the company or natural person shall be taken into consideration as an aggravating circumstance. In conjunction with this determination, particular weight should be attached to whether the infringements are similar in nature, and the time which has elapsed between the various infringements. However, as a mitigating circumstance, consideration should be given to whether the company or the natural persons, to a significant extent, through active cooperation, facilitated the FSA's investigation, and promptly ceased the infringement after it was reported to, or notified by, the FSA.[24]

If the firm has violated the VPM or another statutory instrument that aims to maintain the firm's stability, it should, in principle, be subject to a stricter intervention by the FSA than if the violation is of a provision of less importance to its stability.[25] Examples of less serious violations are those of a more formal nature, such as delayed reporting.[26]

When the FSA is choosing a sanction, the choice should fall on the sanction that is most effective in the individual case under consideration. The injunction should only be used to get the investment firm to rectify something. Remarks can be used where there is nothing to remedy, but the violation should, nevertheless, be sanctioned. Both remarks and injunctions should not be considered for the same infringement.[27]

With regard to the choice between revocation of the company's authorisation and a warning, the latter penalty should be chosen when there are preconditions for revocation, but there are special circumstances whereby a warning appears to be sufficient.[28] If the company has taken measures, initiating changes to its internal routines, computer systems, or risk control, taking measures to strengthen regulatory awareness and compliance, or, where appropriate, making personnel changes, a warning may be sufficient.[29] However,

[24] ibid, 33.

[25] ibid, 53; SOU 2006:50 pt 1, 443. Compare Governmental Proposal to the Parliament, Proposition 2002/03:139 Reformed rules for banking and financial businesses (Reformerade regler för bank- och finanseringsrörelse)', (hereafter prop 2002/03:139), 382.

[26] See prop 2014/15:57, 53.

[27] See SOU 2006:50 p 1, 443, prop 2006/07:155, 636.

[28] See SOU 2006:50 pt 1, 443.

[29] ibid, n 16. Prop 2006/07:115, 499, 636–37.Compare the *travaux préparatoires* to the Banking and Financial Business Act, prop 2002/03:139, 383, where it is stated that a warning can be regarded as a

the FSA itself determines when the circumstances are such that the firm's authorisation should be revoked. It should not be done, however, without special reasons.

In another case from 2018, the FSA decided to revoke all authorisations for a company named Remium Nordic to conduct securities operations in accordance with VPM.[30] Previously, in 2017, the company had received a warning associated with a fine of SEK 3.5 million, as the company had serious deficiencies in its credit management and credit risk management. These deficiencies were related to risk management, risk classification, credit scoring, and documentation of decisions. The deficiencies were so serious that the FSA considered withdrawing the company's authorisation to operate finance operations, but settled for a warning and a fine. This decision was based on the fact that the company had decided to discontinue its financing operations, and had declared that it would return its permit. The liquidation of the financial operations was to be completed on 31 December 2017. However, in December 2017, the company announced that the liquidation would not be finished until the end of the year, but would instead be completed on 31 August 2018.

However, the shortcomings in the company's financial operations were still serious and systematic. The question, however, was whether the shortcomings in the financing operations also affected the company's securities operations so that the firm in general was exposed to risks, which could harm customers and society at large. On this matter, the FSA believed that the company had shown systematic deficiencies in its risk management. In addition, the company had unacceptable standards regarding internal control, which had led to large losses for the financing operations, which, in turn, would affect the securities operations. The company had also risked reporting an incorrect financial position, which, in turn, had risked the company not having enough capital to maintain its financial position. In addition, it was difficult to review the actual ownership of the company. In the FSA's opinion, there were owners who exercised a significant influence over the management, and who had not obtained permission from the FSA do so. The FSA had not investigated whether there were specific breaches in the securities operations, but the clear deficiencies in the company's overall governance and control affected the entire company's operations, and thus also the securities operations. In the FSA's opinion, the violations showed that the company lacked the ability, and perhaps even the

sufficient measure if the company is unlikely to repeat the infringement, and that the forecast for the institute is, therefore, good, or that the institute understood no better when the infringement occurred.

[30] See the decision of the FSA, *Remium Nordic*: FI Dnr 17-19013, 17 April 2018.

desire, to follow basic rules that existed on the securities market to protect consumers and other customers, as well as society at large. The deficiencies were of such a nature that there were no grounds for the company to conduct any licensed financial operations at all.

If an infringement is of a less serious nature, the FSA may issue a remark. There are no examples given in the *travaux préparatoires* of the Banking and Financial Business Act [31] or the VPM of when a remark may be an appropriate sanction.[32] According to Chapter 25 section 2 VPM, the FSA may also refrain from intervening if the infringement is minor or excusable, or if the firm, or a natural person involved with the firm, has taken measures to rectify the infringement. The FSA can also refrain from intervening if another authority has taken measures against the investment firm or natural person concerned, and these measures are considered sufficient, even from the perspective of the FSA.[33]

8.2.4 Intervention in certain cases

According to Chapter 25, section 5 VPM, the FSA is obliged to revoke an investment firm's authorisation if certain specific situations arise. These situations are:

(1) the company has been granted authorisation by providing false information or in any other inappropriate manner;
(2) within one year from the granting of authorisation, the company has not commenced the operations to which the authorisations pertain;
(3) the company has declared that it declines the authorisation;
(4) during a consecutive six-month period, the company has not conducted such operations to which the authorisation pertains; or
(5) with respect to a Swedish limited company which has been granted authorisation to operate a regulated market or clearing operation, the company's equity is less than two-thirds of the registered share capital and the deficiency has not been covered within three months from the date on which it became known to the company.

[31] Banking and Financial Business Act (Bank- och finansieringsrörelselagen (2004:297)).
[32] Compare prop 2006/07:115, 636,639, prop 2002/03:139, 383,548.
[33] See prop 2006/07:115, 491,497, 500-501, 639 and prop 2002/03:139, 384.

According to Chapter 25, section 5, the FSA may, prior to revocation of the firm's authorisation due to infringements under (1), (2), (4) or (5) above, determine whether it is sufficient just to issue a warning. Where authorisation is revoked, the FSA may order the way in which the company's operations shall be wound up. A revocation decision may also include an injunction against continued operations (Chapter 25, section 6 VPM).

8.2.5 Punitive fines

Where an investment firm is notified of a decision regarding an adverse remark or warning, the FSA may order the company to pay a punitive fine (Chapter 25, section 8 VPM). The fine shall accrue to the State (Chapter 25 Section 9(4)). According to the *travaux préparatoires* of VPM, it is stated that the intention of such a fine is that it should impose a financially immediate, sensible penalty, and give the FSA the opportunity to grade the violation.[34] The FSA may determine itself how large the fine should be and, thus, does not need to go to court to get it approved.

According to Chapter 25, section 9, the punitive fine shall not exceed:

(1) an amount in Swedish kronor, which as of 2 July 2014, was five million euro;
(2) ten per cent of the company's turnover or, where applicable, corresponding turnover on a group level during the immediately preceding financial year;
(3) two times the profit which the company realised as a result of the regulatory infringement, where this amount can be ascertained.

The amount may not be set at less than SEK 5,000. Where the infringement occurred during the company's first operational year, or where information regarding turnover is otherwise absent or insufficient, turnover may be estimated. The fine may not be so large that the firm cannot fulfil the requirements regarding solvency and liquidity in Chapter 8, section 3 or Chapter 6, section 1 of the Banking and Financing Business Act.

[34] See prop 2014/15:57, 34. Compare prop 2002/03:139, 387 regarding the Banking and Financing Business Act, where it is stated that a punitive fine further refines the FSA's available sanctions, in addition to other sanctions such as revocation, adverse remarks, and warnings. The punitive fine relates to the same behaviour that caused, eg the adverse remark, but makes the sanction immediately financially noticeable to the firm.

When determining the amount of the punitive fine, according to Chapter 25, section 10, special consideration shall be given to circumstances such as the seriousness of the infringement that caused the remark or the warning, and for how long the infringement has been going on (see Chapter 25, sections 2 and 2a). The size of the penalty should be seen as a way of further grading the warning or the adverse remark. In other words a severe infringement results in a larger fine signalling a grave misconduct compared to a warning or remark in combination with a small fine.

8.3 Administrative procedure in supervision

8.3.1 The process in a case of non-compliance

The financial crisis of 2007 to 2010 exposed weaknesses in the functioning and transparency of financial markets. The adoption of MiFID II and MiFIR reflected the need to address those weaknesses. According, for example, to paragraphs 4 and 137 of the preamble in MiFID II, the need to strengthen the framework for the regulation of markets in financial instruments included increasing transparency, better protecting investors, rebuilding confidence, addressing unregulated areas, and ensuring that supervisors were granted adequate powers to fulfil their tasks, all of which were imminent. It seemed necessary to increase the convergence of the powers at the disposal of the competent authorities, to pave the way towards an equivalent intensity of enforcement throughout the integrated financial market. A common minimum set of powers, coupled with adequate resources, ought to guarantee supervisory effectiveness. Those powers should be exercised, where the national law so required, by application of the competent judicial authorities.

It is, further, clear from the preambular texts of MiFID II that the supervisory powers specified were to be exercised within a complete system of national law that guaranteed the respect for fundamental rights, including the right to privacy. For the exercise of those powers, which may amount to serious interferences with the right to respect for private and family life, home and communications, member states ought to have in place adequate and effective safeguards against any abuse.[35] However, if the supervisory authority does not use the powers it has been granted, against a particular firm committing

[35] See paragraph 138 of the preamble.

infringements, there are no safeguards for customers, other firms or the public at large, which could lead to injustice.

In order to ensure that decisions made by supervisory authorities have a dissuasive effect on the public at large, they should normally be published. It is generally understood that the publication of decisions is also an important tool for authorities to inform market participants of what types of behaviour are considered to infringe MiFID II and, therefore, to promote good behaviour amongst market participants. If such publication would cause disproportionate damage to the persons involved, or jeopardise the stability of financial markets, or an ongoing investigation, the competent authority should publish the sanctions and measures on an anonymous basis in a manner that complies with national law, or delay the publication. However, the publication itself is not an issue, according to paragraph 146 of the preamble, in case of minor issues where the publicity damage would not be disproportionate.

Supervision is one of the most important tools to achieve the objectives set out in preamble 4 of MiFID II, and to ensure compliance with the regulations. It follows from the government's instruction to the FSA that:

> '[the FSA] shall contribute to a robust financial system marked with trust, with well-functioning markets answering to household and companies need of financial services coinciding with a high protection of consumers. The financial system shall also contribute to sustainable development'.[36]

This instruction coincides with the objectives of MiFID, and it is clear that the Swedish instruction match the EU policy and intentions in this area.

However, the administrative processes involved in applying sanctions are not regulated in the MiFID-, nor in the delegated acts from the EU Commission, or in the supplementary acts on technical standards from the ESMA. The relevant rules and principles are, in essence, to be found in general national administrative acts applicable to national authorities: in this case, the FSA.[37]

[36] Ordinance (2009:93) with Instruction to the FSA (Förordning (2009:93) med instruktion för Finansinspektionen), section 2.

[37] For analysis of such regime, see, eg Dirk Schoenmaker and Sander Oosterloo, *Financial Supervision in Europe: A Proposal for a New Architecture* (ResearchGate 2008), with a focus on home-country supervision; Diana-Urania Galetta, *Procedural Autonomy of EU Member States: Paradise Lost* (Springer 2010), with a focus on suppression of national rules; Paul Craig, *EU Administrative Law* (3rd edn, OUP 2018); Eberhard Schmidt-Assman and Fruzsina Molnár-Gábor, European Administrative Law (*Oxford Public International Law*, October 2019) https://opil.ouplaw.com/view/10.1093/law:epil/9780199231690/law-9780199231690-e1819. 2021-08-09.; and Dacian C. Dragos, Polonca Kovaĉ, and Hanna D Tolsma (eds), *The Sound of Silence in European Administrative Law* (Palgrave Macmillan 2020), with a focus on the effects of passivity in decision-making. Although these sources are enlightening in their

The handling of a case is governed, in Sweden, by the principles of the Swedish Administrative Act.[38] The prime principles are transparency in the process and communication with the party involved, objectivity and equal treatment in decision-making, and safeguards to prevent an authority from stalling the process. The principle of transparency shall apply to all actions taken against individual parties. Further, a right to appeal is assured. All of these principles are in line with the European Convention on Human Rights and the *acquis communautaire*. Other principles, guaranteed by one of Sweden's fundamental constitutional laws, the Freedom of the Press Act[39] , focus on protecting the public interest in dealings with authorities, in particular the right of access to public files.[40]

The process in a non-compliance cases is largely the same among Swedish supervisory authorities. In general, the administration of a case is initiated by the authority itself, a notice from another authority, or a claim from a member of the public. If the magnitude of the case is sufficient, and the issue is of importance to many, the authority has the discretion to open a case.[41]

The first step is a comprehensive assessment of the facts at hand. This assessment weighs pros and cons, benefits to the public, and takes into account whether more than one person has complained. The financial market actor under scrutiny, can be contacted in the search for information to establish the breach. Second, if the information gathered indicates non-compliance or other wrongful behaviour, the financial market actor is given the opportunity to respond. The actor is supposed to present a plan of action. The third and final step is a conclusion from the authority on whether a sanction is to be imposed upon the actor, or if the actor's plan of action is sufficient. If the actor agrees with the conclusions reached by the authority, the case is closed. It is possible for the authorities to institute proceedings, or to close the file without imposing sanctions, if non-compliance is not evident.

analyses of principles and case law, common to them all is a focus on the application of legal principles, wrongful or not, in contrast to our focus on effects of non-application.

[38] The Administrative Act (Förvaltningslagen (2017:900)).

[39] Chapter 2, section 1, Tryckfrihetsförordningen (1949:105).

[40] For a review of administrative law in general in the EU, see Chapter 6 of this book, by Jane Reichel.

[41] For a short briefing on administrative procedures at the FSA, see Riksrevisionen RIR 2020:18, 'Finansinspektionens arbete för att motverka intressekonflikter, 2020' (hereafter 'RIR 2020:18') 37. See also a short review in Justitieombudsmannen (Legal Ombudsman), Kritik mot FI för bl.a bristande dokumentation och bristfälligt utformade styrdokument, beslutsdatum, 9 November 2020, Dnr 8490-2018 (hereafter 'JO decision 2020').

As set out in MiFID II, the EU Commission and ESMA report on the application of various articles in the member states. The latest report on sanctions was issued in July 2020.[42] It follows from the statistics that Sweden is one of fifteen member states that did not report a single case of sanctions imposed for non-compliance during 2019. The report is merely a compilation of figures, and an analysis is not provided, but it is suggested here that a particular practice by the FSA, as discussed below, might be part of a background explanation to the lack of sanctions in Sweden for non-compliance with MiFID II.

8.3.2 Alternative supervision—use of discretion

The principles mentioned above, contained in administrative regulations, are designed primarily to safeguard due process in case-handling by authorities. If a case is opened, the law will ensure that any individual concerned will receive fair handling of their case. However, there is a window of discretion granted to authorities, whether a case has been formally opened or not. If a case is not opened, the authorities will cease to deal with the matter and further handling with the circumstances will not take place. If a decision is taken to proceed, the issue has to be registered in the diary of the authority, meaning that a case is at hand, and protective regulation will, accordingly, be activated. Also, when it comes to the important right of appeal, when an individual has been the subject of proceedings but disagrees with the authority about the outcome of the case, the decision must be challengeable in the administrative courts. This follows from the European Convention on Human Rights. A prerequisite, however, is that a formal case has been opened, and that a public decision has been reached by the authority.

Many supervisory authorities in Sweden use discretionary powers in a tradition of 'communicative letters', in the sense of informing actors about decisions that have been taken as to whether there will be formal procedures for non-compliance, or whether the issue will be closed after explanations have been provided for the acts in question.[43]

[42] ESMA, 'Report on Sanctions and measures imposed under MiFID II in 2019', 13 July 2020, ESMA35-43-2427.

[43] See, eg the case from the Swedish Supreme Administrative Court (HFD 2020 ref 12 (6 March 2020)) about Skogsstyrelsen (the Forest Authority), which involved a letter of guidance being sent to a landowner instead of a formal decision. The issue before the Court was whether this handling was appealable. The Court ruled that it was not.

The Swedish FSA has taken the issue further and developed its own practice of 'final letters', as an alternative to formal legal sanctions. This practice involves the FSA having a dialogue with the suspect of potential non-compliance, but not opening a formal registered case. The dialogue commences with communication from the FSA to the actor who is the subject of their interest. Remarks are put forward and, depending on the actor's response, an informal decision is taken on whether to proceed or not. If the FSA decides to proceed, a formal case is opened, with registration and formal administrative routines as described above; if the authority decide not to proceed, an informal 'final letter' is sent to the actor, containing the opinions and remarks of the FSA on issues that it have identified. If alterations are not in place within a certain time frame, the FSA will indicate its intention to open a formal case against the actor. Once the final letter has been issued, the actor cannot object to, or complain about, the opinions of the FSA.

A final remark concerns time-consuming administration. When the Swedish Administrative Act came into force on 1 July 2018, one of the positive reforms it introduced was the possibility for a party to force the authorities to reach a decision, rather than prolonging the handling of the involved actors case.[44] If the FSA uses the practice with a final letter rather than to proceed with issuing a formal decision, the process is dictated by the FSA. The actor cannot halt the dialogue with the FSA, which can continue for years,[45] or demand a decision from the authority. There is no case filed, thus the rules in the Administrative Act, the VPM or any other legislation are not applicable.

This practice of issuing 'final letters' does not follow MiFID II, but has been developed by the Swedish FSA. It has been criticised for both objective reasons (for not being transparent to the public) and subjective reasons (appeal is not possible). A third criticism is that the method is not in conformity with the objectives of MiFID II: the preventive function of having a catalogue of available sanctions is obstructed if authorities simply find their own ways of deciding whether to apply the sanctions or not.

[44] See the background papers to the Act, 'Governmental Proposal to the Parliament, Proposition 2016/17:180 En modern och rättssäker förvaltning—ny förvaltningslag' (hereafter prop 2016/17:180), Ch 9.

[45] One example is the case of HQ Bank, where the FSA communicated with the bank for several years until its licence was finally withdrawn in 2010. The crash of the bank is one of the biggest scandals of the Swedish financial markets in modern times. Court proceedings went on until 2016. See insights by the awarded journalist on financial matters in her thriller/novel, Caroline Neurath, Fartblinda (Speed blind), Piratförlaget, 2016.

8.3.3 Application and practice

A review by Riksrevisionen (the Swedish Audit Authority)[46] explored the supervisory practices of the FSA and the Consumer Protection Agency (CPA). The CPA has taken the approach of setting goals, mapping out inconsistencies, and prioritizing and evaluating its administrative procedures. According to the Audit Authority, the supervision performed by CPA is efficient in its use of resources, the path from non-compliance to sanctions is easy to follow, and the supervisory practices are transparent to the actors on the market.

The FSA, in contrast, has developed a strategy for supervision based on three pillars: a risk-based approach focused on identified risks on the market; a comprehensive supervision regime in relation to all actors on the financial markets, whether they are subject to the requirement of authorisation or not (honouring the principle of equality under the law); and a communicative supervision approach, educating the market actors about regulations and practices.

The FSA identifies between five and ten risks in its annual strategy, subject to priority, and publishes the results of its ongoing supervision in annual and thematic reports. The Audit Authority noted the process adopted by the FSA whereby supervisory actions can be concluded by confidential 'final letters' addressed to the parties involved. It was noted that the FSA did not keep statistics or adopt other follow-up procedures about the efficiency of, or compliance with, the 'recommendations' included in the final letters.

However, the main purpose of supervision is not to fuel sanctions, but to prevent obstacles and problems on the market. This principle is also expressed in the preamble to MiFID II, as noted above. It is clear that final letters do not contribute to the development of case law or other public practices on the market. As the final letters are confidential to a particular actor, other actors cannot be aware of the obstacles or problems raised. The purpose of supervision expressed in MifID are then bound to fail. It is very hard to prevent obstacles and problems if they are not known to the actors on the market. At the same time, there is a need for guidance and advice from the FSA on complex regulation and how to act accordingly, also in the interests of avoiding non-compliance on the financial markets. In the opinion of the Audit Authority, there is potential for the supervision to become efficient, but to be able to achieve this, the FSA needs to further develop its evaluations and follow-up procedures. A further

[46] Riksrevisionen, 'Konsumentskyddet på det finansiella området—förutsättningar och statlig tillsyn' (RIR 2019:32). The Audit Authority has the mandate to review and scrutinise all governmental authorities in Sweden.

development of case law by the courts is desirable, in order to strengthen the rule of law.[47] Market actors are not inclined to take up court proceedings challenging the FSA, in order to avoiding being seen as defiant and resulting in the FSA becoming an adversarial. This may be to the benefit of individual actors, but it is at the expense of loss of guidance to the market.

8.3.4 Comments: Is dialogue improper or desired?

In response to the review by the Audit Authority, the FSA developed a supervisory strategy in 2020.[48] The FSA made it clear that supervision is the most important tool of the authority, that a risk-based approach is self-evident, and that communication is desirable in order to develop compliance. The FSA made it clear that their role is not to act as legal counsel to the market, but that education is still essential. The bulk of cases arising from their supervisory activities are, therefore, run by way of dialogue and communication. The purpose of the FSA's supervision is to ensure revised practices and routines on the financial markets. The FSA noted that their recommendations, in the form of final letters, had led to subjects revising their actions in line with the recommendations.[49]

In its defence of the practice of issuing final letters, the FSA refer to its activities in connection with the ongoing supervision, auditing, and in-depth analysis of about 25,000 financial market actors (around 1,800 of which were subject to authorisation).[50]

In the opinion of the FSA, final letters containing recommendations are part of a communicative supervision approach that aims at dialogue with, and provision of advice to, market actors. They appear to be an important tool for the FSA to gather market information, and to identify risks at an early stage, and thereby to conduct efficient supervision in line with the goals set up for the authority.

In a recent decision, Justitieombudsmannen (the Legal Ombudsman or 'JO') expressed much the same criticism as the Audit Authority regarding the practice of issuing final letters. The JO expects the FSA to make it absolutely clear to market actors that recommendations and decisions included in such letters are

[47] Riksrevisionen, 'Konsumentskyddet på det finansiella området—förutsättningar och statlig tillsyn' (RIR 2019:32). 53- 54.
[48] FSA, 'Tillsynsstrategi, FI Dnr 20-2646, 3 February 2020. (hereafter 'FI Tillsynsstrategi 2020').
[49] FSA press release, 'FI om kritik i media: Vi ingriper när bristerna är allvarliga', 11 December 2018.
[50] FI Tillsynsstrategi 2020.

by no means binding, and must only be voluntary, for actors to accept at their own choice.

It is clear that the FSA should maintain, and even intensify, dialogue with market actors, as well as promoting self-regulation by financial market organisations. Regulation of the financial markets is complex, diversified, and hard to comprehend, and the role of FSA as an authority recommending and giving advice should be developed. Informal contacts are useful and necessary, but cannot be allowed to obstruct the rule of law, and the application of regulations. From the actor's point of view, perhaps the most severe criticism of the use of final letters is that it reduces the possibilities of appealing or complaining about the 'recommendations' included in the letters. There is no formal case filed and, therefore, there is no formal decision taken by the FSA to appeal against.

From a MiFID point of view, perhaps the most severe criticism is the lack of publicity, which is particularly mentioned as an objective of MiFID II. The lack of publicity means that an important deterrent is absent. Further, given the lack of filing of cases, incidents cannot be analysed and compared to establish whether equal treatment and just and non-discriminatory decision-making are being applied.

A further line of discussion needs to be addressed. The Swedish FSA has a high staff turnover. During the period from 2014 to 2018, the turnover was, on average, 16 per cent, which can be compared with 11 per cent for Swedish authorities in general. The authority has a lot of relatively new employees joining from the financial industry. However, even more of these employees return to the financial industry, especially the FSA managers, after their employment at the authority is terminated. 31 per cent of the FSA's administrators came from the financial industry, and 43 per cent went there when they left their employment. Every third manager came from the financial industry, and two out of three went there when they left their employment.[51]

The high staff turnover—or, in other words, exchange of personnel between the FSA and the financial industry—can undermine confidence among both the financial industry and the public in the authority's ability to carry out its mission efficiently and reach decisions without taking undue consideration of the interests of the financial industry.[52] There is extensive international research on the problems that can arise when employees move back and forth

[51] RIR 2020:18, 18–26.
[52] ibid, 6.

between the private and public sectors: so-called 'revolving doors' problems.[53] This problem is often highlighted as an important explanation for authorities starting to represent different special interests instead of the public interest. There may, therefore, be suspicions that staff, individual civil servants, or certain groups or functions begin to act based on interests that are not in line with the authority's responsibilities.

Therefore, it is important that the authority takes effective and transparent measures to counteract conflicts of interest, and to report openly and clearly on how these measures are applied, and are functioning.[54] Many administrators at the FSA (82 per cent) believe that decision-making and preparation processes there work well, and are applied essentially as intended. At the same time, 8 per cent of administrators experience problems with objectivity on decisions. These administrators state, for example, that they thought the FSA did not at all or not particularly sufficient take decisions on objective and factual grounds.[55]

In addition to this vulnerability to potential conflicts of interest, the review also showed that, even in this regard, there were shortcomings in the record-keeping and documentation of the management of cases.[56] Deficiencies in documentation reduced the possibilities for follow-up actions. The Audit Authority concluded, in its report, that the FSA needs to follow up and check that rules, guidelines, and processes are being applied, and are functioning as intended. To facilitate follow-up and control, the FSA should, to a greater extent document, for example, notifications and decisions on non-compliance, and enhance internal education of staff in ethics, particularly when such individuals are trusted with discretion in decision-making. Poor handling of

[53] See, eg Lawrence G Baxter, 'Capture in Financial Regulation: Can we Channel it Toward the Common Good?' (2011) 21(1) Cornell Journal of Law and Public Policy 175; Philip Bond and Vincent Glode, 'The Labour Market for Bankers and Regulators' (2014) Review of Financial Studies 27 (9) 2539–2579.; Jess Cornaggia and Kimberly J Cornaggia and Han Xia, 'Revolving Doors on Wall Street' (2016) 120 Journal of Financial Economics 400; Daniel Carpenter and David A Moss, *Preventing Regulatory Capture: Special Interest Influence and how to Limit it* (CUP 2014); Denis Veltrop and Jakob de Haan, 'I Just Cannot get you Out of my Head: Regulatory Capture of Financial Sector Supervisors' (2014) De Nederlandsche Bank Working Paper no 410; Kevin L Young, Tim Marple, and James Heilman, 'Beyond the Revolving Door: Advocacy Behavior and Social Distance to Financial Regulators' (2017) 19(2) Business and Politics 327. See also Wirsching, Elisa Maria, 'The Revolving Door for Political Elites: An Empirical Analysis of the Linkages between Government Officials' Professional Background and Financial Regulation, OECD. (2018), https://www.oecd.org/corruption/integrity-forum/academic-papers/Wirsching.pdf; accessed 10 August 2021, Janos Bertok and Organisation for Economic Co-operation and Development (OECD), 'Post Public Employment: Good Practices for Preventing Conflict of Interest' (2010); James Kwak, '4—Cultural Capture and the Financial Crisis' in Daniel Carpenter and David A Moss (eds), *Preventing Regulatory Capture: Special Interest Influence and How to Limit It* (CUP 2014) 75–80; Eva Lindström and Niklas Bruun, 'Svängdörr i staten—en ESO-rapport om när politiker och tjänstemän byter sida' ESO 2012:1, 77, 93–94, 109–11.

[54] RIR 2020:18, 54–55.

[55] ibid, 27, 37, 41–42.

[56] ibid, 43, 55–56.

internal administrative routines and record-keeping was also subject to criticism from the JO in the recent decision regarding FSA.[57] In fact, the JO questioned whether shortcomings in case-handling were systematic or of a more casual, case-by-case nature.

8.4 Concluding remarks

The FSA has a number of different sanctions that it may resort to in order to rectify an investment firm's infringements of the financial regulations. Although the FSA has these powers, they are not always used. This brief exposition of practice shows that the FSA often chooses to communicate with the investment firm's management, and to discuss matters with them, rather than using formal sanctions. In most cases, the FSA, in dialogue with the firm, is able to influence the firm to change its behaviour. The actor has few incentives not to do as the FSA is asking. The FSA is, therefore, seeking to maximise efficiency in supervision and minimise the use of resources, but this reduces proactive effects, and also loses the deterrent effects of public decision-making.

In some cases, however, the shortcomings and non-compliance are so serious that the FSA must intervene with sanctions. In order to create a flexible system, the legislator has given the FSA, to a fairly large extent, the discretion to decide which sanction is appropriate in a given situation. In addition to the catalogue of sanctions that the FSA has at its disposal, it may also decline to intervene in certain cases. The threshold of when an infringement requires a more forceful intervention, rather than being dealt with by the FSA in another way can, therefore, in some cases, be difficult to identify.

In addition to the criticism of poor administrative routines within the FSA, it seems clear that the practice by the FSA of issuing 'final letters' needs to be further analysed and scrutinised over time, particularly due to its potential to obstruct the rule of law and the objectives of the MiFID regime. The high turnover of staff makes the practice even more delicate, and creates the room for another kind of potential conflict of interest: a person may be a colleague one day and subject to administrative action by the FSA the next. Ultimately, the financial markets are built on trust, and the FSA needs to take its role as 'gatekeeper' seriously, for the benefit of the whole financial industry. Supervisory arbitrage is not a blessing for anyone.

[57] See JO decision 2020 (n 32).

9

Not Suitable to Lead an Investment Firm

Fit and Proper Assessments as an Instrument of Accountability

Britta Behrendt Jonsson

9.1 Introduction

Undertakings in the financial market are subject to a comprehensive body of regulatory requirements aimed at customer protection and market stability. To ensure compliance with these requirements, undertakings must have suitable management personnel who set the right 'tone at the top', and establish an appropriate organisational structure.

Accordingly, MiFID II[1] and other pieces of EU legislation require members of administrative, management, or supervisory bodies of regulated undertakings in the financial sector to be suitable for their positions, or 'fit and proper'. The European Insurance and Occupational Pensions Authority (EIOPA) describes fit and proper requirements as 'a cornerstone of prudential supervision in today's world'.[2] Supervisory approval of board members is not new, and in both EU and national legislation, earlier examples of requirements for suitability assessments of board members for certain types of regulated undertakings can be found.[3] In the aftermath of the financial crisis, increased governance

[1] Directive 2014/65/EU of the European Parliament and of the Council on markets in financial instruments and amending Directive 2002/92/EC and Directive 2011/61/EU [2014] OJ L 173/349 (hereafter 'MiFID II').

[2] EIOPA, 'Results of the Peer Review on Propriety of Administrative, Management or Supervisory Body Members and Qualifying Shareholders' (18 February 2020) 35 (hereafter 'EIOPA, Results of the Peer Review').

[3] See, for instance, with regard to investment firms, art 9(1) of Directive 2004/39/EC of the European Parliament and of the Council on markets in financial instruments amending Council Directives 85/611/EEC and 93/6/EEC and Directive 2000/12/EC of the European Parliament and of the Council and repealing Council Directive 93/22/EEC [2004] OJ L 145, 30 April 2004, or, for the insurance sector, art 8(3) of First Council Directive 73/239/EEC on the coordination of laws, regulations and administrative provisions relating to the taking-up and pursuit of the business of direct insurance other than life assurance [1973] OJ L 228, enabling member states to require directors and managers of non-life insurance undertakings to have 'technical qualifications'.

Britta Behrendt Jonsson, *Not Suitable to Lead an Investment Firm* In: *Legal Accountability in EU Markets for Financial Instruments*. Edited by: Carl Fredrik Bergström and Magnus Strand, Oxford University Press. © Britta Behrendt Jonsson 2021. DOI: 10.1093/oso/9780192849281.003.0009

requirements have been a focus of EU financial legislation. These include fit and proper requirements that demand more sophisticated processes for the assessment of members of management bodies. Where the assessment of a board member previously merely required the provision of a few documents, such as a CV, a criminal record certificate, and a certificate of non-bankruptcy,[4] applicants today need to provide much more detailed documentation, and national competent authorities (NCAs) may search information on the Internet, or conduct interviews with prospective board members.[5]

Supervisory decisions featuring negative assessments are not rendered very frequently. One reason is that institutions often choose to withdraw an application if the NCA expresses concerns, without waiting for a formal decision. Furthermore, negative assessments are seldom challenged in court. Article 74 (1) of MiFID II, and corresponding provisions in other EU directives, require member states to ensure that an NCA's decision to reject the appointment of a board member, or to require a person's removal from the board can be appealed before a tribunal. To give full effect to these provisions, they must be interpreted in such a way that the person who is negatively assessed has the right to appeal such a decision even if it is addressed to the investment firm only.

An example of a negative assessment concerned a person whom the UK's Financial Conduct Authority deemed to be unsuitable for a board membership due to lack of integrity, because the person had repeatedly used public transport without a valid ticket.[6] Another person was held unsuitable by the Swedish Financial Supervisory Authority because the financial holding company of which she was a non-executive director failed to ensure that its banking subsidiary had adequate risk management processes, which led to the near-bankruptcy of the bank.[7] In both cases, the NCA's decisions can be seen as instruments to hold the persons in question accountable for prior actions or omissions.

As outlined by Carl Fredrik Bergström in Chapter 1, accountability has many different facets. With regard to the accountability of existing or

[4] With regard to German insurance supervision law, see Anke Waclawik, 'Zuverlässigkeit und fachliche Eignung von Geschäftsleitern' in Gunne W Bähr (ed), *Handbuch des Versicherungsaufsichtsrechts* (CH Beck 2011) 94 para 50 ff.

[5] EIOPA, 'Results of the Peer Review' (n 2) 30. Concerning interviews, see EBA, 'Report on the Peer Review of the Guidelines on the Assessment of the Suitability of Members of the Management Body and Key Function Holders' (EBA/GL/2012/06) (16 June 2015) 43 ff. (hereafter 'EBA Peer Review Report').

[6] Financial Conduct Authority, 'Final Notice against Jonathan Burrows', 15 December 2014 <www.fca.org.uk/publication/final-notices/jonathan-paul-burrows.pdf> accessed 17 February 2021.

[7] The NCA's decision was upheld by the Swedish Supreme Administrative Court: HFD 2013 ref 74. The case is discussed in Rebecca Söderström, *Sound Banking* (Uppsala Universitet 2017) 155 ff, and in Britta Behrendt Jonsson, *The Solvency II Capital Requirement for Insurance Groups - On the Tension Between Regulatory Law and Company Law* (Linköping University 2018) 418 ff.

prospective board members, this chapter builds on a relatively wide notion of accountability, namely on accountability as involving some form of negative legal consequence for prior unlawful or inappropriate behaviour. For example, when suitability is denied because of previous behaviour or failures, the fit and proper assessment may become an instrument for holding managers accountable for these actions by justifying their removal from a board membership, or preventing them from taking up a new position.

Another subordinated accountability aspect applied in this chapter concerns an NCA's accountability towards an appointee or existing board member for harm induced by a wrongful negative assessment. In this respect, accountability is applied in a narrower sense, being limited to the possibility of the NCA's liability for damages towards the person in question. This aspect forms the background of the section on the applicability of the procedural guarantees laid down in the ECHR and the EU Charter of Fundamental Rights ('the Charter') in the context of a fit and proper assessment, in order to further depict the legal requirements for a correct fit and proper assessment.

The requirements for an eventual concrete liability claim against an NCA will not be discussed. That an NCA could be held accountable in this sense by investors, for instance, for having approved a manager that later on transpires to be unsuitable, and causes harm to the investment firm's customers, is very unlikely, since an adequate causal link between the wrongful positive assessment and the failure will be difficult to establish.[8] The same is true of liability claims by investors against investment firms for wrongful internal assessments. Equally, a liability claim by a board member against an investment firm for a negative internal assessment that has been conducted in good faith seems rather far-fetched. These aspects are, therefore, not dealt with any further in the remainder of this chapter. Since internal fit and proper assessments belong to the regulatory duties of investment firms, non-compliance may result in supervisory action against investment firms. While the requirements for supervisory action lie outside the focus of this chapter, the commentary herein will suggest where differences between the fit and proper assessments to be conducted by investment firms and NCAs exist.

Mismanagement does not very often lead to criminal or administrative sanctions against members of a management body, nor are personal liability claims often successful. In some cases, the possibilities of at least being able to remove an unsuitable person from the management body, or prevent him or her from taking a new position, may be the only ways to hold a manager accountable for

[8] Iris H-Y Chiu, *Regulating (From) the Inside* (Hart Publishing/Bloomsbury 2018), 191.

deficiencies in the management of a regulated entity. A negative fit and proper assessment during an ongoing assignment may also lead to the loss of variable remuneration for past periods: the failure to meet fit and proper standards is one of the criteria that investment firms must address in their remuneration policies.[9] For these reasons, some managers may regard the consequences of being deemed unfit or improper for an existing or future management position in the financial industry to be more severe than eventual administrative sanctions (in particular when these are directed against the undertaking, and not against themselves). The possible consequences of being deemed unfit or improper may, therefore, have a deterrent effect on board members, and reduce overly risky behaviour.

The other side of the coin is that a negative assessment due to past conduct may have a severe impact on a person's reputation, and may interfere with the person's freedom to choose an occupation, as protected in Article 15 (1) of the Charter . A negative assessment could even be considered a criminal sanction, in which case the presumption of innocence and the *ne bis in idem* principle, ie the right not to be tried and convicted twice for the same action, would apply.

In the following sections, the main focus will lie on fit and proper requirements for members of management bodies of investment firms, but since these requirements are used throughout the financial sector, legislation and doctrine concerning other financial sectors are also taken into consideration.

9.2 Bans and negative assessments

A person held responsible for certain breaches of regulatory law may be explicitly banned from management positions in investment firms, either permanently or for a certain amount of time. Article 70(6)(d) of MiFID II allows, and requires member states to provide for, the possibility of such a ban for the infringement of certain provisions in MiFID II, 'subject to national law'. Similar provisions can be found in Article 67(2)(d) of CRD IV and Article 18(2)(c)

[9] Directive 2013/36/EU of the European Parliament and of the Council on access to the activity of credit institutions and the prudential supervision of credit institutions and investment firms, amending Directive 2002/87/EC and repealing Directives 2006/48/EC and 2006/49/EC [2013] OJ L 176/338 (hereafter 'CRD IV'), art 94 (n) (ii); Directive (EU) 2019/2034 of the European Parliament and of the Council on the prudential supervision of investment firms and amending Directives 2002/87/EC, 2009/65/EC, 2011/61/EU, 2013/36/EU, 2014/59/EU and 2014/65/EU [2019] OJ L 314/64 (hereafter 'IFD'), art 32 (2) (m). See also Rebecca Söderström, in Chapter 10 of this book.

IFD, both of which, however, only provide for temporary and not permanent bans. The Solvency II[10] and IORP[11] Directives lack explicit provisions on bans. National laws in different jurisdictions differ both in the prerequisites for bans, as well as in the minimum and maximum length of temporary bans. German law, for instance, allows BaFin to ban a person from the management board of an investment firm for a maximum of two years,[12] whereas the Swedish supervisory authority may impose a ban for a duration of three to ten years.[13] A ban is, thus, construed as a sanction for a breach of certain regulatory law requirements: it is a direct legal reaction to certain qualified actions or omissions, ie infringements, attributable to a person. In Article 70(6) of MIFID II, a ban is listed as one of the administrative sanctions that competent national authorities shall be able to impose.

A decision by an NCA to require the removal of a board member due to unsuitability differs from a ban in at least three aspects: (1) it concerns the removal from a specific position in a specific undertaking; (2) it addresses this specific undertaking and not the board member, even if this person is undoubtedly affected by the decision; and (3) it is based on a negative assessment of this person's fitness and propriety, ie on a condition, rather than on whether the person is responsible for a breach of law. The person's actions or omissions are, of course, one important factor (next to others) that may (indirectly) lead to a negative assessment. Recital 53 of MiFID II states that the management body of an investment firm must have the 'knowledge, skills and experience to be able to understand the firm's activities including the main risks', and indicates that the assessment's objective is to ensure the sound and prudent management of investment firms. This requires a forward-looking assessment, so that suitability assessments are prudential in nature.[14] A forward-looking assessment necessarily requires a prognosis for the future. This prognosis needs to take into account the complexity of the relevant investment firm's business

[10] Directive 2009/138/EC of the European Parliament and of the Council on the taking-up and pursuit of Insurance and Reinsurance [2009] OJ L 335/1 (hereafter 'Solvency II').

[11] Directive (EU) 2016/2341 of the European Parliament and of the Council on the activities and supervision of institutions for occupational retirement provision (IORPs) [2016] OJ L 354/37 (hereafter 'IORP').

[12] § 6 (7) and (8) Wertpapierhandelsgesetz.

[13] Chapter 25 § 1d Lag (2007:528) om värdepappersmarknaden.

[14] EBA and ESMA, 'Final Report: Joint ESMA and EBA Guidelines on the the assessment for the suitability of members of the management body and key function holders under Directive 2013/36/EU and Directive 2014/65/EU' (26 September 2017) para 50 (hereafter 'EBA and ESMA, Final Report: Joint Guidelines').

and the specific tasks and responsibilities attributed to the board position in question.[15] Past behaviour is, of course, an important basis for this prognosis, but it will normally be insufficient to justify a negative assessment only with past deficiencies, without suggesting why those negative circumstances lead to a negative prognosis.

In an initial fit and proper assessment, a ban that has already been imposed on the person in question is, of course, an important circumstance, and, if the ban applies to the position in question, the person is already unsuitable on formal grounds. If the position in question concerns a position not formally encompassed by the ban, for instance a person banned from taking up positions in the management body of a bank is being appointed to become a member of the management board of an investment firm, the ban is one of the circumstances that is to be taken into consideration. It does not, per se, lead to unsuitability, since the reasons for the ban must be assessed with regard to their relevance for the prognosis of the person's expected performance.

As we have seen, there are considerable differences between a ban imposed on a member of a management body, and the removal of the member from the same management body as a consequence of a negative suitability assessment. Whereas the former is clearly a sanction, in the sense that a ban is imposed by an authority as a reaction to an infringement of a legal requirement, the latter is more difficult to classify. There are various ways to categorise sanctions (for instance, into administrative and criminal sanctions).[16] Of high practical relevance, in this respect, is the case law of the ECHR on the assessment of criminal sanctions, since some of the procedural guarantees laid down in the ECHR and the Charter are only applicable in criminal proceedings. This chapter will, therefore, limit its analysis to the question of whether an NCA's decision, following a negative fit and proper assessment, may constitute a criminal sanction, in the sense meant by the ECHR. This analysis will be based on the description, in the following sections, of the elements of a fit and proper assessment, with the main focus lying on those aspects that involve an accountability dimension.

[15] See also, with regard to the rules applying in the insurance sector: Jürgen Bürkle, 'Personelle Anforderungen und behördliche Überwachung' in Frank S Diehl (ed), *Versicherungsunternehmensre cht* (CH Beck 2020) § 13 para 121.

[16] On different theories on the distinction between criminal and administrative sanctions, see Petter Asp, *EG:s sanktionsrätt* (Iustus 1998) 243 ff.

9.3 Fit and proper requirements in EU financial legislation

EU legislation requires members of management bodies of regulated entities in the financial sector to be 'fit and proper' for their positions. Supervisory authorities have the competence to deny the appointment or continued engagement of persons who are deemed unsuitable.

Despite the existence of European legislation in this field, and a trend towards increasing convergence, national rules and their application by the NCAs differ considerably.[17] Even among the EU directives, differences can be noted, both with regard to the scope of application, and to the requirements themselves. For example, EU legislation at level one requires fit and proper assessments by the supervisory authority of key function- holders of insurance undertakings and institutions for occupational retirement provision (IORPs), but not of MiFID II investment firms. Vos and others suspect that the reasons for these 'arbitrary' differences lie in 'careless drafting rather than a conscious policy choice', and advocate uniform rules across the financial sector, both in terms of level one and two regulation, and level threeguidelines issued by the ESAs.[18] In essence, however, the fit and proper requirements laid down in different pieces of EU legislation are comparable: members of the management body of a regulated entity must be sufficiently qualified, experienced, and skilled to perform their duties, and be of good repute and integrity.[19] In the insurance sector legislation, the latter two requirements are referred to as requirements of propriety, and the others as aspects concerning the fitness of a person.[20] For market operators, Article 41(2) of MiFID II, and, for credit institutions, Article 91 of CRD IV also explicitly mention independence of mind, the ability to devote sufficient time to the management position, and the requirement that the management body collectively possesses sufficient knowledge, skills, and experience. By means of a reference in Article 9 of MiFID II, the fit and proper requirements in Article 91 of CRD IV also apply to investment firms. The rules are supplemented by the European Banking Authority (EBA) and European

[17] With regard to insurance supervision, see EIOPA, 'Peer Review' (n 2) 5. With regard to banking supervision, see EBA, 'Peer Review Report' (n 5) 5.

[18] Tom Vos and others, 'A Cross-Sectoral-Analysis of Corporate Governance Provisions: About Forests and Trees' in Veerle Colaert, Danny Busch, and Thomas Incalza (eds), *European Financial Regulation: Levelling the Cross-Sectoral-Playing Field* (Hart 2019) 180 ff.

[19] See, eg Solvency II, art 42 (1); Commission Delegated Regulation (EU) 2015/35 supplementing Directive 2009/138/EC of the European Parliament and of the Council on the taking-up and pursuit of the business of Insurance and Reinsurance (Solvency II) [2015] OJ L 12/1, art 273 (2); MiFID II, art. 41.1; CRD IV, art 91.

[20] Solvency II, art 42 (1) (i) and (ii).

Securities and Markets Authority (ESMA)'s Joint Guidelines on the assessment of the suitability of members of the management body and key function holders.[21]. Even after the entry into force of the new investment firms regime under the IFD and Investment Firms Regulation,[22] on 26 June 2021, the CRD IV fit and proper requirements continue to apply to all investment firms.[23]

The Joint Guidelines address the circumstances that should be taken into consideration when assessing the honesty and integrity of a manager. These include past convictions for criminal offences, and ongoing investigations. Fit and proper requirements, thus, may function as an instrument to hold managers indirectly accountable for misconduct.

9.4 The personal scope of fit and proper requirements

According to Article 9(1) of MiFID II, the provisions in Article 91 of CRD IV apply to the members of the management body of investment firms falling under MiFID II. In contrast to other EU instruments, for instance Articles 3(7) and (8) of CRD IV, Article 4(36) of MiFID II requires member states to identify which organ or organs fall under the definition of 'management body' therein. Accordingly, they have to decide whether non-executive directors (in a single-tier board system) or members of a supervisory board (in two-tier systems) are encompassed or not. Even though the provision may give the impression that member states are entirely free to choose which organs should be considered management bodies, this is not the case. In order to ensure an implementation in conformity with the objectives of the directive, member states cannot

[21] EBA and ESMA, 'Guidelines on the Assessment of the Suitability of Members of the Management Body and Key Function Holders' (21 March 2018) (hereafter 'Joint Guidelines'). On the legal character of guidelines issued by the ESAs, see Dominique Ritleng, in Chapter 4 of this book and Britta Behrendt Jonsson, 'EIOPA's Guidelines and Recommendations: Mere Proposals or some kind of Binding Law?' Europarättslig Tidskrift 266.

[22] Regulation (EU) 2019/2033 of the European Parliament and of the Council on the prudential requirements of investment firms and amending Regulations (EU) No 1093/2010, (EU) No 575/2013, (EU) No 600/2014 and (EU) No 806/2014 [2019] OJ L 314 (hereafter 'IFR').

[23] Depending on their size, investment firms will, after 26 June 2021, either fall directly under Titles VII and VII of CRD IV, including fit and proper requirements (IFR, art 1(2)), because they will be reclassified as credit institutions, or be subjected to prudential supervision according to the CRD IV rules by an NCA (IFD, art 5), or they will have to continue to apply art 9 of MiFID II, which refers to art 91 of CRD IV. The only investment firms not subject to fit and proper requirements laid down in EU legislation are those that member states have exempted from the scope of MiFID II by making use of art 3(1) of MiFID II. However, member states are obliged to subject these firms to prudential supervision rules analogous to some of the MiFID II rules, including fit and proper requirements (see MiFID II, art 3(1)(a)).

exclude organs or members of a company organ that, without doubt, fall under the definition of 'management body'.[24]

In contrast to the Solvency II and IORP Directives, MiFID II does not extend the application of the fit and proper requirements to key function holders or senior management.[25] Insofar as the Joint Guidelines concern key function holders, they are, therefore, not applicable to investment firms. Of course, this does not prevent investment firms from implementing similar internal assessments in the recruiting processes for certain employees.

9.5 Assessment of fitness and propriety

Compliance with the fit and proper requirements is subject to assessment by both the investment firm and, in certain situations, the NCA.[26]

Credit institutions and investment firms have to comply with the fit and proper requirements at all times (Article 91 (1) of CRD IV). In order to safeguard compliance with this obligation, paragraphs 24 to 30 of the Joint Guidelines require institutions to conduct their own assessments at certain moments, namely when applying for authorisation, when new members of the management body are appointed, or are reappointed and the 'requirements of the position have changed', and on an ongoing basis, in particular when circumstances arise that may have an impact on the suitability of the persons concerned.

These self-assessments precede, and to some extent coincide with, the assessment procedures to be conducted by the NCA, especially when the investment firm is seeking authorisation (Article 9(4) of MiFID II), or upon the election of a new member of the management body (Article 9(5) of MiFID II).

The Joint Guidelines specify the aspects that need to be taken into account during a fit and proper assessment, and address the calculation of the number of eligible directorships, and when a member of the management body can be

[24] Dirk Zetsche, 'Art. 9 MiFID II', para 6 in Matthias Lehmann and Christoph Kumpan, *European Financial Services Law: Article-By-Article Commentary* (Nomos 2019); Compare Vos and others (n 18) 195: 'member states can choose'.

[25] See the comparison in Vos and others (n 18) 195.

[26] For significant credit institutions falling under the Single Supervisory System, the assessment is undertaken by the ECB instead of the NCA, applying applicable national law. On fit and proper assessments by the ECB, and this aspect in particular, see Danny Busch and Annick Teubner, 'Fit and Proper Assessments within the Single Supervisory Mechanism' (2019) European Banking Institute Working Paper Series 2019/34 <https://ssrn.com/abstract=3346976> accessed 17 February 2021.

deemed to be able to dedicate sufficient time to the new position. They also deal with collective suitability of all members of the management body, and independence of mind. Of particular interest here are the guidelines on the assessment of adequate knowledge, skills, and experience (as part of the fitness assessment), and of a person's reputation, honesty, and propriety (as part of the propriety assessment).

9.5.1 Knowledge, skills, and experience (fitness)

Knowledge, skills, and experience are criteria assessed on the basis of the board member's activities and behaviour in the past and may, therefore, in case of a negative assessment, imply a notion of accountability. They must be assessed against the background of the position and institution in question, taking into account the institution's risk profile, business model, size, and complexity.[27]

Assessment of knowledge and experience includes objective, formal aspects that can be assessed quite easily by obtaining information on a person's work experience and education, documented by university diplomas or degree certificates. The Joint Guidelines stress, however, that assessment should not be limited to these aspects. Knowledge gained from previous occupations also needs to be analysed thoroughly (paragraph 63). Board members are also required to have specific knowledge about the investment firm, for instance concerning its governance arrangements, and about their own respective roles and responsibilities (paragraph 59). It is permissible for this undertaking that specific knowledge be acquired during a training programme after the appointment.[28] Equally, when a member of the management body is deemed not to have sufficient knowledge in a particular area, or lacks certain specific skills, NCAs may grant conditional approval, requiring the person to acquire this knowledge or skill within a certain time.

If a person is deemed unfit due to a lack of sufficient knowledge or experience, this does not necessarily imply a negative judgement of the person's previous professional conduct. A prospective board member may have outstanding university degrees and proven leadership skills, but if the NCA deems him or her unfit because their work experience is deemed to be too limited to provide the necessary experience for the board position in question, the negative assessment merely implies that the person is not yet deemed suitable. The

[27] See EBA and ESMA, Final Report: Joint Guidelines (n 14) paras 21 and 27.
[28] This can be derived from Joint Guidelines (n 21) paras 94 and 95.

criteria of knowledge and experience are, thus, not aspects with an 'accountability dimension'.

The third criterion, 'skill', is not defined in the Joint Guidelines, but their Annex II contains a non-exhaustive list of relevant skills that institutions are expected to assess: authenticity, language skills, decisiveness, communication, judgement, customer- and quality-orientation, leadership, loyalty, external awareness, negotiation skills, persuasiveness, teamwork skills, strategic acumen, stress resistance, sense of responsibility, and chairing of meetings. Again, the exact requirements depend on the position in question. The list contains, without doubt, useful criteria for a nomination committee in the process of recruiting new members of a management body, as it stresses the importance of these skills for sound management, and encourages an explicit assessment rather than mere reliance on intuition or reputation. Its suitability for carrying out internal assessment on an ongoing basis is more doubtful. When existing board members are subject to an internal assessment, it seems rather unlikely that their skills will be assessed more negatively in an ongoing assessment than in an initial assessment, unless the person has shown severe shortcomings and shall be removed from his or her position.

NCAs are formally competent to reject a person on the basis of insufficient skills, but given the difficulties of an objective assessment of most of the skills mentioned, this should be applied only in exceptional cases, and conclusions on a person's lack of skills need to be based on facts. It is far from self-evident that NCAs should have the possibility of rejecting people due to a lack of skills that are assessed in a subjective way. This puts NCAs in a position where they become a sort of 'super-recruiter': where the supervisory authority's judgement on a person's skills may override the nomination committee's recommendation. EBA and ESMA obviously do not expect NCAs to assess a person's skills themselves, since the list of documentation to be provided for initial appointments in Annex III of the Joint Guidelines does not require any documentation concerning skills. The requirement to provide a list of referees, and to include institutions' own suitability reports, however, open up the possibility that NCAs may revise institutions' own assessments of skills.

Regardless of whether it is done internally, or by an NCA, the assessment of a person's skills may contain elements of accountability for past actions. This is because: (1) severe problems in an institution are more likely to draw attention to insufficient management skills of the persons responsible; and (2) because the NCA does not usually have enough insight to be able to assess a person's skills. A negative assessment of 'soft skills' will, therefore, probably be based on the conduct of a person in a crisis, rather than under ordinary circumstances.

9.5.2 Reputation, honesty, and integrity (propriety)

More clearly than in the context of the fitness criteria, an accountability dimension can be found in the criteria belonging to the requirement of propriety: reputation, honesty, and integrity. These criteria have in common that they require a moral judgement on the person in question.

The Joint Guidelines mention three different types of information to be taken into account in propriety assessments. These can be summarised as information on: (1) the person's criminal and administrative record, including any ongoing investigations; (2) past and present business performance, and the person's own financial soundness; and (3) the person's manner of dealing with competent authorities, as well as any prior refusals of an authority to carry out a certain profession. Also belonging to this last category is information concerning any 'disqualification by any relevant competent authority from acting as a member of the management body'.[29] This seems to include both bans that an NCA has imposed on a person (which are already encompassed by the obligation to provide information on measures taken by a regulatory body for non-compliance with regulatory law), and prior negative fit and proper assessments by an NCA (but not negative internal assessments by a regulated entity). If a person has been deemed unsuitable by an NCA before, this is supposed to be taken into consideration as an aspect of honesty and integrity. The rationale behind this seems to be that an NCA in a member state ought to be informed about another member state's NCA's negative assessment before taking its decision, so that negative circumstances revealed by one NCA do not remain undiscovered by another authority. The assessments, however, are to be undertaken by applying national law. Different outcomes of suitability assessments in different states, therefore, are not necessarily attributable to divergent knowledge about the relevant circumstances, but may be the result of differences in national law. Such differences may concern, for instance, the time period for rehabilitation after a criminal conviction.[30]

The Joint Guidelines state, in paragraph 73, that 'a member of the management body should be deemed to be of good repute and of honesty and integrity if there are no objective and demonstrable grounds to suggest otherwise'. In the final report on the guidelines, the ESA's presented their view of the burden of proof: when concerns have been raised, the burden of proof for a person's suitability lies with the institution.[31]

[29] Joint Guidelines (n 21) para 78.
[30] Busch and Teubner (n 28) 22.
[31] EBA and ESMA, Final Report: Joint Guidelines (n 14) para 50.

This is not without concern, for several reasons. Some of the criteria to be taken into account give only a very vague indication of a person's suitability. There is a risk of them being given too much weight by institutions or the NCAs. For instance, the business performance, bankruptcy, or winding-up of entities directed by a person may be indicators of that person's suitability, but it must be assessed against the background of the person's contribution to the situation.[32] Investment firms may be overly cautious and refrain from nominating a person if their internal assessment reveals any circumstances in the person's past that may lead to discussions with the NCA. With 'suitability' of a person being a concept involving proportionality, discretion, and moral judgements, it is impossible to be fully proven. If the presumption of suitability is rebutted, and the burden of proof is reversed as soon as concerns are raised, there is a risk that NCAs will not live up to their obligations to also take mitigating circumstances into account. With regard to the banking sector, the need to uphold the public's confidence in the banking system and, ultimately, to contribute to financial stability has been cited as a justification for the reversal of the burden of proof.[33] Since the business activities of investment firms differ from those of banks, it is submitted that the confidence argument is less convincing in a MiFID II context. It is arguable that only under very exceptional circumstances would a board appointment in an investment firm potentially impact severely on the public's confidence in the financial system. This aspect, therefore, risks being overinterpreted.

Fitness and propriety aspects may be interrelated, since administrative procedures against a person may have their background in regulatory breaches caused by insufficient knowledge or skills. If a new position requires similar knowledge and skills to the one under which the person was responsible for infringements of regulatory law, the NCA must assess whether the person has acquired the necessary knowledge, skills, and experience in the meantime.[34]

An issue not explicitly addressed in the Joint Guidelines is the existence of a health condition or conditions that may impair the suitability of a member of a management body. None of the documents that need to be provided include information on the physical or psychological health of an appointee, and, considering the sensitivity of such information, this is understandable. However,

[32] Joint Guidelines (n 21) para 77.

[33] Söderström (n 7) 156.

[34] An example of such a negative assessment is the decision by the Financial Conduct Authority, 'Final Notice against Elizabeth Marie Walker', 21 February 2020 <www.fca.org.uk/publication/final-notices/elizabeth-marie-walker-2020.pdf> accessed 17 February 2021. The assessment concerned an application of approval to perform a so-called 'controlled function'.

known continuing health problems need to be taken into account insofar as they affect the amount of time a member of the management body can dedicate to the position—for instance due to frequent health-related absences—or impair the skills necessary for performing his or her tasks, such as judgement, decisiveness, or resilience to stress.[35]

9.6 Fit and proper requirements and proportionality

In the view of EBA and ESMA, 'all members of the management body must be of good repute, regardless of the nature, scale and complexity of the institution and their specific position'.[36] This has been described as leaving no room for the application of the proportionality principle in the assessment of propriety, as, in contrast to the fitness assessment, a person's reputation can only be assessed as either good or bad.[37] This understanding is supported by EIOPA: 'the proportionality principle does not result in different standards in the case of the propriety requirement'.[38] EIOPA's statement is correct if proportionality is understood as a mechanism only to justify the application of different levels of standards depending on the specific features of an undertaking, and especially more lenient requirements for small undertakings with low, homogeneous risk profiles. It does not mean, however, that a person who is considered unsuitable for one position would also necessarily be unsuitable for another position. Paragraph 74 of the Joint Guidelines acknowledges that not only mitigating circumstances such as the minor nature of a relevant offence, or the time that his elapsed since, but also the relevance of the offence to the member's role should be considered.[39] Thus, propriety is not an absolute concept, but can be regained over time, and is dependent on the tasks that are to be performed.

It is doubtful whether a differentiation between the application of the proportionality principle to the criteria belonging to the fitness requirements and those belonging to the propriety requirements is useful. If both sets of criteria are understood as relating to the requirement to be fit and proper for a specific position in the management body of a specific investment firm, it may

[35] 'Physical and psychological impairments' need to be taken into account: Christian Armbrüster in *BeckOK VAG* (10th edn, CH Beck 2020) § 24 para 19. See also Waclawik (n 4) 89 paras 27 and 28.

[36] EBA and ESMA, 'Final Report: Joint Guidelines' (n 14) para 38; see also EIOPA, 'Final Report on Public Consultation no 14/017 on Guidelines on System of Governance' (28 January 2015) (hereafter 'EIOPA, Final Report: Governance') para 2.57.

[37] Busch and Teubner (n 28) 13.

[38] EIOPA, Final Report: Governance (n 38) para 2.58.

[39] Joint Guidelines (n 21) para 74.

also be said that knowledge, skills, and experience are not subject to proportionality assessments. All members of the management body must have adequate knowledge, skills, and experience, but what is adequate depends on the respective role and of the nature, scale, and complexity of the investment firm, ie the proportionality assessment is inherent in, and not additional to, the fitness assessment.

9.7 Fit and proper assessments as criminal sanctions?

The Joint Guidelines mention fundamental rights, and particularly the presumption of innocence, in the chapter on the assessment of a person's reputation, honesty, and integrity.[40] When NCAs conduct a fit and proper assessment, both the ECHR and the Charter are applicable. We have seen that an appointee or board member's criminal record, and any ongoing investigations to which they are subject, are aspects that need to be taken into account in a fit and proper assessment. With this in mind, we can return to the question of whether an NCA's decision to refuse the appointment, or demand the removal, of a board member constitutes a criminal sanction, in the sense of the ECHR. If this were the case, the procedural guarantees applicable to criminal proceedings would apply, which would have consequences for the way that NCAs have to conduct their assessments. In the context of a fit and proper assessment, this concerns the right to a fair trial and, particularly, the right not to incriminate oneself (Article 6 (1) of the ECHR and Article 47 of the Charter), and the *ne bis in idem* principle, ie the right not to be convicted twice for the same action (Article 4 of Protocol 7 of the ECHR and Article 50 of the Charter).

The right not to incriminate oneself may be relevant when there are ongoing investigations against the person in question, or against the regulated entity of which the person was a board member. In the fit and proper assessment, a person's attitude concerning prior mismanagement may have an impact on the outcome: is the person regretful, takes responsibility, and therefore can be expected to act differently next time? Or is the person denying any failure and can be expected to act in a similar way again, and what does this say about the person's leadership skills? It is important to note, however, that a denial of a previous breach does not necessarily indicate a person's obstinacy and unwillingness to learn. It may simply be motivated by the wish to escape personal

[40] EBA and ESMA, Final Report: Joint Guidelines (n 14) paras 74–76.

liability, or by concerns over losing protection from directors' and officers' liability insurance, in the event that the person faces or fears liability charges connected with the situation. And even if a manager is convinced that he or she has not acted unlawfully, he or she might still have learnt a lesson.

Also, if an NCA removes a person from his or her position for alleged criminal behaviour, or denies a new position, may he or she still be prosecuted? If the *ne bis in idem* principle hindered prosecution after such decision, it could be counterproductive to base a removal or denial on such allegations since the suspect would could not be convicted to (potentially harsher) criminal sanctions.

The fundamental rights referred to above are only guaranteed in criminal proceedings. That a fit and proper assessment, or rather the denial of membership in, or removal from, the management body of an investment firm could be considered a criminal proceeding, seems far-fetched at first sight, since there are considerable differences between this and 'ordinary' criminal proceedings, as follows:

(1) The supervisory measure is not the direct consequence of a law infringement, but of an assessment of a person's qualification or condition (where his or her prior actions play a role, besides other aspects). In other words, the typical description of an offence is lacking.
(2) With regard to an initial suitability assessment, the assessment process is started only after an appointee accepts a position on the management body of an investment firm, in contrast to ordinary criminal procedures, where proceedings are initiated without the cooperation of the accused.
(3) The 'sanction', ie removal from the management body or denial of appointment, differs from 'ordinary' criminal sanctions such as fines or imprisonment.
(4) If done correctly, the assessment is forward-looking rather than backward-looking, so that a negative assessment should never be based only on past actions without a prognosis for the future.
(5) A person can be denied appointment due to lack of knowledge, in which case there is no connection to any offence at all.

However, despite these considerable differences, the application of the procedural guarantees cannot be entirely excluded, as the analyses of the case law of the European Court of Human Rights (ECtHR) and the European Court of Justice conducted by van Bockel,[41] and Lamandini, Ramos Muñoz, and Solana

[41] Bastiaan van Bockel, 'Fundamental Rights Aspects of the SSM: Differentiated Standards of Protection under the Charter of Fundamental Rights of the EU' (ECB Legal Conference 2015, From

Álvarez[42] show. Both of these studies concerned the ECB's competences under the Single Supervisory Mechanism, but their results can also be applied to the fit and proper assessments conducted by the NCAs.

According to the jurisprudence of the ECtHR, the classification as 'criminal' is autonomous from national law, and subject to the same criteria, namely those developed in the *Engel* case.[43] These criteria are: (1) the legal classification under national law; (2) the nature of the offence; and/or (3) the degree or severity of penalty.

The first criterion refers to the classification at national law, but the classification is only conclusive if the proceedings or sanctions are classified as criminal according to national law. In that case, they are also considered criminal for the purposes of the ECHR, and the two other criteria are not tested.[44] Only if the proceedings are not considered criminal according to national law are the two other criteria relevant. Assuming that the ESA's view that the suitability assessment is 'distinct from criminal or administrative infringement procedures'[45] is shared in national law, recourse to the other two criteria is necessary.

The second criterion is the nature of the offence, where, among other factors, the punitive or deterrent purpose[46] of the rule in question plays a role, ie whether it protects the general interests of society usually protected by criminal law,[47] and whether it is generally applicable rather than directed to a specific group of people.[48]

General applicability is used to differentiate criminal proceedings from disciplinary proceedings, which are not considered criminal in the sense of the ECHR.[49] The ECtHR has considered as disciplinary proceedings, among others, the withdrawal of the pension rights of a retired judge who was convicted of murder,[50] the temporary suspension of the right to practise as an

Monetary Union to Banking Union, on the way to Capital Markets Union 2015) 112 <www.ecb.europa.eu/pub/pdf/other/frommonetaryuniontobankingunion201512.en.pdf> accessed 17 February 2021.

[42] Marco Lamandini, David Ramos Muñoz, and Javier Solana Álvarez, 'Depicting the Limits to the SSM's Supervisory Powers: The Role of Constitutional Mandates and of Fundamental Rights' Protection' (Quaderni di Ricerca Giuridica, October 2015) 97.

[43] *Engel and Others v The Netherlands* App nos 5100/71; 5101/71; 5102/71; 5354/72; 5370/72, 8 June 1976, paras 81–85.

[44] ibid, para 81.

[45] EBA and ESMA, 'Final Report: Joint Guidelines' (n 14) para 50.

[46] *Öztürk v Germany* App no 8544/79, 21 February 1984, para 53.

[47] *Grande Stevens v Italy* App no 18640/10, 4 March 2014, para 90.

[48] *Bendenoun v France* App no 12547/86, 24 February 1994, para 47; *Müller-Hartburg v Austria* App no 47195/06, 19 February 2013, para 44.

[49] See the references to cases concerning various professional groups in *Ramos Nunes de Carvalho E SÁ v Portugal* App nos 55391/13, 57728/13, and 74041/13, 6 November 2013, para 123.

[50] *Kremzow v Austria* App no 16417/90 (Commission Decision), 7 November 1990.

accountant,[51] and the loss of the right to work as a lawyer.[52] Proceedings are deemed to have a disciplinary rather than criminal nature when they are based on provisions that 'are designed to protect the profession's honour and reputation and to maintain public trust' in the profession.[53] Ongoing fit and proper assessments only apply to current members of management bodies of investment firms, and not to the general public. Initial assessments apply to anyone who is to be appointed and are, arguably, general in nature because, in theory, anybody could be appointed, and thereby subjected to a suitability assessment. Even if the main objective of the fit and proper requirements is to safeguard the stability of the financial market by requiring managers to be suitable, the good reputation of managers, as an element to enshrine trust in the financial markets, is also reflected in the rules on fit and proper assessments.

Based on the aforementioned cases, it seems that a decision following a negative suitability assessment will not be considered a criminal proceeding, even if it is based on prior behaviour. However, the *Grande Stevens* case leaves room for some doubt. This case concerned administrative fines, temporary bans, and withdrawal of a licence, as sanctions imposed by an independent administrative body for market manipulation. The Court held that the body's task was to protect investors, and to ensure the 'effectiveness, development and transparency of the stock markets', which were general interests of society, 'usually protected by criminal law'.[54] Whether or not the rules applied to a limited group of professionals was, thus, irrelevant.[55]

When examining the third *Engel* criterion in the *Grande Stevens* case, the Court also considered the possible sanctions as a whole to be sufficiently severe to constitute criminal rather than administrative sanctions, and assumed that the intention of the sanctions was the punishment of unlawful conduct.[56] In the *Matyjek* case, a person's prohibition from taking up certain government positions as a sanction for having lied about collaboration with the Polish secret service during the Cold War was considered to be a sanction with a criminal character since 'the prohibition to practising certain professions (political or legal) for a long period of time may have a very serious impact on a person, depriving him or her of the possibility of continuing professional life'.[57] Some

[51] *Luksch v Austria* App no 37075/97, 21 November 2000.
[52] *Grande Stevens* (n 49) para 96.
[53] *Ramos Nunes de Carvalho* (n 51) para 125.
[54] *Grande Stevens* (n 49) para 96.
[55] van Bockel (n 43) 111 at fn 24.
[56] *Grande Stevens* (n 49) paras 96 and 97. The case is also discussed by Lamandini, Muñoz, and Álvarez (n 44) 97.
[57] *Matyjek v Poland* App no 38184/03, 30 May 2006, para 54. See also van Bockel (n 43) 112.

similarities to the outcome of a negative fit and proper assessment can be noted: the consequences for an individual's possibility of continuing his or her professional life may be similarly severe for a board member or appointee as in the *Matyjek* case, and the procedure in the *Matyjek* case also served to ensure that civil servants had the necessary moral qualification for their position, ie an unblemished reputation.[58] However, there are also differences that justify another classification. In contrast to fit and proper assessments, the proceedings in the *Matyjek* case bore similarities to criminal procedure: the sanction consisted of a temporary ban for a variety of public positions, and was the consequence of a very specific instance of wrongdoing, namely submitting a false declaration.

To identify the purpose of a measure, the Court identifies the presumed intention behind the measure. A negative fit and proper assessment could be considered a criminal sanction based on the *Grande Stevens* judgment, at least if it is part of a bundle of sanctions against a person.[59] However, if NCAs conduct their assessments correctly, with a forward-looking prospect, rather than simply justifying the removal of a board member by reference to prior breaches, it seems rather unlikely that a suitability assessment will be considered a criminal proceeding.

9.8 Ongoing proceedings and the presumption of innocence

As already described, the presumption of innocence, laid down in Article 6(2) of the Convention and Article 48(1) of the Charter, could be violated if a negative fit and proper assessment is based on alleged criminal behaviour. According to the case law of the ECtHR, the presumption of innocence is a fundamental right of a person charged with a criminal offence, and also applies in parallel proceedings[60] or, if the accused has been acquitted, in subsequent civil, administrative, or disciplinary actions.[61]

In the course of a fit and proper assessment, it is therefore clear that the NCA must not presume the person to be guilty because there are ongoing criminal proceedings. This is also recognised in paragraph 76 of the Joint Guidelines, and should be quite obvious when the criminal proceedings concern an act

[58] *Matyjek* (n 59) para 54.
[59] Lamandini, Muñoz, and Álvarez (n 44) 97.
[60] *Böhmer v Germany* App no 37568/97, 3 October 2002, para 67.
[61] *Kemal Coşkun v Turkey* App no 45028/07, 28 June 2017, para 41.

or omission that is unrelated to the person's professional conduct, for instance criminal charges following a car accident. The same principle should apply when a person is subject to ongoing administrative procedures that could be considered criminal in the sense meant by the Charter, for instance procedures that may result in a temporary ban or a fine. NCAs could potentially be given the possibility of postponing a fit and proper assessment during ongoing investigations against the person in question until the investigation or proceedings are finished. This could be a way to deal with insecurity, but, in an initial assessment, there is a considerable risk that a postponement would have the same effect on the individual as a negative assessment.

However, the presumption of innocence does not hinder the NCA from taking the underlying circumstances of the proceedings into consideration, as the ECB states in its *Guide to Fit and Proper Assessments*.[62] This is particularly important given the difficulty of holding managers criminally or civilly liable, otherwise manifest mismanagement would have to be disregarded in the assessment merely because the threshold for personal sanctions was not attained. For instance, repeated breaches of regulatory law by an investment firm may indicate organisational failures or an unsound management culture that may be attributed to certain members of the management body, even if their own personal involvement in a particular breach cannot be proven. Not to take such circumstances into account would sit badly with the requirement to assess soft skills, for example. A negative assessment requires that such failures can, in fact, be attributed to a certain person. In other words, there is no automatic link between regulatory breaches in an undertaking and a manager's insufficient management skills. It is therefore insufficient for an NCA to question the suitability of a person solely on the basis of regulatory breaches. However, it should be easier to demonstrate concrete instances of insufficient management skills than to provide the evidence required for imposing a sanction against an individual.

The ECB also mentions in its guide that ongoing legal proceedings must also be assessed in the context of the ability of the affected person to commit sufficient time to their position.[63] It is certainly true that defending legal or criminal proceedings is often time-consuming, but consideration of this aspect may lead to a circumvention of the presumption of innocence. A negative suitability assessment of a member of a management body should not, therefore, be based solely on this factor .

[62] European Central Bank, 'Guide to Fit and Proper Assessments' (May 2018) 13.
[63] ibid, fn 14.

9.9 Conclusions

Fit and proper assessments of members of management bodies of investment firms may serve as instruments of accountability, alongside administrative sanctions and criminal or civil liability, since regulatory breaches or other misconduct of the firm or the person may have a negative impact on fitness and propriety. The risk of being assessed negatively and being removed from the management body, or being denied a new position may, therefore, have a deterrent effect on managers, and foster sound (risk) management. The objective of the fit and proper assessment is to ensure that investment firms are managed by competent persons, in order to protect investors and market stability. The assessment must, therefore, be forward-looking, even if past circumstances must, of course, play a role. A negative assessment has severe consequences for the person in question, both in terms of reputation, and with regard to his or her professional career. Assessments, therefore, need to be conducted in a professional manner, taking into account proportionality aspects and mitigating circumstances. Past behaviour or observed misconduct may lead to a negative assessment despite acquittal from criminal or other charges, but the forward-looking character of the assessment requires a negative prognosis for the future. A person who has been deemed responsible for illegal acts should not be automatically be considered unsuitable, although this constitutes an important circumstance to be considered in the course of the assessment. If an NCA undertakes a thorough forward-looking analysis, the risk of their fit and proper assessment being considered a criminal proceeding, within the meaning of the ECHR and the Charter, is very small.

10

Remuneration Policies in Investment Firms

Incentives, Regulation, and Accountability

Rebecca Söderström

10.1 Introduction

> *There is agreement among regulatory bodies at international level that weaknesses in corporate governance in a number of financial institutions, including the absence of effective checks and balances within them, have been a contributory factor to the financial crisis. Excessive and imprudent risk taking may lead to the failure of individual financial institutions and systemic problems in Member States and globally. Incorrect conduct of firms providing services to clients may lead to investor detriment and loss of investor confidence.*
>
> MiFID II, recital 5.

Corporate governance is a crucial and central component for any company's successful conduct of its business. There are many aspects to how corporations are owned, controlled, and operated; aspects that are included in the wide research field of corporate governance. Legal as well as societal, economic, and political structures and dimensions can be included in this discussion. Corporate governance or, rather, the observed *lack* of corporate governance, became highly topical during the financial crisis of 2007 to 2008. As the recital quoted above shows, flawed governance of financial institutions has been identified as playing a major role in the crisis.[1] The main focus in the subsequent

[1] See Federal Reserve Bank, *Guidance on Sound Incentive Compensation Policies* (Board of Governors of the Federal Reserve System 2010); Jacques de Larosière, *Report of the High-level Group on Financial Supervision in the EU* (2009) 24; Commission, 'Green Paper: Corporate Governance in Financial Institutions and Remuneration Policies' COM (2010) 284 final; Lucian A Bebchuk and Holger Spamann, 'Regulating Banker's Pay' (2020) 98 Georgetown Law Journal 247.

Rebecca Söderström, *Remuneration Policies in Investment Firms* In: *Legal Accountability in EU Markets for Financial Instruments.* Edited by: Carl Fredrik Bergström and Magnus Strand, Oxford University Press. © Rebecca Söderström 2021.
DOI: 10.1093/oso/9780192849281.003.0010

discussion and, indeed, also in the regulatory responses following the crisis, has been on risk, incentives, and accountability, with the purpose of restoring good corporate governance in financial institutions and firms.

One important tool by which owners may affect a company is through *compensation* of the company's executive staff. By using incentive programmes and other types of variable remuneration policies, incentives can be imposed on managers (executives) of the company to work for the owners' interests. Such incentive programmes are quite common, not least in publicly traded companies with dispersed owners. The programmes consist of bonuses, in cash or in shares, which are paid when certain business parameters are met or fulfilled. By means of such arrangements, executives are induced to achieve the company's business goals. Executive compensation through variable remuneration is often an effective way to govern a company and, thus, a central part of discussions on corporate governance.

In the wake of the financial crisis, variable remuneration has, however, become widely problematised as a factor forcing companies into unsound risk-taking and short-sighted business decisions; actions that may bring detrimental consequences to investors and society.[2] Regulation has become adopted as the answer to these problems.

This Chapter will elaborate on the post-crisis regulation of remuneration policies in investment firms. The main focus will be on variable remuneration, because such compensation schemes have the conflict between owners' governance, on one hand, and financial stability and investor protection, on the other, at their heart.[3] The regulation of remuneration in investment firms is one of many attempts to regulate that has the purpose to improving corporate governance. The main aim of this chapter is to discuss how MiFID II and related regulation impacts corporate governance of investment firms, with remuneration policies as an example, and a focus. As accountability has been identified as being central to good corporate governance, the analysis draws on arguments from the research area of accountability.[4]

[2] See, eg Frederico Della Negra, *MiFID II and Private Law—Enforcing EU Conduct of Business Rules* (Hart Publishing 2019) 7 --26; Lucian A Bebchuk, Alma Cohen and Holger Spamann, 'The Wages of Failure: Executive Compensation at Bear Stearns and Lehman 2000–2008' (2010) 27 Yale Journal on Regulation 257; Rüdiger Fahlenbrach and René M Stulz, 'Bank CEO Incentives and the Credit Crisis' [2010] Journal of Financial Economics.

[3] In this chapter, the relationships between shareholders and managers are in focus. This is the main relationship in firms with dispersed ownership. In family-owned firms or firms with higher ownership concentration, the relationships between shareholders and managers are not as problematic. See Katarzyna Cieślak, 'Agency Conflicts, Executive Compensation Regulations and CEO Pay-performance Sensitivity: Evidence from Sweden' (2018) 22 Journal of Management and Governance 535.

[4] For a review on accountability research in a European context, see Chapter 11 of this book, by Frederico Della Negra.

The chapter links two different levels of accountability already established in the literature: the firm level of accountability and the regulatory level of accountability. The research question that will be discussed in the chapter is whether MiFID II and related regulation on remuneration in investment firms successfully achieve a higher degree of accountability in investment firms, both as regards firm-level accountability and regulatory-level accountability.

The chapter will not deal with external remuneration issues, where investment firms are targeted with regulation because of payments from third parties. In investment firms, inducements in relation to the provision of services to clients give rise to conflicts of interest. An investment firm may, by giving customers advice on which product or service to choose, receive fees, commissions, or other benefits from a third party in relation to the provision of the third party's service to clients. Therefore, MiFID II restricts third-party payments, and even bans the use of such remuneration for some types of investment businesses.[5] The regulation aims at protecting customers' interests and to manage the information asymmetry between investment firms and investors. This chapter is restricted to structures of remuneration *within* investment firms, and the relationships between owners and directors and other executive staff. As already described, the overarching question is whether regulation of remuneration in investment firms is effective in achieving the regulatory goals of financial stability and investor protection.

Reforms of the regulation of investment firms[6] also give reasons to discuss whether EU regulatory policy on the financial markets is changing. A decade ago, the EU began regulating the financial markets, after the greatest financial crisis since the Great Depression in the 1920s. Now, ten years later, the EU markets for financial services are thoroughly harmonised—it is, indeed, one internal market. The introduction of Regulation 2019/2033 and Directive 2019/2034 raises questions on how the regulatory path for the EU legislator will develop in the coming decade.

[5] Directive (EU) 2014/65 of the European Parliament and of the Council of 15 May 2014 on markets in financial instruments and amending Directive 2002/92/EC and Directive 2011/61/EU (MiFID II), art 24.

[6] Directive (EU) 2019/2034 of the European Parliament and of the Council of 27 November 2019 on the prudential supervision of investment firms and amending Directives 2002/87/EC, 2009/65/EC, 2011/61/EU, 2013/36/EU, 2014/59/EU, and 2014/65/EU (hereafter 'Directive 2019/2034'); Regulation (EU) 2019/2033 of the European Parliament and of the Council of 27 November 2019 on the prudential requirements of investment firms and amending Regulations (EU) No 1093/2010, (EU) No 575/2013, (EU) No 600/2014, and (EU) No 806/2014 (hereafter 'Regulation 2019/2033').

10.2 Regulatory structures

Certain requirements on remuneration are specified as central *operating conditions* for investment firms. Article 9 of MiFID II sets out requirements for the member states to 'ensure that the management body of an investment firm defines, oversees and is accountable for the implementation of the governance arrangements that ensure effective and prudent management of the investment firm including the segregation of duties in the investment firm and the prevention of conflicts of interest, and in a manner that promotes the integrity of the market and the interest of clients'. In Article 23 of MiFID II, the investment firm's 'own remuneration and other incentive structures' are highlighted in relation to conflicts of interest within the firm, including managers, employees, tied agents, clients and other persons linked to the firm. Member states are obligated to require investment firms to take all appropriate steps to identify, and to prevent or manage, such conflicts of interest.

Remuneration within investment firms is, additionally, addressed by specific *prudential requirements* at the EU level, through Directive 2013/36/EU, the Capital Requirements Directive (CRD IV).[7] The purpose of the rules on remuneration is to foster sound and effective risk management, and to align remuneration policies with the risk appetite, values, and long-term interests of the investment firm. In short, the rules restrict the scope for determining executive compensation, making remuneration policies a matter for legislators and supervisors, and not exclusively for the company (usually the board of directors) to decide.

Since 26 June 2021, reformed rules on the prudential regulation of investment firms have been implemented in the member states. The EU has adopted a new regulation (EU/2019/2033) and directive (EU/2019/2034), which contain specific prudential rules for investment firms.[8] Under this new package of rules, investment firms are regulated by separate rules from those applicable to banks.[9] The main reason for this regulatory reform is to adapt the rules to ensure that the regulatory requirements are proportionate to the nature, scope,

[7] Directive (EU) 2013/36 of the European Parliament and of the Council of 26 June 2013 on access to the activity of credit institutions and the prudential supervision of credit institutions and investment firms, amending Directive 2002/87/EC and repealing Directives 2006/48/EC and 2006/49/EC (hereafter 'Directive 2013/36').

The Directive collectively refers to credit institutions and investment firms as 'institutions'.

[8] Directive (EU) 2019/2034; Regulation (EU) 2019/2033.

[9] The largest investment firms, being those with a total value of consolidated assets of 30 billion euros or more, will be included within the definition of credit institutions, and continue to be included within Regulation (EU) 2019/2033, art 62.3, amending Regulation (EU) No 575/2013, art 4.1.

and complexity of the activities of the investment firms.[10] The rules on remuneration have been slightly amended, as well, excluding small and non-interconnected investment firms from the requirements.[11]

In the next section, variable remuneration is defined and described.

10.3 Definitions of variable remuneration

Variable remuneration can be contrasted with fixed remuneration, which consists of salaries or fees where the recipient cannot affect the amount through his or her own performance. Today, legislation contains precise definitions for fixed and variable remuneration. Under EU law, remuneration is either fixed or variable; there is no third category of remuneration.

The European Banking Authority (EBA) defines variable remuneration in *Guidelines on sound remuneration policies*[12], by setting out the components for fixed remuneration:

Remuneration is fixed where the conditions for its award and its amount:

1. are based on predetermined criteria;
2. are non-discretionary, reflecting the level of professional experience and seniority of staff;
3. are transparent with respect to the individual amount awarded to the individual staff member;
4. are permanent, ie maintained over a period tied to the specific role and organisational responsibilities;
5. are non-revocable; the permanent amount is only changed via collective bargaining, or following renegotiation in line with national criteria on wage setting;
6. cannot be reduced, suspended, or cancelled by the institution;
7. do not provide incentives for risk assumption; and
8. do not depend on performance.

If the remuneration does not meet the components set out above, it is considered to be variable remuneration. The EBA guidelines are non-binding, but

[10] Commission, Inception Impact Assessment - Ares(2017)1546878; Regulation (EU) 2019/2033, recital 13.

[11] Directive (EU) 2019/2034, recital 22; Regulation (EU) 2019/2033, art 12(1).

[12] European Banking Authority, 'Guidelines on sound remuneration policies under Articles 74(3) and 75(2) of Directive 2013/36/EU and disclosures under Article 45', (EBA/GL 2015/22) p. 117.

the competent authorities of the member states, and the financial institutions, should make every effort to comply with the guidelines and recommendations.[13] The EBA is responsible for reviewing and updating the guidelines for all firms that are compelled to comply with Directive 2013/36/EU and the remuneration rules.

Variable remuneration relates the amount of remuneration to performance. Often, persons in managerial positions or other key positions benefit from variable remuneration policies.

In this chapter, the executive management (CEOs and other persons in executive roles) of a company, as well as the board of directors, are included in the discussion, and discussed on equal terms. Members of the board of directors of a company may receive variable remuneration for their assignments, and may thereby be induced to increase risk-taking in their decisions. Even though the most evident problems arise when executives are compensated through variable remuneration, since executive managers are responsible for a company's day-to-day operations and take most of the business decisions, and the majority of the discussion on remuneration has addressed executive compensation,[14] this chapter does not distinguish between executive managers and directors on the board of investment firms. The incentives for both executives and directors are considered in relation to the incentives of owners.[15]

Variable remuneration takes many forms. Most prevalent are incentive programmes, featuring, for example, bonuses and/or equity-based compensation. Usually these programmes apply to CEOs, directors, and other key staff in a company. The persons included receive compensation in the form of cash, shares, or other fungible assets. Equity-based programmes involve executives and other persons benefitting from the programmes receiving shares in the company where they are employed, or having the opportunity to purchase the shares at a favourable price. This chapter will use the term 'variable remuneration', since that is the term prevalent in the legislation. However, different types of variable remuneration give rise to various problems, and may need to be managed with differing methods and levels of intensity.

[13] See, eg Regulation (EU) No 1093/2010 of the European Parliament and of the Council of 24 November 2010 establishing a European Supervisory Authority (European Banking Authority), amending Decision No 716/2009/EC and repealing Commission Decision 2009/78/EC, art 16 (3).

[14] See, eg Lucian Bebchuk and Jesse Fried, *Pay without Performance—the Unfulfilled Promise of Executive Compensation* (Harvard University Press 2006).

[15] Note that the directors on the board are principals in relation to the executive managers. This relationship does not feature as large a divergence in the incentives, as compared to when owners are discussed as principals. In this chapter, conflicts of interest arising from the relationship between directors and executives are not discussed.

Section 10.4 below continues with a summary of the prudential requirements on variable remuneration.

10.4 Prudential requirements on variable remuneration

Good governance structures, transparency and disclosure are essential for sound remuneration.

The Capital Requirements Regulation,[16] recital 97

Remuneration in credit institutions and investment firms was harmonised at EU level in 2014, through the implementation of the Capital Requirements Directive IV (CRD IV) and the Capital Requirements Regulation (CRR) (together 'the CRD IV package').[17] This comprehensive package of rules included credit institutions as well as investment firms. From June 2021, the prudential requirements for investment firms are to be found in Regulation EU/2019/2033 and Directive EU/2019/2034.[18] In the summary below, both legal packages are referred to in each individual point.

Variable remuneration in investment firms is subject to prudential requirements as regards:

(1) *Disclosure*: investment firms are mandated to disclose certain information regarding their remuneration policies and practices, for example how remuneration is decided, the ratios between fixed and variable remuneration, the link between pay and performance, aggregate quantitative information (the amounts of fixed and variable remuneration), and the most important design characteristics of the remuneration system.[19]
(2) *Categories of staff*: the rules on remuneration have, as their starting point, categorisation of which staff are included in the regulation, namely staff whose professional activities have a material impact on the risk profile of the investment firm.[20] These are the members of the management body and senior management team, staff members with

[16] Regulation (EU) No 575/2013 of the European Parliament and of the Council of 26 June 2013 on prudential requirements for credit institutions and investment firms and amending Regulation (EU) No 648/2012 (hereafter 'Regulation 575/2013').
[17] The CRD IV package consists of Directive 2013/36 and Regulation 575/2013.
[18] Regulation (EU) 2019/2033; Directive (EU) 2019/2034.
[19] Regulation (EU) No 575/2013, art 450; Regulation (EU) 2019/2033, art 51.
[20] Directive 2013/36, art 92(3); Directive 2019/2034, art 30(4).

managerial responsibility over the institution's control functions or material business units, and certain staff members entitled to significant remuneration.[21] Competent authorities in the member states are required, in addition to the categories set out in the legislation, to identify whether there are other staff categories with a material impact on the firm's risk profile, and, if there are, these individuals also are required to comply with the rules.[22]

(3) *Remuneration policy:* investment firms are obliged to have remuneration policies and practices that are consistent with, and promote, sound and effective risk management. The remuneration policy is required to be gender-neutral.[23] The remuneration policy must be in line with the business strategy, objectives, and the long-term effects of investment decisions taken, and must incorporate measures to avoid conflicts of interest.[24] Investment firms are required to apply the principles to the extent that is appropriate to their size, internal organisation, and the nature, scope, and complexity of their activities.[25]

(4) *Implementation and review*: the management body, in its supervisory function, is responsible for adopting and overseeing the implementation of the remuneration policy in the firm, and must periodically review the general principles of the policy.[26] The policy must, additionally, be subject to central and independent internal review, at least annually.[27] The remuneration policy must also make a clear distinction between criteria for setting basic fixed remuneration and variable remuneration.[28]

(5) *Restrictions on variable remuneration:* variable remuneration is restricted in various ways. There are requirements as to what instruments the variable component may consist of[29] and how performance is assessed,[30] and a requirement that the total variable remuneration is

[21] These are the staff categories set out in Directive 2013/36, art 92.3. EBA will, as regards investment firms, develop draft regulatory technical standards to specify appropriate criteria to identify the categories of staff whose professional activities have a material impact on the risk profile. EBA were to submit those draft regulatory technical standards to the Commission by 26 June 2021 (see Directive 2019/2034, art 30(4)).

[22] Commission Delegated Regulation (EU) No 604/2014 of 4 March 2014 supplementing Directive 2013/36/EU of the European Parliament and of the Council with regard to regulatory technical standards with respect to qualitative and appropriate quantitative criteria to identify categories of staff whose professional activities have a material impact on an institution's risk profile, art 2.

[23] Directive 2013/36, art 92(2)(a); Directive 2019/2034, art 30(1)(b)–(c).

[24] Directive 2013/36, art 92(2)(b); Directive 2019/2034, art 30(1)(d).

[25] Directive 2013/36, art 92(2); Directive 2019/2034, art 30(1)(a).

[26] Directive 2013/36, art 92(2)(c); Directive 2019/2034, art 30(1)(f).

[27] Directive 2013/36, art 92(2)(d); Directive 2019/2034, art 30(1)(g).

[28] Directive 2013/36, art 92(2)(g); Directive 2019/2034, art 30(1)(j).

[29] Directive 2013/36, art 94(1)(l); Directive 2019/2034, art 32(j).

[30] Directive 2013/36, art 94(1)(a)–(b); Directive 2019/2034, art 32 (a)–(c).

not allowed to limit the ability of the investment firm to strengthen its capital base.[31] There are also restrictions on the paying out of variable remuneration. At least 40 per cent of the variable remuneration component is required to be deferred over a period of not less than three to five years. The deferral period must be aligned with the nature of the business, the business cycle, the risks of the institution, and the activities of the member(s) of staff in question. In the case of a 'variable remuneration component of a particularly high amount', the deferral must comprise at least 60 per cent of the amount.[32]

The above provides a summary of the prudential requirements on variable remuneration in investment firms. The chapter now proceeds to presenting theoretical departure points, which will form the basis for the coming analysis and final discussion.

10.5 Variable remuneration in investment firms: theory

10.5.1 Agency theory

Incentive programmes consist of bonuses or other pay arrangements, in cash or in shares, which are designed to serve shareholders' interests. The employment of such programmes has increased during recent decades.[33] Variable remuneration has the purpose of aligning executives' incentives with shareholders' incentives by inducing them to create the largest possible turnover for the company. Equity-linked compensation has rapidly become more frequently used in all sectors.[34] This type of remuneration of executive staff takes the form of grants of the firm's shares, or call options on the firm's equity. There may also be long-term compensation, often functioning as a type of pension, consisting of a fixed sum or payment per share, which is obtained at a future point in time.

Executive compensation, including various types of variable remuneration, may serve as a mechanism to reduce the conflict between the shareholders and managers of a firm. Shareholders (*principals*) transfer a large part of the control

[31] Directive 2013/36, art 94(1)(c); Directive 2019/2034, art 32(d).
[32] Directive 2013/36, art 94 (m); Directive 2019/2034, art 32(l).
[33] Jens Hagendorff, 'Corporate Governance in Banking' in Allen N Berger, Philip Molyneux, and John O S Wilson (eds), *Oxford Handbook of Banking* (2nd edn, OUP 2014) 146.
[34] ibid.

of the business to the managers (*agents*). The relationship between those who contribute with resources and those who administer the resources is called the principal–agent relation.[35] There is a risk of conflicts of interest in this type of relationship. The shareholders have an interest in gaining the profit of their invested capital in the firm. Most commonly, shareholders invest in many companies; they have a limited personal liability for corporate obligations and, because of this limited risk, are willing to invest. Since shareholders are only rarely exposed to the risks of one firm alone, they may secure their investments even if one firm's situation develops negatively.

The executive management team members have interests related to the company where they work, in maximizing their own income through their positions in the firm. They are, however, not as willing to take on risk as the shareholders. The managers, and sometimes also the board of directors, invest their time and their work efforts, usually in one company. The managers' pursuit of their own interests may lead to actions that are at the expense of the best interests of shareholders.[36] The managers may optimise their positions by gaining large salaries for minimal work effort, or decreasing the quality of their work. Managers may also procure economic advantages at the expense of the company, or act to develop the company in a way that makes themselves appear favourably, so as to gain new employment at another firm, with a better salary.

The risk of managers acting in their own interests increases if they have an information advantage in relation to the shareholders. The risk also increases in firms with dispersed owners, where there is a separation of ownership and control. In smaller, owner-managed companies, there is usually not as great a potential for conflicts of interest.

When agents do not act in a way that is optimal for the principals, costs arise for the principals, since the value of the management of resources is diminished.[37] Conflicts of interest in firms where ownership and control are separated also bring a need for principals to monitor the agents in order to make sure the management of the firm is in line with the interests of the shareholders. This monitoring induces agency costs, which are costs for the principals. Principal–agency theory elaborates on how agency costs can be minimised, through either monitoring systems or reward systems. Monitoring the management is often costly and difficult to enforce for most shareholders (at least

[35] Michael C Jensen and William H Meckling, 'Theory of the Firm: Managerial Behavior, Agency Costs and Ownership Structure' (1976) 3(4) Journal of Financial Economics 305, 309–10.

[36] Bebchuk and Fried, (n 14) 15–17; Frank H Easterbrock and Daniel R Fischel, 'The Corporate Contract' in Lucian A Bebchuk (ed), *Corporate Law and Economic Analysis* (CUP 1990) 182.

[37] Jensen and Meckling (n 36) 309–10.

when ownership is dispersed). Executive compensation through variable remuneration has the purpose of diminishing agency costs by aligning the incentives of agents with those of the principals. Shareholders may more readily trust the management to optimise their invested capital in the firm if those who control and manage the firm receive compensation connected to the firms' performance. Variable remuneration functions as a tool to govern companies, and is often discussed in relation to effective corporate governance.[38]

10.5.2 Remuneration in investment firms

Corporate governance issues in financial firms generally cannot be dealt with in the same ways as in non-financial firms.[39] Risk-taking in financial firms can have systemic implications, and effects on society. If financial firms take deposits from the public, they are engage in business in which their customers need special protection. Depositors have very restricted opportunities to influence a financial firm. Moreover, financial firms are, typically, at an information advantage vis à vis their customers.

Monitoring executive managers in a financial firm is important, both so that risk- taking does not have systemic effects, and in order to achieve customer protection. Incentive programmes and other forms of variable remuneration have the purpose of decreasing agency costs by aligning the management's incentives with the shareholders' incentives. Arguably, variable remuneration may bring new problems, however. Since variable remuneration creates incentives for managers to take business decisions from an investment perspective, according to the preferences of shareholders, one effect may be increased risk-taking by managers and others who benefit from incentivisation programmes and other types of variable remuneration.[40] If corporate governance is sound, on an overall level in the firm, and the risk-taking is, thus, controlled, incentive programmes may function well, if designed in a long-term, transparent, and controllable manner.[41] In such situations, shareholders' interests become decisive in the business decisions of the firm's management, which affects the firm's

[38] See, eg George P Baker, Michael C Jensen, and Kevin J Murphy, 'Compensation and Incentives: Practice vs Theory' (1987) 43(3) The Journal of Finance 593; Jensen and Meckling (n 36) 305–60.

[39] Hagendorff (n 34) 139–.

[40] Another problematic aspect discussed in the wake of the corporate scandals around the turn of the millennium, not least in the US, were that these programmes were shown to be flawed in aligning the incentives, and were, therefore, not functioning as desired. See, eg Bebchuk and Fried (n 14) ix.

[41] Joakim Bång and Daniel Waldenström, 'Rörlig ersättning till vd—vad säger forskningen?' (2009) IFN Policy Paper no 27 and 37 Ekonomisk Debatt 5, 52–53.

financial development and performance in a beneficial way. In other situations, however, where corporate governance is generally poor, or incentivisation programmes are flawed, the enhanced risk-taking induced by variable remuneration may become too high, in regard to the firm's business.

Risk-taking, incentives, and implications for corporate governance become highly interesting in financial firms. As already described, financial stability and investor protection may be threatened by excessive risks in financial firms, at least in some cases. The regulation discussed in section 10.4, up until the reforms of 2021, targeted credit institutions and investment firms. Credit institutions, such as banks and other companies whose businesses involve deposit-taking in combination with lending, are very typically regulated on the basis of stability concerns. Here, individual prudential requirements on capital, exposures, risks, and governance have been complemented with macroprudential regulation, in order to fully combat excessive build-up of risks in the financial system.[42] The special nature of banks, and their potential to be affected by systemic risks, form the basis for such regulation. Banks are, among other things, highly leveraged firms with deposit guarantee schemes and other governmental support mechanisms surrounding their business.

Investment firms, on the other hand, are not subject to the same amount of regulation, as such firms may engage in many different types of businesses, and are not inherently critical to the financial system. Investment firms are not targeted by capital requirements and other prudential rules to the same extent as banks and credit institutions. Investment firms do, however, compete with banks and credit institutions, and conduct many types of activities containing risks. They offer investment services such as giving their customers access to markets in securities and derivatives through brokerage, they provide investment advice, perform portfolio management, they conduct execution of orders, proprietary trading, and underwriting.

Even though investment firms are not subject to such strict regulation as banks, they have become increasingly regulated since the financial crisis, and, as shown, they have been included in the CRD IVpackage. As also shown, financial stability and investor protection are the regulatory aims of the CRD IV-package. As investment firms generally do not pose the same risks to the system, or to investors, as banks, it is of interest to scrutinise the regulation of investment firms. Perhaps an especially interesting discussion relates to a regulation, such as the one regarding variable remuneration, which specifically

[42] See Rebecca Söderström, 'Sound Banking' (Academic Dissertation, Uppsala University 2017) 100–37.

targets excessive risk-taking as a means to prevent the societal effects of failure. The next section aims to develop this section, with particular reference to the regulatory reforms of 2021.

10.6 Investment firms' remuneration policies and the need for regulation

10.6.1 The regulatory reforms of 2021

The Regulation EU/2019/2033 and the Directive EU/2019/2034[43] that are being implemented in the EU basically contain the same material rules on remuneration as the previous regulation for investment firms, under the CRD IV package. The biggest change relates to the differentiation of which firms are obliged to comply with the rules. Recital 22 of the Directive EU/2019/2034 states (author's emphasis) that:

> To align remuneration with the risk profile of investment firms and to guarantee a level playing field, investment firms should be subject to clear principles with regard to corporate governance arrangements and remuneration rules, which are gender neutral and which take into account **the differences between credit institutions and investment firms.** Small and non-interconnected investment firms should, however, be exempt from those rules because the provisions on remuneration and corporate governance laid down in Directive 2014/65/EU are sufficiently comprehensive for those types of investment firms.

Recital 23 continues (author's emphasis):

> Similarly, the Commission report of 28 July 2016 on the assessment of the remuneration rules under Directive 2013/36/EU and Regulation (EU) No 575/2013 demonstrated that the requirements on deferral and pay-out in instruments laid down in Directive 2013/36/EU **are not appropriate for small**

[43] Regulation (EU) 2019/2033 of the European Parliament and of the Council of 27 November 2019 on the prudential requirements of investment firms and amending Regulations (EU) No 1093/2010, (EU) No 575/2013, (EU) No 600/2014 and (EU) No 806/2014; Directive (EU) 2019/2034 of the European Parliament and of the Council of 27 November 2019 on the prudential supervision of investment firms and amending Directives 2002/87/EC, 2009/65/EC, 2011/61/EU, 2013/36/EU, 2014/59/EU, and 2014/65/EU.

> **and non-complex investment firms or for staff with low levels of variable remuneration.** Clear, consistent and harmonised criteria for identifying investment firms and individuals that are exempt from those requirements are necessary to ensure supervisory convergence and a level playing field.

Recital 25 also states that it is appropriate to offer some flexibility to investment firms in the ways that such firms may use non-cash instruments to pay variable remuneration.

The Regulation EU/ 2019/2033 specifies the criteria for defining *small and non-complex investment firms*, in Article 12. A number of cumulative standards are prescribed, which all have to be met in order for a firm to be exempted. The criteria relate to the comprehensiveness of client assets under management and client orders handled.[44]

Another important difference with the new regulation is the absence of a cap on the amount of variable remuneration, which Directive 2013/36/EU (CRD) laid down in Article 94(g). The variable component was, according to the CRD, not allowed to exceed 100 per cent of the fixed component of the total remuneration for each individual. Following the changes effected by the reforms of 2021, no such cap will be imposed on investment firms.

Directive 2019/2034, however, requires investment firms to set appropriate ratios between the variable and fixed components of the total remuneration specified in their remuneration policies, taking into account the business activities of the investment firm and their associated risks, as well as the impact that different categories of staff have on the risk profile of the investment firm.[45] The fixed component must represent a sufficiently high proportion of the total remuneration so as to enable the operation of a fully flexible policy on variable remuneration components, including the possibility of paying no variable remuneration component at all.[46]

The directive also introduces a number of other exemptions for investment firms, related to variable remuneration. The rules on deferral of 40 or 60 per

[44] All investment firms should calculate their own funds requirement by reference to a set of so-called K-factors. Small and non-interconnected firms are defined as such if all of the following factors are met: (1) Assets under (K-AUM) is less than 1.2 billion euros; (2) client orders handled (K-COH) is less than either 100 million euros per day for cash trades, or 1 billion euros per day for derivatives; (3) assets safeguarded and administered (K-ASA) is zero; (4) client money held (K-CMH) is zero; (5) daily trading flow (K-DTF) is zero; (6) net position risk (K-NPR) or clearing margin given (K-CMG) is zero; (7) trading counterparty default (K-TCD) is zero; (8) the on- and off-balance sheet total of the investment firm is less than EUR 100 million; (9) the total annual gross revenue from investment services and activities is less than 30 million euros.

[45] Directive 2019/2034, art 30(2).

[46] ibid, art 30(1)(k).

cent of variable remuneration, and the rules on the type of instruments allowed, do not apply to firms with off-balance sheet assets equal to or less than 100 million euros over a four-year period.[47] Also, individuals are exempted if their annual variable remuneration does not exceed 50,000 euros, and does not represent more than one-quarter of that individual's total annual remuneration. Member states are allowed to increase or decrease these thresholds under certain conditions.[48]

10.6.2 Enhanced flexibility and fewer requirements

The 2021 reforms of the prudential regulation of investment firms contains many details, and this chapter will not further elaborate on their exact content. The section above describes the most important changes, from a remuneration point of view. The new directive and regulation represent a different approach to rulemaking in the financial sector. The scope of the acts is narrowed down, exempting small and non-interconnected firms. The reforms also bring more flexibility to how member states implement the rules on variable remuneration. As recital 5 of Regulation 2019/2033 points out, investment firms are different from banks and other credit institutions. The requirements in the CRD IV package are calibrated from a banking business point of view, and aim at preserving the lending capacity of credit institutions through economic cycles, and protecting depositors and taxpayers from possible business failure. Investment firms, if they fail, are not as likely to impact on overall financial stability as negatively as credit institutions. Here, it can be noted that very large investment firms are still included in the CRD/CRR regulation regime, for stability reasons, as they are very likely to impact on stability, in the event of failure.

A major change is the removal, for all investment firms, of the cap on the amount of variable remuneration. Disclosure, deferral, and staff categorisation remains, as does a long list of other detailed rules on the structures and content of firms' remuneration policies. Since the CRD-IV rules on the cap is, perhaps, the most invasive part of the remuneration regulation of the EU, it is interesting that it is no longer considered necessary for investment firms under the new directive.

[47] ibid, art 32(1), (j), and (l).
[48] ibid, art 32(4), (5), and (6).

Stability reasons for regulation, in relation to market failures in the form of negative externalities connected to a firm's business, have, conversely, been used as motivations for the reform. Investment firms do not need such extensive regulation as credit institutions for a stable and functioning EU market for financial services.

The other main reason for capital markets regulation is investor protection. Regarding small and non-interconnected investment firms, the provisions on remuneration and corporate governance contained in MiFID II are referred to, in the new directive, as being sufficiently comprehensive for small and non-interconnected investment firms.[49] These firms are already required to fulfil investor protection rules, and need not be subject to additional restrictions on variable remuneration in order to adequately manage the risks to investors.

Risks are lower, but also different, in investment firms, as compared to the regulatory aims of the CRD/CRR requirements. The reforms, therefore, also address the lack of appropriate management for the risks that do exist in investment firms. There are various risks concerning this category of firms. As pointed out, investment services include giving customers access to markets in securities and derivatives through brokerage, and other services such as investment advice, portfolio management, execution of orders, proprietary trading, and underwriting. The main definition of an investment firm is found in MiFID II, Article 4.1: 'Investment firm means any legal person whose regular occupation or business is the provision of one or more investment services to third parties and/or the performance of one or more investment activities on a professional basis'. Many different types of services may be included in this definition, and may be conducted by investment firms, bringing challenges as to how to design their regulation. What is clear is that the reforms aim to ensure that the different risks are clearly reflected in the prudential framework of the EU.

10.7 Accountability and its relation to remuneration

Accountability is a central component for a sound business or company. Clear structures for accountability are one irreplaceable aspect of adequate risk management in a financial firm. Variable remuneration of managers relates to accountability in a direct way, since such compensation schemes aim at aligning

49 ibid, recital 22.

managers' incentives with shareholders' incentives. Shareholders are, as pointed out previously, interested in gaining profit from their invested capital, and usually have a diverse portfolio. Shareholders are, further, not personally liable for the obligations of the firms they invest in. Shareholders, thus, generally invest from departure points of high risk, and almost no requirements related to accountability. Managers, on the other hand, are liable to a higher extent, especially in firms operating under authorisation or licence.

Aligning managers' interests with owners' interests by means of variable remuneration risks resulting in an increased incentive for managers to act in a less accountable manner. As accountability is one of the central aims of MiFID II, as described in the first part of this chapter, there is a legitimate reason to develop this concept a little deeper in relation to corporate governance, remuneration, and applicable EU regulation.

Article 9 of MiFID II pinpoints that managers are accountable for implementing governance arrangements that 'ensure effective and prudent management of the investment firm including the segregation of duties in the investment firm and the prevention of conflicts of interest, and in a manner that promotes the integrity of the market and the interest of clients'. MiFID II, and the prudential regulation of investment firms described in section 10.4 above, is designed to achieve accountability by the implementation of various rules in the member states. Legislation, as discussed above, is thus used to foster corporate governance. The inclusion of corporate governance rules in MiFID II is a distinctive difference in relation to the original MiFID regulation .

Accountability, at firm level, may include legal liability for firms to comply with regulation and accountability requirements through fiduciary responsibilities between firms and their clients. Firm-level accountability refers to the relationship between the firm and a regulatory or supervisory authority, or between the firm and its customers. Firm-level accountability also includes internal relations within the firm, not least between owners and managers, typically envisaged by the principal–agency theory described in section 10.5 above.

Accountability may, however, also refer to administrative procedures and processes whereby legitimate rules are formulated and enacted. Another procedural aspect of accountability comes in the form of political accountability mechanisms. Administrative and political procedures can be viewed as a regulatory level of accountability, where the relation addressed is between various levels of political, legislative, and regulatory entities. Political accountability and its procedural aspects are elaborated by Héritier in Chapter 2 of this book. Héritier applies a principal–agent approach to explain political accountability: a political actor (the 'principal') delegates a task to an executive actor (the 'agent'), for example a regulatory or supervisory authority, and is able to monitor the performance of the task if the principal has sufficient information on the quality of the execution of the task. It is important from an accountability point of view that unsatisfactory performance of the task by the agent can be penalised by the principal. Héritier points to the fact that, in practice, the sanctioning element is often missing or weak in relation to regulatory authorities, resulting in weaker political accountability.

As Héritier concludes in Chapter 2, all actors—politicians, regulators, investors, fund managers, and investment firms—are involved in the regulatory process, and are linked together by various political and administrative accountability mechanisms. This chapter has elaborated on MiFID II's ambition of enhancing accountability mechanisms *within* investment firms by requiring corporate governance structures and regulating remuneration policies. It is interesting to relate the firm's level of accountability to the regulatory level of accountability, not least the perspectives developed by Héritier.

On both levels, the principal–agent relation constitutes a fruitful structure for discussing the various types of regulation. The principal–agent relation also relates to the overarching goals of MiFID II. At the level of the firm, accountability can be referred to theories of the company and the relation of entities within a firm ('company bodies'). On a regulatory level, accountability can be analysed from theories of political science.[50] MiFID II strives to foster accountability on both levels. The enactment of rules and structures for delegation of powers to legislative and regulatory authorities, and the requirements for sanctions at member state supervisory level through MiFID II and related regulation of investment firms, includes many elements of political accountability. Accountability for regulatory authorities, in the sense that they are accountable for their own actions, is vital for effective fulfilment of the regulatory aims and purposes of any legal act.

The content of rules, for example MiFID II Article 9, and the prudential regulation of investment firms' remuneration arrangements, may foster accountability at the firm level. Here, the internal structures, the division of powers, and the incentives for the various company bodies in a firm are affected by legal rules and instruments. Important departure points in economic life are the free market, and the ability to conduct business with limited liability. Markets are far from 'free', in the sense of being non-regulated, but businesses carried out in companies and firms, driven by profit and on the terms of owners, is a

[50] See Héritier, in Chapter 2 of this book.

cornerstone of all market economies.[51] Corporate governance is, first and foremost, in the interests of the owners of a company. Legal rules and instruments may affect corporate governance in various ways, but usually the legislator imposes legal rules with parameters other than those already prevalent due to the firm's owner. Financial stability and investor protection are two parameters which often are not, or at least not fully, included in owners' preferences and, thus, not necessarily reflected in the corporate governance of an investment firm.

What are the effects on firm accountability and political accountability when legal instruments are used? Good corporate governance, which is emphasised in MiFID II, is considered necessary for the overarching goals of investor protection and systemic stability. Legal instruments are deployed to achieve these goals. The regulatory reforms of 2021 ease certain requirements, as presented above, and make national implementation more flexible. However, to a large extent, variable remuneration is still under strict regulation in investment firms. Remuneration is, it will be recalled, regulated to decrease agency costs, as elaborated in section 10.5. Variable remuneration constitutes a powerful tool for incentivizing managers to act in the interests of shareholders, whereby excessive risk-taking and short-sightedness are two potential effects. These effects may cause governance failure in a firm, where long-term perspectives on business are shifted to short-sighted business decisions, spurred by incentivisation programmes or bonuses. However, these types of negative effects of risk-taking do not, typically, constitute reasons for legislators to act. The negative consequences for individual firms must, potentially or actually, give rise to problems with certain characteristics, to legitimate legal rules and regulation. Such characteristics, as explained above, include effects on market stability or a need for investor protection.[52] If excessive risk-taking, resulting from a firm's compensation structures, brings detrimental consequences to investors, to the market, or to society, there are reasons for regulation by means of external and binding rules.

The regulatory reforms of 2021 in relation to investment firms pinpoint the differences in economic reasons for legal rules on the financial markets. As regards credit institutions, the case is clear. Stability concerns are central, and banks' potential to spread systemic risk has been shown, both theoretically and

[51] See Easterbrock and Fischel (n 37) 182–94.

[52] Emilios E Avgouleas, *The Mechanics and Regulation of Market Abuse: A Legal and Economic Analysis* (OUP 2005) 24;

Peter-Jan Engelen, *Remedies to Informational Asymmetries in Stock Markets* (Intersentia 2005) 28; Hendrik S Houthakker and Peter J Williamson, *The Economics of Financial Markets* (OUP 1996) 284.

empirically.[53] Investment firms, as discussed above, are not automatically exposed to the same risks. Remuneration, and especially variable remuneration can, to a larger extent in comparison to banks, be employed in investment firms to align the interests of managers with the interests of shareholders without putting market stability or investors at risk.

Enforcing sound corporate governance through legislation can be questioned generally.[54] Also, the regulation of credit institutions has been criticised for being too detailed.[55] Even though stability concerns necessitate regulation, in the case of banks and other credit institutions, the design of the regulation could be questioned. Remuneration structures that give rise to a problematic level of risk-taking may be a symptom of flawed corporate governance in a firm. The EU approach to financial market regulation has, thus far, had the ambition of regulating every symptom of unsound governance in financial firms. The result is a large, draconian, and non-reviewable body of rules. Legal provisions will never, however detailed and strict, fully reflect or foster soundness in financial firms, or on financial markets. Legal rules may, of course, be necessary in the efforts to ensure soundness, but soundness cannot be ensured by legal rules addressing symptoms of unsoundness. Soundness, which, like confidence and stability, is a regulatory aim, must permeate every aspect, business decision, and employee of a financial firm's organisation. Sound financial business is a moving target, especially in times when markets change constantly due to technical innovations, artificial intelligence, new currencies, and digitalisation of services, to mention just a few areas.

Compliance with prudential regulation will, however, never in itself foster perfectly accountable and sound management in a firm. Variable remuneration could be, but is not automatically, negative due to its risk-incentivizing and accountability aspects. If management is sound on an overall level, compensation (including incentive programmes or bonuses) will fit into a sound business profile. Legal instruments may promote soundness and accountability,

[53] George J Benston and George G Kaufman, 'The Appropriate Role of Bank Regulation' (1996) 106 The Economic Journal 436, 688–97; Mathias Dewatripont, Jean-Charles Rochet, and Jean Tirole, 'Balancing the Banks: Global Lessons from the Financial Crisis' (Princeton University Press 2010) 1; Söderström (n 43) 92–99.

[54] Roberta Romano, 'The Sarbanes-Oxley Act and the Making of Quack Corporate Governance' (2004) European Corporate Governance Institute (ECGI)—Finance Working Paper No 52/2004, NYU Law and Economics Research Paper No 04-032, Yale ICF Working Paper No 04-37, Yale Law and Economics Research Paper No 297.

[55] Luca Enriques and Dirk A Zetzsche, 'Quack Corporate Governance, Round III? Bank Board Regulation Under the New European Capital Requirement Directive' (2014) European Corporate Governance Institute (ECGI)—Law Working Paper No 249/2014, Oxford Legal Studies Research Paper No 67/2014.

but cannot replace investment firms' own pursuit of sound business structures and accountability mechanisms at all levels in a firm.

Given all of this, issues on the regulatory level of accountability arise when legal instruments are used to regulate financial markets. The detailed and vast amount of financial regulation, in conjunction with far-reaching supervisory powers, at both EU- and member state-level risk increasing the expectations, or even the demands, on political accountability. There is a danger that very detailed regulatory approaches, such as extensive reporting requirements or, indeed, detailed requirements on remuneration, foster a 'tick-box' mentality in regulated entities. Instead of addressing business-specific needs in a holistic and long-term perspective, firms may be pushed into short-sighted reporting standards that are highly time- and resource-consuming. There is no scope for wider reflection on regulatory goals or soundness. With all the regulatory boxes 'ticked', firms may tend to find themselves taking a mechanical approach towards accomplishing what is required by them, leaving the regulatory or supervisory authority accountable for finding flaws or deficiencies in their businesses. Political accountability is, thus, affected by invasiveness in the area of financial regulation, and arguably not in a solely positive way.

Political accountability is vital, but cannot replace firm-level accountability. The very essence of good corporate governance is that a firm and its owners, directors, and managers take responsibility for governing the business in accordance with various business goals, and not at the expense of its clients or society in large. Excessively detailed and far-reaching legal requirements risk increasing the need for political accountability, in the sense that political and regulatory entities must take a larger responsibility for the fulfilment of the goals of financial stability and investor protection, at the expense of strong accountability mechanisms at firm level.

It is tricky to achieve all of the aims and purposes of MiFID II. No one would deny the importance of financial stability and investor protection. The EU has, since the wake of the financial crisis of 2008, walked down an increasingly detailed and strict regulatory path. One alternative, when designing regulations to enhance accountability in investment firms, would be to promote a culture of self-accountability and proactive compliance with rules. This is discussed in Chapter 7 of this book by Pieter van Cleynenbreugel. In his chapter, van Cleynenbreugel shows that the MiFID II framework and its compliance organisational requirements function as a tool for facilitating external accountability mechanisms, such as sanctioning by supervisory authorities. Little attention has been paid to how financial firms themselves comply with the increasing amount of rules, and to what extent such internalisation can be used to accomplish accountability. A well-functioning compliance framework within an investment firm could be a sign of the firm having internalised a culture of respect for the rules. Making firms responsible for internalizing compliance structures could provide a useful complementary accountability mechanism, according to van Cleynenbreugel, whereby firms can be held accountable without the authorities having to resort exclusively to sanctions or supervisory decisions. Van Cleynenbreugel also argues that another effect of the focus on sanctions and external accountability in MiFID II is that there is no room to treat the existence of 'internalised compliance-oriented behaviour' as a mitigating factor, in a situation where a sanction is being imposed on such a firm. Respect for compliance requirements by means of a dedicated compliance framework is not explicitly a mitigating factor, from an EU regulatory point of view. There is, thus, no clear link, in MiFID II, between compliance and sanctions. Establishing such a link in law, or by policy approaches from ESMA, would make the legal accountability regime within the EU more coherent.

Internalised accountability mechanisms, where firms are empowered to set up structures that promote a sound corporate culture, could complement, but also to some extent replace, external accountability and the need for supervisory interference. Also important, as has been argued in this chapter, is the need for a sane view on what can be accomplished by means of legal rules and supervision. The regulatory aims and purposes of MiFID II—financial stability and investor protection—need firm-level accountability and a robust internal corporate culture, both of which can be promoted and supported, but not fully and exclusively achieved, by legal instruments.

The reforms of the prudential requirements for investment firms implemented in 2021 show a slightly new approach to regulating the EU financial markets. This chapter concludes with some remarks on this development.

10.8 Financial regulation in the EU in the next decade

The harmonisation of the European Capital Markets Union (CMU) has frequently been criticised for leading to legislation with a 'one-size-fits-all' approach. Directives such as MiFID are often used to exemplify this approach.[56]

[56] FSA report, 'UK response to the Commission Services' consultation on the Review of the Markets in Financial Instruments Directive (MiFID)'(February 2011); 'Why MiFID II is a Menace to Investment Banking in Europe' *Financial Times* (Andrea Vismara, London, 12 May 2019).

Such legislation is criticised for imposing high costs, for being inflexible in view of the market differences between various member states, and for being too far-reaching as regards comprehensiveness and volume of rules. The regulatory reforms of 2021 for investment firms point to a new regulatory approach within the EU. Flexibility is stressed, as is the need to differentiate between different types of financial firms. The degree of interconnectedness and the size of the firm are decisive factors in which regulation applies to any particular firm. Non-interconnected and small investment firms need not be addressed with regulation of intensity equal to that applicable to larger firms whose failure might potentially impact on wider financial stability.

This is a most welcome development, from a regulatory approach point of view. Regulating in order to foster accountability within financial firms, and on political and regulatory levels, is legitimate to a greater extent if rules addressing, for example, corporate governance are adapted to the types of firm they address. The higher the potential impact on market stability is, the higher the need for regulatory intervention. The same is valid regarding investor protection: investors with access to less information— not least, consumers—require protection to a larger extent in comparison to more sophisticated or professional investors. The introduction of firm-specific prudential regulation within the CMU is, hopefully, not the last step in reforming EU legal acts to better reflect the aims and purposes of financial market regulation.

PART IV

INVESTMENT FIRMS IN HORIZONTAL ACCOUNTABILITY

11

The Investment Firm's 'Horizontal Accountability' towards Clients

Standards and Institutional Mechanisms of Control

*Federico Della Negra**

11.1 Setting the scene

The theme of accountability in EU financial markets has, traditionally, attracted much attention from legal scholars. A rich body of literature flourished after the EU reforms following the 2008 global financial crisis (GFC), which granted new tasks and powers to EU institutions and agencies for the supervision and oversight of financial markets.[1] These studies analysed the adequacy of the legislative mechanisms that have been put in place to ensure that these public bodies (accountors) can effectively answer to, and be held accountable for their acts and conduct by, parliaments and other fora (accountees).

* Senior Legal Counsel at the European Central Bank (ECB). The views expressed are purely personal, and do not reflect those of the ECB.

[1] The literature on this topic is abundant. For the accountability of the European Central Bank (ECB), see, in particular, Jonathan Zeitlin and Filipe Brito Bastos, 'SSM and the SRB Accountability at European Level: Room for Improvements?—Banking Union Scrutiny', study requested by the ECON committee of the European Parliament (PE 645.747, May 2020); René Smits, 'SSM and the SRB Accountability at European Level: Room for Improvements?—Banking Union Scrutiny', study requested by the ECON committee of the European Parliament (PE 645.726, April 2020); Fabian Amtenbrink and Menelaos Markakis, 'Towards a Meaningful Prudential Supervision Dialogue in the Euro Area? A Study of the Interaction between the European Parliament and the European Central Bank in the Single Supervisory Mechanism' (2019) 44 European Law Review 3. With regard to the European Supervisory Authorities (ESAs) within the European System of Financial Supervision (ESFS), see Iris H-Y Chiu, 'Power and Accountability in the EU Financial Regulatory Architecture: Examining Inter-agency Relations, Agency Independence and Accountability' (2015) 8 European Journal of Legal Studies 68. With regard to the accountability mechanisms within the European Monetary Union (EMU), see Menelaos Markakis, *Accountability in the Economic and Monetary Union: Foundations, Policy, and Governance* (OUP 2020) (hereafter Markakis, *Accountability*).

Federico Della Negra, *The Investment Firm's 'Horizontal Accountability' towards Clients* In: *Legal Accountability in EU Markets for Financial Instruments*. Edited by: Carl Fredrik Bergström and Magnus Strand, Oxford University Press.
 DOI: 10.1093/oso/9780192849281.003.0011

Less attention has been paid to the potential applications of the concept of accountability in horizontal relationships. Generally speaking, horizontal accountability refers to those cases where account-giving takes place in the absence of formal obligations on the accountor to account for their conduct. The accountor can be either a public body or a private institution. For example, for a public body, horizontal accountability might mean consulting the public before adopting an act or a new policy.[2] For a private corporation or organisation, horizontal accountability is often associated with social responsibility, for its business practices, towards citizens and interest groups, but can also comprise relationships between firms and their clients that are subject to legal standards of conduct.

Credit institutions and investment firms (together also referred to as 'financial intermediaries') play a crucial role in the economy and society by providing funding to individuals and businesses, facilitating their access to capital markets, and, thus, contributing to economic growth. The erosion of the welfare state has further increased the role of financial intermediaries in our society. Access to capital markets has become crucial for funding the basic financial needs of ordinary citizens, for example pension schemes, healthcare, and educational plans.[3] The financialisation of the economy creates opportunities, but also exposes ordinary citizens to new risks, and requires financial intermediaries to account more frequently for their conduct to their clients, and to society at large.[4]

Against this background, this chapter aims to explore the ways in which investment firms can be held accountable for their conduct when they provide investment services to clients. More specifically, the aim is to describe the substantive standards and institutional mechanisms available to clients in order to hold investment firms accountable when they provide such services.[5] It will be submitted that investment firms' scope of accountability has been broadened by new substantive standards set out in MiFID II[6], non-binding (or so- called 'soft law') standards set out by supervisory authorities, and new or reinforced institutional mechanisms (firms'

[2] Markakis, 'Accountability' (n 2) 12.

[3] Alastair Hudson, *The Law of Finance* (2nd edn, Sweet & Maxwell 2013) 34.

[4] See, in particular, Joanna Gray and Jenny Hamilton, *Implementing Financial Regulation: Theory and Practice* (Wiley 2006) 187; Dimity Kingsford-Smith, 'Regulating Investment Risk: Individuals and the Global Financial Crisis' (2009) 32 University of New South Wales Law Journal 518.

[5] Investment services can be provided by both investment firms and credit institutions, if authorised to do so.

[6] Directive 2014/65/EU of the European Parliament and of the Council of 15 May 2014 on markets in financial instruments and amending Directive 2002/92/EC and Directive 2011/61/EU [2014] OJ L 173, 349–496 (hereafter 'MiFID II').

internal functions, alternative dispute resolution (ADR) mechanisms, and national courts).

11.2 Horizontal accountability and civil liability: Differences

The building of a new EU administration to supervise and oversee financial markets has fuelled scholarly debate on the adequacy of the mechanisms of control and accountability.[7] Legal research has gradually expanded the concept of administrative accountability. This is no longer understood only as a legal mechanism whereby an agent (an administrative agency) gives account for his actions to a principal (a parliament), but more broadly as 'a relationship between an actor and a forum in which the actor has an obligation to explain and to justify his or her conduct, the forum can pose questions and pass judgement, and the actor may face consequences'.[8] In this broader meaning, accountability can also include relationships where the accountee has not delegated powers to the accountor,[9] and can comprise, besides the most studied forms of political and administrative accountability,[10] also horizontal accountability.

There are several forms of horizontal accountability. For public entities, horizontal accountability describes cases where the account-giving takes place on a voluntary basis.[11] For private entities and, more specifically, for financial intermediaries, horizontal accountability has a broad social or political dimension and a narrower formal-legalistic dimension. In a broad sense, horizontal accountability refers to the collective responsibility that financial intermediaries have, by reason of their economic function, not only to their clients, but also to third parties and society at large. In a narrower sense, horizontal

[7] See, in general, on the process of agencification in the EU, Edoardo Chiti, 'European Agencies' Rulemaking: Powers, Procedures and Assessment' (2013) 19 European Law Journal 93 ss. With regard to the financial sector, see Edoardo Chiti and Pedro Gustavo Teixeira, 'The Constitutional Implications of the European Responses to the Financial and Public Debt Crisis' (2013) 50 Common Market Law Review 690 et seq.

[8] Mark Bovens, 'Analysing and Assessing Accountability: A Conceptual Framework' (2007) 13 European Law Journal 447 (the author excludes from the concept of accountability those relationships where there is no scrutiny by a specific forum, ie transparency, responsiveness, and participation).

[9] ibid 451 (which cites the example of a court, in cases of legal accountability, or a professional association, in cases of professional accountability).

[10] See, for more detail, the contributions in this volume by Carl Fredrik Bergström and Adrienne Héritier.

[11] Bovens (n 9) 460; and compare Guillermo O'Donnell, 'Horizontal Accountability in New Democracies' in A Schedler, L Diamond, and MF Plattner (eds), *The Self-Restraining State: Power and Accountability in New Democracies* (Lynne Rienner Publishers 1999) 29–51.

accountability describes the instances where financial intermediaries are called upon to account for their conduct on the basis of a legal standard. The relationship between financial intermediaries and their clients is highly regulated by rules of law (disclosure, distribution, product regulation, contract law rules) and soft law instruments (guidelines and recommendations. A deviation from these standards could trigger a form of horizontal accountability and, in certain cases, civil liability. Liability, sometimes also termed 'legal accountability', could be regarded as one of 'the most unambiguous type of accountability, as the legal scrutiny will be based on detailed legal standards, prescribed by civil, penal or administrative statutes, or precedent'.[12]

However, civil liability should be conceptually distinguished from horizontal accountability. While, in both accountability and liability relationships, an accountor has to account for his/her conduct to an accountee and, in both relationships, the standard of control can be based both on detailed and general duties,[13] the various rationales for and consequences of accountability arising from this duty to respond are very different from one another.

Accountability results in a scrutiny over the conduct of a public authority that is not based on strict concepts of legality, and not court-centred.[14] By contrast, civil liability, in relation to both public and private entities, ensures the enforcement of contracts, or protects, in cases of non-contractual liability, the specific pecuniary or non-pecuniary interests identified by legal enactments.

Moreover, civil liability not only enables the accountee to ask questions or demand explanations; it also empowers the accountee to acquire a remedy from a court and, as a result, the accountor may face financial consequences, for example a duty to pay damages, to return a profit, or to refrain from certain conduct. This type of financial consequence can arise also as a result of accountability relationships, but is not a constitutive or necessary element of these.[15]

[12] Bovens (n 9) 451–56 (arguing that the possibility of the accountee imposing sanctions, and not the actual imposition of sanctions, is a constitutive element of accountability).

[13] Administrative accountability can be based on detailed duties, on which financial and administrative compliance is assessed, and civil liability can be based not only on detailed duties, but also on general clauses (eg good faith and reasonableness).

[14] Wolfgang C Müller, Torbjörn Bergman, and Kaare Strøm, 'Parliamentary Democracy: Promise and Problems' in Kaare Strøm, Wolfgang C Müller, and Torbjörn Bergman (eds), *Parliamentary Democracy: Promise and Problems* (OUP 2006) 19. See also Giacinto della Cananea, 'The EU Administration: Imperium and Dominium' in Carol Harlow, Päivi Leino, and Giacinto della Cananea (eds), *Research Handbook on EU Administrative Law* (Edward Elgar Publishing 2017) 68.

[15] Bovens (n 9) 451.

11.3 Substantive standards of accountability

11.3.1 Market- and social-based accountability

Having clarified the meaning of horizontal accountability, we turn now to examine the main forms of horizontal accountability that investment firms are subject to.

Market discipline requires financial intermediaries, much like other corporations, to inform their shareholders, creditors, and investors about their financial situations, and to explain their business strategies, in order to receive sufficient funding for their businesses.[16] However, unlike non-financial corporations, commercial banks rely primarily on short-maturity debt (ie deposits), and much less on equity, to fund their businesses.[17] Reliance on borrowed money, in combination with the generally illiquid nature of the asset side of their balance sheets, makes the banking business inherently risky, and requires banks to instil a high level of trust in their customers, in order to ensure that existing and new depositors continue to provide funding, and to avoid existing depositors withdrawing their money simultaneously (bank runs).[18] Trust is also of paramount importance for the supply of investment services. While in most of the investment services provided to retail clients (ie execution of orders, reception and transmission of orders, investment advice and portfolio management) firms do not risk their own capital but gain a fee or commission from the service provided, clients need to trust investment firms to handle their funds honestly, fairly, and professionally.[19] Misconduct in the supply of financial services weakens customers' confidence in financial markets, and could lead, in practice, to

[16] For the public role of private regulation, see Fabrizio Cafaggi, 'Transnational Private Regulation and the Production of Global Public Goods and Private "Bads"' (2012) 23 European Journal of International Law 695.

[17] See, in particular, Anat Admati and Martin Hellwig, *The Bankers' New Clothes: What's Wrong with Banking and what to do about it* (Princeton University Press 2013) 31.

[18] As Luigi Zingales reminds us, 'the word "credit" comes from the Latin *credere*, which means to trust'. See Luigi Zingales, 'The Future of Securities Regulation' (2009) 47 Journal of Accounting Research 396. On the concept of trust in financial markets, see Peter O Mülbert and Alexander Sajnovits, 'The Element of Trust in Financial Markets Law' (2017) 18 German Law Journal 1.

[19] However, an important difference between traditional banking business (deposit taking and credit granting) and investment services business is that, with the former, the depositor loses an ownership right over his or her funds, and obtains only a credit towards the bank. By contrast, investors keep their ownership rights in the funds that they entrust to investment firms, since these funds have to be segregated by those firms.

consumers' withdrawal of funds from the financial sector (ie through redemption of instruments, or runs on banks). This could, in turn, provoke systemic effects, thus also affecting citizens and firms that were not part of the financial transactions in question.[20]

Financial institutions are also subject to forms of collective, social responsibility. It is widely acknowledged that the business of banks and, albeit to a lesser extent, investment firms, can produce negative externalities because the social costs of insolvency or illiquidity exceed the private costs for the shareholders of such institutions, and also affect parties that are not depositors or customers.[21] In the aftermath of the GFC, this consideration has driven the new macroprudential focus of financial regulation in the EU, and internationally.[22] A strand of legal scholarship has acknowledged that financial intermediaries should also have some form of social responsibility for financial inclusion, broader economic development, and equalisation of economic opportunity,[23] and environmental sustainability[24]. Following international political initiatives towards sustainability and the transition to a low-carbon economy,[25] EU institutions have integrated Environmental,

[20] See, on the systemic effects of misconduct on the financial sector: European Systemic Risk Board, 'Report on Misconduct Risk in the Banking Sector' (June 2015); Commission, 'European Financial Stability and Integration Review' SWD(2015)98 (April 2015) 173; Letter from Mark Carney (Governor of the Bank of England and Chair of the G20 Financial Stability Board) to G20 finance ministers and central bank governors (4 February 2015). See also, for recognition in legislative texts and CJEU's case law, of the importance of consumers' confidence in financial markets: recital no 5 of MiFID II; recital no 3 of the Directive 2014/17/EU on credit agreements for consumers relating to residential immovable property [2014] OJ L 60, 34–85); judgment of 10 May 1995 in Case C-384/93 *Alpine Investments BV v Minister van Financiën* EU:C:1995:126, para 42.

[21] See, in particular, Steven L Schwarcz, 'Systemic Risk' (2008) 97 Georgetown Law Journal 207 and Kern Alexander, *Principles of Banking Regulation* (CUP 2019) 40.

[22] See, for more detail on the EU reforms aimed at ensuring financial stability: Jan H Dalhuisen, *Dalhuisen on Transnational, Comparative, Commercial, Financial and Trade Law* (vol 3, 7th edn, Hart Publishing 2019) 509–12, Gianni Lo Schiavo, *The Role of Financial Stability in EU Law and Policy* (Wolters Kluwer 2017) 12 et seq, Luca Amorello, *Macroprudential Banking Supervision & Monetary Policy: Legal Interaction in the European Union* (Palgrave Macmillan 2018) 11 et seq; Ignazio Angeloni, 'Towards a Macro-prudential Framework for the Single supervisory Area, Remarks by Ignazio Angeloni, Member of the Supervisory Board of the European Central Bank, Belgium Financial Forum, Brussels, 20 April 2015', available at <https://www.bankingsupervision.europa.eu/press/speeches/date/2015/html/se150420.en.html> accessed 15 October 2021.

[23] See, in particular, Mads Andenas and Iris H-Y Chiu, *The Foundations and Future of Financial Regulation: Governance for Responsibility* (Routledge 2014) 238 and 469; Alan M White, 'Banks as Utilities' (2016) 90 Tulane Law Review 1274. See also Commission (n 21) 143; Commission, 'A Digital Finance Strategy for the EU' COM/2020/591 final, 5; Basel Committee on Banking Supervision, 'Guidance on the Application of the Core Principles for Effective Banking Supervision to the Regulation and Supervision of Institutions Relevant to Financial Inclusion' (September 2016) 33.

[24] Alexander (n 22) 326.

[25] See the Paris Agreement conclusions of December 2015, available at: <http://unfccc.int/paris_agreement/items/9485.php> accessed 15 October 2021; and the United Nations UN 2030 Agenda for Sustainable Development, available at: <https://sustainabledevelopment.un.org/post2015/transformingourworld> accessed 15 October 2021.

Social, or Governance (ESG) criteria into the regulatory approach to financial services, in order to support the path towards sustainable economic growth.[26] As a consequence, ESG risks have now become part of the Single Rulebook, with the 2019 amendment of the Capital Requirements Regulation (CRR), Capital Requirements Directive (CRD),[27] and the ESAs' founding regulations.[28] Moreover, the European Commission proposed to introduce sustainability factors in the suitability assessment and into the organisational requirements and risk management policies set out in MiFID II.[29]

11.3.2 Regulation-based accountability

Contracts between credit and investment firms and their clients are regulated by a multi-layered framework, in which contract law rules (ie rules on the formation, validity, interpretation of contracts and remedies for breach of pre-contractual and contractual obligations) represent only one level of contract governance. The other tiers are based on requirements that have been imposed internationally, or at EU level, in order to achieve three goals: a high level of client protection (conduct regulation), the safety and soundness of individual firms (microprudential regulation), and the financial system as a whole (macroprudential regulation). The main rationale for conduct or investor protection regulation, which is the focus of this contribution, is to protect clients

[26] See, in particular, Commission, 'Action Plan: Financing Sustainable Growth' COM/2018/097 final; Commission, 'The European Green Deal' COM/2019/640 final.

[27] See art 98(8) of the CRD (ESG risk to be included in the supervisory review and evaluation process (SREP) as amended by Directive (EU) 2019/878 as regards exempted entities, financial holding companies, mixed financial holding companies, remuneration, supervisory measures and powers and capital conservation measures [2019] OJ L 150, 253–95.

[28] See art 449a of the CRR (disclosure requirements for ESG risks), art 501c (prudential treatment of exposures to environmental and/or social objectives), as amended by Regulation (EU) 2019/876 of the European Parliament and of the Council of 20 May 2019 amending Regulation (EU) No 575/2013 as regards the leverage ratio, the net stable funding ratio, requirements for own funds and eligible liabilities, counterparty credit risk, market risk, exposures to central counterparties, exposures to collective investment undertakings, large exposures, reporting and disclosure requirements, and Regulation (EU) No 648/2012 [2019] OJ L 150, 1–225. See also ESMA, 'Strategy on Sustainable Finance' ESMA 22-105-1052, 6 February 2020; and, with regards to credit institutions, see ECB, 'Guide on Climate-related and Environmental Risks Supervisory Expectations relating to Risk Management and Disclosure' (May 2020).

[29] European Commission, Delegated Regulation (EU) …/... amending Delegated Regulation (EU) 2017/565 as regards the integration of sustainability factors, risks and preferences into certain organisational requirements and operating conditions for investment firms, C/2021/2616 final. This draft regulation is based on ESMA, Technical advice to the European Commission on integrating sustainability risks and factors in MiFID II, Final Report, 30 April 2019 ESMA35-43-1737.

from market failures (information asymmetries, agency problems, and imperfect competition),[30] firms' misconduct,[31] and clients' own behavioural limitations.[32] The regulation of retail markets in the EU has been motivated, especially prior to the GFC, by the need to address market failures, and has, traditionally, been geared towards the long-term goal of strengthening the cross-border exchange of financial products and services.[33] An important point that should be stressed, for present purposes, is that, even when this form of regulation does not harmonise contract law aspects of financial transactions, it may—and, in certain cases, should—affect the interpretation of national contract and tort law. The possibility of clients obtaining private law remedies for breaches of these standards could be described, as we shall see below, as a form of hybrid civil liability,[34] whereby regulation expands the scope of financial institutions' liability before national courts, and ADR mechanisms raise the standard of care that firms must observe in private law relationships.

11.3.3 Soft law-based accountability

An important form of investment firms' accountability stems from soft law instruments.[35] Soft law has played a foundational role in international financial regulation,[36] and plays a central role in the European System of Financial Supervision (ESFS). Within this new framework for financial supervision, the national competent authorities (NCAs) remain responsible for the day-to-day supervision of market participants, while the European Supervisory Authorities (ESAs)—the European Banking Authority (EBA), the European Securities and Markets Authority (ESMA), and the European Insurance and

[30] See, for more detail, David Llewellyn, 'The Economic Rationale for Regulation' (1999) Financial Services Authority Occasional Paper Series no 1.

[31] See, in particular, David C Lagenvoort, 'Selling Hope, Selling Risk: Some Lessons for Law from Behavioural Economics About Stockbrokers and Sophisticated Customers' (1996) 84 California Law Review 627.

[32] See, in particular, Christine Jolls, Cass Sunstein, and Richard Thaler, 'A Behavioral Approach to Law and Economics' (1998) 50 Stanford Law Review 1476; FCA, 'Applying Behavioural Economics at the Financial Conduct Authority' (2013) Occasional Paper Series no 1.

[33] See, in particular, Emilios Avgouleas, 'The Global Financial Crisis and the Disclosure Paradigm in European Financial Regulation: The Case for Reform' (2009) 4 European Company and Financial Law Review 441 et seq.

[34] See, for more detail, Federico Della Negra, *MiFID II and Private Law: Enforcing EU Conduct of Business Rules* (Hart Publishing 2019) 173 (hereafter Della Negra, *MiFID II and Private Law*).

[35] On the concept of soft law, see, in particular, Fabien Terpan, 'Soft Law in the European Union—The Changing Nature of EU Law' (2015) 21 European Law Journal 68.

[36] See, in particular, Lucia Quaglia, *The European Union and Global Financial Regulation* (OUP 2014) 47.

Occupational Pensions Authority (EIOPA)—have been granted new tasks and powers to ensure a consistent application of regulatory and supervisory standards across the EU.[37] These powers include, in particular, the adoption of non-legally binding acts of general application, such as guidelines and draft regulatory and implementing technical standards, as well as supervisory convergence instruments (for example, Questions and Answers (Q & As)).

Although these acts are not intended to create binding legal effects on market participants, they do produce some legal effects on the authority that adopted them, on the NCAs addressed by the acts, and on the market participants themselves.[38] In particular, market participants should make every effort to comply with the ESAs' recommendations and guidelines and, if required by those guidelines or recommendations, financial institutions must report, in a clear and detailed way, whether they comply with the provision in question. More importantly, national courts should take recommendations into consideration for the purposes of deciding disputes before them.[39] Therefore, the ESMA 'handbook' on MiFID II conduct of business rules and investor protection regulations can expand, even further, the scope of accountability of these firms, leading national courts to take greater account of retail clients' need for protection.

The forms and intensity of judicial review of soft-law instruments have been extensively discussed in literature and cannot be elaborated further in this context.[40] Suffices to recall that while recommendations and guidelines cannot be subject to an action for annulment under Article 263 TFEU, Article 19(3)(b) TEU and the first paragraph of Article 267(b) TFEU enable the CJEU to give preliminary rulings on the validity of these acts.[41]

[37] See, for more detail on the ESAs' objectives, tasks, and powers: Niamh Moloney, *EU Securities and Financial Markets Regulation* (3rd edn, OUP 2014) 973–1007.

[38] See, for more detail, Della Negra, 'MiFID II and Private Law' (n 34) 85.

[39] Judgment of 13 December 1989 in case C-322/88 *Grimaldi* EU:C:1989:646, para 8; judgment of 15 September 2016 in case Case C-28/15 *Koninklijke KPN NV et al v Autoriteit Consument en Markt (ACM)* EU:C:2016:692, para 43. See also, with regard to the effects of EBA recommendations, the opinion of AG Campos Sanchez-Bordona of 17 September 2020 in Case C-501/18 *BT v Balgarska Narodna Banka* EU:C:2020:729, point 95.

[40] For an overview of the main issues see in particular Linda Senden, *Soft Law in European Community Law* (Oxford and Portland Oregon, Hart Publishing, 2004); Joanne Scott, 'In Legal Limbo: Post-Legislative Guidance as a Challenge for European Administrative Law' (2011) 48 *Common Market Law Review*, 329; Stefan, O., *Soft Law in Court. Competition Law, State Aid and the Court of Justice of the European Union* (Kluwer, Alphen aan den Rijn, 2013).

[41] See, with regard to recommendations, Case C-322/88, *Grimaldi*, para 8; Case C-16/16 P, *Belgium v Commission*, EU:C:2018:79, para 44 and Case C-501/18 *BT v Balgarska Narodna Banka*, EU:C:2021:249, para 83. With regard to guidelines issued by the European Banking Authority (EBA), the Case C-911/19 *Fédération bancaire française (FBF) v Autorité de contrôle prudentiel et de résolution (ACPR)*, ECLI:EU:C:2021:599, para 57.

11.4 Institutional mechanisms for accountability

11.4.1 Firms' internal complaints-handling functions

Moving now to the mechanisms that trigger financial institutions' horizontal accountability, it is possible to identify, in MiFID II, three distinctive institutional arrangements making these firms accountable for their conduct towards clients. The first level of horizontal accountability is based on firms' internal complaints-handling functions. MiFID II has strengthened these complaints-handling obligations in comparison with the original MiFID,[42] and ESMA has launched a consultation on new guidelines on the compliance function.[43] An important novelty of MiFID II is that the complaints-handling function not only plays its traditional, prudential role as a firm's internal control mechanism (the so-called 'second line of defence'),[44] but that it is also instrumental in ensuring the effective protection of clients.[45] Two aspects of this new objective, assigned by EU law to firms' internal functions, can be observed. First, not only do firms have the duty to publish details of their complaints procedures,[46] but they must also communicate their positions on complaints to clients and potential clients, and inform clients and potential clients about their options, including referral of a complaint to an ADR mechanism, or taking civil action.[47] The reference to civil actions shows that, even if MiFID II did not harmonise civil law consequences for breaches of conduct of business rules, it certainly accepted that breach of these duties can give rise to civil actions. Moreover, firms must provide information on complaints and complaints-handling procedures to relevant competent authorities and, where applicable under national law, to alternative dispute resolution (ADR) mechanisms.[48]

[42] Art 10 of the Commission Directive 2006/73/EC of 10 August 2006 implementing Directive 2004/39/EC of the European Parliament and of the Council as regards organisational requirements and operating conditions for investment firms and defined terms for the purposes of that Directive [2006] OJ L 241, 26.

[43] ESMA, 'Guidelines on Certain Aspects of the MiFID II Compliance Function Requirements' (Consultation Paper) ESMA35-43-2019, 15 July 2019.

[44] For details on the 'three lines of defence' model for the governance of risks, see EBA, 'Guidelines on Internal Governance under Directive 2013/36/EU' EBA/GL/2017/11, 26 September 2017, p 9.

[45] Art 22(2)(d) and recital no 38 of the Commission Delegated Regulation (EU) 2017/565 of 25 April 2016 supplementing Directive 2014/65/EU of the European Parliament and of the Council as regards organisational requirements and operating conditions for investment firms and defined terms for the purposes of that Directive [2017] OJ L 87, 1 (hereafter, 'MiFID II Delegated Regulation').

[46] ibid, art 26(2).

[47] ibid, art 26(5).

[48] ibid, art 26(6).

11.4.2 Out-of-court dispute resolution

11.4.2.1 Main innovations of MiFID II and the ADR Directive

The second level of firms' accountability for compliance with conduct of business obligations is based on out-of-court dispute resolution. MiFID II also made significant changes to the framework for out-of-court dispute resolution of retail client disputes. The directive provides for two types of out-of-court scheme. First, it requires member states to set up procedures for the out-of-court settlement of consumer disputes on investment services. A similar rule was laid down in the original MiFID, but MiFID II now requires (rather than merely encouraging) member states to set up these procedures. Second, it requires the establishment of mechanisms to ensure that compensation can be paid, or other remedial action taken, in accordance with national law, for any financial loss or damage suffered as a result of an infringement of MiFID II or Regulation (EU) No 600/2014.[49]

It is debatable what the legal implications of this rule are for civil law. Specifically, it has been debated whether it is intended to harmonise national contract law remedies, or whether its role is, instead, limited to out-of-court dispute resolution procedures. It is submitted that this provision cannot be interpreted as harmonizing national civil liability regimes, for several reasons.[50] First, the term 'remedial action', used in the English language version of the directive, is translated by the Italian, French, and Spanish versions into the term 'corrective measures', which is a broader concept, not restricted to a private law remedy, which may encompass any administrative measure taken by a competent authority.[51] The term 'remedy' is also used in this sense by the first paragraph of Article 69 of MiFID II, which concerns the powers of competent supervisory authorities. Second, in its initial version, this article, which was added by the European Parliament to the Commission's proposal, granted the competent authorities a supervisory power to set up mechanisms to compensate clients.[52] Subsequently, the provision was amended, transforming the

49 MiFID II, arts 75(1) and 69(2).

50 For more detail on this provision, see Della Negra, 'MiFID II and Private Law' (n 34) 92, and the contribution by Magnus Strand in Chapter 12 in this volume. See, for the differing view that this provision also affects private law remedies, Evariest Calliens, 'Recalibrating the Debate on MiFID's Private Enforceability: Why the EU Charter of Fundamental Rights is the Elephant in the Room' (2020) 21(4) European Business Organization Law Review 759 and Danny Busch and Cees van Dam, 'A Bank's Duty of Care: Perspectives from European and Comparative Law' in Danny Busch and Cees van Dam (eds), *A Bank's Duty of Care* (Hart Publishing 2017) 420.

51 The German version reads *Abhilfemaßnahmen*, which could be translated as 'measure to remedy'.

52 This provision was originally included by the EU Parliament in art 72(ha) (named 'Remedies to be made available to competent authorities') of the Commission MiFID II proposal ('require that

supervisory power into an obligation on member states. Third, according to Article 69(2) of MiFID II, compensation should be made, or other remedial action taken, 'in accordance with national law'. Hence, MiFID II relies on detailed national private law rules, in particular on causation, evidence, and measures of damages, for the functioning of this special mechanism. It is, therefore, plausible that Article 69(2) MiFID II was drafted having in mind the model of the consumer redress schemes that the UK Financial Conduct Authority (FCA) can decide to set up to compensate investors, in cases of large-scale mis-selling.[53]

These new MiFID II provisions complement the framework for consumer ADR procedures laid down in 2013 by the ADR Directive and the ODR Regulation.[54] But there is an important difference between the two out-of-court settlement mechanisms included in MiFID II. The 'Article 75 mechanisms' do not necessitate the grant of a private law remedy on the basis of legal rules, and can rely on considerations of equity, or any other criteria.[55] By contrast, the 'Article 69(2) mechanisms' require adjudicators to grant a remedy to clients only if there is an infringement of the directive. This should be without prejudice to remedies that are available under national private law. A model of so-called 'light law enforcement'[56] and a model of quasi-judicial enforcement can, of course, coexist in the same jurisdiction, as we shall see below.

11.4.2.2 Permanent ADR mechanisms

The minimum harmonisation approach taken by the ADR Directive in this area has favoured the emergence of a wide variety of ADR mechanisms and schemes in member states.[57] While it is not possible to examine them in detail here, it suffices to say that ADR mechanisms can be set out either by industry

compensation be paid or other remedial action be taken to correct any financial loss or other damage suffered by an investor as a result of any practice or conduct that is contrary to this Directive or to Regulation (EU) No —/— [MiFIR]').

[53] Financial Services and Markets Act 2000 (FSMA), s 404G, and FCA CONRED 'Consumer Redress Schemes Sourcebook' (FCA 2016/32).

[54] Directive 2013/11/EU of the European Parliament and of the Council of 21 May 2013 on alternative dispute resolution for consumer disputes [2013] OJ L 165/63 (hereafter 'ADR Directive') and Regulation (EU) No 524/2013 of 21 May 2013 of the European Parliament and of the Council on online dispute resolution for consumer disputes [2013] OJ L 165/1 (hereafter, 'ODR Regulation').

[55] See ADR Directive, arts 6(1)(b) and 7(1)(i).

[56] Gerhard Wagner, 'Private Law Enforcement through ADR: Wonder Drug or Snake Oil?' (2014) 51 Common Market Law Review 177.

[57] Member States shall ensure compliance with the principles of equivalence and effectiveness. See Joined Cases C-317/08, C-318/08, C-319/08, and C-320/08 *Alassini and Others* EU:C:2010:146, paras 47–67; Case C-75/16 *Menini and Rampanelli v Banco Popolare Società Cooperativa* EU:C:2017:457, paras 53–55.

associations, or by the competent supervisory authorities, can be funded from the public budget or by the industry, can decide disputes on the basis of legal or non-legal standards, and can lead to binding or non-binding decisions. The procedures can take the form of a mediation scheme, where a potential non-binding solution is suggested to the parties, or an ombudsman scheme, where a third party takes a decision. The decision may involve the award of damages, pecuniary or non-pecuniary, or other types of remedy. The procedure can be voluntary for the parties, or a mandatory precondition of accessing a judicial proceeding. For present purposes, a very relevant distinction, when determining a firm's accountability, is that between permanent (or ordinary) and special (or ad hoc) ADR mechanisms.

Permanent ADR mechanisms are set up within NCAs, as well as private industry associations, and resolve retail client disputes without limit of time, or restriction as to the type of dispute. These ADR bodies can be based on mediation schemes (as in France, for example)[58] and adjudicative schemes (for example, the UK[59], Italy,[60] and Spain).[61]

While consumer ADR proceedings have been often associated with a non-legalistic and informal approach to dispute resolution, research has shown that, in the investment and banking services sectors, ADR bodies tend to rely on legal standards to resolve disputes. These standards are based both on regulations (ie national laws transposing MiFID, or soft law acts by competent authorities), and on private law rules. Therefore, these procedures do not simply produce 'a settlement for the parties', but determine how regulatory duties and supervisory expectations should be interpreted in the concrete case; in this sense, they truly complement the investors protection mandate of supervisory authorities.[62] For example, in Italy, the banking and investment service ombudsmen rely greatly on private law concepts and case law to decide cases.[63] A different but valuable dispute resolution approach is that of the UK Financial Ombudsman Service (FOS), which is statutorily required to take decisions based on what is 'fair and reasonable in all the circumstances of the case'.[64]

[58] See the mediation scheme of the AMF (Médiation de l'Autorité des Marchés Financiers) and the private schemes set up by the Fédération bancaire française (FBF) and the Association des Sociétés Financières (ASF).

[59] Financial Ombudsman Service (FOS).

[60] Arbitro per le Controversie Finanziarie (ACF).

[61] Servicios de Reclamaciones—CNMV.

[62] See Hans-W Micklitz, 'The Transformation of Enforcement in European Private Law: Preliminary Considerations' (2015) 4 European Review of Private Law 502.

[63] See, for more detail, Della Negra, 'MiFID II and Private Law' (n 34) 107.

[64] FSMA, s 228.

11.4.2.3 Special ADR mechanisms

Special ADR mechanisms have been set up in the wake of the GFC by NCAs, or by legislators, to provide redress to clients for specific and serious cases of mis-selling. Hence, these schemes are time-limited, access is restricted to specific classes of plaintiffs, and they are normally set up in the form of an adjudicative scheme (arbitration, or an ombudsman). Examples of these schemes can be found in the UK, Spain, and Italy.[65]

In the UK, the FCA has the power to set up consumer redress schemes ('CRSs') to compensate clients under certain conditions.[66] In the wake of the GFC, the FCA also set up another type of scheme to compensate investors for losses suffered as a result of the mis-selling of interest rate hedging products (IRHPs)[67] and payment protection insurance (PPI).[68] Compensation was provided by banks, after an assessment based on regulatory standards.

In Italy, three special redress schemes were set up by law, in order to compensate retail holders of subordinated debt instruments issued by credit institutions that were subject to resolution and compulsory liquidation. A first scheme (Fondo di Solidarietá), set up in 2016, was funded by the Fondo Interbancario di Tutela dei Depositi (FITD). Other schemes were set up in 2017 (Fondo di Ristoro Finanziario),[69] and in 2018 (Fondo Indennizzo Risparmiatori), and funded out of the public budget.[70] Compensation of clients' losses is based on an assessment made by a special commission appointed

[65] Investors' compensation schemes are in place also in Australia. See detailed discussion in Kingsford-Smith (n 5) 542.

[66] Rules for the CRSs are set out in the FCA handbook 'Consumer Redress Schemes Sourcebook' (June 2020).

[67] For a criticism of this scheme, see Richard Samuel, 'Tools for Culture Change: FCA, now you are Listening! Time to Build an Independent, Low-cost Forum for Conduct Dispute Resolution' (2017) 12 Capital Markets Law Journal 281. See also Richard Samuel, 'Tools for Changing Banking Culture: FCA are you Listening?' (2016) 11 Capital Markets Law Journal 129.

[68] PPI is an 'insurance against a borrower becoming unable to make credit repayments for specified reasons, such as accidental injury'. See, for discussion in detail, Eilís Ferran, 'Regulatory Lessons from the Payment Protection Insurance Mis-selling Scandal in the UK' (2012) 13 European Business Organization Law Review 247, 250 et seq. The scheme rules are set out in DISP app 3 of the FCA Handbook DISP app 3.1.3. In *BBA v FSA and FOS* [2011] EWHC 999 (Admin), the High Court of England and Wales held that this special redress scheme, while different from a CRS, is legally sound. The UK Supreme Court in *Plevin v Paragon Personal Finance Ltd* [2014] UKSC 61 [18] held that a firm's failure to disclose the amount of its commission made the contractual relationship with its client unfair under s 140A(1)(c) of the Consumer Credit Act 1974. In order to provide guidance on the impact of this ruling on PPI dispute resolution, the FCA amended the rules on the PPI redress scheme on 1 March 2017, but set a deadline of 29 August 2019 to submit a complaint, unless there were exceptional circumstances, with the aim of bringing the PPI issue to an orderly conclusion, and bring finality and certainty for consumers and firms.

[69] Legge del 27 dicembre 2017, no 205, art 1, commi 1106–09).

[70] Law of 30 December 2018, no 145, art 1, paras 493–507. This new fund replaced the previous Fondo di Ristoro Finanziario, and increased the amount of compensation that the Fondo di Solidarietà can award to clients from 80 to 95 per cent of the purchase price of the financial instrument, requesting the FITD to integrate the compensation already given to clients by 31 December 2019.

by the Italian government, and is limited to a percentage of the purchase price of the financial instruments.

Like Italy, Spain has experienced widespread cases of the large-scale mis-selling of financial instruments issued and distributed by credit institutions. A first special arbitration scheme was set up to resolve disputes on the mis-selling of *participationes preferentes* and other hybrid financial instruments held by retail clients and distributed by credit institutions (Bankia, CatalunyaCaixa, and Novacaixagalicia (NCG)), where the Fondo de reestructuración ordenada bancaria (FROB) owned a majority capital stake.[71] A commission was tasked with ensuring that this procedure was kept transparent, by publishing periodic reports on the functioning of the procedure (Comisión de seguimiento de instrumentos híbridos de capital y deuda subordinada).

Another special out-of-court dispute resolution mechanism was set up in 2016 to compensate clients who had suffered losses as a result of unfair floor clauses (*cláusulas suelo*) included in mortgage contracts.[72] Credit institutions make a proposal for the amount to be given back to the consumer and, if the consumer accepts this proposal, he or she cannot later make the same claim in a court. In order to increase the efficiency of judicial resolution of floor clause disputes, the Spanish General Council of the Judiciary (Consejo General del Poder Judicial), on 25 May 2017, put in place an extraordinary measure mandating fifty-four first instance courts (at least one per province) to decide only disputes on floor clauses in mortgage contracts.[73]

Even if anecdotal evidence suggests that regulatory and private law standards both played a role in the Spanish arbitration on *participationes preferentes*, it is difficult to make a conclusive assessment about the standards used by these ad hoc ADR mechanisms, due to the limited publicity that characterises the processes and final decisions of these special schemes.[74]

[71] The scheme was set up by the Real Decreto-ley 6/2013, de 22 de marzo, de protección a los titulares de determinados productos de ahorro e inversión y otras medidas de carácter financiero (BOE no 71, de 23 de marzo de 2013, p 22901). On 18 December 2013, the FROB resolved to sell all of its shareholding in NCG Banco SA (88.33 per cent) to Banco Etcheverría SA/Grupo Banesco.

[72] Real Decreto-ley 1/2017, de 20 de enero, de medidas urgentes de protección de consumidores en materia de cláusulas suelo (BOE no 18 de 21 de enero de 2017). The scheme was set up after the CJEU judgment in Joined Cases C-154/15, C-307/15, and C-308/15 *Francisco Gutiérrez Naranjo et al* EU:C:2016:980.

[73] The measure was in force from 1 June until 31 December 2017.

[74] While the aggregate data on the numbers of complaints and decisions are generally available, the text of the decisions are not available, thus making it difficult for complainants and researchers to analyse how these disputes were resolved. See, for more detail, Della Negra, 'MiFID II and Private Law' (n 34), 125 et seq.

11.4.3 National courts

11.4.3.1 Civil law effects of conduct of business obligations from an EU law perspective

Civil liability for breaches of conduct of business obligations could be regarded as the strongest form of investment firms' horizontal accountability.

To understand this point, it is useful to remember that EU law does not have general private law rules to govern private relationships. It has harmonised specific aspects of private law relationships, mainly in consumer, public procurement, and competition law, on the basis of Article 114 of the Treaty on the Functioning of the European Union (TFEU), with the aim of strengthening the internal market.[75] The same legal basis was used, after the GFC, to harmonise specific aspects of the civil liability of depository institutions, credit rating agencies, firms offering packaged retail and insurance-based investment products (PRIIPs), providers of pan-European personal pension products (PEPPs), and managers of European long-term investment funds (ELTIF), to ensure an effective protection of investors.[76] Yet, there is no EU general liability regime for investment losses caused by investment service providers (investment firms and credit institutions). In the absence of EU law rules on this matter, the question that has arisen across national jurisdictions after the GFC is whether MiFID conduct of business rules ought only to have effect between firms and their supervisory authorities, or whether they should also produce effects between firms and their clients (so-called 'civil law effects').

In the *Bankinter* and the *Banif Plus Bank* judgments, the CJEU has held that it is for the internal legal order of each member state to determine the contractual consequences of non-compliance with the obligations of Article 19(4) and (5) of MiFID I, subject to observance of the principles of equivalence and effectiveness.[77] It is submitted that these judgments confirm that member states

[75] Art 21 of Directive 2011/61/EU on Alternative Investment Fund Managers [2011] OJ L 174/1; Art 11 of Regulation (EU) No 1286/2014 on key information documents for packaged retail and insurance-based investment products [2014] OJ L 352/1; Art 35(a)(4) of Regulation (EU) No 462/2013 on credit rating agencies [2013] OJ L 146/1; Art 7(3) of Regulation (EU) 2015/760 on European long-term investment funds [2015] OJ L 123/98; Art 31 of Regulation (EU) 2019/1238 on a pan-European Personal Pension Product (PEPP) [2019] OJ L 198/63. See also Art 12(3) of Regulation (EU) No 648/2012 of the European Parliament and of the Council of 4 July 2012 on OTC derivatives, central counterparties and trade repositories [2012] OJ L 201/1.

[76] See, for discussion in more detail, Federico Della Negra, 'The Regulatory Design and Goals of Civil Liability in EU Securities Regulation after the Global Financial Crisis: Trends and Perspectives' in Olha O Cherednichenko and Mads Andenas (eds), *Financial Regulation and Civil Liability in European Law* (Edward Elgar Publishing 2020) 160–80.

[77] Case C-604/11 *Genil v Bankinter* EU:C:2013:344, para 57; Case C-312/14 *Banif Plus Bank Zrt v Márton Lantos* EU:C:2015:794, para 79.

are not only allowed, but also required, to provide for private law remedies for breaches of these rules.[78] This interpretation reflects the very purpose of the principles of equivalence and effectiveness, which is to ensure the effective application of EU law before national courts.

These principles apply only when the EU law provision grants rights to individuals.[79] Otherwise, member states retain full discretion to regulate the matter. Therefore, by referring to these principles in *Bankinter* and *Banif Plus Bank,* the CJEU implicitly held that the MiFID appropriateness and suitability rules are rights-conferring provisions and, for this reason, member states should ensure that investors have at their disposal a private law remedy to enforce these rules. Only the executive conditions of this remedy (causation, measure of damages, and evidence) are to be determined on the basis of the principles of equivalence and effectiveness.[80] The question of whether conduct of business obligations confer rights on investors has to be answered by national courts, with regard to the specific rule(s) at stake. The guiding criteria is whether a rule has a transactional function, namely whether the rule is imposed on the credit or investment institution in so far as it is part of a contractual transaction.[81] In this regard, a transactional function can be associated to pre-contractual information duties, appropriateness and suitability rules given that this type of rules, for their content and purpose, require, as a pre-condition for their application a relationship between the firm and a client or potential client. By contrast, rules that have primarily an organisational function may not be able to grant an individual right to investors because they produce their effects mainly within the credit or investment firm as an organisation, irrespective of its relationship with a client or potential client (eg most of the conflict of interest and product governance rules).

[78] See, for more details, Della Negra, 'MiFID II and Private Law' (n 34) 180. See also Stefan Grundmann, 'The *Bankinter* Case on MiFID Regulation and Contract Law' (2013) 9 European Review of Contract Law 278. For the differing opinion that this case law would only allow member states to establish civil law consequences for breaches of conduct of business rules, see Elke Vandendriessche, *Investor Losses: A Comparative Legal Analysis of Causation and Assessment of Damages in Investor Litigation* (Intersentia 2015) 103.

[79] For the concept of a right in EU law, see Thomas Eilmansberger, 'The Relationship between Rights and Remedies in EC Law: In Search of the Missing Link' (2004) 41 Common Market Law Review 1199.

[80] For the notion of constitutive and executive remedial conditions, see Walter van Gerven, 'Of Rights, Remedies and Procedures' (2001) 37 Common Market Law Review 525.

[81] See in more details Federico Della Negra, *MiFID II and Private Law,* 178. The proposed criterion of the transactional function or nature could be regarded as a specific application of the *Schutznormtheorie* which is applied also by the CJEU, to identify right-conferring rules. For the use of this theory in EU law, see Norbert Reich, 'Horizontal Liability in EC Law: Hybridisation of Remedies for Compensation in case of breaches of EC Rights' (2007) 44 Common Market Law Review 719. In more details on the type of rules granting rights to investors, see Takis Tridimas, 'Financial regulation and private law remedies: an EU law perspective', in Olha O. Cherednichenko and Mads Andenas (eds.), *Financial Regulation and Civil liability in European Law*, 57 ss.

The formulations of some of the provisions of MiFID II corroborate the argument that its conduct of business rules are, in principle, rights-conferring. Articles 75 and 69(2), as well as the reference made in Article 26 of Commission MiFID II Regulation to 'civil actions', all indicate that the EU legislators have 'accepted' that breaches of these rules can give rise to compensation and private law consequences, although they decided not to harmonise these. Therefore, the silence of MiFID II on private law harmonisation does not demonstrate that conduct of business obligations have only 'public law effects', or that they are irrelevant to private law relationships. It is also relevant to mention that, where EU legislators intend to limit civil law effects of regulatory duties, they enact an express provision, like they did in respect of the conduct of business rules laid down in the EMIR.[82] In the absence of such an express legislative limitation of civil liability, the general principles of EU law (effectiveness and equivalence) should apply, as specified above.

Finally, the mere existence of supervisory or sanctioning measures (public enforcement mechanisms) for breaches of conduct of business obligations would not offer a sufficiently effective application of these provisions, which are also aimed at protecting the individual investor.[83]

11.4.3.2 National law divergences

The crucial role that national private law plays in mis-selling disputes could be one reason why, so far, national courts have only twice decided to refer a question for a preliminary ruling to the CJEU on the interpretation of MiFID conduct of business rules.

There is a significant difference between the adjudication approaches taken in continental jurisdictions, and in the UK. In continental jurisdictions, courts have accepted that conduct of business obligations qualify as contract law rules, or as rules that determine the content of contract law duties, and hence that their breach can give rise to contract law remedies. In the UK, courts maintain that conduct of business obligations cannot be regarded as contract law duties, and only in exceptional cases can they influence the content of the duty of care of credit and investment firms (in particular, where an advisory contract was concluded).[84] Within continental jurisdictions, the main divergence is between compensatory and restitutionary remedies: 'the competing

[82] Regulation (EU) No 648/2012 of the European Parliament and of the Council of 4 July 2012 on OTC derivatives, central counterparties and trade repositories [2012] OJ L 201/1, art 12(3). See, for a reference to this issue in the context of competition law, Magnus Strand, 'Competition Damages Betwixt and Between Past and Future: Cogeco' (2020) 57 Common Market Law Review 579.

[83] See in this regard the opinion of AG Kokott of 14 November 2019 in Case C-616/18 *Cofidis SA v YU and ZT* EU:C:2019:975, para 82 and judgment in Case C-679/18 *OPR-Finance s. r. o. v GK*, ECLI:EU:C:2020:167, para 38.

[84] While in France, Italy and Spain national courts have consistently held that MiFID I conduct of business rules have a contractual or tortious nature and thus directly produce civil law effects, in the

paradigms of damages in securities law'.[85] While in most jurisdictions, including France and Germany, a breach of conduct of business rules can lead only to compensatory remedies, either in tort or contract law, courts in some jurisdictions (Spain, Italy, and Austria) accept that such breaches may, in some circumstances, lead to the annulment of the investment service contract. The financial burden for the firm is clearly very different in these two outcomes: the annulment of a contract requires a firm to pay, to its client, not only money to compensate their investment loss, but also a payment corresponding to the purchase price of the financial instrument.[86]

These divergences clearly reflect different doctrinal approaches to private law and private enforcement cultures within each national jurisdiction. However, irrespective of these differences, national private law remedies ought to be interpreted in order to ensure compliance with the principles of equivalence and effectiveness. As far as MiFID II is concerned, it is important to distinguish between the suitability rule and the other conduct of business rules. The suitability rule, which applies only to investment advice and portfolio management services—services that entail a quasi-fiduciary relationship between firm and client—requires firms to assess their client's knowledge and experience, their financial situation and objectives, their risk tolerance, and their ability to bear losses, before recommending a financial instrument. If the firm cannot obtain this information from its client, it should not carry out the transaction, and should not make a recommendation, or decide to trade, where none of the services or instruments are suitable for the client.[87]

This prohibition, which stands out in the EU regulatory framework, primarily based on the existence of pre-contractual disclosure duties, aims to ensure a higher level of protection for clients in services where the firm takes, in practice, the investment decision. Therefore, given the fact that these prohibitions are directly applicable between private parties,[88] they should be interpreted as

Netherlands and in Germany national courts follow a more cautious approach, denying in particular an automatic, direct effect of regulatory duties on private law. See in more detail on the Dutch and German case law, Marninx Wallinga, 'Why MiFID & MiFID II Do (not) Matter to Private Law: Liability to Compensate for Investment Losses for Breach of Conduct of Business Rules' (2019) 3 European Review of Private Law 528-538.

[85] Frank H Easterbrook and Daniel R Fischel, 'Optimal Damages in Securities Cases' (1985) 52 University of Chicago Law Review 634.

[86] See, for an overview, Busch and van Dam (n 48) 373.

[87] MiFID II Delegated Regulation, art 52(8) and (10).

[88] See, for the effects of provisions prohibiting certain conduct, the Opinion of AG Bobek of 5 June 2018 in Case C-167/17 *Volkmar Klohn v An Bord Pleanála* EU:C:2018:387, para 40; Judgment of 15 April 2008 in Case C-268/06 *Impact* EU:C:2008:223, para 60.

prohibitions on concluding the contract, and member states should ensure, in light of the principle of equivalence, that a breach of this rule is 'sanctioned' with the same remedy that, under national law, applies to the conclusion of a contract that should not have been concluded. It could be added that a private law remedy with restitutionary effects would ensure, better than a compensatory remedy, the deterrent effect of this prohibition, as the restitution of the price paid by the client would put the client in the pre-contract situation they would have been in had no contract been concluded, and, thus, would be in line with the principle of effectiveness, as interpreted by the CJEU in the *Hirmann* judgment.[89]

MiFID II does not provide any consequences, aside from the possibility of competent authorities taking supervisory measures and sanctions, for breaches of other conduct of business obligations, such as fair treatment, disclosure, appropriateness, and product governance rules. Therefore, a breach of these rules would not prevent firms from distributing the financial instrument to their clients, and a civil law remedy compensating the actual loss suffered by investors (ie out-of-pocket damages) would be more in line with the rationale of these rules.

11.5 Assessing horizontal accountability: Implications and the way forward

11.5.1 Substantive law aspects

MiFID II has strengthened the accountability of financial services providers, beyond the traditional boundaries of national private law. From a substantive law perspective, the interpretation of private law concepts in the light of conduct of business obligations broadens firms' civil liability towards their clients and, thus, makes them more accountable, given that regulatory duties are more stringent than national private law duties. Private law adjudication is, therefore, turned into a form of hybrid or mixed private and regulatory enforcement that has the effect of holding firms accountable for their effective compliance with conduct of business obligations.[90] A similar development has been observed in the field of EU competition law, where private enforcement complements the

[89] Case C-174/12 *Hirmann v Immofinanz AG* EU:C:2013:856, paras 43–44. See also, for the relevance of the deterrent effect of private law remedies, Naranjo et al (n 70).

[90] On the aspect of hybridisation of remedies, see, in particular, Reich (n 79) 705–42.

public enforcement actions taken by the Commission and the national competent authorities.[91] However, in contrast with EU competition law, national courts cannot rely on a EU private law remedy to enforce breaches of conduct of business obligations. Rather, they have to apply their national private law, and interpret it in the light of EU conduct of business obligations and EU general principles (for example, effectiveness and equivalence). In the financial sector, therefore, private enforcement is fragmented, and responds to the rationale of each nation's own private law.

Lack of private law harmonisation brings about a degree of fragmentation and divergence in the field of adjudication, across jurisdictions. Although the level of cross-border trade of retail financial services remains low,[92] the existence of different private enforcement approaches undermines the credibility of these common regulatory standards. This is even more so where conduct of business rules have been laid down in directly applicable acts. However, harmonisation of contract law is not on the EU regulatory agenda, and 'judicial' harmonisation via CJEU preliminary rulings appears unlikely in this field, since very few requests have been sent to the CJEU so far. National courts and legal doctrine, therefore, has a crucial role in this regard. General principles of EU law, in particular equivalence and effectiveness, but also the principle of conforming interpretation, could and should play a more central role in national law adjudication, thus contributing to levelling the playing field.

The emergence of hybrid private law dispute resolution should be welcomed, because this ensures that not only courts, but also ADR bodies, can contribute to strengthening the effectiveness of the conduct of business rules, thereby mitigating the risk that these procedures increase legal uncertainty.[93]

Hybrid private law could, potentially, implement the MiFID II requirement of a law enforcement-driven ADR procedure (Article 69(2) of MiFID II), and could achieve the right balance between 'discretion and consistency'.[94] Regulatory principles (such as suitability) allow ADR bodies to deviate from the strict application of legal rules where necessary to ensure a fair outcome in the individual case, but ensure that decisions are compliant with regulatory

[91] See, inter alia, Andrea Renda, 'Private Antritrust Damages Actions in the EU: Chronicle of an Attempted Golpe' in H-W Micklitz and A Wechsler (eds), *The Transformation of Enforcement: European Economic Law in a Global Perspective* 273.

[92] Commission, 'European Financial Stability and Integration Review (EFSIR)', Brussels, 3 March 2020 SWD(2020) 40 final, 55.

[93] See, for this risk especially, Olha O Cherednichenko, 'Public and Private Enforcement of European Private Law in the Financial Services Sector' (2015) 4 European Review of Private Law 640.

[94] Rt Hon Lord Hunt of Wirral MBE , 'The Hunt Review—The Independent Review of the Financial Ombudsman Service—Opening up, Reaching out and Aiming High—An Agenda for Accessibility and Excellence in the Financial Ombudsman Service' 18.

duties, and that outcomes are fairly predictable for retail clients, as well as investment firms.

11.5.2 Institutional aspects

A private enforcement regime that is increasingly based on regulatory standards takes up a function that is, in a sense, 'public': the outcome of adjudication is influenced or determined by public regulatory goals. In out-of-court dispute resolution, this entails striking a fair balance between ensuring 'justice' in the individual case, and securing a sufficient level of predictability and consistency of decisions.

While the imposition of detailed legal rules and doctrine would stifle ADR bodies, and reduce the benefits of an informal, efficient adjudication process for retail clients,[95] informal, non-legalistic forms of dispute resolution may give excessive discretion to ADR bodies, undermining the predictability of out-of-court dispute resolutions, and calling the fairness of the procedures into question.[96] A good compromise between these two approaches might be to ask ADR bodies to follow, as far as possible, regulatory principles which are already binding on firms. In addition, ADR bodies should be requested to publish their decisions and make them easily accessible: transparency of decision-making could benefit both clients and investment firms, making the ADR adjudication process more predictable.

The increasing involvement of administrative authorities in dispute resolution creates a form of administrative enforcement of private law,[97] which calls for a new understanding of traditional categories of private enforcement, such as compensation and deterrence.[98] On the one hand, compensation granted via public funds seems to be the only way to remedy *ex post* a negative externality (loss of clients' funds and confidence in financial markets) that has been created by the failure of the financial intermediary, and cannot be remediated through traditional private enforcement mechanisms. On the other hand, this form of extraordinary public financing of compensation can create moral

[95] See for this point the judgment of the High Court in *BBA v FSA and FOS* [2011] EWHC 999 (Admin), para 82.

[96] See Christopher Hodges and Naomi Creutzfeldt, 'Transformations in Public and Private Enforcement' in H-W Micklitz and A Wechsler (eds), *The Transformation of Enforcement. European Economic Law in a Global Perspective* (Hart Publishing 2016) 132.

[97] Micklitz (n 60) 516.

[98] For an analysis of this trend, see Andrea Wechsler and Boško Tripkovic, 'Conclusions: Enforcement in Europe as a Market for Justice' in H-W Micklitz and A Wechsler (eds), *The Transformation of Enforcement: European Economic Law in a Global Perspective* 378.

hazard, fragment the effectiveness of financial regulation across the EU (since each jurisdiction has adopted a different approach), and weaken the deterrent effect of conduct of business obligations. The national experiences that have been examined suggest that more systematic EU regulatory intervention is needed to set uniform conditions for the use of *ex post* remedies (investors' compensation funds) to address systemic mis-selling, so that ADR schemes set up on an ad hoc basis can ensure an independent, fair, and transparent adjudication process.

11.5.3 Reshaping and redefining investment firms' horizontal accountability

Bringing together the different strands of the analysis above, we may ask what the practical and conceptual implications are of broadening investment firms' horizontal accountability towards their clients. Three main corollaries can be observed. First, the technocratic, expert-based governance of ESMA,[99] which has been intensively assessed via the vertical, public law perspective of accountability, also creates new accountability links for investment firms in their relationships with their clients. Soft law, which has, usefully, been characterised as a layer in-between the contract and the law[100], becomes a yardstick to interpret general private law concepts (for example good faith, reasonableness, and skill and care). In practice, the interpretation of binding law in the light of soft law tightens the private law requirements for investment firms but, at the same time, ensures a more consistent application of these requirements across the EU.

A second consequence is a 'juridification' and formalisation of social and non-legal forms of accountability. This is certainly not a new phenomenon in financial regulation. Conduct of business rules themselves derive from non-binding codes of conduct that encapsulated 'moral' standards of good behaviour for broker-dealers and advisers.[101] A similar trend is visible nowadays with regard to ESG risks, which are no longer left to firms' internal corporate

[99] See, in particular, Niamh Moloney, 'EU Financial Market Governance and the Retail Investor: Reflections at an Inflection Point' (2018) 37 Yearbook of European Law 277.

[100] Klaus J Hopt, 'Contract Governance, Disclosure, and Rule-setting between the Market and the Law: A View from Commercial and Company Law' in Stefan Grundmann, Florian Möslein, and Karl Riesenhuber (eds), *Contract Governance: Dimensions in Law and Interdisciplinary Research* (OUP 2015) 467.

[101] See, in particular, Andrew F Tuch, 'Conduct of Business Regulation' in N Moloney, E Ferran, and J Payne (eds), *The Oxford Handbook of Financial Regulation* (OUP 2015) 547.

cultures, or their social responsibility, but have gradually been made subject to regulatory and supervisory standards.

A third consequence is that investment firms are not only accountable or answerable for their conduct, but can also be held liable on the basis of national private law for breaches of EU regulatory/soft law standards. Although, theoretically, civil liability could be considered the strongest manifestation of accountability, the different rationales of, and consequences deriving from, accountability and civil liability suggest that a clear distinction should be kept between these two concepts. Thus, in our opinion, the concept of hybrid civil liability could provide more precise normative guidance on the conditions on which investment firms may deviate from regulatory as well as soft law standards, and the consequences of such deviation.

11.6 Concluding remarks

After the GFC, financial intermediaries' accountability, in their relationships with their clients (what we defined as 'horizontal accountability'), has been strengthened, in order to ensure a higher level of investor protection. The level one and level two conduct of business rules set out in MiFID II have been supplemented by the ESMA's guidelines, recommendations, and other soft law instruments, all of which have to be taken into account by national courts when interpreting the relevant EU law.

The intensification of horizontal accountability mechanisms is a consequence of the incrementally increasing focus of EU law on retail financial markets governance.[102] However, this governance remains based on a two-layer regulatory framework, composed of EU-derived conduct of business rules, and national private law rules. The actual implementation of these accountability regimes is, therefore, based on national courts' and ADR bodies' application of national private law rules in retail client disputes. Where EU conduct of business rules are interpreted in the light of their investor protection purposes, firms' horizontal accountability translates effectively into civil liability. But there are divergences across national jurisdictions as regards the intensity of the civil law effects of these rules. While a certain degree of divergence reflects social, cultural and dogmatic differences that characterise national private laws in each country, the existence of different private law remedies for the breach of the same rule risks reducing the retail clients' confidence in regulation.

[102] See Moloney (n 98) 259.

Going forward, harmonisation of national private law rules would be beneficial, in order to increase legal certainty for both investment firms and their clients, and to level the playing field. However, at this current juncture, uniformity of judicial decisions across the EU could be achieved only by ensuring an effective, consistent application of EU general principles to national retail client disputes. The principles of full effectiveness of EU law, effectiveness, and equivalence can assist national courts in choosing the private law remedy that best reflects the rationale of each specific conduct of business rule. Recourse to the preliminary ruling proceedings is crucial to ensure a higher degree of consistency of national courts' judicial decisions in mis-selling litigation across the Union.

12

Damages Liability as a Dual Opportunity to Promote Accountability

Magnus Strand

12.1 Introduction: Accountability and damages liability

Accountability comes in such varied shapes and sizes that it does not seem feasible to even start listing them. Arguably, the same goes for accountability in the form of legal liabilities, even when the scope of an accountability study is kept strictly delineated to a specific substantive legal subfield, such as MiFID II[1] and MiFIR[2] and the dual role of investment firms in safeguarding accountability. For the purposes of this chapter, the focus will be on accountability in the form of compensation for harm caused by an infringement of MiFID II or MiFIR (or relevant law in this context, such as primary EU law).

Investment firms hold both obligations and rights under MiFID II and MiFIR.[3] This means that they can be held accountable for any lack of compliance with legal obligations conferred on them. The proper functioning of the internal market for trade in financial instruments is, thus, protected by EU and member state authorities monitoring the conduct of investment firms and other businesses on that market. However, it also means that if the legal rights of investment firms are infringed, these firms are capable of holding others accountable for such infringements. As consistently pointed out by the Court of Justice of European Union (CJEU), the rule of law in the EU is dependent on the vigilance of individuals and businesses such as investment firms, as

[1] Directive 2014/65/EU of the European Parliament and of the Council of 15 May 2014 on markets in financial instruments [2014] OJ L 173/349.

[2] Regulation (EU) No 600/2014 of the European Parliament and of the Council of 15 May 2014 on markets in financial instruments [2014] OJ L 173/84.

[3] For a mapping exercise in this regard, see Magnus Strand, 'The Choice of Instrument for EU Legislation: Mapping the System of Governance under MiFID II and MiFIR' in Adrienne Héritier and Magnus G Schoeller (eds), *Governing Finance in Europe: A Centralisation of Rulemaking?* (Edward Elgar Publishing 2020) (hereafter Strand, 'Choice of Instrument').

Magnus Strand, *Damages Liability as a Dual Opportunity to Promote Accountability* In: *Legal Accountability in EU Markets for Financial Instruments*. Edited by: Carl Fredrik Bergström and Magnus Strand, Oxford University Press. © Magnus Strand 2021. DOI: 10.1093/oso/9780192849281.003.0012

they invoke rights conferred on them by EU law before competent offices and courts. Investment firms, therefore, have a dual role to play in the implementation of the system under MiFID II and MiFIR: they are subjects of oversight and enforcement, but also agents in the maintenance of the rule of law.

Damages liability is a very specific form of accountability. It is retrospective, in the sense that it deals with past events and has only indirect repercussions on what is to come.[4] It is narrowly pecuniary, since it can only operate by putting a monetary value on harm suffered through an infringement, although there is, arguably, a dimension of moral opinion being expressed through decisions on whether claimants should be awarded damages. Finally, it is governed by stringent conditions for liability that have been developed in the European civil law tradition. It is often said that these conditions illustrate that the main rule is that anyone who suffers harm will have to bear that harm without compensation, while the payment of compensation is an exception—subject to a number of stringent conditions—to that main rule.[5] This point of departure is certainly appropriate, but we should not, therefore, underestimate the opportunities for accountability that are offered by contractual and non-contractual damages actions. On the contrary, it will be argued below that damages liability should be promoted, in order for accountability through private enforcement to complement other forms of accountability. Infringements of financial markets law can cause great economic harm and it is, consequently, appropriate to maintain both compensation for victims and accountability for delinquents.[6] Damages liability offers a combination of these two elements.

In this chapter, I will explore the dual role of investment firms in accountability through damages claims. First, the opportunities to promote accountability for the investment firms themselves will be examined, focusing on the relevant passage in MiFID II (Article 69(2)(3)) and the conditions to be satisfied. Second, it will turn to the opportunities for investment firms to act as agents for the rule of law by holding EU and national authorities accountable through actions for damages. These issues will be examined in turn. The underlying theory in this presentation is, as mentioned, that damages liability can contribute to accountability, and thereby to deterrence

[4] Such indirect repercussions arise from the fact that a judgment granting an award of damages puts the claimant in the right, which may have an impact on the future behaviour incentives of the parties, and of others in similar situations.

[5] Such conditions have been developed in European private law traditions that can be traced back to the Roman Empire, most impressively so, perhaps, in Reinhard Zimmermann, *The Law of Obligations: Roman Foundations of the Civilian Tradition* (Clarendon Press/OUP 1996).

[6] Commission, 'Reinforcing Sanctioning Regimes in the Financial Services Sector' (Communication of 12 December 2010) COM(2010) 716 final, 10.

from infringements of MiFID II and MiFIR. Consequently, it is argued that damages liability should be promoted as an instrument of the rule of law in the financial markets.

12.2 Damages liability for investment firms under MiFID II and MiFIR?

12.2.1 Introduction

Accountability in the form of damages liability comes in two main guises. An investment firm can be liable in contractual damages, in the event that it has acted in breach of a contract. In such an action for damages, the claimant might, for instance, be an investor, and the action would predominantly be governed by the contract and national contract law. Alternatively, where there is no contractual relationship between the investment firm and the injured party, the action would be for non-contractual damages. In this case, the claimant might, for example, be a competing investment firm that has been blocked from information, in breach of Article 37(5) MiFIR, and the action would be governed by national tort law. In the latter case, in particular, the systems of the member states are notoriously different from one another. Therefore, the EU has sometimes been prompted to harmonise aspects of tort damages rules, such as through Directive 2014/104/EU on competition damages.[7]

There is no such harmonisation under MiFID II and MiFIR, however. Indeed, commentators disagree on whether the member states are required to offer contractual or non-contractual damages (as the case may be) at all, as courses of action for claimants suffering injury by reason of a breach of the substantive rules in MiFID II and MiFIR. Indeed, some readers might wish to settle for accountability mechanisms under EU law to be of a public law character. Granted, claimants can also rely on the private law remedies that are available to them under their national systems; national law fills the gap, it might be said. However, as noted above, these private law mechanisms for accountability can be very different across European jurisdictions.

[7] Directive 2014/104/EU of the European Parliament and of the Council of 26 November 2014 on certain rules governing actions for damages under national law for infringements of the competition law provisions of the Member States and of the European Union [2014] OJ L 349/1.

Therefore, under the consistent case law of the CJEU, the general principles of EU law may require certain remedies to be made available in the event that national remedies prove insufficient for the effective judicial protection of a substantive EU law right.[8] It is, nonetheless, important to note that the CJEU will not, in such situations, require every suitable remedy common to the member states to be available, but will require some appropriate and effective remedy to be available to the aggrieved party. This section will explore whether such interventions by the CJEU can be expected under MiFID II and/or MiFIR. It will also be argued below that, if damages actions are not available, there may be a lack of accountability for the actions of investment firms.

Title VI, Chapter I of MiFID II outlines 'redress procedures' under the twin instruments of MiFID II and MiFIR. Among the provisions in this Chapter, the closest thing to a provision on damages liability is Article 69(2)(3). Much of the debate on liability under MiFID II and MiFIR, therefore, turns on the proper interpretation of this Article, which reads:

> Member States shall ensure that mechanisms are in place to ensure that compensation may be paid or other remedial action be taken in accordance with national law for any financial loss or damage suffered as a result of an infringement of this Directive or of Regulation (EU) No 600/2014.

Three questions will be addressed in the analysis below. Firstly, should Article 69(2)(3) be read as instructing the member states to offer a remedy of damages (contractual or non-contractual damages, as the case may be) to parties injured through a breach of the substantive rules in MiFID II/MiFIR? Secondly, if damages are not available in the national system of a member state, are there any situations in which EU law might require its national courts to make a damages remedy available nonetheless? This issue may arise not only in the event of an affirmative answer to the first question examined here, but also in connection with a breach of MiFIR and/or a breach of primary law connected to MiFID II and MiFIR. Thirdly, what are the applicable criteria for liability (whatever its form)? These three interpretative issues under Article 69(2)(3) will be analysed, in turn.

[8] Such as in Case C-213/89 *Factortame* EU:C:1990:257; Joined Cases C-6/90 and C-9/90 *Francovich* EU:C:1991:428; and Case C-453/99 *Courage v Crehan* EU:C:2001:465. For a detailed discussion by this author, see Magnus Strand, *The Passing-on Problem in Damages and Restitution under EU Law* (Edward Elgar Publishing 2017) (hereafter Strand, 'The Passing-on Problem') paras 2.010–2.029.

12.2.2 Does Article 69(2)(3) mean that damages should be available?

The first main issue to be addressed relates to the type of actions to be made available in order for claimants to find redress. In comparison with Article 35a of the Credit Rating Agencies Regulation (CRAR),[9] which is very explicit on civil liability in damages for credit rating agencies,[10] Article 69(2)(3) of MiFID II is more generally framed, and does not specify a damages remedy, as such. Further, the provision is part of a directive addressed to the member states. It is an inherently constitutional instruction to the member states to make sure that compensation or the like is available, in the event of an infringement of the rules in MiFID II and/or MiFIR. Investment firms are not directly addressed by Article 69(2)(3) or, indeed, by any provision in MiFID II, because it is a directive.[11]

The interpretative question asked can, therefore, be rephrased with more precision: does a proper transposition of Article 69(2)(3) require member states to make a damages remedy available to claimants?

This issue has been debated. Proceeding from an analysis of the legislative process behind Article 69(2)(3), it has been argued by Della Negra that, although this provision was designed to offer compensation in the event of a breach of the rules in MiFID II or MiFIR, it was not intended to impose a duty on member states to introduce private law remedies such as damages in contract or tort. Instead, the intention was for competent national authorities to set up compensation mechanisms such as public or private funds or other redress schemes.[12] The same author also stresses that Article 69(2)(3) remains under the heading 'Supervisory powers' rather than the subsequent heading 'Sanctions for infringements' (above Article 70), and that it does not refer to 'courts' in the manner of Articles 74 and 81.[13] For these reasons, Della Negra

[9] Regulation (EC) No 1060/2009 of the European Parliament and of the Council of 16 September 2009 on credit rating agencies.

[10] On damages liability for credit rating agencies, see Emil Nästegård, *The Liability of Credit Rating Agencies to Investors: A Swedish Perspective* (Iustus 2016).

[11] Art 288(3) TFEU.

[12] Federico Della Negra, *MiFID II and Private Law: Enforcing EU Conduct of Business Rules* (Hart Publishing 2019) 92–93 (hereafter Della Negra, 'MiFID II and Private Law').

[13] Federico Della Negra, 'The Effects of the ESMA's Powers on Domestic Contract Law' in Mads Andenaes and Guidula Deipenbrock (eds), *Regulating and Supervising European Financial Markets: More Risks than Achievements* (Springer 2016) 155–56. With regard to the rule being placed in art 69, it can be pointed out that, according to anecdotes from negotiations that carry on into the wee hours of the morning, the precise placing of a rule in an instrument can sometimes be due to happenstance. Our analysis must, nonetheless, take seriously such things as the placing of rules within the systematic whole of a legislative instrument.

concludes that, although member states may choose to comply with Article 69(2)(3) by introducing damages remedies, there are alternative options that would, likewise, maintain full and proper transposition.[14] Similarly, Callens has submitted that Article 69(2)(3) 'does not necessarily oblige member states to provide private law mechanisms'. Nonetheless, Callens argues that such an obligation follows from the general principles of judicial protection, as interpreted by the CJEU.[15] By contrast, but essentially reaching the same conclusion, Busch and van Dam have invariably argued that Article 69(2)(3) is a codification of the principle of effectiveness. The Article should, therefore, according to Busch and van Dam, be construed as imposing a duty on member states to safeguard the effectiveness of MiFID II and MiFIR by ensuring that damages actions are available to claimants who have been harmed by an infringement.[16] In a recent contribution, Nikolai Badenhoop has also subscribed to the latter interpretation, but reserved it for circumstances where the delinquent investment firm has acted in breach of a prudential duty, and an award of damages 'is necessary to ensure individual depositor and investor protection'.[17]

The contributions of all of these authors are compelling. The issue of whether general principles on judicial protection of rights conferred by EU law constitute a requirement for damages actions to be made available will be analysed below. This section is concerned with the meaning of Article 69(2)(3) and what would constitute a proper transposition. In this matter, I would respectfully agree with Della Negra that the wording of the provision is open to transposition not only in the form of contractual and non-contractual damages remedies, but also in the form of alternative remedies that ensure compensation for claimants. Article 69(2)(3) stops short of designating a specific remedy to be made available in the event of 'financial loss or damage suffered'; it merely indicates that there should be 'compensation ... or other remedial action'. Damages liability seems the obvious choice of remedy, but plausible alternatives include insurance or compensation fund schemes, restitutionary awards, and possibly even declaratory judgments.

[14] ibid 156.

[15] Evariest Callens, 'Recalibrating the Debate on MiFID's Private Enforceability: Why the EU Charter of Fundamental Rights is the Elephant in the Room' (2020) 21 European Business Organization Law Review 759–87, 783.

[16] Danny Busch and Cees van Dam, 'A Bank's Duty of Care: Perspectives from European and Comparative Law' in Danny Busch and Cees van Dam (eds), *A Bank's Duty of Care* (Hart Publishing 2017) 416–17 (also available in Danny Busch and Cees van Dam, 'A Bank's Duty of Care: Perspectives from European and Comparative Law – Part II' (2019) 30 European Business Law Review 367–416, 385–86); and Danny Busch, 'The Private Law Effect of MiFID: The *Genil* Case and Beyond' (2017) 13 European Review of Contract Law 70–93, 74–75.

[17] Nikolai Badenhoop, 'Private Law Duties Deriving from EU Banking Regulation and its Individual Protection Goals' (2020) 16 European Review of Contract Law 233–66, 265.

With regard to compensation fund schemes, such a scheme is in place under the Investor Compensation Schemes Directive (ICSD).[18] Under its Article 2(1), compensation schemes protecting investors must be in place in all member states. Under Article 14 of MiFID II, the national competent authorities must ensure that all investment firms meet the requirements in the ICSD at the time of their authorisation. The ICSD further sets out the minimum requirements for such schemes in the EU. It is beyond the scope of this chapter to go into the details of this instrument,[19] however it should be noted that the ICSD, first and foremost, aims to protect small investors in the event of the insolvency of an investment firm (see Articles 2(2) and 4, and recital 11). The scope of protection from the ICSD is, therefore, limited. As pointed out by Moloney, 'conflict-of-interest breaches, negligent advice (mis-selling), or misleading advertisement are all excluded'.[20] Nevertheless, as previously mentioned, the requirements in the ICSD are minimum requirements, and member states are able to introduce more wide-ranging compensation schemes for investors, as well as for other stakeholders.

In situations not covered by the ICSD (or an extended national scheme of its kind), Article 69(2)(3) of MiFID II still includes a requirement for compensation in the event that one investment firm has caused harm to another through an infringement of MiFID II or MiFIR. Will remedies other than damages suffice to satisfy this requirement? The answer to this question is contingent on the circumstances of the situation and, in particular, on the character of the rule infringed, but also turns on whether Article 69(2)(3) requires member states to ensure that claimants are able to recover not only losses as such (*damnum emergens*) but also lost profits (*lucrum cessans*). To illustrate, let us assume that an investor places an order with an investment firm. For some reason, the investment firm fails to execute the order in accordance with Article 27(1) of MiFID II: in other words, the order is executed at an unfavourable price, with unnecessary extra costs, too slowly to ensure a favourable transaction, or in some similarly deficient way. The financial losses suffered by the investor may come in various shapes and sizes. If an unnecessary extra cost was incurred, this would be a straightforward loss (*damnum emergens*) for which compensation comes in the form of the investment firm paying an amount to the investor that is equivalent to the financial loss. There can be no doubt that such

[18] Directive 97/9/EC of the European Parliament and of the Council of 3 March 1997 on investor-compensation schemes [1997] OJ L 84/22 (Investor Compensation Schemes Directive (ICSD)).

[19] For an overview and discussion, see Niamh Moloney, *EU Securities and Financial Markets Regulation* (3rd edn, OUP 2016) 835–46.

[20] ibid 839.

losses are covered by Article 69(2)(3). However, if the financial loss is due to a failure of the investment firm to seize a favourable opportunity to buy or sell financial instruments, as was intended by the investor, matters would be more complicated. Does Article 69(2)(3) cover a loss of profits (*lucrum cessans*)? If it does not, restitution in the form of a reversal of the failed transaction will suffice to satisfy the rule.[21] If it does cover a loss of profits, however, the investment firm will also need to pay compensation in damages for the profits proven to have been lost by the investor. An educated guess in relation to this issue is that damages should be made available for a loss of profits, and consequently that Article 69(2)(3) of MiFID II should be interpreted as including a requirement for the member states to ensure that such damages are available to claimants. The bases for making such an assumption are the facts that damages are available for a loss of profits under Article 340(2) TFEU,[22] must not be excluded in damages from a member state,[23] and must be available in competition damages.[24] From the perspective of the CJEU, this seems to be part and parcel of its long-established emphasis on full compensation.[25] As a consequence, remedies other than damages may meet the requirement in Article 69(2)(3) of MiFID II, provided that they are effective remedies in the situation before the national court, and that, where relevant, they include compensation for both direct losses (*damnum emergens*) and lost profits (*lucrum cessans*), plus interest.[26]

To conclude, it is submitted that Article 69(2)(3) is open to transposition not only in the form of contractual and non-contractual damages remedies, but also in the form of alternative remedies to ensure compensation for claimants. Precisely what will amount to full compensation depends, to a large extent, on the particularities of the given situation. Where relevant, however, it is submitted that the remedy available must include compensation for both direct losses (*damnum emergens*) and lost profits (*lucrum cessans*), plus interest. The fact that compensation for the injured party might not be connected to liability

[21] This should, of course, also suffice if the failure of the investment firm did not, in fact, give rise to financial losses for the investor, for example because the expected movements on the financial market never occurred.

[22] Provided that the loss of profit is real and certain: Joined Cases 5/66, 7/66, and 13–24/66 *Firma E Kampffmeyer* EU:C:1967:31; Joined Cases C-104/89 and C-37/90 *J M Mulder and others* EU:C:1992:217.

[23] Joined Cases C-46/93 and C-48/93 *Brasserie du Pêcheur* EU:C:1996:79, paras 86–87.

[24] Joined Cases C-295/04–298/04 *Vincenzo Manfredi and others* EU:C:2006:461, Operative part, para 5: still good law under Dir 2014/104/EU, in this respect, by indication in its recital 12.

[25] See Case 14/83 *von Colson and Kamann* EU:C:1984:153, para 28.

[26] For case law where the CJEU has been clear that interest must be payable, see Case C-271/91 *Marshall II* EU:C:1993:335; and *Manfredi* (n 22). For the purposes of competition damages, the right to interest has since been codified in art 3(2) of Dir 2014/104/EU.

on the part of the infringer, and the question of whether this is a missed opportunity for accountability, will be addressed below.

12.2.3 Might national courts be required to make damages available?

It has been acknowledged above that there is a clear option of transposing Article 69(2)(3) MiFID II into national law through the introduction of contractual and non-contractual damages remedies that fulfil its requirements. Many member states have done so (subject to varying criteria).[27] This section, however, will outline a few different situations in which EU law may require—irrespective of this analysis of Article 69(2)(3)—national courts to allow claimants to use contractual or non-contractual damages remedies to protect their rights. The section's focus is, thus, on litigation rather than on constitutional issues, although, of course, there are constitutional reasons for the demands of EU law on national courts.

Constitutional law does not (usually) help claimants who, by reason of the failures of a member state, find themselves with few or no useful national remedies to use for the safeguarding of their rights. For example, let us say that a stakeholder suffers harm through an infringement of MiFID II and/or MiFIR by an investment firm, and seeks to hold that investment firm accountable by seeking compensation. The action brought against the investment firm would be based on national rules on liability for the investment firm, and those national rules would constitute the member state's transposition of Article 69(2)(3) into national law. What if a member state has failed to adopt rules transposing Article 69(2)(3) into national law? Or if the national rules adopted are not a full transposition, because they do not ensure full compensation? Petitioning your MP for a review of national legislation will do no good. However, this is when the intricate doctrines of interaction between EU law and national law come into play.

One scenario would be that there is no redress mechanism available at all under national law. As has been stressed, MiFID II is a directive, and cannot, as such, create legal obligations for individuals. Under recent case law, a directive cannot even serve as the basis for setting aside national rules that are incompatible with the rules of the directive.[28] Consequently, Article 69(2)(3)

27 Including France, Italy, and Spain: see Della Negra, 'MiFID II and Private Law' (n 10) 169.

28 Case C-122/17 *Smith v Meade* EU:C:2018:631, para 49.

cannot, as such, suffice to give injured parties a right of redress against investment firms before national courts. Nonetheless, if there is a national law that can, in accordance with national principles of interpretation, be construed, in light of the wording and purpose of MiFID II, so as to fulfil the requirement on the member state laid down in Article 69(2)(3) of the directive, a national court hearing an action must make such an interpretation.[29] Accordingly, the generally applicable rules on contractual or non-contractual damages liability (as the case may be) could apply and, if so, should then be interpreted in light of the wording and purpose, not only of Article 69(2)(3), but of MiFID II and MiFIR as a whole. This might solve the problem by ensuring compensation for the injured party, and accountability on the part of the investment firm.

In another scenario, the transposition may be flawed due to the redress mechanism in place not allowing claimants full compensation. Provided that the substantive rights at issue are faithfully implemented, this problem can be solved by requiring the national court to remove the bars to full compensation by reference to the EU law principles of equivalence and effectiveness.[30]

In an extreme case, there could be a national rule barring the liability of investment firms for contractual or non-contractual damages (for whatever reason). If this meant that an injured party was left with no means of redress at all, could the CJEU intervene? The problem would be that MiFID II cannot create obligations for an investment firm. Therefore, there would be two sub-scenarios, one in which the substantive rule at issue had been faithfully transposed into national law, and one where it had not been. In the former situation, the CJEU could point to the substantive right and the right to an effective remedy in Article 47 of the EU Charter of Fundamental Rights[31] to strike down the prohibition. In the latter situation, the odds are that there would be no remedy available to the injured party against the investment firm.[32] That said, however, a few qualifications are necessary.

The first such qualification is that an infringement of MiFID II and/or MiFIR may also constitute an infringement of some other EU law rule or principle, and that liability may arise by reason of the latter infringement. For instance, should an investment firm have a policy of habitually targeting women and men with different investment advice, this might constitute an infringement

[29] Joined Cases C-397/01–C-403/01 *Pfeiffer and others* EU:C:2004:584, para 116; Case C-441/14 *Dansk Industri* EU:C:2016:278, para 31.

[30] *Manfredi* (n 22).

[31] Charter of Fundamental Rights of the European Union [2016] OJ C 202/389.

[32] The injured party might nonetheless be able to bring an action for damages against the member state under the so-called *Francovich* doctrine (see below).

of both Article 25(2) of MiFID II and the general EU law principle of non-discrimination on grounds of sex, enshrined in Article 21 of the EU Charter (as well as in many other legislative acts). With regard to this general principle, the CJEU has been prone to require stringent remedies to be made available, in the event of its infringement.[33] An investment firm might, accordingly, be liable, as a matter of EU law, for an infringement of MiFID II and/or MiFIR if it also constitutes an infringement of another EU law rule or principle that is simultaneously applicable, and which can serve as a basis for such liability.

The second qualification is that an infringement of MiFIR might plausibly serve as a basis for liability, in contrast with an infringement of MiFID II. Under Article 288 TFEU, regulations are binding and directly applicable in all member states. Constitutionally, they are capable of giving rise to legal obligations for individuals. A breach of such legal obligations may give rise to liability, for infringers.[34] However, for liability to attach to an investment firm in relation to another person under EU law, as such, the case law clearly indicates that it is, further, necessary for the rule breached to confer a right onto the claimant.[35] In many national systems, this is expressed differently: the rule breached must be intended to protect the interests of individuals rather than the interests of the general public or the broader European economy.[36] Against the backdrop of these conditions, it is noteworthy that the EU legislator does not seem keen to use regulations (as opposed to directives) to impose legal obligations on individuals. When a regulation does so, the rules at issue seldom correspond to rights for other individuals, but tend, instead, to be requirements for due process in relations with authorities. Recently, I conducted a survey of the legal character of the rules in MiFID II and MiFIR, concluding that the legal obligations for individuals in MiFIR are, with few exceptions, instructions to provide national and EU authorities with information, or to publish information. By contrast, MiFID II includes many substantive obligations (to be transposed into national law by the member states).[37] Granted, it

[33] See *von Colson* (n 23); *Marshall II* (n 24); Case C-180/95 *Draehmpaehl* EU:C:1997:208; and Case C-81/12 *Asociaţia Accept* EU:C:2013:275.

[34] Case C-253/00 *Muñoz* EU:C:2002:497.

[35] Such a criterion is part and parcel of the right to damages under art 340(2) TFEU, and of the right to damages from a member state under the *Francovich* doctrine: see, eg Joined Cases C-178/94, C-179/94, C-188/94, C-189/94, and C-190/94 *Dillenkofer* EU:C:1996:375, para 21.

[36] See, in non-contractual damages, art 823(2) BGB (German Civil Code) and the so-called *Schutznormtheorie* included in that provision. In contractual damages, it has been argued that the contract rule or legal rule breached ought to have a 'transactional nature', ie it should be directly relevant to the decision to enter into the contract: see Della Negra, 'MiFID II and Private Law' (n 10) 178. The discussion on these issues mirrors the classical discussion on competition law enforcement in the 1960s. See, for an overview, Enric Picañol, 'Remedies in National Law for Breach of Articles 85 and 86 of the EEC Treaty: A Review' (1983) 10 Legal Issues of Economic Integration 1–37, 4–6.

[37] Strand, 'Choice of Instrument' (n 1) 104.

is plausible that an investment firm's failure to comply with publishing and reporting requirements may lead to misinformed decision-making on the part of investors and other stakeholders, which may, in turn, cause financial losses. However, the vast majority of such rules do not confer rights on stakeholders to be individually informed. Therefore, it is debatable whether they are designed to protect the interests of individuals in the manner necessary for a breach of those rules to give rise to liability on the part of the investment firm. The few obligations on private parties in MiFIR that seem to me to be eligible for giving rise to liability vis-à-vis other private parties are the following:

(1) Article 15(2) on the duty of investment firms who are systematic internalisers to execute received orders at quoted prices at the time of reception of the order (with certain exceptions in sub-paragraph 2 and in paragraphs 3 and 4).
(2) Plausibly, certain duties of systematic under Articles 17 and 18 to give access to their firms' quotes to their clients, and to give access to their quotes on the basis of commercial policy, but also in a non-discriminatory manner.
(3) Article 35 on the duty of investment firms who are central counterparties (CCPs)[38] to clear financial instruments on a non-discriminatory and transparent basis.
(4) Article 36 on the duty of trading venues to provide trade feeds to CCPs on a non-discriminatory and transparent basis.
(5) Article 37(5): a prohibition on CCPs and others from taking certain measures that would block competitors from gaining equivalent information and licensing.

These five rules are comparatively clear-cut legal obligations, laid down in order to protect the interests of easily identifiable investors, or, in the case of Article 37(5), competitors. I would, however, exclude reporting and publishing requirements, as well as requirements for certain trading to take place in specified trading venues, since such rules seem to be designed merely to ensure general transparency on the financial markets.

To summarise, even if Article 69(2)(3) MiFID II has not been transposed into national law in the form of damages provisions, a breach of the rules contained in MiFID II or MiFIR may still give rise to damages liability in certain

[38] Defined in art 2(1) of Regulation (EU) No 648/2012 of the European Parliament and of the Council of 4 July 2012 on OTC derivatives, central counterparties and trade repositories [2012] OJ L 201/1.

circumstances. In essence, as long as the substantive rules of MiFID II have been faithfully transposed into national law, national courts can be required either to ensure full compensation through consistent interpretation of general liability rules, or to remove hindrances to the full effectiveness of such rights by reference to the EU law principles on judicial protection now enshrined in Article 47 of the EU Charter. In more extreme situations, damages may still be available if the rules breached are mirrored by EU primary law, or if they are MiFIR rules. The latter alternative should, however, be the subject of a preliminary reference to the CJEU under Article 267 TFEU, as it has not been explicitly held by the Court that a breach of a rule in a regulation can give rise, as a matter of EU law, to liability between private parties.

12.2.4 The conditions for liability

The third theme to be addressed regards the relevant criteria for compensation to be available pursuant to Article 69(2)(3) MiFID II. This Article instructs member states that remedial action should be made available where (1)'financial loss or damage [is] suffered' (2) 'as a result of' (3) 'an infringement of this Directive or of Regulation (EU) No 600/2014'. The three criteria specified therein mirror quite precisely the common features of tort law. There should be: (1) a tort (here an infringement of MiFID II or MiFIR); (2) harm eligible for compensation (the 'financial loss or damage' discussed above); and (3) a causal link between the tort and the harm suffered. However, the seeming simplicity of this model covers a plethora of intricate legal issues, and the relevant issue, for our purposes, is to decide whether those issues are governed by Article 69(2)(3), or by national law. The Article seems—albeit rather unclearly—to indicate the latter, as it says that the action should be 'taken in accordance with national law'.[39] This would mean that, in principle, the detailed assessment of whether there is a tort, a causal link, and harm eligible for compensation will rest with the national systems of the member states. Nonetheless, Article 69(2)(3) may have an impact, and so may the EU principles of judicial protection.

[39] Interpretative problems include whether the reference to national law pertains to payments of compensation, too, or only to 'other remedial action', and what is meant by having 'mechanisms ... in place to ensure that compensation can be paid' (a phrase which appears in a total of twelve EU legal acts, the other eleven being unrelated to damages liability). It is submitted that these should be seen as flaws in the drafting of the legislative text. Consequently, I will proceed on the assumption that the reference to national law includes compensation in damages, and that 'ensuring' means respecting the right to an effective remedy under art 47(1) of the Charter.

Firstly, with regard to the tort, Article 69(2)(3) specifies that liability shall arise in the event of an infringement of MiFID II or MiFIR. A relevant question, in that regard, is whether additional criteria under national law, such as a criterion of fault or culpability, can be added, or whether the infringement alone is enough?[40] It is submitted that this question should be answered mainly by reference to the character of the rule breached. As explained above, liability towards another entity will be relevant only in situations where the rule breached confers a relevant legal obligation on the defendant (the investment firm), and a corresponding legal right that has been frustrated because of the breach, on the claimant. This assessment rules out liability for insignificant and irrelevant transgressions. Still, there may well be situations where an investment firm is convinced that it has acted in good faith and with due diligence, but is nevertheless deemed to have committed an infringement capable of giving rise to liability in damages. For instance, it may have trusted a well-reputed third party with certain important operational functions (see Article 16(5) of MiFID II), but have then suffered a disruption of the third party's services, causing financial harm to the firm's clients. When the firm's conduct is scrutinised before the competent court, it will be necessary for the court to decide what sort of precautions the investment firm should have taken in order to comply with its duty to 'take reasonable steps to avoid undue additional operational risk'. This is, inherently, a balancing assessment including business judgement, and views on this matter may differ. In such situations, it would make sense for courts to avoid second-guessing the business choices made by investment firms by using national criteria such as culpability, or by adding 'manifest error' or the like to the criteria. In principle, such an issue ought to be referred to the CJEU for a preliminary ruling. For present purposes, it suffices to say that it makes sense to use such additional liability criteria to maintain a reasonable balance between risk-taking and accountability in financial business.

Secondly, the financial harm must be incurred 'as a result of' the infringement of MiFIR II or MiFID. This is clearly a reference to the tort law concept of causation. It must immediately be noted that causation is, in itself, a complex concept with several distinct components. Most importantly, it can be subdivided into so-called legal and factual causation, although these components are not always easily distinguished from one another. Ideally, the issue of factual causation concerns the establishment of facts through an assessment of evidence: has it been established that the financial harm was caused by the

[40] There is some variance among the member states with regard to whether there are conditions added to the finding of a breach, as such: see Della Negra, 'MiFID II and Private Law' (n 10) 190.

infringement of the rule, or is it more plausible that it was caused by some other event? By contrast, legal causation consists of an evaluation of the proximity between cause and effect, which can be phrased in many different ways. Was it foreseeable, for instance, that the kind of financial harm sustained would arise from the infringement? Is this kind of financial harm within the scope of the infringed rule's protective purpose? Does the financial harm have a sufficiently direct link to the infringement?[41] To what extent EU law governs the assessment of factual and legal causation is a matter of some debate.[42] The CJEU has been reluctant to enter into detailed and systematic reasoning on causation, even in cases falling under its exclusive jurisdiction, such as actions under Article 340(2) TFEU.[43] In situations where the action falls under the jurisdiction of national courts, as would be the case in relation to Article 69(2)(3) of MiFID II, the Court has been prone to leaving the details of causation issues to the national courts. Still, the Court has made a number of relevant statements. In essence, the case law indicates (and scholars usually agree[44]) that factual causation—at least in its ideal form—is to be established by the national courts on the basis of the evidence presented to them.[45] By contrast, national rules on legal causation have been scrutinised by the Court on several occasions, usually by reference to the EU law principles of effectiveness and equivalence.[46] The case law essentially indicates that the CJEU will allow reasonable national criteria that set legal causation standards, even if these may lead to the failure of some claims.[47] However, where the national criteria constitute absolute bars against whole classes of claimants, the Court has been inclined to intervene.[48]

[41] For further reading a good starting point is Cees van Dam, *European Tort Law* (2nd edn, OUP 2013) ch 11.

[42] See Pekka Aalto, *Public Liability in EU Law:* Brasserie, Bergaderm *and Beyond* (Hart Publishing 2011) 11; Takis Tridimas, *The General Principles of EU Law* (2nd edn, OUP 2006) 533 (hereafter Tridimas, General Principles'); and Andrea Biondi and Martin Farley, *The Right to Damages in European Law* (Kluwer Law International 2009) 59.

[43] See Strand, 'The Passing-on Problem' (n 6) paras 3.043–3.060.

[44] Takis Tridimas, 'Liability for Breach of Community Law: Growing Up and Mellowing Down?' (2001) 38 Common Market Law Review 301, 310; Biondi and Farley (n 39) 55.

[45] Case C-446/04 *FII* EU:C:2006:774, para 218, in relation to damages from a member state; Case C-435/18 *Otis II* EU:C:2019:1069, para 33, in relation to competition damages. This approach would arguably follow from the role of the CJEU under Art 267 TFEU, as it is not supposed to apply the law, but only to interpret it, however strained that distinction may be, both in theory, and in the Court's interpretive practice. Cases that blur the lines include Case C-319/96 *Brinkmann* EU:C:1998:429; and Case C-420/11 *Leth* EU:C:2013:166.

[46] Much more can, and has, been said on these principles, which have been developed since Case 33/76 *Rewe* EU:C:1976:188, and Case 45/76 *Comet* EU:C:1976:191. For a concise recent contribution, in a damages context, see Katri Havu and Liisa Tarkkila, 'EU Competition Litigation and Member State Procedural Autonomy—Current Issues' (2018) 11 Global Competition Law Review 65. For further analysis, see, eg Anthony Arnull, *The European Union and its Court of Justice* (OUP 2006) ch 9, or Strand, 'The Passing-on Problem' (n 6) s 2D.

[47] *Leth* (n 42).

[48] Case C-557/12 *Kone* EU:C:2014:1317; *Otis II* (n 42).

It is to be expected that such an approach would also apply to national criteria of legal causation when applied to actions brought by reason of infringement of MiFID II and/or MiFIR.

Thirdly, the financial harm or damage suffered must be eligible harm, estimated, and proven. It has been explained above that eligible harm should include both direct losses (*damnum emergens*) and lost profits (*lucrum cessans*), plus interest. Detailed assessment should, however, be left to the national courts, on the basis of the evidence presented to them, just as it is in even the most far-reaching of the EU's efforts to harmonise damages assessments: Directive 2014/104/EU on competition damages.[49] This follows the established pattern with regard to causation, in the sense that factual assessments are for the national courts, although national standards governing the exercise of those assessments may be subject to scrutiny under the EU law principles of effectiveness and equivalence.[50] This means that stringent national rules limiting the use of certain evidence, setting limits on the amounts recoverable or the like (costs, delays, impracticalities, or bars) might be struck down by the CJEU. This might be on the basis of effectiveness, if the rules make the exercise of the right to compensation virtually impossible or excessively difficult, and/or on the basis of equivalence, if the rules treat claims connected to MiFID II and MiFIR less favourably than similar claims with no EU law dimension.

To summarise, the general criteria for liability are set out in Article 69(2)(3), but must be fleshed out using national legal rules and traditions on liability. The latter will, however, be subject to scrutiny by the CJEU, the case law of which offers some guidance on what to expect.

12.2.5 Is there still a gap with regard to accountability?

Before criticizing the law, I tell my students, you must be very sure that you understand what the law is. Otherwise, you risk creating a 'straw man', and criticizing a flaw that does not exist. At this point, however, I feel confident enough to point out a flaw in the system of enforcement under MiFID II and MiFIR as regards compensation. The flaw is that compensation is not—or at least

[49] See art 17(1). The Commission has issued some non-binding documents with guidance on the estimation of harm in competition litigation. However, these are not intended to govern the details of the assessment, but only to present various methods and how they can be employed.

[50] See *Marshall II* (n 24) para 30; *Draehmpaehl* (n 30) para 40. These are both sex discrimination cases, however, and it could be argued that the CJEU would be even more cautious in contexts where there is a less firm basis in primary law and general EU law principles. In relation to damages from a member state, the balance is almost identical: see *Brasserie* (n 21) Operative part, para 4.

should not be—the only aim of a system of private enforcement. The 'elephant in the room' is accountability. If those who have suffered harm are compensated through a public compensation fund for injuries caused by an investment firm's infringement of MiFID II or MiFIR, where does that leave accountability for the wrongdoing of the investment firm? At best, the competent supervisory authority will take public enforcement action, but there is no guarantee that it will do so. In the absence of accountability through public or private enforcement, there will be no deterrence, and the rule of law in the financial markets will be jeopardised.[51]

Indeed, research from competition law enforcement indicates that private enforcement through damages claims can make a significant contribution to ensuring accountability in the event of a breach of law.[52] The theory, which is supported by empirical research,[53] is that public authorities will only discover a certain proportion of transgressions (even with the help of whistle-blowers and complaints from competitors). Moreover, and perhaps most importantly, public authorities do not have sufficient resources to follow up all reports and complaints. Therefore, private litigants can make a significant contribution to the rule of law by holding delinquent firms accountable through private enforcement action. There is no reason to presume that it would be otherwise in circumstances where an investment firm acts in breach of MiFID II or MiFIR. Certainly, the scarcity of resources for public supervision authorities to follow up on reports is well known.[54] As pointed out by Shruti Kashyap in her contribution to this book, effective accountability mechanisms prompt compliance, as a form of risk control measures in investment firms. Therefore, it is crucial to ensure that infringements of law are risk-enhancing measures, from an accountability point of view, so that investment firms have an incentive to have in place stringent compliance management practices in relation to MiFID II and MiFIR. Exposure of firms to damages liability can contribute to this.

For these reasons, it is submitted that the better choice for member states is to transpose Article 69(2)(3) MiFID II by adopting damages liability mechanisms for investment firms, rather than choosing any minimum option. Arguably,

[51] Similarly, see Moloney (n 17) 968.

[52] There is abundant literature on this matter, but a good starting point is OECD, 'Roundtable on Public and Private Enforcement in Competition, 2015' <http://www.oecd.org/daf/competition/antitrust-enforcement-in-competition.htm> accessed 16 September 2020.

[53] Emmanuel Combe, Constance Monnier, and Renaud Legal, 'Cartels: The Probability of Getting Caught in the European Union' (*Cahiers de Recherche PRISM-Sorbonne*, March 2008) <https://ssrn.com/abstract=1015061> accessed 14 October 2021.

[54] Recently this was pointed out by the Swedish Finansinspektionen in a statement on possible accession to the European Banking Union: Finansinspektionen FI Dnr 20-1970, 'Sverige och bankunionen' (SOU 2019:52).

the intentions of the EU legislator in this respect can be seen as less important. Rather than looking at what the author of the text intended, and trying to ascertain those intentions as faithfully as possible, it might be preferrable to look at the opportunities presented by the text, and to try and make the most of these, in order to have the best possible accountability measures in place.[55]

12.3 Public liability in connection with MiFID II

12.3.1 Introduction

There will always be shortcomings of public authorities. Mistakes are made because public authorities are made up of human beings, who make mistakes now and then. What matters is how we react to mistakes that have been made, and whether we allow those who have been adversely affected by them an opportunity to hold public authorities accountable, in the interests of both transparency in public administration and reparation for the individual. This is acknowledged by public accountability mechanisms such as, for example, Article 17 of the ESMA Regulation,[56] which concerns accountability for national authorities (albeit from ESMA's perspective) by determining how ESMA can deal with breaches of EU law by national supervisory authorities. The mechanism in Article 17 is a form of accountability mechanism, but is also relevant to the division of powers between ESMA and national authorities, as it allows ESMA to intervene in such cases.

Such public law mechanisms should not, however, be allowed to preclude the possibility of national and EU authorities being held accountable through liability in damages. Private enforcement actions by investment firms can make a significant contribution when the firms' rights, in connection with their freedom to conduct business in the financial markets,[57] have been frustrated in ways that have caused them harm. To find the rules on non-contractual public liability, though, it is necessary to look beyond MiFID II and MiFIR, to the damages liability of member states under the *Francovich* doctrine, and to

[55] On these different interpretative perspectives, see Richard Rorty, 'Nineteenth-century Idealism and Twentieth-century Textualism' (1981) 64 The Monist 155, 166–68. For clarity, 'textualism', in Rorty's paper, has nothing to do with the so-called textualist movement in the interpretation of the Constitution of the United States of America.

[56] Regulation (EU) No 1095/2010 of the European Parliament and of the Council of 24 November 2010 establishing a European Supervisory Authority (European Securities and Markets Authority) [2010] OJ L 331/84.

[57] This freedom is protected by art 16 of the EU Charter, and by the TFEU articles on free movement on the internal market.

the damages liability of the EU under Article 340(2) TFEU. These subjects will be explored below.

12.3.2 Public liability for member states and their agencies

Under settled case law, the EU member states can be held liable in damages for harm caused to individuals—a concept including corporate entities such as investment firms—by a breach of EU law by some emanation of the state in question.[58] The conditions for such liability are that: (1) the EU law rule breached must be intended to confer a right on the claimant; (2) the breach must be sufficiently serious; and (3) there must be a direct causal link between the breach and the damage sustained.[59] These conditions are sufficient for the establishment of liability, but member states are free to use less stringent conditions.[60] In other words, member states are not allowed to introduce additional conditions, such as the existence of fault, over and above the establishment of a sufficiently serious breach.[61] Of course, it will also be necessary for an investment firm acting as a claimant to establish that a harm that is eligible for compensation has been suffered.

With regard to the first criterion, and its application under MiFID II and MiFIR, it should be pointed out that these instruments contain very few rules designed to confer substantive rights on investment firms. There are some, though. For example, Article 6(3) and Articles 34 to 35 of MiFID II establish that an authorisation to operate as an investment firm in one member state gives a right of establishment, and freedom to provide services, for that authorised investment firm in all member states. Under Articles 36 to 38, investment firms must be authorised to execute client orders, and must have access to regulated markets, clearing facilities and the like. Investment firms also have the right, under Article 29, to appoint tied agents to promote and/or solicit on behalf of their businesses. Less commonly, there are rules in MiFIR affording

[58] The concept of the 'state' under EU law is an extended one: see Case C-188/89 *Foster* EU:C:1990:313. For analysis, see Sacha Prechal, *Directives* (2nd edn, OUP 2005) 58–61.

[59] *Brasserie* (n 21) para 51.

[60] Case C-429/09 *Günter Fuß* EU:C:2010:717, paras 65–66. Indeed, if such more lenient criteria for public liability exist, in the event of a breach of national law by the state, it follows from the principle of equivalence that they must be extended to a breach of EU law: *Brasserie* (n 21) para 66; Strand, 'The Passing-on Problem' (n 6) para 6.024.

[61] *Brasserie* (n 21), Operative part, para 3.

discretions that could perhaps be construed, in certain circumstances, as rights for investment firms that are systematic internalisers or the like.[62]

Irrespective, however, of the scarcity of rights conferred on investment firms by MiFID II and MiFIR, as such, it must be kept in mind that those instruments are part and parcel of an internal market for trade in financial instruments that rests on the fundamental rights and freedoms established in the TFEU. Importantly, the EU financial market encompasses the freedom to invest in company shares, including portfolio investments,[63] and the freedom to grant credit on a commercial basis.[64] Such fundamental freedoms under EU internal market law, which are crucial to the business of investment firms, and are protected by Articles 49, 56, and 63 TFEU, may also, more broadly, be construed as rights for investment firms. It is of no consequence in this regard that the TFEU provisions may be designed to protect general interests rather than individual interests.[65] This also means that an infringement of those freedoms by a member state may cause liability for damages to attach to that infringing state. Such an infringement could consist in hindering investment firms from offering financial services in another member state,[66] hindering mortgages from being registered in the currency of another member state,[67] or prohibiting investment firms from other member states from trading in shares in certain domestic companies.[68]

The second criterion, that the breach of EU law by the member state must be sufficiently serious, indicates a rather flexible assessment, and its application is contingent on the degree of discretion enjoyed by the member state under the provision breached.[69] In *Brasserie*, the CJEU held that the factors to be taken into account

> include the clarity and precision of the rule breached, the measure of discretion left by that rule to the national or Community authorities, whether the infringement and the damage caused was intentional or involuntary, whether any error of law was excusable or inexcusable, the fact that the position taken by a Community institution may have contributed towards the omission, and the adoption or retention of national measures or practices contrary to Community law.[70]

[62] See, eg art 15 of MiFIR.

[63] Joined Cases C-282/04 and C-283/04 *Commission v Netherlands* EU:C:2006:608, para 19.

[64] Case C-452/04 *Fidium Finanz* EU:C:2006:631, para 43.

[65] See, eg *Brasserie* (n 21) para 23, where art 30 EEC (now art 34 TFEU) was concerned (and cf, in that case, the Opinion of AG Tesauro, EU:C:1995:407, para 75); *FII* (n 42) para 211, where arts 43 and 56 EC (now arts 49 and 63 TFEU) were concerned.

[66] As in Case C-384/93 *Alpine Investments* EU:C:1995:126.

[67] As in Case C-222/97 *Trummer and Mayer* EU:C:1999:143.

[68] Similarly to Case C-367/98 *Commission v Portugal (Golden Shares)* EU:C:2002:326.

[69] Case C-5/94 *Hedley Lomas* EU:C:1996:205, para 28.

[70] *Brasserie* (n 21) para 56. The dictum on positions taken by EU institutions is particularly interesting, and will be discussed further below.

In essence, is the CJEU was outlining an assessment of culpability. In this regard, the fundamental freedoms conferred on investment firms under the core provisions of EU internal market law must be seen as quite clear, in particular as they have been elaborated upon by the CJEU in abundant case law.[71] The clarity of the provisions in MiFID II and MiFIR that confer rights on investment firms varies. As mentioned above, some provisions clearly confer a right, while others give investment firms a discretion that may be construed as a right. In the latter case, the ambiguity may be such as to exclude liability, in the event of a breach of those provisions by a member state.

The third criterion—a direct causal link—is somewhat elusive, as it concerns both a substantive assessment and an evaluation of the facts. These two elements of causation are usually referred to as 'legal causation' and 'factual causation', respectively. As remarked above, there has been precious little guidance from the CJEU on how to carry out the causation test. With regard to factual causation, this is only to be expected, as the final assessment of the facts lies with the national court, in the context of a reference under Article 267 TFEU. Concerning legal causation, however, it has been insisted that the existence of an assessment of foreseeability or the like should be governed by EU law, and that the CJEU should, therefore, be more clear on legal causation.[72] It suffices here to point out that the Court seems to have focused on whether the tortious act or omission at issue was capable of causing the alleged harm,[73] but has mostly been content to leave the final assessment to the national courts.[74] In that vein, the Court held in *FII* that it was for the national court to assess whether the loss and damage being claimed flowed sufficiently directly from the breach of [EU] law for the state to be liable to compensate the claimants.[75]

In sum, in the event that the rights of an investment firm under the TFEU, or under MiFID II/MiFIR, have been infringed by a member state, that the above three conditions are satisfied, and that the investment firm can also prove the existence of harm eligible for compensation,[76] that member state will be liable in damages to the investment firm. In this sense, investment firms can use

[71] ibid, para 57.

[72] Tridimas, 'General Principles' (n 39) 533; Biondi and Farley (n 39) 59.

[73] This is arguably a *conditio sine qua non* ('but for') test of causal capacity. See, further, Strand, 'The Passing-on Problem' (n 6) paras 6.053–6.071.

[74] In *Brinkmann* (n 42), and in *Leth* (n 42), however, the Court came very close to making the assessment itself.

[75] *FII* (n 42) para 218.

[76] There is precious little case law on this point, but an award of damages payable by a member state for a breach of EU law must be commensurate with the loss or damage sustained: *Brasserie* (n 21) para 82. See, further, Katri Havu, 'Full, Adequate and Commensurate Compensation for Damages under EU Law: A Challenge for National Courts?' (2018) 43 European Law Review 24; and Strand, 'The Passing-on Problem' (n 6) paras 6.081–6.090.

damages actions to protect their rights, thereby also acting as agents of the rule of law, whether or not that may be their primary purpose in pursuing such an action.

12.3.3 Public liability for EU institutions and agencies

In the context of an action brought by an investment firm with regard to an infringement of its rights under MiFID II or MiFIR, ESMA or the Commission are most likely to be the defendants at EU level. The key provision on liability in damages for ESMA is Article 69(1) of the ESMA Regulation:[77]

> In the case of non-contractual liability, the Authority shall, in accordance with the general principles common to the laws of the Member States, make good any damage caused by it or by its staff in the performance of their duties. The Court of Justice of the European Union shall have jurisdiction in any dispute over the remedying of such damage.

Identical provisions are included in Article 69(1) of each of the regulations establishing the other two ESAs;[78] indeed, it is a standard provision in the setting up of EU agencies. It is based on Article 340(2) TFEU, which stipulates liability in damages for EU institutions:

> In the case of non-contractual liability, the Union shall, in accordance with the general principles common to the laws of the Member States, make good any damage caused by its institutions or by its servants in the performance of their duties.

The purpose of drafting such similar provisions for EU agencies is to be clear that claimants, such as investment firms, who find themselves harmed by an infringement of EU law by an EU agency can bring an action for damages

[77] Regulation (EU) No 1095/2010 of the European Parliament and of the Council of 24 November 2010 establishing a European Supervisory Authority (European Securities and Markets Authority) [2010] OJ L 331/84.

[78] Art 69(1) of Regulation (EU) No 1093/2010 of the European Parliament and of the Council of 24 November 2010 establishing a European Supervisory Authority (European Banking Authority) [2010] OJ L 331/12; Art 69(1) of Regulation (EU) No 1094/2010 of the European Parliament and of the Council of 24 November 2010 establishing a European Supervisory Authority (European Insurance and Occupational Pensions Authority) [2010] OJ L 331/48.

before the Court of Justice of the European Union, even though agencies are not institutions within the meaning of Article 340(2) TFEU.[79] The wording of these provisions on non-contractual liability is not, however, very helpful to those looking for conditions for liability. The provisions offer only a vague reference to common general principles of the member states. Therefore, they must be read in light of the case law of the CJEU. The General Court has stated, in *European Dynamics Luxembourg*, that the 'principles' of liability in Article 340(2) TFEU apply *mutatis mutandis* to the non-contractual liability of agencies under the specific rules applicable to them (in that case, the agency in question was EUIPO).[80] Consequently, case law on the conditions for liability under Article 340(2) TFEU should apply *mutatis mutandis* to the ESAs, including ESMA.

It was settled by the Court in *Bergaderm* that the conditions at issue are the same as for member states. It must, thus, be demonstrated that: (1) the EU law rule breached is intended to confer a right on the claimant; (2) the breach is sufficiently serious; and (3) there is a direct causal link between the breach and the damage sustained.[81] In principle, these conditions should also be applied in an equivalent manner. However, the application of the second criterion (to establish a 'sufficiently serious breach') may vary, to some extent, due to different contexts.[82] Also, there will inevitably be some variance due to the fact that the final application of the conditions is for the national courts, in relation to member state liability, but exclusively for the EU Courts under Article 340(2) TFEU. This may, for instance, have an impact on the application of the third element (causation), as explained above. In the absence of case law on the ESAs' liability, it suffices here to refer back to the discussion on the conditions for member state liability.

[79] The concept of 'institutions' is limited to those listed in art 13(1) TEU. It has been debated whether the EU should, nonetheless, be liable under art 340(2) for the acts and omissions of agencies. It is plainly arguable that an exclusion of such liability would (in light of the expansion of agencies in recent years, the delegation of powers to those agencies on a scale that was unforeseen in 1957, and the lack of jurisdiction for national courts) amount to a circumvention of the intentions expressed in art 340(2) TFEU. For similar reasoning by the ECJ, see Case C-15/00 *Commission v EIB* EU:C:2003:396, para 75. See also Case C-234/02 P *European Ombudsman v Lamberts*, Opinion of AG Geelhoed, EU:C:2003:394, para 108; Case C-160/03 *Spain v Eurojust*, Opinion of AG Poiares Maduro, EU:C:2004:817, para 16; Biondi and Farley (n 39) 90; and Merijn Chamon, *EU Agencies: Legal and Political Limits to the Transformation of EU Administration* (OUP 2016) 355–61. See also Dominique Ritleng's Chapter 4 in this book.

[80] Case T-556/11 *European Dynamics Luxembourg* EU:T:2016:248, para 264.

[81] Case C-352/98 P *Bergaderm* EU:C:2000:361, para 42.

[82] As with member state liability, the point of departure is the discretion of the EU institution (or agency) concerned: see Case C-198/03 P *CEVA and Pfizer* EU:C:2005:445, paras 64–66. For further analysis of the case law of the EU Courts, see Aalto (n 39) 134–48; and Koen Lenaerts, Ignace Maselis, and Kathleen Gutman, *EU Procedural Law* (OUP 2014) 522–28.

Before moving on, it should be pointed out that ESMA will assume liability under Article 69(1) of the ESMA Regulation for harm 'caused by it *or by its staff* in the performance of their duties' (italics added). This means that ESMA is liable in damages for harm caused by a breach of EU law, not only through acts officially adopted by the ESMA as such (for example, policy decisions and enforcement actions), but also for harm caused by its staff members. The latter is sometimes referred to as 'vicarious liability' of employers for their employees.[83] The case law is scarce, but indicates that the EU 'is only liable for those acts of its servants which, by virtue of an internal and direct relationship, are the necessary extension of the tasks entrusted to the institutions'.[84] This should apply *mutatis mutandis* to EU agencies. A point to consider in this connection is whether ESMA (for example) would be liable in damages if one of its staff members abused her or his powers as a representative of the authority. A strict interpretation of the dictum just cited would seem to indicate that, under such circumstances, the staff member would be liable, but not ESMA. It is submitted that a claimant-friendly interpretation would be more suitable, whereby ESMA would be liable as long as it reasonably seemed, from the claimant's perspective, that the staff member was acting on behalf of ESMA, and within the powers attributed to the staff member by ESMA.

12.3.4 Concurrent and joint public liability

It is a matter of some debate—a debate that can be expected to continue in light of the development of the EU—how the system of judicial protection in the EU ought to cope with instances of concurrent (or joint) liability for member states and the EU.[85] In this book, the issue of concurrent liability is analysed in detail

[83] On this concept and its history, see Zimmermann (n 3) 1118–26. See also Christian von Bar and Eric Clive (eds), *Principles, Definitions and Model Rules of European Private Law: Draft Common Frame of Reference (DCFR) Full Edition* (6 vols, Sellier 2009) VI–3:201, with comments and notes.

[84] Case T-124/04 *Ouariachi* EU:T:2005:378, para 18. cf Case 5/68 *Sayag* EU:C:1968:42, where the ECJ ruled that 'immunity [for servants] only covers acts which, by their nature, represent a participation of the person entitled to the immunity in the performance of the tasks of the institution to which he belongs' and that 'driving a motor vehicle is not in the nature of an act performed in an official capacity', save for in exceptional circumstances.

[85] Contributions include Trevor Hartley, 'Concurrent Liability in EEC Law: A Critical Review of the Cases' (1977) 2 European Law Review 261; Peter Oliver, 'Joint Liability of the Community and the Member States' in Henry G Schermers, Ton Heukels, and Philip Mead, *Non-Contractual Liability for the European Communities* (Martinus Nijhoff Publishers 1988); Wouter Wils, 'Concurrent Liability of the Community and a Member State' (1992) 17 European Law Review 191; Maartje de Visser, 'The Concept of Concurrent Liability and its Relationship with the Principle of Effectiveness: A One-way Ticket to Oblivion?' (2004) 11 Maastricht Journal of European and Comparative Law 47; Lenaerts, Maselis, and Gutman (n 79) paras 11.24–11.32; and, more recently, Melanie Fink, 'EU Liability for Contributions to Member States' Breaches of EU Law' (2019) 56 Common Market Law Review 1227. Please note that

in the contribution by Dominique Ritleng. I would, nevertheless, like to offer some brief notes on the same issue. In essence, the problem is to find a system for distinguishing EU and member state liability as different courses of action, rather than adopting a coherent system for joint liability. To that end, the CJEU held, in *SGEEM*, that liability in damages for the (then) Community could only arise in connection with 'acts through a Community body established by the Treaty and authorised to act in its name and on its behalf'.[86]

Lenaerts et al have submitted that the 'decisive criterion seems to be the respective decision-making powers of the Union and the Member States'.[87] As a consequence, the allocation of accountability would coincide with the allocation of power. This is a very straightforward and, as such, appealing model, which also finds support in the case law.[88] It does not, however, account for more complex situations, such as in *Kampffmeyer* where national authorities could adopt certain decisions if the decisions were authorised by the Commission.[89] The decision, in this case, was subsequently quashed as illegal by the Court. In relation to such 'joint' decision-making, it has been submitted by Oliver that the EU should only assume 'residual liability', arguing that it is better for the member states to compensate claimants, and for the states then to turn to the EU for recourse. In this model, actions against the EU would be admissible only in very exceptional cases, if any.[90] Fink, by contrast, has identified a need for 'loosening the conditions for liability' applicable to the EU, in order to avoid claimants being deprived of an effective remedy to protect their rights under EU law.[91]

I would agree with Wils that the time has come for a system of joint and several liability to be introduced.[92] The EU system is becoming ever more complex and integrated at EU and national level, and private parties such as investment firms should not be suspended in a 'blame game' between the two levels. Authorities such as ESMA and the national financial authorities are working closely together, and with a very high degree of mutual trust. It is time for non-contractual liability in damages to follow suit, and, therefore, it is time for the

restitution has been distinguished here, and will not be addressed. With regard to concurrent liability in restitution for member states and the EU, see Strand, 'The Passing-on Problem' (n 6) para 4.007.

[86] Case C-370/89 *SGEEM* EU:C:1992:482, para 15.

[87] Lenaerts, Maselis, and Gutman (n 79) para 11.25.

[88] Case law cited by the authors includes *Mulder* (n 20), para 9, and Joined Cases 89/86 and 91/86 *L'Étoile commerciale* EU:C:1987:337, para 18.

[89] *Kampffmeyer* (n 20).

[90] Oliver (n 82) 142.

[91] Fink (n 82) 1263.

[92] See Wils (n 82) 206.

EU to introduce a system of joint and several public liability. This would ensure that opportunities for promoting accountability and the rule of law through damages liability are not lost in a 'blame game' between the EU and member state levels.

12.4 Conclusions

This chapter has been dedicated to an analysis of the conditions applicable in situations where damages liability can be used as an instrument of accountability in the event of an infringement of MiFID II, MiFIR, or related law (such as primary law). It has been demonstrated that investment firms have a dual role to play: they can, and should, be held accountable for their breaches by claimants bringing actions for damages, but they can also bring actions of their own against member state authorities and/or EU authorities, if they have suffered harm caused by those public authorities.

It has been pointed out that liability in damages has its limits as an instrument of accountability: it is retrospective, and is essentially pecuniary in character. Nonetheless, it is widely accepted that damages actions can add to deterrence from infringements of law, and thereby serve not only as instruments for individual compensation, but also as instruments for the rule of law. The relevant provision in MiFID II, Article 69(2)(3), is quite vague, and relies heavily on national law and national remedies for compensation. Nonetheless, through a systematic interpretation, and a comparison with other EU law contexts, a number of indications on how the provision can be read have been presented. In this connection, and with respect to the ongoing debate on whether contractual and non-contractual damages actions should be available in the event of infringements of the rules in MiFID II and MiFIR, it has been submitted that the better choice for member states is to transpose Article 69(2)(3) of MiFID II by adopting damages liability mechanisms for investment firms. Essentially, my reason for adopting this view is that the alternatives do not sufficiently promote accountability. Supervisory authorities will not detect all infringements: they are not able even to pursue all reports of infringements that they receive. Therefore, private enforcement can contribute to accountability and, thereby, to deterrence, and the upholding of the rule of law. Member states should seize the interpretative opportunities offered by the text of MiFID II. If compensation fund schemes are used, an opportunity to promote the accountability of investment firms is lost. It is crucial to ensure that infringements of law are risk-enhancing measures for investment firms, so that firms have an incentive to have in place stringent compliance management in relation to MiFID II and MiFIR. Exposure to damages liability can contribute to this.

Liability conditions for national and EU authorities have also been explored. In this context, it has been suggested that a system of joint and several liability for EU and national authorities should be put in place. ESMA and the national financial authorities are now working closely together, and it has come to a point where the division of powers between the two levels is not easily discernible by (for example) investment firms. When powers are intertwined, accountability should, perhaps, be so too. This point is relevant, not only in the context of MiFID II and MiFIR, and the non-legislative acts adopted pursuant to them, but to EU law as a whole. Accountability measures in the public sphere are relatively weak in the EU law system as it currently stands. The example of MiFID II and MiFIR has served to illustrate the broader issue.

In sum, and connecting to the thematic questions explored in this book, this chapter has outlined the possibilities for accountability, in the forms of damages liability and the dual role of investment firms when appearing as defendants and claimants, respectively, in private enforcement litigation. It has been submitted that the rule of law in EU financial markets law can be served by promoting private enforcement, as it is not possible for public enforcement agencies, at either EU or national level, to detect and pursue every transgression that has caused harm. Private enforcement can complement public enforcement in this way, and synergies between the two (as with follow-on actions, in the context of competition law enforcement) can further the rule of law in EU financial markets.

PART V

INVESTMENT FIRMS AND ACCOUNTABILITY: CONCLUSIONS

13

Investment Firms, Accountability, and the Effective Rule of Law

Magnus Strand and Carl Fredrik Bergström

13.1 A return to our thematic questions

The overall project underlying this book has identified significant patterns of changes in EU rulemaking, during and after the financial crisis. These changes relate to the choice of the form of legal acts, and to the introduction of institutional innovations and simplified procedures. Most obviously, we see more intense rulemaking by the EU legislator than was the case before the crisis, and rulemaking that leaves national parliaments and authorities less room to adapt resulting legal acts 'to the varying constitutional preconditions in each individual Member State'.[1] But, in parallel with this centralisation of rulemaking, we also find a new focus on collective involvement of national authorities in EU rulemaking. This reflects a central idea in the reform agenda: that 'the way new legislation will be implemented is to be taken into account already during its design and well before its adoption'.[2] This, in turn, affects the preconditions for accountability, and the appropriateness of existing mechanisms: for example, the lack of judicial review over 'shadow rule-making',[3] in the form of guidelines and other soft law instruments that coordinate national authorities' application of EU law.[4] It also affects the positions of the actors involved. For example, national authorities gain collective influence over the drafting of rules that they

[1] Swedish Parliament's Constitutional Committee, Repqrt 2014/15:KU5.

[2] Commission, 'Monitoring the Application of European Union Law: 2015 Annual Report' COM (2016) 463 final, 12.

[3] See Heikki Marjosola, 'Shadow Rulemaking: Governing Regulatory Innovation in the EU Financial Markets' (pending publication in the German Law Journal).

[4] There is strong industry support for furthering the accountability of ESMA in this regard, see Niamh Moloney, *The Age of ESMA: Governing EU Financial Markets* (Hart 2018) 351.

Magnus Strand and Carl Fredrik Bergström, *Investment Firms, Accountability, and the Effective Rule of Law* In: *Legal Accountability in EU Markets for Financial Instruments.* Edited by: Carl Fredrik Bergström and Magnus Strand, Oxford University Press. © Magnus Strand and Carl Fredrik Bergström 2021. DOI: 10.1093/oso/9780192849281.003.0013

themselves will apply, and EU agencies gain access to direct relationships with investment firms and other private actors.

The book is based on the work of a group of scholars with expertise from different legal disciplines, but a shared interest in the EU internal market and the way in which it develops. The underlying idea was to integrate a high-level focus on the form and function of EU rulemaking in the internal market after the financial crisis with an evaluation of core aspects of rulemaking in the financial market, and, in that way, provide a cross-cutting treatment of modern EU law. Now that we are able to see the results, we think that this has been successful. In this final chapter, we will return to the thematic questions that we set out to answer in our book. We will carefully highlight some of the answers that our authors have offered, and formulate some general conclusions.

The thematic questions we set out to answer at the start of the work, for all authors to address, were the following:

Question 1: what are the legal mechanisms for accountability within the regulatory framework on markets in financial instruments, and what is the role of investment firms in the operation of those mechanisms?

Question 2: what are the implications of the answers to Question 1 for EU law and the EU legal system?

Question 3: how do our findings contribute to the understanding of the concept of accountability?

The results confirm that there are a wide range of legal mechanisms for accountability within the regulatory framework on markets in financial instruments, and that some of these are more visible than others. They also demonstrate the crucial, and sometimes novel, role of investment firms. In particular, the results address how investment firms can be held accountable (Part II), hold EU agencies and national authorities to account for their actions (Part III) and, indeed, appear in another dual role in a private law context (Part IV). The book in its entirety, thus, presents the reader with answers to the first thematic question in its full complexity. Obviously, we do not purport to have exhausted the matter, but we are satisfied that we have provided new insights and ideas that can be built on—by ourselves and others—in new studies of EU rulemaking in the financial market and, indeed, the internal market.

Notwithstanding the many ways in which accountability has been shown to come into play within the regulatory framework on markets in financial instruments, it seems clear that there is a certain lack of coherence and effectiveness of the mechanisms that are in place. Those findings pertain to the second thematic question. In this connection, we wish to remind the reader that our focus on this particular regulatory framework is motivated by methodological considerations, and is intended to enable us to deepen our study of accountability in the context of centralisation of rulemaking, and the implications for the EU legal system. For those reasons, our concluding comments are primarily intended to address this broader dimension of the accountability mechanisms.

Before we return to the second thematic question, we will address, briefly, the third thematic question. In seeking to explain how our findings contribute to the understanding of the concept of legal accountability in EU law, we will introduce the notion of an 'infrastructure' for accountability.[5] It is a theoretical tool that is helpful in explaining how the rule of law in the EU can be kept efficient by promoting and maintaining clear and precise pathways for accountability. The underlying premise is that such infrastructure is fundamental for every form of accountability. Furthermore, the concept of an infrastructure for accountability is sufficiently general to encompass most policy fields, and yet still flexible enough to apply in a specific context.

13.2 The concept of accountability

13.2.1 Some points of departure

It is a fundamental trait of accountability that it concerns holding someone to account for a *past event*.[6] There cannot, logically, be proactive accountability: it is, by definition, reactive. At the very least, it would be contrary to general principles of law to hold anyone to account for a *possible future event*; in other words, for something that you are concerned that they *might* do. This is not to say that accountability does not have any proactive function. A stringent and well-functioning system of transparency and accountability will disincentivise (and thereby proactively deter) misfeasance and infringements of law.

Together, our authors have illustrated how accountability is—to borrow from the song by Sammy Fain and Paul Francis Webster—a many-splendoured

[5] We acknowledge our indebtedness to Dorothea Agnostopoulos, Stacey A Rutledge, and Rebecca Jacobsen, from whom we have adopted this concept, which they coined with regard to accountability in the sector of education, and introduced in the title of their book: Dorothea Agnostopoulos, Stacey A Rutledge, and Rebecca Jacobsen (eds), *The Infrastructure of Accountability: Data Use and the Transformation of American Education* (Harvard Education Press 2013).

[6] Mark Bovens, 'Analysing and Assessing Accountability: A Conceptual Framework' (2007) 13 European Law Journal 447, 467.

thing. This comes across even more clearly if we broaden the view of what can constitute accountability, in a range of different contexts. There can be political accountability, which may, in turn, be subdivided into internal accountability mechanisms (such as holding the member of a political party to account for publicly speaking against party policy), and external accountability mechanisms (such as voting out an MEP who has not delivered on campaign promises, or media pressure for resignations if a scandal arises). In the workplace, and in business partnerships, there are contractual mechanisms for accountability in the event of disloyalty (such as the termination of an agreement), but also softer business mechanisms for accountability (such as confronting an underperforming partner) that can be just as effective. We would point out that all of these forms of accountability share a need, if the mechanisms are to be effective, for a context in which accountability can be enforced. For instance, in order for us to be able to vote out any MEP who does not deliver, we must be informed of what is going on in the European Parliament, and we must have a right to vote.[7] It has been said that accountability must be understood as a process including several stages, from the obtaining of information, via a judgement on the contents of that information, to a decision on the consequences.[8] In light of the findings in this book, we would push the argument further, and assert that accountability is a shorthand for a variety of processes, and that stakeholders, such as investment firms, may appear in more than one role in those processes, depending on the circumstances.

In this book, we have focused on legal accountability, which we have defined as a legal means of holding somebody (be it an investment firm, a national or EU agency, or a person) to account. Such legal means of achieving accountability follow the same logic, *mutatis mutandis*, as other accountability mechanisms: they are only workable if aggrieved parties can obtain information concerning infringements of the law or duty of care at issue, if they can present that information to a competent authority or court, if the complaint is fairly processed, and if there are, ultimately, consequences for the party being held accountable. These elements and, in particular, the safeguards that a legal system has in place in order to protect the integrity of a fair and transparent process are what we would call the infrastructure of legal accountability. The EU Treaties supply a number of accountability mechanisms for various situations (most

[7] See, further, ibid 454–462.

[8] Elizabeth Fisher, 'The European Union in the Age of Accountability' (2004) 24 Oxford Journal of Legal Studies 495, 497 (citing Anne Davies, *Accountability: A Public Law Analysis of Government by Contract* (OUP 2001) 81).

prominently, Articles 258–260, Article 263, and Article 340(2) TFEU), and the CJEU has developed further mechanisms whereby accountability could, in the view of the Court, be considered inherent in the Treaties.[9] Nonetheless, the EU system of accountability has consistently been criticised as lacking in availability (for instance in criticisms of the limitation of standing for non-privileged applicants under Article 263(4) TFEU)[10], and in coherence (for instance by comparing the broad accountability of member states under Articles 258–260 TFEU to the narrower accountability of EU institutions and agencies under Article 263 TFEU). Nevertheless, the accountability mechanisms laid down in the Treaties do, after all, offer a rather comprehensive system of accountability, in spite of these weaknesses. The most blatant incoherencies in the EU system of accountability are, it is submitted, those that concern accountability mechanisms laid down in secondary law. This is a result of two mutually reinforcing factors: reliance on national enforcement under national procedures, and a rather ad hoc harmonisation of (certain aspects of) legal remedies in the member states. The result is a fragmented range of tailor-made solutions for various policy areas.[11] Contributions in this book serve to illustrate that this also applies to accountability in the EU financial market: coherence, comprehensiveness, and effectiveness, in the senses that we would expect through the notion of an infrastructure of accountability, are just not quite there.

Adrienne Héritier offers a summary of parallel insights from studies of political accountability in the context of the EU financial reform. The picture she paints comes close to the view presented here. In her words:

> The overall picture is that of a patchwork of accountability channels. In response to this patchwork, the Commission and [the European Parliament] have made efforts to centralize accountability channels by empowering ESMA, but also by introducing new measures … These top-down endeavours are, to some extent, counteracted by the regulatory competition from the bottom, in the case of fintechs, their varying regulation across member states and the UK, and the ways in which they are held politically and privately accountable. Making the picture even more complex is the increasing reliance on self-regulation of private actors.

[9] For example, the damages action against member states (Joined Cases C-6/90 and C-9/90 *Francovich and Bonifaci* EU:C:1991:428), and the action for repayment of unlawfully levied charges (Case 177/78 *Pigs and Bacon* EU:C:1979:164).

[10] See the sometimes rather heated debate on Case 25/62 *Plaumann* EU:C:1963:17, recently reignited pursuant to Case C-565/19 P *Carvalho* EU:C:2021:252.

[11] Compare, eg the disparate designs of the anti-discrimination law, competition law, and intellectual property law systems.

From these points of departure, we will proceed to summarise the lessons we have learned on accountability, in writing this book. Thereafter, we will return to the issue of the infrastructure for accountability, and how to promote it.

13.2.2 Lessons on accountability

In order to move from the particular conclusions of different authors into general patterns of findings, we have used the position of the investment firm in accountability processes to structure our analyses. This ought to be evident even from the ordering of the chapters in the book into parts representing separate themes. Investment firms can, thus, appear as agents of accountability, promoting the accountability of public bodies at both EU and national level (Part II). But they can also be held accountable for their own infringements of financial markets law (Part III). Furthermore, in some circumstances, their positions are also decided by their (horizontal) relationships to other private actors (Part IV). In this part, we will explore the implications of the findings in this book within the contexts of each category, beginning with investment firms as agents for accountability of public bodies.

In his chapter, Merijn Chamon observes that investment firms are able, under certain circumstances, to use the Joint Board of Appeal of the three EU agencies or ESAs, operating in different sectors of the financial market, as an accountability mechanism. The Joint Board of Appeal is, in his words, 'a forum in which the agency is required to explain and justify its decisions, with the possibility of its behaviour (ie its decisions) being subject to sanctions'. But, according to Chamon, the potential of the Joint Board of Appeal is hampered by two main factors. Firstly, a significant part of the ESAs' rulemaking output consists of non-binding acts that are not reviewable. Secondly, the jurisdiction of the Joint Board of Appeal (like that of other EU agencies' Boards of Appeal) is defined more narrowly than the jurisdiction of the EU Court, and there are binding acts that the Board is not competent to examine. Therefore, Chamon suggests that the jurisdiction of the Joint Board of Appeal should be extended, to realise its full potential, and that the ESAs' powers to adopt non-reviewable soft laws are superseded by powers to adopt reviewable hard law. In both cases, these improvements can be made via EU legislative acts and, thus, the power of reform lies in the hands of the EU legislator. Dominique Ritleng reaches very similar conclusions, albeit from a broader survey of judicial protection for investment firms. In his words:

> The question of whether the remedies available to litigants, especially investment firms, to challenge action taken by ESMA under MIFID II or MIFIR are liable to ensure effective judicial protection cannot be answered definitively ... adjustments would certainly be welcome for meeting the needs of effective judicial protection ... with respect to the direct reviewability of guidelines issued by ESMA, whose effects make it clear that they are the result of quasi-regulatory powers.

Even though Ritleng identifies and discusses several accountability mechanisms, he nevertheless concludes that their effectiveness is uncertain. Like Chamon, it is submitted by Ritleng that this uncertainty pertains, in particular, to the lack of judicial review of non-binding acts and, thus, of soft law.

In response to this, we would point out that the participation of ESMA in rulemaking mainly takes place in two ways that should be distinguished from one another. Firstly, ESMA drafts regulatory and implementing technical standards, to be adopted by the Commission in the form of delegated or implementing acts (under Article 290 or 291(2) TFEU). As these non-legislative acts are binding, they are reviewable under Article 263 TFEU. However, this system creates an impression that rulemaking for the financial system is under the control of the Commission, while it is, by and large, actually under the control of ESMA, who draft the non-legislative acts to be adopted. This may become a problem, as it does not quite fit the constitutional design intended by the EU Treaties, and Regulation 182/2011.[12] Secondly, ESMA drafts guidelines, Q & As, and other soft law instruments, which ESMA subsequently publishes as part of the Single Rulebook. These are neither formally binding nor (consequently) reviewable under Article 263 TFEU. Nonetheless, they are usually accepted by member state agencies and investment firms (and other stakeholders) as norms that should be followed. There is, in other words, an expectation of compliance among stakeholders, but no possibility for them to challenge the normative soft law instruments at issue. Thus, as Chamon and Ritleng have stressed, accountability is compromised.

Helene Andersson and Jane Reichel both take different perspectives, scrutinizing the safeguards available to investment firms when they are subject to investigations or sanctioning by public agencies, at EU and national levels. Andersson asks to what extent investment firms can hold EU agencies

[12] Regulation (EU) No 182/2011 of the European Parliament and of the Council of 16 February 2011 laying down the rules and general principles concerning mechanisms for control by Member States of the Commission's exercise of implementing powers [2011] OJ L 55/11.

accountable for transgressions of their rights, in such circumstances. Reichel focuses on agency accountability for deviations from principles of good administration. In her chapter, Andersson observes that there is a significant lack of safeguards available to investment firms when subjected to the scrutiny of public agencies:

> [The EU] legislator appears confident that a general reference to the Charter in the recitals, combined with a right to appeal, is sufficient to ensure adequate fundamental rights protection. This absence of explicit safeguards is remarkable for a number of reasons. First, given the strict regulation of these markets, defining the appropriate level of protection may, at times, be difficult . . . Second, member states have also been required to introduce extremely tough sanctions against natural persons, and this calls for even stricter safeguards against abusive or arbitrary measures from the NCAs . . . Absent minimum safeguards, and effective possibilities of holding supervisory authorities accountable for any transgressions of these safeguards, there is an apparent risk that the level of protection will vary between member states. This, in turn, means that the desired level playing field will not materialize, as the risks involved in carrying out financial services are not consistent throughout the Union.

In the same vein, Reichel asks:

> [W]hy has the EU legislator not laid down at least minimum rules to ensure that the principle of good administration can be upheld within composite decision-making procedures? . . . Administrative cooperation is central for ESMA to achieve its mission and objective, but focus seems to have been placed on efficiency in carrying out the supervision, whereas the need for legal certainty, transparency, and good administration has been underestimated . . . In the end, the prioritization of efficiency may not only undermine the conditions for an adequate judicial accountability regime, but, further down the line, the legitimacy of EU financial markets law.

In sum, there are remedies in place that can be used by investment firms in order to ensure accountability and the rule of law vis-à-vis public bodies, at both EU and national levels. But these accountability mechanisms are underdeveloped, uncertain, and, generally, seem to have been a lesser priority than the interests of a coordinated system of supervision and reporting. Given the fact that much of the supervision is carried out in accordance with soft law measures adopted by ESMA, and that there are limited possibilities for judicial review of those measures, the overall impression is less than satisfactory. To quote the famous dictum of the CJEU: 'the vigilance of individuals concerned to protect their rights amounts to an effective supervision'.[13]

We now turn to lessons learned with regard to accountability, in relation to compliance and non-compliance by investment firms. In the third part of the book, Pieter van Cleynenbreugel explores the requirements in MiFID II for investment firms to set up compliance management structures, and these structures' links to accountability. He notes:

> [T]he principles-based, rules-centred approach to MiFID II compliance has been drafted in such a way that the objective to instil an internalized compliance culture in investment firms has not been made as explicit as it could have been ... neither do the ESMA guidelines make any link whatsoever with the sanctioning apparatus at the disposal of member states' supervisory authorities, and to the relationship between respect for compliance and the consequences this may have for the imposition of sanctions.

Making a case for positive promotion of compliance, or, in other words, the adoption of a system of leniency towards investment firms that have clearly tried to ensure compliance with MiFID II, he continues:

> In practice, and as a matter of policy, linking compliance to sanctions is not self-evident, as the example of EU competition law compliance demonstrates. It was submitted that those obstacles should not limit ESMA from at least considering linking compliance and sanctioning tools more explicitly. At the same time, however, setting up such a linked and more coherent legal accountability framework would require a more elaborate conceptualization of, and reflection as to how, accountability can best be ensured within the framework of EU financial services regulation as a whole.

In addition to this, van Cleynenbreugel offers two policy strategies for ESMA to consider: the 'wait and see' strategy, in which ESMA continues to give significant leeway to national agencies to strike the appropriate balance, and the 'coordinated experimentalism' strategy, in which ESMA intervenes by adopting an opinion or recommendation under Article 16 of the ESMA founding regulation, with which national agencies must 'comply or explain'.

[13] Case 26/62 *van Gend & Loos* EU:C:1963:1.

Malou Larsson Klevhill and Annina Persson are similarly concerned with the coordination of supervisory efforts—or rather lack thereof—and the consequences for the EU financial market. Introducing the concept of supervisory arbitrage, to mirror the well-known phenomenon of regulatory arbitrage,[14] the authors present a case study of *Finansinspektionen;* the competent national authority in Sweden (FSA). They note that FSA has a number of sanctioning tools at its disposal that all serve as mechanisms of accountability but emphasise that these tools are not always used:

> [T]he FSA often chooses to communicate with the investment firm's management, and to discuss matters with them, rather than using formal sanctions. In most cases, the FSA, in dialogue with the firm, is able to influence the firm to change its behaviour. The actor has few incentives not to do as the FSA is asking ... In some cases, however, the shortcomings and non-compliance are so serious that the FSA must intervene with sanctions ... Ultimately, the financial markets are built on trust and, the FSA needs to take its role as 'gatekeeper' seriously, for the benefit of the whole financial industry. Supervisory arbitrage is not a blessing for anyone.

Larsson Klevhill and Persson would, thus, favour further intervention by ESMA in order to level the playing field and avoid supervisory arbitrage.

The assessment of whether investment firm managers are 'fit and proper' for their tasks is an area in which the public agencies have far-reaching powers. To some extent, these powers serve proactive purposes, insofar as they stipulate supervisory approval of directors and managers, but they can also be used as mechanisms of accountability. As Britta Behrendt Jonsson explains further, national authorities can order the removal of board members and, in the case of managers, even impose permanent or fixed-period bans on them acting as managers in an investment firm. She summarises:

> Fit and proper assessments of members of management bodies of investment firms may serve as instruments of accountability, alongside administrative sanctions and criminal or civil liability ... The risk of being assessed negatively and being removed from the management body, or being denied a new

[14] On regulatory arbitrage in financial markets law, see eg Heikki Marjosola, 'The Problem of Regulatory Arbitrage: A Transaction Cost Economics Perspective' (2021) 15(2) Regulation & Governance 388.

> position may... have a deterrent effect on managers, and foster sound (risk) management.

In her chapter, Rebecca Söderström focuses on some other aspects of internal organisation and accountability: the need to balance internal incentive schemes in investment firms with sound risk management, and the possibility of national agencies holding managers accountable, if a proper balance is not struck. She acknowledges that there can be scepticism towards regulation and supervision concerning corporate governance issues, and asks whether the perspective adopted is capable of attaining the aim pursued:

> Legal provisions will never, however detailed and strict, fully reflect or foster soundness in financial firms, or on financial markets ... If management is sound on an overall level, compensation (including incentive programmes or bonuses) will fit into a sound business profile. Legal instruments may promote soundness and accountability, but cannot replace investment firms' own pursuit of sound business structures and accountability mechanisms at all levels in a firm ... Internalized accountability mechanisms, where firms are empowered to set up structures that promote a sound corporate culture, could complement, but also to some extent replace, external accountability and the need for supervisory interference... Regulating in order to foster accountability within financial firms, and on political and regulatory levels, is legitimate to a greater extent if rules addressing, for example, corporate governance are adapted to the types of firm they address. The higher the potential impact on market stability is, the higher the need for regulatory intervention.

Söderström, thus, calls for some refinement and differentiation in supervision and, perhaps in a similar vein to van Cleynenbreugel, for a lenient approach where investment firms themselves have sound systems of internal accountability mechanisms. But Söderström also stresses the market position of the firm as an important variable in setting the standard of supervisory scrutiny, in such a differentiated approach.

Summarizing these contributions on external accountability for investment firms and internal accountability systems therein, it is clear that the authors see a system in need of further reflection and development. It seems unclear to what extent ESMA and the national agencies wish to coordinate the monitoring, supervision, and accountability measures that they take towards investment firms. Moreover, it is unclear what role internal compliance management and accountability mechanisms could, and should, play in the EU system.

In the fourth part of the book, private law accountability is considered. This is a field where, perhaps, the concept of 'accountability' has not traditionally been used. But, in our view, the concept of accountability also helps, in a private law context, to highlight the role of vigilant individuals and firms as agents of the rule of law, when they use private law remedies to hold their counterparts accountable for misfeasance. Here, investment firms truly have a dual role, both holding other firms accountable, and being held accountable. Federico Della Negra considers carefully how the intense rulemaking at EU level may have an impact in a private law context:

> Soft law, which has, usefully, been characterized as a layer in- between the contract and the law, becomes a yardstick to interpret general private law concepts (for example good faith, reasonableness, and skill and care). In practice, the interpretation of binding law in the light of soft law tightens the private law requirements for investment firms but, at the same time, ensures a more consistent application of these requirements across the EU ... Conduct of business rules themselves derive from non-binding codes of conduct that encapsulated 'moral' standards of good behaviour for broker-dealers and advisers ... [I]nvestment firms are not only accountable or answerable for their conduct, but can also be held liable on the basis of national private law for breaches of EU regulatory/soft law standards ... But there are divergences across national jurisdictions as regards the intensity of the civil law effects of these rules ... Going forward, harmonization of national private law rules would be beneficial, in order to increase legal certainty for both investment firms and their clients, and to level the playing field.

Finally, Magnus Strand, focusing on damages liability as an accountability mechanism, stresses that public liability in damages should also be considered:

> [I]nvestment firms have a dual role to play: they can, and should, be held accountable for their breaches by claimants bringing actions for damages, but they can also bring actions of their own against member state authorities and/or EU authorities, if they have suffered harm caused by those public authorities ... Supervisory authorities will not detect all infringements: they are not able even to pursue all reports of infringements that they receive. Therefore, private enforcement can contribute to accountability and, thereby, to deterrence, and the upholding of the rule of law.

Further, in connection with the role of investment firms in ensuring accountability for public agencies, at EU and national levels, Strand also emphasises the usefulness of public liability in damages, and asks whether joint and several liability for agencies at both levels should be an option:

> ESMA and the national financial authorities are now working closely together, and it has come to a point where the division of powers between the two levels is not easily discernible by (for example) investment firms. When powers are intertwined, accountability should, perhaps, be so too. This point is relevant, not only in the context of MiFID II and MiFIR, and the non-legislative acts adopted pursuant to them, but to EU law as a whole. Accountability measures in the public sphere are relatively weak in the EU law system as it currently stands. The example of MiFID II and MiFIR has served to illustrate the broader issue.

This brings us back, full circle, to the starting point, and gives us a chance to summarise the results of this book, and, in that way, to provide some answers to questions 1 and 2 above. To us, it is evident that the authors have described a system of legal accountability—in all its aspects, and in all directions—that holds many promises, but which is very much lacking in coherence and effectiveness. A wide range of mechanisms are in place, but it is unclear how they can, and should, be used, and there is a striking lack of coordination. There has been an intense period of reform, and there is a need for the new system to settle. Perhaps it is now time to 'wait and see' (as van Cleynenbreugel suggests). But, still, this process presupposes that there are actors pushing matters forward. Not only public bodies can contribute, but private bodies, too. Our book shows that investment firms have a crucial responsibility. We will now elaborate on some further implications of our findings, and, thereby, attempt not only to answer the third question set out above, but also to provide some suggestions for the future.

13.3 In search of a comprehensive model of accountability

13.3.1 The need for an accountability infrastructure

What, then, should be our answer to the third question asked above? It is submitted that the findings of the contributing authors have yielded the conclusion that accountability in the EU financial market remains, at present, a paradox. Although there are many different accountability processes within the regulatory framework on markets in financial instruments, there are, nonetheless, a great number of deficits in the system. The overall impression is that accountability mechanisms are lacking in comprehensiveness and systematic reflection: in other words, the accountability system is immature. Our conclusions, with regard to the third question, are therefore that *isolated accountability mechanisms are insufficient*, and that *accountability must be construed through a comprehensive system* of such mechanisms. This brings us back to the need for an infrastructure of accountability. Consider again the comparison with political accountability, where we assume that there is an MEP who has voted contrary to her or his promises. What kind of infrastructure needs to be in place for there to be accountability? First of all, it must be possible for journalists and the public to find out how she or he has voted. Second, media outlets must be able: (a) to contact the MEP and request answers on why she or he has not delivered on campaign promises; and (b) to tell the electorate how she or he has voted, that the pattern runs contrary to these promises, and to report on any explanations she or he has offered. Third, it must be possible for the electorate to vote the MEP out in the next election. The factors involved—transparency, freedom of the press, and democratic elections—are all part of the infrastructure necessary for political accountability to work.

The same is also true for legal accountability. It must be possible to identify an infringement of the regulatory framework on markets in financial instruments or other relevant provisions of EU law (transparency), it must be possible to identify a course of action for the aggrieved party to pursue (an effective remedy), and that course of action must be reasonably accessible (within the meaning(s) of the general principles of judicial protection and Article 47 of the EU Charter).

Reflecting on this, it becomes clear that legal accountability, in this sense, is a flip side to judicial protection, which has been abundantly discussed in EU law.[15] We submit that judicial protection and accountability are two separate perspectives on the same set of issues. Judicial protection analyses set out to scrutinise whether EU law has an appropriate system in place for the enforcement of substantive rights. This includes ensuring that, where there is a right, there is also a remedy (which is sufficiently effective), and that the conditions *de fond et de forme* for the exercise of that remedy are compliant with Article

[15] For a 'nutshell' summary with references, see Magnus Strand, *The Passing-on Problem in Damages and Restitution under EU Law* (Edward Elgar Publishing 2017) paras 2.001–2.005.

47 of the EU Charter, and the twin principles of equivalence and effectiveness. By contrast, accountability focuses on duties and obligations, and on the detection and sanctioning of misfeasance. In this way, judicial protection can be said to act mainly in the interests of ensuring justice for the individual, whereas accountability is more immediately concerned with the general interest of maintaining transparency and, in the legal context, the rule of law. This, admittedly, pushes the differences between the two concepts rather far, but we believe that a stark juxtaposition of the two perspectives clarifies the benefits of switching perspectives (as Mr Keating illustrates in *Dead Poets Society* (1989), by standing up on his desk to have a new look at the classroom). The more common 'rights perspective' is less capable of identifying the bigger picture, whereas the accountability perspective arguably highlights precisely the need for a full system of protection for the rule of law.

The regulatory framework on markets in financial instruments includes a range of mechanisms for accountability, but these are lacking in coherence and effectiveness. The accountability perspective allows us to see this clearly, and to reflect on what sort of infrastructure reforms are needed to enhance the system. In order to make some constructive suggestions on how to move forward, we would like to return to the rulemaking model presented by the Lamfalussy Group before the financial crisis.

13.3.2 Can the interests of coordination and accountability be combined?

In order for national authorities to hold investment firms to account in an effective and uniform way, the authorities need coordination of their supervisory practices and interpretations. We have seen, in the introductory chapter, how the process launched by the Lamfalussy Group, and later elaborated on by the de Larosière Group, seeks to further European integration (and centralisation) in rulemaking, but also—and perhaps even more conspicuously—in formal and informal contacts between national authorities. Most significantly, the ideas of the de Larosière Group ensure that this process builds on ESMA and the other ESAs coordinating a permanent network with many functions. One such function is to ensure that national authorities exchange information relating to the implementation and application of EU law. Another is to semi-regulate the market, through common guidelines and Q & A's. This, in turn, is intended to lead to uniform results in the member states, with high compliance rates and, therefore, less need for enforcement. In the introductory chapter, Bergström demonstrated how this is reflected in a decreasing number of Commission actions against member states, under Article 258 TFEU.

It seems to us that this model has proven a tremendous success, in the sense that national authorities have gained a collective influence over EU rulemaking. In this way, it may be said that the legal acts that are being adopted by ESMA within the regulatory framework on markets in financial instruments are also 'owned' by their national counterparts. This not only boosts the consistency of national interpretations of common rules but, arguably, also the legitimacy of the EU system in the member states. But, importantly, the de Larosière Group did not take any particular interest in legal accountability mechanisms. As demonstrated by Bergström, their main aims, which continue to echo through EU rulemaking, were to coordinate rulemaking through more forceful instruments (regulations rather than directives), and to ensure that supervision and enforcement were carried out by politically independent authorities, coordinated by equally independent EU agencies (no longer controlled by the Commission). If you search the de Larosière Report looking for keywords such as 'court', 'judicial', 'justice', or 'appeal', you will come out empty-handed. Searching for 'accountability' produces more results, but all of these are concerned with political accountability. If you look for 'sanctions', you will find reasoning on the importance of strong sanctioning powers for authorities vis-à-vis investment firms (and others), but no mention of the sanctioning of transgressions by public authorities, at EU or national level.

The next question to be asked, therefore, is whether the current model for rulemaking and supervision could not be combined with an equally comprehensive model for accountability at the various levels. Indeed, using that model to structure the analysis seems to us to be a helpful way of clarifying which aspects work well, and which aspects need further attention.

13.3.3 Accountability at level one

At the first level of the Lamfalussy model, we find the legislative acts adopted by the EU, laying down general principles and structures for the functioning of the financial market. The EU Treaties include a well-known framework for accountability, in the event of any transgressions in this context. The legislative acts can be annulled, under the procedure in Article 263 TFEU, 'on grounds of lack of competence, infringement of an essential procedural requirement, infringement of the Treaties or of any rule of law relating to their application, or misuse of powers'. Further, indirect action is possible through Article 267

TFEU. In certain circumstances, an investment firm that has been injured by an irregularity in a legislative act can also bring an action for damages, under Article 340(2) TFEU.[16]

The main problem, at this level, is the well-known and much debated issue of the standing of non-privileged applicants such as investment firms, under Article 263 TFEU, and whether or not the possibilities of securing a reference for a preliminary ruling, or bringing a damages action, are sufficient alternative means of holding the EU legislator to account.[17]

13.3.4 Accountability at level two

The Lamfalussy model speaks next of non-legislative acts of general application, which provide detailed rules for the financial market. These are the delegated and implementing acts adopted by the Commission (often at the request of ESMA, which also drafts the acts). Constitutionally, this level also encompasses binding acts adopted by ESMA, which are mostly decisions of individual application, but may sometimes also be decisions of general application.[18]

For these non-legislative acts, the same articles of the Treaties apply, mainly under the same criteria. There is, however, an exception with regard to non-legislative acts that do not 'entail implementing measures'. This exception, thus, concerns any regulations (but not directives, although these are scarce) that have been adopted as non-legislative acts. In regard to these, a non-privileged applicant such as an investment firm will only have to demonstrate a direct concern, in order to bring an action for annulment, but will not bear the onus of proving individual concern. The *Plaumann* test is, thus, relaxed, and an investment firm will have standing to challenge the act if, as stated by Chamon above, 'the legal situation of the applicant is directly affected' by the act.

[16] For a brief summary of relevant case law developments, with references to further reading, see ibid paras 3.012–3.028.

[17] cf n 9: this debate is too vast to be done any justice here, but interested readers can find a summary in any EU law textbook.

[18] Such as the ESMA decisions adopted to temporarily restrict contracts for differences (CFDs), eg European Securities and Markets Authority Decision (EU) 2018/796 of 22 May 2018 to temporarily restrict contracts for differences in the Union in accordance with Article 40 of Regulation (EU) No 600/2014 of the European Parliament and of the Council [2018] OJ L 136/50 (followed by several others, all expired at the time of writing).

13.3.5 Accountability at level three

Some of the core problems identified in this book pertain to level three of the Lamfalussy model, in which national authorities coordinate their interpretations of the regulatory framework provided by levels one and two, and their approaches to its application in level four. This is done partly through informal discussions, but also (pursuant to the suggestions of the de Larosière Group) through the adoption of common guidelines and other soft law instruments by ESMA.

As discussed by Ritleng and Chamon, these guidelines and instruments are not subjectable to judicial review. Investment firms can only challenge them indirectly, by challenging individual decisions directed at them, in situations where a national authority is relying on an interpretation of law expressed in one of the soft law instruments. However, it is far from certain that the national authority will indicate clearly, in its statement of reasons, that it is, in fact, relying on a soft law instrument; therefore, it cannot be certain that this aspect of the action will be properly identified.

The reasons behind this situation are essentially constitutional in character. In the classic case law of the CJEU, non-binding legal acts that result from a procedure that is only seeking 'to ensure permanent consultation' have not been seen as exercising true powers, since these acts are intended to be taken over, later, by binding acts that are amenable to full review.[19] To the extent that this perspective is still valid—and we cannot find any indication to the contrary—it amounts to a general problem in the approach to accountability that should be addressed in the upcoming review of MiFID II and MiFIR. We would agree with Chamon that the Joint Board of Appeal should be given jurisdiction to hear challenges brought against soft law instruments adopted by ESMA, and we see no reason to limit the standing of investment firms to bring such actions. Indeed, even adopting a criterion of direct concern would potentially rob such an action of any usefulness, as it could then be argued that a soft law instrument cannot have direct concern to anyone until implemented in a concrete authority decision. Why not try these reforms out in the limited context of the MiFID II and MiFIR framework? Let us see if the 'floodgates' argument holds water. A small experiment like this could yield important lessons for the overall EU system of accountability.

[19] See, most notably, the notion of powers discussed in Case 9/56 *Meroni* EU:C:1958:7, p 146, and in Case 25/70 *Köster* EU:C:1970:115, paras 8–9.

13.3.6 Accountability at level four

At level four, we have finally arrived at the point where the dual role of investment firms can be expressed clearly. Our discussion of all of the other levels has, inevitably, concerned accountability for the EU institutions and agencies, and for national agencies, and the possibilities for investment firms to hold these bodies to account. At level four, we can explore not only this aspect, but also the aspect of accountability for investment firms and their managers.

Beginning with the latter aspects, Behrendt Jonsson, Söderström, and van Cleynenbreugel have all described external accountability structures, in terms of public supervision and legal accountability, of investment firms and their managers. The regulatory system under MiFID II and MiFIR is well-developed as regards the availability of sanctions designed to deter and penalise infringements. Behrendt Jonsson, in particular, focused on the details of how individual managers' behaviour is assessed. Söderström and van Cleynenbreugel chose to explore the interrelationship of these external accountability structures, and the internal structures of accountability in investment firms. In these contexts, it seemed to the authors, there was need for further reflection on what incentives are created by the external accountability structures created by the EU system, and whether it would be preferable, instead, to promote the development of sound internal accountability systems in investment firms. We would endorse this position, and add (as implied by van Cleynenbreugel) that a modern and comprehensive system of accountability should not rest on deterrence only, but also on the promotion of positive choices that further the general interest of a rule of law. Furthermore, Larsson Klevhill and Persson illustrate that investment firms with an interest in establishing their activities in a jurisdiction with less intense supervision and sanctioning are able to do so, since the actual practices of sanctioning infringements still differ between member states. In all, and although the system has devoted quite some attention to the accountability of investment firms, there seems to be a need for further refinement, by coordinating further, in order to secure a level playing field, and by reflecting, in that process, on how to promote internal compliance and accountability structures (indeed, internal compliance *cultures*) in investment firms.

In this context, although these are not directly linked to public supervision and enforcement, we would also highlight the role of horizontal accountability mechanisms, to which Della Negra and Strand have devoted their chapters. Public supervision and sanctioning cannot bring compensation to victims of infringements of financial markets law. Only private, horizontal actions can do that. Furthermore, horizontal actions are capable of contributing to the rule of law, as investment firms suffering from infringements may detect the reasons for their losses, and hold the infringers accountable for these losses, in instances where the issue has escaped the attention of the competent national authority, and in situations where the competent national authority has, perhaps, made a budgetary choice not to pursue the issue.

Returning to accountability for public agencies at level four of the Lamfalussy model, it has been demonstrated by Reichel and Andersson that transgressions of the safeguards of administrative and procedural law suffer from inadequately developed systems of accountability, in relation to the national (and EU) agencies concerned. As Reichel submits, 'focus seem to have been placed on efficiency in carrying out the supervision, whereas the need for legal certainty, transparency and good administration has been underestimated'. Our analysis of the de Larosière Report seems to confirm this: attention was fixed on coordination and on enforcement vis-à-vis investment firms, not on securing a role for investment firms in ensuring that national agencies comply with such standards. Importantly, this leaves investment firms with no specific remedies, but only the accountability mechanisms available under national law. We mentioned above that the infrastructure of accountability under EU law suffers, in the national context, from two mutually reinforcing factors: reliance on national enforcement under national procedures, and a rather ad hoc harmonisation of (certain aspects of) legal remedies in the member states. It might be considered whether the EU legislator should intervene further here, making sure that there is an EU system of accountability for 'legal certainty, transparency and good administration' that covers the national context.

13.4 Suggestions for further development of the infrastructure

Anyone who appreciates the rule of law will instinctively want wrongdoings to be corrected. These should be caught in the 'fishing net' of competent law enforcement authorities, and those responsible should be held accountable. But the coarser the mesh, the greater the number of wrongdoers who will slip through. There will, thus, be less accountability, and it will be more difficult to uphold and maintain the legitimacy of the rule of law. It is plainly arguable that the enforcement of EU law generally relies on a very coarse mesh, or rather that the mesh is irregular, and has holes in some places while being quite intact in others. The system in place under Articles 263, 267, and 340(2) TFEU has been debated, but we would point out that the coarseness of the mesh is mostly due to the fact that the EU must often rely on its member states for supervision and enforcement. Therefore, while EU rulemaking in the various sectors of the financial market, but also other fields of the internal market, become more centralised and more detailed, erasing the previous problem of regulatory arbitrage, the system of accountability seems to lag behind. As shown in the contribution by Larsson Klevhill and Persson above, regulatory arbitrage can be replaced by supervisory arbitrage.

It is submitted that the EU, as we know it, will not be able to overcome the underlying problem: that supervision and enforcement cannot be fully centralised and uniform. This is a political impossibility. Nevertheless, we submit that the system must be reformed in order to enhance coherence and effectiveness in accountability. This cannot be done in a simple and general manner, but we will submit a few suggestions on how to proceed with regard to specific issues. These may, in turn, inspire solutions in other fields of EU policy.

Let us admit, first of all, that the issue is complex. The legal remedies that form part of the infrastructure for accountability that we want to address are embedded in a complicated web of jurisdictions and procedures. Therefore, rather than suggesting a single solution for all forms of accountability mechanisms, we need to focus on the fora for accountability, individually or at least thematically, and the institutions that channel accountability.[20]

To begin with, we would suggest that accountability issues in the context of the regulatory framework on markets in financial instruments should be addressed more intensively within ESMA. The issues of coherence and balancing of interests that are highlighted in Part II of this book deserve immediate attention. To quite some extent, it ought to be possible for ESMA to develop uniform and transparent accountability practices, issuing communications on the use of sanctions and leniency assessments in a similar vein as the Commission does for the purposes of competition policy. That way, the model could be extended to matters of accountability that fall within the competence of ESMA.

With regard to the accountability of ESMA, Chamon has concluded that the Joint Board of Appeal can be an effective instrument of accountability, if its jurisdiction is broadened to include soft law measures adopted by ESMA. We second his assessment, but would also suggest boldly that the mandate of the Joint Board of Appeal might be enlarged even further. Why not allow it to transform into a specialised tribunal for complaints and actions against ESMA

[20] Carol Harlow, 'Three Phases in the Evolution of EU Administrative Law' in Paul Craig and Gráinne de Búrca (eds), *The Evolution of EU Law* (2nd edn, OUP 2011) 464; Fisher (n 7) 511.

and the other ESAs, including not only actions for annulment or omissions, but also for damages? Why not allow the member states to nominate one judge each, to be appointed in accordance with the procedure in Articles 254 and 255 TFEU? In this way, the Joint Board of Appeal could be placed in a position that would enable it to truly develop a case law on accountability, for the benefit of the rule of law in the EU financial market.

The question of national authorities' accountability is more difficult, falling within the jurisdiction of national courts (even though they can use the Article 267 TFEU procedure where appropriate). Here we would highlight that complaints often start in administrative proceedings before they reach the courts. In such a context, the Joint Board of Appeal could have a role to play. For instance, perhaps it could issue advisory statements—in national proceedings that are not (or not yet) court proceedings—on how to interpret the EU law at stake? Moreover, where public liability in damages is at issue, the national authorities should be able to communicate within ESMA on legal matters, and on circumstances in which they choose to oppose, or concede to, an action.

Overall, the upcoming review of MiFID II and MiFIR would do well to devote some attention to the issues addressed here. However, as stated above, isolated accountability mechanisms are insufficient, and accountability must be construed through a comprehensive system of such mechanisms. It would be unwise to settle for ticking a few boxes while neglecting the need for a systematic overview. The broader themes we would identify as most crucial in such an overview are threefold. Firstly, reflection on how to design a coordinated system of accountability for investment firms that promotes an internal culture of compliance. Secondly, to enable formal coordination (at levels two and three of the Lamfalussy model) of mechanisms designed for the accountability of national agencies, including not only appeals, but also public liability. Thirdly, to ensure that investment firms and other crucial stakeholders have proper standing in appeals procedures, at both national and EU levels.

Such a comprehensive overview of the infrastructure of accountability would take time and energy, both of which are scarce resources. But let us have hope. Strengthening the infrastructure of accountability in EU financial market law in this way will, after all, mean furthering the rule of law in the financial market. All lessons learned from such an endeavour will, moreover, be useful for the future general development of the infrastructure of accountability in the EU.

Index

For the benefit of digital users, indexed terms that span two pages (e.g., 52–53) may, on occasion, appear on only one of those pages.